Adolf Hitler screamed,

"I DEMAND TO KNOW. YES OR NO? IS PARIS BURNING?"

"The bridges of the Seine, Notre Dame, the Arc de Triomphe, the Louvre, even the Eiffel Tower, were to be blasted to oblivion. The conquerors were to find that, in its dying gasp, the Thousand-Year Reich had leveled a thousand years of Western history's most treasured monuments, leaving Paris, in Hitler's words, 'nothing but a blackened field of ruins.'

"IS PARIS BURNING? is the extraordinary story of what happened in the next 19 days before Paris was taken by the Allies. . . . It is the absorbing story of Von Choltitz' lonely drama of decision." —*Time*

"A CLIFF-HANGER, BRILLIANT . . . AN ABSORBING SUSPENSE STORY"
  —*San Francisco Chronicle*

IS PARIS BURNING?

—ADOLF HITLER
August 25, 1944

Larry Collins
and
Dominique Lapierre

A KANGAROO BOOK
PUBLISHED BY POCKET BOOKS NEW YORK

IS PARIS BURNING?

POCKET BOOK edition published February, 1966

12th printing.....................October, 1977

This POCKET BOOK edition includes every word contained in
the original, higher-priced edition. It is printed from brand-
new plates made from completely reset, clear, easy-to-read type.
POCKET BOOK editions are published by
POCKET BOOKS,
a Simon & Schuster Division of
GULF & WESTERN CORPORATION
1230 Avenue of the Americas,
New York, N.Y. 10020.
Trademarks registered in the United States
and other countries.

ISBN: 0-671-81833-3.

Printed in the U.S.A.

ACKNOWLEDGMENTS

Is PARIS BURNING? is the result of almost three years of work and, above all, of the combined efforts of the authors, their numerous collaborators, and the hundreds of individuals, official and nonofficial, who offered their help and cooperation in the work. The research for the book divided into two phases. The first was based on locating, translating and studying all the material available on the subject. The second involved a patient, long and difficult effort to track down and interview the French, American, English and German actors in the drama of Paris's liberation.

For the success of this latter effort, we owe a particular debt to Jean Sainteny, France's Minister of Veterans Affairs, George McIntyre, Secretary of the Fourth U.S. Infantry Division's Veterans Association, and the editors of *Caravan*, the official publication of the veterans of the 2nd French Armored Division. M. Sainteny located for us the handwritten records of each of the more than two million German soldiers held prisoner in France during and after the war. On the record for each soldier was his name, rank, unit, serial number, the address of his next of kin and the place of his capture. M. Sainteny set eight of his staff to work on those files. In three weeks of patient effort they located for us the names and addresses of over 2,000 Germans taken prisoner during Paris's liberation.

Their names and addresses were checked against the current mailing list of the WAST organization in Berlin, a German Army organization responsible for re-establishing the destroyed personnel records of the Wehrmacht. From that cross-checking came a list of more than 200 current addresses for German soldiers who had served in Paris at the time of the liberation. They were added to another list of names—of men who had responded to a series of articles on our search very thoughtfully published by the Berlin daily paper *Bild Zeitung*. All of the individuals on the two lists were contacted either by mail or in person by our German collaborators working under the direction of Vladimir Benz of the Armed

Forces Network in Berlin. Benz, who also translated for us during almost two weeks of conversations with General von Choltitz in his home in Baden-Baden, was assisted by Dieter Wagner of *Der Spiegel* in Hamburg and Nina Silianof of *Paris Match* in Munich.

George McIntyre, Secretary of the Fourth Division Association, and Joseph Summa, its president, provided us with a copy of their membership rolls listing over 4,000 division veterans. To each we sent a detailed questionnaire. Over 500 veterans of Paris's liberation replied. More than a hundred of them were interviewed in person or by telephone. Similarly, the editors of *Caravan* opened their pages to us and helped us locate over 350 veterans of the 2nd French Armored Division.

In our search for documentation for the book we owe first a special debt of gratitude to Sherrod East, director of the U.S. National Archives depot in Alexandria, Virginia, and his pleasant and helpful associates. They made available to us the enormous mass of SHAEF and U.S. Army files relating to our subject, and then helped guide us through the voluminous material they had put before us. They also forwarded to us thirteen precious—if lengthy—rolls of microfilm of captured German records. In evaluating that data, we were given great assistance by Martin Blumenson of the U.S. Army's Department of Military History (himself the author of two excellent works on France's liberation) and his department chief, Israel Wice.

In Paris, Pierre Messmer, Minister of Defense, and General Pierre Koenig were kind enough to authorize our entry, the first of its kind, into the archives of the B.C.R.A. (Bureau Central des Renseignements et Actions), the service that handled all Free French communications, intelligence and operations in occupied France. Colonel Jean Le Goyer, head of the Contemporary Branch of the French Army's Historical Service, helped us study and evaluate the material we found therein. Edgar Pisani, now France's Minister of Agriculture, very generously turned over to us for our use the minute-by-minute logbooks kept in the Prefecture of Police during the insurrection, records that were immensely valuable to us in reconstructing the fight around the building. In addition, M. Pisani and Yves Bayet gave us unsparingly of their own time in our effort to recapture the details of the struggle at the Prefecture. Emmanuel d'Astier de la Vigerie, Minister of the Interior in General de Gaulle's provisional French government first in Algiers and later in Paris, very generously placed at our disposition his own collection of copies of the cables exchanged between his ministry and the French underground.

Altogether, in compiling the material for this book, we interviewed over 800 people in person, by telephone or by correspondence, and used parts of the experiences of 536 of them. To all of them we owe our gratitude, and to some we acknowledge a special debt.

General Dwight Eisenhower took a morning from his busy schedule to submit to an interview in his railroad car while he was en route to Palm Springs in December 1963. Allen Dulles in Washington and Robert Murphy in New York City both gave us of their time, as did General Omar Bradley. Generals Harold Blakeley, John G. Hill, Richard Lee and William Helmick, all veterans of the V Corps, offered their time and help in reconstructing the Corps's march on Paris. General Thomas Betts in Washington and General Sir Kenneth Strong in London, senior officers in SHAEF's G2 section, each helped us by scouring their memories for us, and General Julius Holmes, now U.S. Ambassador to Iran, took time for a lengthy telephone conversation during one of his brief visits to Washington.

To dozens of others, former G.I.'s and officers, who wrote detailed replies to our letters, sent us copies of the letters they had mailed home in 1944, their diaries or their own postwar notebooks, we offer our thanks.

In France, we must thank first Mme. la Maréchale Leclerc for her gracious assistance and her kindness to us in showing us her private mementos of her late husband. Jacques Chaban-Delmas, now President of France's National Assembly, and Colonel Henri "Rol" Tanguy each sat through four lengthy interviews. Alexandre Parodi, Vice President of France's Conseil d'État, gave us generously of his time, then read and helped us correct our manuscript. Geoffroy de Courcel, France's Ambassador to London; General Alain de Boissieu, General de Gaulle's son-in-law; and Claude Guy, his aide, all assisted us in reconstructing the General's movements in August 1944. Major Aimé Bully gave us a detailed description of the General's return to France and even found for us his logbook of the Lodestar "France's" return.

André "Passy" de Wavrin, first director of the B.C.R.A., and Henri "Vernon" Zeigler, his successor, helped us reconstruct the atmosphere of London at the time. Zeigler also revealed to us the details of the famous premature announcement of Paris's liberation on the BBC.

A very special debt must be acknowledged to Édouard Fievet, the nephew of the late Swedish Consul General Raoul Nordling, and to Nordling's brother Rolf. The two men very kindly helped complete the story Nordling had begun to tell us before his death in October 1963.

To General Dietrich von Choltitz must go, of course, a special word of thanks. Patiently, uncomplainingly, he submitted to our long and wearing interviews as we tried to recreate again, hour by hour, his brief but crucial stay in Paris. Also of great help to us in that task were his second-in-command, Colonel Hans Jay; his aide-de-camp, Colonel Dankvart von Arnim; his orderly, Corporal Helmut Mayer; and his secretary, Cita Krebben.

General Walter Warlimont proved particularly helpful in our efforts to re-create the atmosphere of OKW and Hitler's fanatical determination to raze Paris. To supplement his own memory, he offered us access to his voluminous personal notes and papers. Among the other German officers who were especially helpful to us, mention must be made of Generals Günther Blumentritt and Hans Speidel; Captain Theo Wulff, aide to General Hubertus von Aulock, who furnished us his detailed personal diary; and Emil "Bobby" Bender.

But above all, we must thank the devoted band of colleagues who worked with us tracking down people, interviewing and re-interviewing them day after day. Theirs was a difficult job, sometimes frustrating, occasionally unrewarding, always demanding a high degree of zeal and perseverance. Through it all, they worked with great competence and grand cheer. We owe them much. Michelle Ristich headed the team, correlated their efforts and put the mass of documents they uncovered into organized form. Working with her were Manuela Andreota, Colette Brault, Mai Jumblatt, Olivier Fleuriot de Langle, Lisette Edery and Michel Renouard in France; Vladimir Benz, Dieter Wagner and Nina Silianof in Germany.

Martine Louis cross-referenced their reports into ten loose-leaf folders comprising a minute-by-minute chronology of the liberation. She, Manuela Andreota, Colette Brault, and Christiane Ciezko spelled each other in Saint-Tropez typing our manuscript during the four months required to write the book.

We would also like to thank Dimitri Panitza of the *Reader's Digest* in Paris for his help and his early faith in our project; our employers at *Newsweek* and *Paris Match* for the leaves of absence they generously accorded which made it possible for us to write *Is Paris Burning?*; and our éditors, Tony Schulte at Simon and Schuster and Henri Nogueres at Editions Robert Laffont in Paris for their valuable counsel and criticism.

To all of them, and to all those who helped in the preparation of this book, go once again our thanks. We hope they will join with us in our satisfaction at having attempted to add one small page to the lengthy legend of a city we all love.

L.C. AND D.L.

Les Bignoles
Ramatuelle, Var
France

CONTENTS

TABLE OF COMPARATIVE GERMAN AND AMERICAN OFFICER RANKS

U.S. ARMY	WEHRMACHT	SS (*Schutz Staffeln*)
General of the Army	Generalfeldmarschall	SS Reichsführer
General	Generaloberst	Oberstgruppenführer
Lt. General	General	Obergruppenführer
Maj. General	Generalleutnant	Gruppenführer
Brig. General	Generalmajor	Brigadeführer
———	———	Oberführer
Colonel	Oberst	Standartenführer
Lt. Colonel	Oberstleutnant	Obersturmbannführer
Major	Major	Sturmbannführer
Captain	Hauptmann	Hauptsturmführer
First Lieutenant	Oberleutnant	Obersturmführer
Second Lieutenant	Leutnant	Untersturmführer
Warrant Officer	Unteroffizier	Hauptscharführer

On August 23, 1944, at 11 A.M., the following order was transmitted from Adolf Hitler's Supreme Headquarters in East Prussia to the Commanding General of Greater Paris. Designated Top Secret and Very Urgent, with copies for the Commander in Chief of the Armies of the West, Army Group B, the First Army, the Fifth Panzer Division, and the Fifteenth Army, it set forth Hitler's final decision on the fate of Paris.

Geh. Kommandosache Chefsache
Nur durch Offizier
KR Blitz

O.B. West Ia
Okdo d. H. Gr. B. Ia
A.O.K. 1
Pz. A.O.K. 5
A.O.K. 15

The defense of the Paris bridgehead is of capital importance from both a military and political standpoint. The loss of the city would lead to the loss of the entire coastal plain north of the Seine and would deprive us of our rocket-launching sites for the long-distance war against England.

In all history, the loss of Paris has inevitably brought with it the loss of all France.

The Führer therefore categorically reaffirms his order: Paris must at all costs be defended by locking the city inside a strong position. He reminds the Commander in Chief of the West that reinforcements have been designated for this purpose.

In the city itself, the most energetic tactics, such as the razing of entire city blocks, the public execution of ringleaders, the forced evacuation of any quarter of the city which appears menacing, must be used to smash the first signs of an uprising; this is the only way to prevent such movements from spreading.

The destruction of the city's Seine bridges, will be prepared.

Paris must not fall into the hands of the enemy, or, if it does, he must find there nothing but a field of ruins.

O.K.W./W.F.St./Op. (H)
Nr. 772989/44

23.8.44
11.00 Uhr

PART ONE

THE MENACE

1

He was never late. Each evening when the German arrived with his old Mauser, his frayed leather binocular case and his dinner pail, the inhabitants of the village of May-en-Multien knew it was six o'clock. As he walked across the cobbled town square, the first notes of the evening Angelus invariably rang out from the Romanesque belfry of the little twelfth-century church of Notre-Dame-de-l'Assomption looking down on May-en-Multien's gray slate roofs from its perch on a ridge over the River Ourcq, 37 miles northeast of Paris.

The German, a graying Luftwaffe sergeant, always marched straight toward that peaceful sound. At the door of the church, he tugged off his cloth cap and walked inside. With a slow step, he climbed up the narrow, circular staircase to the top of the belfry. There at its summit were a table, a gas burner, and a chair requisitioned from the church below. Carefully laid out on the table were a German General Staff map, a notebook, a calendar, and a gray-green field telephone. The belfry of Notre-Dame-de-l'Assomption was a Luftwaffe observation post.

Here, with his binoculars, the German could survey the whole region. From the spires of the cathedral of Meaux to the south, to the medieval stone walls of the Château de la Ferté-Milon in the north, his gaze swept over 13 miles past a graceful arc of the Marne River, the terra-cotta walls of the town of Lizy-sur-Ourcq and back, finally, to the poplar-studded banks of the Ourcq dropping away below his eyes.

In a few hours, night would fall over that peaceful scene

spread out under the sergeant's binoculars. Scanning the horizon, peering into the shadows around him, he would then begin another night's vigil, his fifty-eighth since the invasion. In the first light of dawn, he would pick up his field telephone and report to Luftwaffe regional headquarters in Soissons. Since the last full moon, twelve days earlier, the sergeant's reports had invariably been the same: "Nothing to report for my sector."

The German knew the Allies always made their parachute drops to the French Resistance in the light of a full moon. The moon would not be full again, the calendar on his table showed him, for sixteen more nights, not until the evening of August 18.

Nothing, the German was sure, would happen that night in this tiny pocket of occupied France entrusted to his care. That night of August 2, 1944, the sergeant felt certain that he could doze in safety on the shaky table before him. The German was wrong.

While he slept, two miles away in a wet field of shocked wheat, two men and a woman staked themselves out into the triangular pattern that marked a Resistance drop zone. Each clutched a flashlight wrapped in a tin sleeve. Pointed overhead, these shrouded flashlights could send out a thin pillar of light visible only from above. The trio waited. Shortly after midnight they heard the sound they were waiting for. It was the low drone of the throttled-down motors of a Halifax bomber sweeping softly over the valley of the Ourcq. They switched on their lights.

Staring down into the blacked-out river valley, the pilot of the plane above sighted their blinking triangle. He pressed a button on the panel before him. In the fuselage of his bomber a glowing light switched from red to green. As it did, a man grasped the sides of the plane's open hatch and flung himself into the night.

As he drifted silently home to French soil, young medical student Alain Perpezat could feel at his waist the tug of a money belt containing five million francs. But it was not to deliver that impressive sum that he had plummeted into this dark August night.

Fitted into the sole of Alain Perpezat's left shoe was a gossamer-thin strip of silk. It contained eighteen blocks of coded figures. So important and so urgent did his superiors in

London consider the message stamped on it that, against all their rules, they had sent Alain Perpezat plunging into this moonless night to deliver it.

Perpezat did not know what was in the message he carried. All he knew was that he was to deliver it as quickly as possible to the head of the British Intelligence Service in France, whose code name was "Jade Amicol." His headquarters were in Paris.

It was seven o'clock the next morning when Perpezat shook off the last slivers of hay from the haystack in which he had hidden for the night. To get to Paris, the young medical student chose the quickest means open to him. He decided to hitchhike.

The first truck that rolled past him on France's Route 3 stopped. It belonged to the Luftwaffe. Four helmeted German soldiers hanging to the wooden slats of its open van stared down at him.

Perpezat watched the door of the truck open. The driver beckoned to him. It seemed to Perpezat at that instant that his bulky money belt weighed a hundred pounds. The German studied him. "Nach Paris?" he said. Perpezat nodded and numbly slid onto the warm seat beside him. Then the German shifted gears, and, from the cab of the Luftwaffe truck, the young agent with his message for the head of British intelligence for France watched the road to Paris begin to slide past.

• • •

Kneeling in the cool shadows of their chapel, the nine sisters of the order of the Passion of our Blessed Lord were reciting their third rosary of the day when the three long and one short rings jabbed through the stillness of their convent. Immediately two of them got up, blessed themselves, and left. To Sister Jean, the mother superior, and Sister Jean-Marie Vianney, her assistant, three long and one short rings of the old doorbell of their convent at 127 rue de la Santé meant "an important visit."

For four years the Gestapo had searched desperately for a man this convent concealed. There, behind the sitting room of this scabrous old building built at the juncture of a vacant lot and the high stone walls of the insane asylum of Sainte-

Anne, was the headquarters of "Jade Amicol," the head of
British intelligence for occupied France. Protected by these
old stones and the tranquil courage of a handful of nuns, his
headquarters had survived all the Gestapo's relentless hunts.°

Sister Jean opened the judas window cut into the convent's
heavy oak door, and saw outside the face of a young man.

"My name is Alain," he said. "I have a message for the
colonel."

Sister Jean unbolted the door and stepped out onto the
doorstep herself to make sure the young man was alone and
that he had not been followed. Then she beckoned him inside.

In the sitting room, under an austere portrait of the unknown Lazarite priest who had founded the order of the
Passion of our Blessed Lord, Alain Perpezat took off his left
shoe. With a knife Sister Jean handed him, Perpezat pried
apart its sole and slipped out the scrap of silk for which he had
just risked his life. He handed it to the balding giant with
blue eyes sitting in the armchair next to him.

Colonel Claude Ollivier—"Jade Amicol"—glanced at the
black letters stamped on it, and asked Sister Jean to bring
him the grid with which he decoded his messages. It was
printed on a razor-thin handkerchief made of a digestible
fabric that would dissolve on his tongue in seconds if he had
to swallow it. Sister Jean kept it hidden in the chapel, below
the altar stone under the tabernacle of the altar of the Good
Thief.

Ollivier fitted the grid to the message Perpezat had brought
him. The Allied Command, it said, was determined to "bypass
Paris and to delay its liberation as long as possible." Nothing,
it added, could be allowed to change those plans. It was
signed "General," the code name for the head of the intelligence service, a signature reserved for messages of extreme
importance.

The colonel looked up at Perpezat.

"My God!" he said. "This is a catastrophe!"

° In 1943, the convent was even the site of a secret meeting between
Admiral Wilhelm Canaris, head of the Abwehr, Germany's military intelligence, who was taken there blindfolded, and the chief of the intelligence
service in France. Canaris wanted to find out from Churchill what might
be the terms of an eventual peace treaty between the Allies and a Germany
free of Hitler. Fifteen days later, the answer came back from Churchill. It was
"unconditional surrender." Eighteen months later, Canaris was executed for
his role in the plot against Hitler.

2

FOR THE CITY, SPREAD beyond the walls of "Jade Amicol's" convent, this warm August morning marked the 1,503rd day of its German occupation.

Exactly on the stroke of twelve, just as he had done every day during those four years, Private Fritz Gottschalk and the 249 other men of his First Sicherungsregiment began their daily march down the Champs-Élysées to the place de la Concorde. Ahead of them a brass band broke into the strident notes of "Preussens Glorie"—Prussia's Glory. Few Parisians stood on the sidewalks of that majestic avenue to watch Private Gottschalk's display. They had learned long before to avoid that humiliating sight.

That strutting parade was just one of the many humiliations the capital of France had had to learn to bear since June 15, 1940. The only place a Frenchman could see his country's flag on public display in Paris that day was the musty Army Museum of Les Invalides, where it was locked inside a glass cabinet.

The black, white and red swastika of Nazi Germany defied the city from the top of the monument that was its very hallmark, the Eiffel Tower. From hundreds of hotels, public buildings and apartment houses requisitioned by Paris's conquerors, the same oppressive banner fluttered, a symbol of the regime that had for four years shackled the spirit of the world's most beautiful city.

Along the graceful arcades of the rue de Rivoli, around the place de la Concorde, in front of the Palais du Luxembourg, the Chamber of Deputies, and the Quai d'Orsay, black, white and red Wehrmacht sentry boxes barred Parisians from the pavements of their own city.

Before 74 avenue Foch and 9 rue des Saussaies, before other buildings less clearly marked but no less well known, other men stood guard. They wore the twin silver flashes of the SS on their tunic collars. They guarded the offices of the

Gestapo. Their neighbors did not always sleep well. Sometimes it was not easy to blot out the screams that floated almost nightly from those buildings.

The Germans had even changed the face of the city. Almost two hundred of its handsomest bronze statues had been torn down. They were shipped to Germany to be melted into shell castings.

The architects of the TODT labor organization had replaced them with monuments of their own—less esthetic, perhaps, but more efficacious. Sunk into the pavements of Paris were almost a hundred concrete pillboxes. Their squat forms pimpled the surface of the city like a rash of warts.

And a tangle of white wooden signs had sprouted like beanstalks in the place de l'Opéra, before the wicker chairs of the Café de la Paix. Their black-lettered arms pointed German drivers to such un-Gallic destinations as DER MILITÄRBEFEHL-SHABER IN FRANKREICH, GENERAL DER LUFTWAFFE, and HAUPT-VERKEHRSDIREKTION PARIS. That summer a new one had been added. Its wording cheered the Parisians who passed it. It read ZUR NORMANDIE FRONT.

Never had the city's wide boulevards been so empty. There were no buses. Taxis had disappeared in 1940. The few drivers fortunate enough (or compromised enough) to have a German *Ausweis* for their cars used wood for fuel. Those converted cars were called *gazogènes*, and they burned the wood that powered them in washboilers bolted to their trunks.

The bicycle and the horse ruled the highway. The bicycle had even replaced the taxi. Some cab drivers had converted their taxis into fiacres and themselves into horses by cutting their cabs in half, leaving only their back seats balanced on their rear wheels. They were called "vélo-taxis." The drivers towed them with their bicycles. For express service, there were super-vélo-taxis towed by four riders. The fastest was pulled by a group of veterans of the Tour de France, France's famous bicycle race. Painted on the back of most of these man-powered jitneys was a name. The favorite was LES TEMPS MODERNES.

The métro closed from eleven to three every workday and all weekend. At night it shut down at eleven o'clock. Curfew was at twelve. When the Germans caught a Parisian out after curfew, they took him to the headquarters of the Feldgendarmerie (Military Police) where he spent the night shining their boots. But if a German soldier was shot by the Resistance that night, his price for missing the last métro home might be higher. It would be paid in front of a firing squad. The Germans liked to select victims for their reprisal firings from among the night's curfew violators.

Three days a week there was no alcohol in the city's sidewalk cafés. Instead they served a loathsome ersatz coffee called *café national*. It was made from acorns and chick-peas.

Paris was a city practically without gas and electricity. Its housewives had learned to cook over ten-gallon cans welded together and called the *"réchaud '44."* For fuel they used scraps of newspaper crumbled into tiny balls and sprinkled with water. They burned more slowly that way. A six-page paper, a department store advertised, could bring a liter of water to boil in twelve minutes.

Above all, Paris was a hungry city. It had become the largest country village in the world, and each morning it woke to the crowing of roosters. They called out the dawn from backyards, rooftop pens, garrets, spare bedrooms, even broom closets—from any place where the city's hungry millions could find a few feet to raise them. It was a city in which little boys and old women crept out each morning to chop a few forbidden blades of grass in its parks for the rabbits they kept in their bathtubs.

Parisians that August would get two eggs, 3.2 ounces of cooking oil, 2 ounces of margarine on their ration tickets. The meat ration was so small that, according to a popular joke, it could be wrapped in a subway ticket—provided the ticket had not been used. If it had, went the joke, the meat might fall out through the hole punched in the ticket by the conductor's perforator. Staple of most Parisian diets was the rutabaga, a variety of turnip they had formerly fed to cattle.

For those who had the money, there was the black market. There a meal for four cost 6,250 francs. (A secretary that summer earned 2,500 francs a month.) Eggs were forty cents apiece and butter ten dollars a pound. For those who lacked the money, the only way to stretch a ration card was to bicycle 20, 30 or 40 miles into the country looking for a peasant with a chicken or a handful of vegetables to sell.

Vichy posters urging French workers to "unite with their German brothers," or join the "Legion against Bolshevism" covered the city's walls. The front pages of collaborationist papers like *Le Petit Parisien, Paris-Soir*, and the weekly *Je Suis Partout* (I am Everywhere) proclaimed that "work in Germany is not deportation," and announced from Berlin that "never has the German General Staff been so full of confidence in the future." Inside, discreet advertisements offered "long-distance furniture shipping by horse."

Yet, somehow, Paris had managed to keep its heart, as Elliot Paul remembered it, "light and gay." Never had its beautiful women seemed so beautiful. Four years of lean rations and daily bicycle riding had hardened their bodies and slimmed their legs. That summer they wore their hair wrapped in turbans or swept into wide flowered hats that seemed to come from the paintings of Renoir.

In July, Madeleine de Rauch, Lucien Lelong and Jacques Fath had announced the "*Mode Martiale*." It featured broad shoulders, wide belts, and short skirts—to save material. Some of that material in fabric-short France was made of wood fibers. When it rained, Parisians joked, the termites came out.

At night, Parisiennes wore thick wooden-soled shoes that clopped noisily against the pavement as they walked. They had learned to take them off and walk home barefooted if they were caught out after curfew. Then the Germans patrolling the city could only hear the footfalls of their own hob-nailed boots.

That August, Paris had stayed home. *C'était la guerre*, and no one was able to leave for the traditional country vacation. Schools were open. Thousands sunbathed along the quais of the Seine, and, that summer, the muddy river became the world's largest swimming pool.

For the collaborators and their German friends, for the *nouveaux riches* of the black market, there was still champagne and caviar at Maxim's, the Lido and a few cabarets like Shéhérazade and Suzy Solidor's. That week, with ticket No. 174,184, a lucky Frenchman would win six million francs ($34,300) in the twenty-eighth drawing of the National Lottery, more than Alain Perpezat had brought into Paris in his itchy money belt.

Saturday, Sunday and Monday, the racing season went on at Longchamp and Auteuil. The horses were thin but the stands were full. And from Luna Park, Paris's Coney Island, came the consoling announcement, "Don't feel sorry about missing a vacation. With 99 strokes of your bike's pedals, you can find fresh air and sunshine here."

Yves Montand and Edith Piaf sang together at the Moulin Rouge. Serge Lifar looked back on the ballet season and praised two young unknowns, Zizi Jeanmaire and Roland Petit.

Movie houses kept their projectors running on the current pedaled into their generators by a brace of bicycles. The Gaumont Palace, France's Radio City Music Hall, calculated that four men pedaling at 13 miles an hour for six hours could store enough current for two complete shows. Outside, the theater advertised free parking for 300 bicycles.

Theaters opened at three and closed at dusk. They played to full houses. The city's round green kiosks advertised over twenty different plays. The Vieux Colombier was giving Jean Paul Sartre's *No Exit*. A few blocks from the theater, hidden in an attic bedroom, its author wrote tracts for the Resistance.

But above all, each evening of that memorable summer of 1944, one sacred activity fixed the people of Paris to their homes during the brief half hour when the electric current flickered on. Then, ears pressed to radio sets, an entire city hushed and listened across the crackling static of the German jamming to the forbidden broadcasts of the BBC. That night, August 3, 1944, in the matchless beauty of a Parisian sunset, the people of this city would learn for the first time of an event that would soon become for them a special nightmare.

Warsaw, that night, was in flames. While its Russian liberators paused only a brief march from its gates, its German garrison was brutally crushing a premature uprising of its Resistance movement. When they had finished, 200,000 Poles would be dead, and Warsaw a sad pile of blackened stone.

Any Parisian, looking out his window that night, could gaze upon one of the miracles of the war. Paris was intact. Notre-Dame, Sainte-Chapelle, the Louvre, Sacré-Coeur, the Arc de Triomphe, all the matchless monuments that had made this city a beacon to civilized man, had thus far survived unscathed five years of the most destructive war in history. Now, finally, the hour of Paris's liberation was approaching. The fate that was reducing Warsaw to ruins this August evening, the fate Paris had thus far so miraculously escaped, would soon hang over this, the most beautiful city in the world.

For Paris was the hub around which all France turned.

Into this city converged all France's major roads, railroads, canals. It was the heart from which France was ruled. Its three and a half million citizens, millions of others around the world, might think only of the safety of the treasures it held in escrow for civilized man. To other men separated that night by thousands of miles, Paris was now something else. To them, Paris had become an objective.

3

FOR THE AMERICAN WHO would liberate it, Paris had been a dilemma. General Dwight D. Eisenhower, in a command caravan hidden in a rain-swept grove of trees two miles inland from the Normandy beach of Granville, had finally made a reluctant decision, the most important, perhaps, that he had made since D Day. He would postpone the liberation of Paris as long as possible. He would encircle and bypass the city. Paris, the Supreme Allied Commander estimated, would not be freed for almost two months, not until mid-September at the earliest.

This was not a decision Eisenhower had made lightly. He knew as well as anyone the tremendous emotional impact Paris's liberation would have on the French, on his troops, indeed on all the world. He was aware of the stirring impatience of its population and of General Charles de Gaulle, Free France's imperious leader. But in Eisenhower's mind, the precise military reasoning in a 24-page mimeographed document on his desk weighed more heavily than all the magic in the word "Paris." Its blue manila folder bore the words "Top Secret—Post Neptune Operations Section II—Crossing of the Seine and Capture of Paris." It came from SHAEF's three-man planning board, which furnished the recommendations on which he based his strategic decisions.

Eisenhower was convinced "the Germans would put up a strong fight for Paris." To him, "every strategic and geographic reason dictated it." The three-man planning study on his desk confirmed his own belief. It was one fight he wanted to avoid.

The paper warned that if the Germans held Paris in strength, dislodging them would require "prolonged and heavy street fighting similar to that in Stalingrad," fighting that could end "in the destruction of the French capital."

Eisenhower could not allow that to happen to Paris. Further, he did not want his armor, now rolling free across France, sucked into a wasting city battle.

But above all else, there was one overwhelming reason which, in Eisenhower's mind, had dictated his decision. It was summed up in one paragraph in the paper on his desk.

"If taken early," it said, "Paris will become a serious limitation to our ability to maintain forces in operation."

And, the paper warned, "The capture of Paris will entail a civil affairs commitment equal to maintaining *eight divisions in operation.*"

In other words, to Eisenhower, the capture of Paris meant the risk of drying up the fuel tanks of almost a fourth of the 37 divisions he had already landed in France. It was a risk he would not take. Gasoline that summer was the most precious thing in the world to him. "I hurt every time I had to give up a gallon," he said later. Paris would cost him thousands.

The cost would come not in capturing the city but in feeding and supplying it once it was free. "Paris food and medical requirements alone are 75,000 tons for the first two months, and an additional 1,500 tons of coal daily are likely to be needed for public utilities," the SHAEF study reported. With only Cherbourg and the invasion beaches for ports, with the French railways a ruin, every ton of that would have to be brought from Normandy to Paris by truck, a 416-mile round trip. Avoid that commitment—and avoid liberating Paris—"as long as possible" was the advice of the planners.

They had suggested another plan. It involved a pincer movement north and south of the city, which would also allow the Allies to roll up the launching sites for the V-1 and V-2 rocket bases in the north of France, a task, they felt, that was so urgent it "justified more than normal risks."

Under the plan, General Sir Bernard L. Montgomery's Twenty-first Army Group would strike over the Lower Seine between the Oise and the sea, open the port of Le Havre and menace the V sites in the Pas-de-Calais. Then, at Amiens, 82 miles north of Paris, two corps would break east in a wheeling movement. At the same time, south of Paris, the American

Twelfth Army Group would cross the Seine at Melun, drive northeast to Reims, 98 miles beyond Paris, and wheel west to meet the British forces striking out from Amiens. There the two forces would hook up, closing Paris into a gigantic bag. The date estimated for the operation was between September 15 and October 1.

To Eisenhower, the plan had offered three advantages. It avoided a destructive street battle in Paris; it pushed his troops through the tank country they could use best; and above all, it saved precious gasoline for his overriding objective—a breach in the Siegfried Line and a bridgehead over the Rhine before winter set in.

Only one thing could upset it: some unforeseen event such as an uprising in Paris. But on that point Eisenhower could feel reassured. He had issued General Pierre Joseph Koenig, head of the FFI (French Forces of the Interior), "firm instructions" that "no armed movements were to go off in Paris or anywhere else" until he had given the order. It was essential, he had told him, that "nothing happen in Paris to change our plans."

It would be a difficult burden for the impatient Parisians to bear. But if they could "live with the Germans a little bit longer," he told his brilliant deputy, General Walter Bedell Smith, "their sacrifice may help us shorten the war."

To make sure they did, British intelligence had sent Alain Perpezat parachuting into France on a moonless night.

4

FOR A MELANCHOLY FRENCHMAN waiting restlessly in the sodden heat of an Algiers summer, Paris was the hinge on which the destiny of his country would shortly turn. And with it would turn also the destiny of this lonely man. Better than any of the men around him, Charles de Gaulle knew that Paris was the place where the bold gamble, embodied in his call to his defeated countrymen from London June 18, 1940, would be forever won or lost. What happened there in the next few weeks would decide, de Gaulle was convinced, who would control postwar France. De Gaulle was resolutely determined that that control should be his.

Two factions, de Gaulle believed, conspired to deny it to him: his political enemies, the French Communist party, and his military allies, the Americans.

United States-de Gaulle relations had, after a brief honeymoon in 1940, slipped steadily downhill. United States recognition of Vichy, the deal with Darlan, the fact de Gaulle was not informed of the United States landings in North Africa until they were actually taking place,° a personal antagonism between de Gaulle and President Franklin D. Roosevelt—all had helped build the mistrust and suspicions that plagued Franco-American relations in the summer of 1944.

Nothing, however, irritated de Gaulle more than F.D.R.'s refusal to recognize his Comité Français de Libération Nationale (CFLN) as the provisional government of France. He saw in it an American refusal to acknowledge his leadership of France.†

F.D.R. had defined the United States position in a memo to General George C. Marshall, June 14, 1944. "We should," he wrote, "make full use of any organization or influence that de Gaulle may possess that will be of advantage to our military effort provided we do not by force of arms impose him on the French people as the government of France." He warned Eisenhower that SHAEF "may deal with the CFLN but must not do anything that would constitute a recognition of the CFLN as the provisional government of France."

De Gaulle's relations with Eisenhower were better, although the SHAEF commander could note "he [de Gaulle] was always trying to get us to change this or that to accommodate his political needs," and his chief of staff, General Walter

---

° To insure that the Algiers landings were unopposed, the United States made a much criticized deal with Admiral Jean Louis Darlan, the Vichy master of Algiers. An angry de Gaulle's first words when he was awakened on November 8, 1942 and informed the landings were under way were "I hope Vichy drives them back into the sea."

† De Gaulle was persuaded, as early as the Casablanca conference in January, 1943, that the United States was aiming to keep the control of postwar France out of his hands. He was, according to one diplomat, "literally chased out of London" to Casablanca, and the French leader's first words to his United States host, diplomat Robert Murphy, were an icy declaration of hostility. "Let me assure you, Mr. Murphy," he said, "I should not be here on French soil, behind American barbed wire and American bayonets, if the villa in which we are meeting belonged to a Frenchman." It belonged to a Dane.

Bedell Smith, could testily scrawl on a SHAEF memo in June, 1944: "I should be happy to give him [de Gaulle] a briefing if someone can define for me what his status is with this headquarters. As far as I know, he has none."

There were other irritations, too. De Gaulle's radio communications with his London staff had to pass through Anglo-American hands, and he was aware Churchill had instructed Foreign Minister Anthony Eden to see that they were "examined for political content." The Allied decision to issue invasion currency on D Day had so infuriated the French leader that he withdrew all but twenty of the five hundred French liaison officers trained to help SHAEF administer the liberated portions of the Normandy beachhead.

Above all, de Gaulle was determined no trace of AMGOT (Allied Military Government of Occupied Territories) should take root on French soil. His fears had been partially eased in July during his first official visit to Washington. There, he and F.D.R. had reached an agreement on the administration of liberated France. But it was a tenuous accord. On leaving, de Gaulle remarked to Robert Murphy, "Our agreements end the day the war ends."

Under it, liberated France would be divided into two parts: a Zone of the Interior in which control was to be handed over to de Gaulle's CFLN, and a Zone of Operations in which SHAEF's authority was to be supreme. The responsibility of deciding the boundaries of the two zones was left largely to Eisenhower.

The agreement failed to resolve the basic division between de Gaulle and SHAEF. To de Gaulle, he, as the head of the Free French Government, represented French sovereignty, and therefore his authority, not SHAEF's, was supreme in France. To SHAEF, France was a theater of military operations and de Gaulle's political needs had to be fitted into SHAEF's strategic demands.

The agreement made no provision for Paris. Washington assumed that the city would remain in the Zone of Operations for some time after its liberation. And F.D.R. had no intention of installing in it a government he had not yet recognized. It was a valid assumption. But it overlooked one salient fact —Charles de Gaulle's unyielding determination to install himself and his government in Paris as quickly as possible. On his success in doing that hung, de Gaulle felt, his own and France's fate.

In these critical early August days, de Gaulle had become convinced F.D.R. would make one last effort to block his route to power by sealing him off in Algiers while the State Department connived against him in France.° Those American efforts, de Gaulle was sure, could not succeed. But he feared they might delay him just long enough to allow his real foes, the French Communist party, to embed themselves in the foyers of power that Paris represented. That he would not permit.

For de Gaulle was convinced he was in a race with the French Communist party. The immediate goal was Paris; the victor's prize would be all France.

As early as 1943 he had given orders to "Colonel Passy," André de Wavrin—the industrialist who controlled his arms-dropping organizations—that "no arms are to be parachuted directly to the Communists or dropped in such a way that they might fall into their hands."

Since D Day, he had set into motion a plan to insure that political control in France stayed out of their grasp. As each parcel of France was liberated, all civil authority was placed in the hands of a high commissioner appointed by de Gaulle and responsible only to his government. None of the orders they had received were stricter than those they were given for dealing with local Resistance committees which, de Gaulle felt, were Communist-dominated. They were not to be allowed any direct authority over the liberated areas. And under no conditions were they to become "Committees of Public Safety" patterned after those of the French Revolution. During the Allied sweep into Brittany, de Gaulle received a series of alarming reports. On all sides, the Communists seemed stronger, better organized, more forthright in their bid for power than he had expected.

The decisive test would come in Paris. On June 14 he had ordered an end to all arms drops in the Paris region; he estimated the Communists already had 25,000 armed men in the city.

De Gaulle was sure the party was preparing to launch a

° His suspicions were perhaps not ungrounded. In the summer of 1944, F.D.R. was still, according to Robert Murphy, "perfectly prepared to accept any viable alternative to de Gaulle—providing one could be found."

bloody insurrection in Paris to seize the levers of power, with
which France was ruled, before he could get to them. Then
they would sink their roots down into the governing structures
of France and confront him with an entrenched Red-run
Commune ° when he and his government entered Paris. Thus
solidly installed, they could shunt him and his ministers into
an honorary corner cut off from real authority while they
finished the job of consolidating their hold on France. To his
political representative in Paris, a quiet civil servant named
Alexandre Parodi, it seemed clear de Gaulle expected nothing
less than "an armed Communist challenge to his authority"
in the capital.†

De Gaulle's answer was simple. He would take control of
Paris before the Communists could. If they were permitted
to install themselves before his government, he feared, only
a bloody showdown which France neither wanted nor could
afford could get them out. Whatever the cost, whatever the
means, de Gaulle was determined he would get there first.

At about the same time that Eisenhower, in his Granville
headquarters, reached his decision to delay Paris's liberation,

---

° The Revolutionary authority installed in Paris by an insurrection March
18, 1871, on the heels of the retreating Prussian Army. It had to be over-
thrown in May of the same year by Regular French Army forces and later
became a symbol of Communist hopes for the city.

† It was an allegation the party and many non-Communists were to deny.
How far the Communists were prepared to go in their quest for political
power will probably never be known. At the very least, it seems clear their
aim was to install themselves in the key positions of power from which spring-
board, in Paris as in Prague, they could catapult themselves into authority,
should the opportunity appear in postwar France. Perhaps their true senti-
ments toward de Gaulle were summed up by a Bulgarian Red leader of the
Communist Resistance in the South of France, Yvan Kaleff. "For the moment," he said, "we need de Gaulle. After the war, who knows if de Gaulle
will want to stay or France will want him?" (New York *Herald Tribune*,
August 23, 1944, page 25)

Whatever their aims, the Communists' tactics in those parts of France
in which they gained control tended to bear out de Gaulle's suspicions. In
southwest France, it took the Gaullist movement months to wrest the area from
party control. In some areas de Gaulle even had to use clandestine Resistance
transmitters to communicate with his high commissioners. On October 26,
1944, the OSS in a report compiled from its contacts with de Gaulle's security
agents, wrote: "If the French internal situation remains as bad as it is today,
a Communist *coup d'état* is to be expected." Fifty people a day were being
arrested illegally in Toulouse, it reported, and 40,000 armed and carefully
chosen FTP (the Communist-run militia, Francs-Tireurs et Partisans) were
ready to be sent secretly to Paris. They would "constitute the body of the
party's shock troops in the event of a *coup d'état*. Such a bid, if it comes,
would come in mid-January, when their forces are at full strength and the
population is most miserable [*sic*]. The party believes the operation would
take 8 to 10 days and the Allies would not interfere because it would be an
internal French matter."

de Gaulle in Algiers was drafting a secret memo to General Pierre Koenig, head of the FFI. It was essential, he told Koenig, that, whether the Allies liked it or not, Paris be liberated as soon as possible. As soon as it was free, he intended to enter the city himself and impose his personal authority and the authority of his government on the capital.

He had already made his first preparations. For de Gaulle, just as for Eisenhower, an insurrection in the city of Paris would be a disaster. Like Eisenhower, he too had issued firm orders to prevent just that from happening.

5

FROM AN ATTIC WINDOW of a fifth-floor apartment in the Paris suburb of Auteuil, the man to whom Charles de Gaulle had issued those orders stared into the darkness of an August night. In the somber blackout, his eyes could barely follow the outlines of the jagged shadows stumbling before him down to the horizon. They were the rooftops of Paris. His name was Jacques Chaban-Delmas, and he was twenty-nine years old. He was a general. That day he had received a message mumbled to him on a street corner by a man repairing a bicycle tire. It was the message "Jade Amicol" had decoded in the convent of the Passion of our Blessed Lord a few hours before.

To no one in Paris had the information carried in the sole of Alain Perpezat's left shoe appeared more catastrophic than it did to this brooding young man.

Of all the tasks de Gaulle had given him, none, Chaban knew, was more important in the general's eyes than that he had assigned him in Paris. None of the secret instructions he had received from de Gaulle's military headquarters in London had been clearer or more precise than those he had received for Paris.

He was to retain absolute control of the armed Resistance in the city. He was under no circumstances to allow an insurrection to break out in the capital without de Gaulle's direct authorization.

They were impossible orders.

Chaban did not control the Resistance in Paris. The Communist party controlled it.

The head of the underground army for all France was a Communist general named Alfred Mallaret-Joinville. Its leader for the Paris region was a stocky Breton Communist. His senior deputy was another Communist, named Pierre Fabien, a man who, in the Barbès subway station, had, in 1942, shot the first German soldier killed in the capital. The party dominated the unions and the clandestine press. They ran two of Paris's three Resistance political committees and had turned the third into an ineffectual debating society.° Recently a Communist gang had boldly hijacked a plane full of funds sent to Chaban-Delmas from FFI headquarters in London. For months they had been reinforcing their positions, planting their agents in key posts in every part of the city. Even a senior Resistance doctor complained that the party had forced a watchful deputy on him. Daily Chaban-Delmas watched the ranks of the Communist-run militia, the FTP, swell.

Yet no group had fought harder or paid a higher price in blood in the Resistance than the Communists. Latecomers to the Resistance—they did not throw themselves into the battle against the Germans until after the Nazi invasion of the U.S.S.R. in 1941—they had brought to it its best-organized, best-disciplined, and often its most courageous troops. The party's ranks had swollen enormously during the war. Never had its prestige been so high. It was the most important single political organization in France. Its FTP was the most important single armed body in the Resistance.† Its leadership,

---

° They were the Comité Parisien de Libération (CPL), the Paris Liberation Committee, and the Comité d'Action Militaire (COMAC), Military Action Committee, which they controlled, and the Comité National de la Résistance (CNR), National Resistance Committee, where they were a powerful minority. Founded by de Gaulle in 1943, the CNR was in theory the senior political body of the Resistance. In fact, by the summer of 1944, it had outlived its usefulness to de Gaulle and was, he felt, dominated by the Communists. He scathingly referred to it as "this Comité de Salut Public"—Committee of Public Safety—a reference to the French Revolutionary directorate which ruled France under Maximilien de Robespierre during the Terror.

† On September 6, General Koenig would estimate to Eisenhower that the party had under its discipline in France 250,000 armed men and another 200,000 waiting for arms. France's Regular Army at the time numbered fewer than 500,000 men.

long trained to clandestinity, had survived the war intact. A system of party couriers, drifting in and out of Switzerland, and two secret radio transmitters in southwest France had kept them in contact with Moscow.

Now the time had come for this stirring political giant to claim the price of three hard years of service. It would claim it in Paris.

Staring out at this darkened city which was his ward, Chaban-Delmas knew what the price would be. The leaders of the party were determined to force in the streets of Paris the insurrection he had been ordered to prevent.

"Whatever the cost," he believed, "the Communists would launch their insurrection, even if the result was the destruction of the most beautiful city in the world." Paris, Chaban realized, "was an opportunity the Communists could not afford to miss."

He had tried during the past weeks to persuade them to miss it. He had gotten nowhere. Chaban's archrival, an ascetic Communist architect named Roger Villon, felt the Gaullists wanted to prevent an insurrection so "de Gaulle could march into Paris at the head of a conquering army and find the city gratefully prostrated at his feet." Chaban believed the Communists wanted to stage an insurrection "to seize power in Paris and welcome de Gaulle not as the head of the Free French, but as their invited guest."

Like the rest of Paris, Chaban, too, had heard the news of the Warsaw insurrection on the BBC that night. For weeks he had had one hope for saving Paris from the same destiny. It was that the Allies, once clear of Normandy, would strike straight for Paris and seize the city before the Communists could organize their insurrection. The message in Alain Perpezat's left shoe had ended that hope. In the loneliness of his darkened apartment, this young general now realized the plans of the Allies would play directly into the hands of his Communist foes.

One of two fates, Chaban was sure, awaited Paris.

Either a vengeful Wehrmacht would crush the insurrection and Paris along with it, or its victorious Communist leaders would install themselves in the capital's citadels of power, ready to spread their authority over all France.

To Chaban, that night, there seemed to be only one way out of his dilemma. He must persuade the Allies to change their plans. He must warn de Gaulle of the situation in Paris. Somehow he would have to make the trip Alain Perpezat had just made, but in the opposite direction. He would try to reach London. With the energy of despair and of youth, he would implore Eisenhower to change his plans, and send his armored columns straight to Paris.

• • •

To the twisted reasoning of the German who, from a steel-and-concrete bunker in Rastenburg, East Prussia, directed the armies of the Third Reich, Paris meant perhaps even more.

For four years, from 1914 to 1918, six million Germans like Corporal Adolf Hitler had been kept in the trenches of the Western Front by the magic in the cry *"Nach Paris!"* Two million of them had died.

In 1940, what they had failed to achieve in four years, Hitler had achieved in four stunning weeks. On Monday, June 24, at seven o'clock in the morning, two weeks after his troops had entered the city, Hitler had kept his rendezvous with Paris. Few Parisians that morning had seen his black Mercedes glide to a stop at the edge of the Esplanade of the Trocadéro. For a long and satisfying moment, Paris's conqueror contemplated the historic vista spread before his eyes: the Seine, the Eiffel Tower, the gardens of the Champ de Mars, the golden dome of Napoleon's Tomb at Les Invalides and, to the left, down the horizon, the 800-year-old towers of Notre-Dame.

Now Paris was the last prize of five years of warfare left in Hitler's hands. For the last five days, on the maps of his bunker in Rastenburg, Hitler had followed the advance of the Allied armies flowing through the hole driven in his Normandy defense line near Avranches. Hitler knew the battle of France was upon him. If he lost it, there would be only one battle left for him to fight, the battle of Germany.

Like Charles de Gaulle, Hitler knew Paris was the axis around which all France turned. Twice in his short life, Adolf Hitler had attacked Paris. Soon, the irony of history would place him in another role. This time, Adolf Hitler would be Paris's defender. As the planners of SHAEF knew, he had every reason to clamp desperately to the "natural defensive bastion" Paris and the Seine offered him. Lose it, and he would lose his rocket sites and find the armies of the Allies on the doorstep of the Reich.

Hitler would know how to fight for Paris as he had known how to fight for Stalingrad, Monte Cassino, and Saint-Lô. In a few days, in this bunker in East Prussia, he would order Paris defended to the last man. Then, slamming his fist onto his oaken conference table, he would shriek at his doubting General Staff:

"He who holds Paris holds France!"

6

WARWORN AND WEARY, the soldiers of the Wehrmacht lined the concrete platform paralleling the track, their young faces masks of indifference and resignation. Soon they would clamber aboard the *Fronturlauberzug* idling before them and, in a shroud of escaping steam, slide out of Berlin's Silesia station for the long journey back to the eastern front.

Picking his way slowly down the platform, a short, squat major general of the Wehrmacht eyed their emotionless faces with sympathy. Often he, too, had stood in the silence of this blacked-out station waiting for that same train to carry him back to the war in the east. But this night, Dietrich von Choltitz was catching a different train. With his valet tugging at his suitcase behind him, Choltitz edged past the last row of troops on the platform and turned toward that train. Along the top of one of its blue sleeping cars Choltitz could make out the faded yellow letters of the French words that recalled its other journeys in a more peaceful Europe. Tonight, however, these cars of La Compagnie Internationale des Wagons-Lits et des Grands Express Européens belonged to the "Offizier General Sonderzug D2 Führer," the train which would deliver Choltitz and a select group of distinguished visitors to the headquarters of Adolf Hitler in Rastenburg, East Prussia.

Choltitz climbed into the compartment reserved for him

and began to unbutton his tunic. He watched his valet carefully set out on the polished redwood ledge of his washbasin
his prewar Gillette razor, his soap and a tube of Rivonal sleeping pills. Later, he knew, he would be grateful for the sleep
those pills would give him. The next morning, for the first
time in his life, Generalleutnant Dietrich von Choltitz would
have a personal interview with the man who ruled the Third
Reich.

Rare in that summer of 1944 were the field marshals summoned to Hitler's presence. Rarer still were the generals to
whom he granted his time. Choltitz had been called for a
special reason. This stolid little Prussian general settling onto
the tufted brown upholstery of his sleeping compartment had
been hand-picked by Adolf Hitler to command the defense
of the capital of France.

Three days earlier, in the same headquarters toward which
the Führer's train now carried him, a man had selected the
dossiers of three general officers from the metal filing cabinet
locked in his safe. One of them belonged to Choltitz. General
Wilhelm Burgdorf, chief of officer personnel at OKW (Oberkommando der Wehrmacht), Hitler's headquarters, had been
immediately attracted to Choltitz's file. Above all, it showed
Choltitz was a man whose loyalty to the Third Reich had
never flagged. Burgdorf needed just such a man for Paris.
The rot of defeat and disloyalty was creeping through his
generals' corps, and nowhere had it seemed to have set in
more firmly than in Paris. The senior army man in France,
General Karl Heinrich von Stülpnagel, had been a ringleader
of the July 20 attempt on Hitler's life. Blinded and half dead
from a suicide attempt, he lay that night on a cot in Berlin's
Plötzensee prison. Soon, on Hitler's orders, he would be
strangled to death. The commander of Gross Paris, the dilettantish General Hans von Boineburg-Lengsfeld, seemed little
better to Burgdorf.

Burgdorf knew that OKW would need, for the difficult
days ahead in Paris, a man whose loyalty and capacity were
beyond question, a man who would restore discipline to the
city with an iron hand, a man who would know how to beat
out any civilian uprising without hesitation, a man who would
know how to put up for the city the savage defense Burgdorf
was sure Hitler would demand.

Choltitz had seemed to him to be that man. Burgdorf had

taken his dossier and laid it himself in front of the Führer. Choltitz, he recommended, was the man they should assign to Paris; he was "an officer who had never questioned an order no matter how harsh it was."

The Führer had given his approval. Then, as an afterthought, he appended to it a special request. So important did he feel the Paris assignment was that he told Burgdorf to order Choltitz from his Normandy Corps headquarters to OKW so he could prepare him for the command himself.

For this officer of irreproachable loyalty whom Hitler had decided to send to Paris, the war had begun at 5:30 on May 10, 1940. Jumping out of the first JU-52 to land on Rotterdam airport, Lt. Colonel von Choltitz, at the head of the 3rd Battalion of the 16th Regiment of Airborne Infantry, had that morning led the whole German blitzkrieg in the west. He was the first German officer to invade the Low Countries. His assignment was to seize the bridges over the Nieuwe Maas River just south of the city. After four days and four nights of furious combat, the Dutch continued to resist. At noon on May 14, Choltitz ordered a priest and a grocer into the Dutch lines to convince the Dutch commander to surrender. If he did not do so, he warned them, "Rotterdam will be mercilessly bombed." Two hours later they returned without having found the Dutch commander, and the attack began. When he felt the attack had gone on long enough, Choltitz tried to stop it by firing a signal flare. But the signal was blotted out, he said later, by the smoke of a freighter burning nearby, and the bombing ran its course. It left, according to the Dutch, 718 dead and 78,000 wounded and homeless. It destroyed the heart of Rotterdam.

Later a friend would ask him if it had not bothered his conscience when he led the invasion of a country on which Germany had not declared war.

"Why?" he replied.

Dietrich von Choltitz had not been brought up to ask the question "Why?" From the moment of his birth in his family's timbered estate of Silesia, his destiny had been set. Three generations of Prussian soldiery had preceded him out of its gray slate towers into the army. He had received his schooling in the rigidly disciplined Saxon cadet corps. So well had he performed that he was chosen to serve as a page in the court of Saxony's queen.

Von Choltitz's proudest moments had come during the siege of Sebastopol. It was there that he had won his general's insignia. When the siege of the Black Sea port opened, his regiment had contained 4,800 men. On July 27, 1942, 347 were left. But Dietrich von Choltitz, though bleeding from a wound in his right arm, had taken Sebastopol.

To do it, he had not hesitated to force his Russian prisoners to bring forward the ammunition for his siege guns and charge his batteries. In fact, he found it funny that he had compelled the Russians to stuff his cannons with the shells that would blow their homes apart.

Later, when he was transferred to Army Group Center, it had been the unhappy lot of Choltitz's division to cover the path of a retreating army. As always, he faithfully executed the orders he received. And they were in those hard days of 1943 to leave nothing behind the withdrawing Wehrmacht but a swath of scorched earth and destruction.

This unknown general waiting for the Führer's train to leave the Silesia station would carry with him to Paris the reputation of a smasher of cities. It was not entirely undeserved.

"Since Sebastopol," he would one day confess to a Swedish diplomat in Paris, "it has been my fate to cover the retreat of our armies and to destroy the cities behind them."

•   •   •

Nine hundred miles away another man waited for a train to start. Jacques Chaban-Delmas was probably the only passenger on the train sitting under the metal roofing of Paris's Gare de Lyon that evening who knew that it was scheduled to be derailed twice before it would arrive in Lyon.

Chaban knew because those attacks were part of a plan he himself had helped to work out, "Plan Green," designed to disorganize German rail communications. Since early morning Chaban had tried to cancel them. Sitting in his blacked-out compartment, he could now only wait and hope his orders had reached the knots of men waiting in ambush for this train.

The next night, in a cow pasture near Mâcon, Chaban had a rendezvous with a Lysander. Like all the planes landing in occupied France, that Lysander would have instructions to wait three minutes for its passengers Then, with or without them, it would return to England The safety of Paris, Chaban believed, might depend on his getting to that cow pasture on time.

7

IN THE THIRTEEN YEARS that he had borne arms for the Third Reich, Dietrich von Choltitz had met Hitler only once. It was just a year before, during the summer of 1943 at the field headquarters of Generalfeldmarschall Fritz von Manstein on the banks of the Dnieper outside Dnepropetrovsk. The occasion was a lunch offered to the Führer during one of the German dictator's inspections of the eastern front.

Von Choltitz had sat opposite Hitler. During the silence which accompanied Hitler's habitual lunchtime monologue, Choltitz had had ample time to study the Master of the Third Reich. Three things had struck him about Hitler: the contagious sense of confidence that flowed from his nervous body; the fact that he never smiled; and the fact, shocking to this wellborn aristocrat, that he had the table manners of a Bavarian peasant.

Now, one year later, at the end of this stormy August morning, Choltitz would see Hitler again. This time the circumstances had changed. The Führer's optimistic predictions at the Dnieper luncheon had not materialized. The advance guards of the Red Army were already less than 60 miles from Rastenburg. In the west, as von Choltitz knew as well as any man, the Wehrmacht was losing the battle of Normandy.

Yet this Prussian general stepping off the "Führer Sonderzug" in the somber Rastenburg forest would later admit he was ready that morning to be injected with a new sense of confidence in Germany's destiny. Von Choltitz believed in Germany's destiny. And he still believed on that August morning that Germany could win the war. He had come to Rastenburg, he later recalled, anxious "to be convinced again

by Hitler." Like a believer undertaking a pilgrimage to reawaken his faith, von Choltitz that morning had come to
Rastenburg to have his confidence in the Third Reich re-
newed by the man who ruled it. He wanted, above all, to
leave this meeting "with [his] spirits raised by Hitler, reassured that there was still a chance to change the course of the
war."

It was Hitler's personal aide who greeted him at the Rastenburg siding. Choltitz got into the aide's Mercedes, and the
two men slid under the dense tangle of fir trees that folded
over the *Wolfsschanze*, the "Wolf's Lair." At the first of its
three security rings, all of von Choltitz's baggage was taken
out of the car. It was, the aide apologized, a precaution in
force since July 20. Then, one by one, the car passed through
the three belts of barbed wire, minefields and machine-gun
emplacements that circled the headquarters, until they came
to the final barrier to this Nazi sanctuary. Inside, guarded by
seven companies of the SS Division "Gross Deutschland," in
a handful of buildings bordering a small pond, lived Adolf
Hitler and his principal assistants.

Burgdorf was waiting for him in the gloomy clearing outside Hitler's bunker. Even on that summer day only a few
weak shafts of sunlight filtered through the fir forest shrouding the *Wolfsschanze*. Hands clasped behind their backs, the
two men paced the little lawn next to the bunker, waiting
for the sign that would summon them to Hitler's presence. As
they walked, Burgdorf gestured at a few of the charred ruins
still left from the bomb plot.

Choltitz knew enough not to question Burgdorf too deeply
about his visit. But he did ask him one question.

Why, he wondered, had he been chosen for Gross Paris?

"Because," Burgdorf replied, "we know you can do the job
that has to be done there."

A few instants later, the SS guards at the bunker door signaled and Choltitz stepped into the bunker to receive from
the hands of the Master of the Third Reich the command of
the most beautiful city in the world.

His fingers clutching nervously at the visor of his cap,
Choltitz walked across the windowless neon-lit chamber to
the man leaning against the spare wooden desk at the far end
of the room. He raised his right hand in the gesture that had
been made the mandatory salute for the Wehrmacht since

July 20. Behind him he could feel the heavy breathing of Burgdorf on the nape of his neck.

Choltitz looked into the lusterless eyes of the man before him. In one awful instant he realized this was not the same man who had sat across the luncheon table from him a year earlier. Hitler had become "an old man." His face was worn and drawn. His shoulders sagged. He cupped his left hand in his right to hide the faint trembling in his left arm.[*]

But above all, it was Hitler's voice that shocked Choltitz. This hard raucous voice that had so often held him breathless by his radio, this voice that a year ago had poured new confidence through him, had faded now to the weak whisper of a senile man.

In fact, Choltitz barely heard Hitler's first words as he turned to Burgdorf and asked, "Has he been told of his new assignment?"

Behind Choltitz, Burgdorf answered, "In general terms."

Then Hitler began to talk.

First, he wandered aimlessly through the past, poking into distant corners of his career. He described how he had founded the Nazi party, molded it into a perfect tool with which to control the German people. That party, he insisted, had given Germany the machinery she needed to guide her fighting spirit.

Then his voice began to rise. Choltitz recognized now an echo of the man he had seen a year ago. Hitler spoke of the victories he was preparing. Normandy, he told Choltitz, was only a temporary setback. Soon, with "new weapons," he would reverse the tide.

Brutally, without warning, Hitler switched to another topic. His hands tightened on the edge of the desk under him. He leaned forward until Choltitz blinked at the closeness of his face. He was shrieking.

"Since the 20th of July, Herr General," he screamed, "dozens of generals—yes, dozens—have bounced at the end of a rope because they wanted to prevent me, Adolf Hitler, from continuing my work, from fulfilling my destiny of leading the German people."

Frothy little beads of spittle puffed from the corners of his

---

[*] Some of Hitler's doctors were convinced he suffered from Parkinson's disease.

mouth. Perspiration studded his forehead. His body, von Choltitz saw, was shaking under his nervous exertion.

But nothing, he shouted at Choltitz, would stop him. He would go on, he yelled, until he had led the German people "to their final victory."

On and on he raged at "the clique of Prussian generals" who had tried to kill him, and the tortures that he would use to send them to their graves.

Finally, jerking in little spastic bursts, Hitler sank back down into his chair.

After a long pause, he began to speak again. He was calm now. This time his voice was a faint whisper, just as it had been when the audience opened. It was as though the whole scene von Choltitz had just witnessed had not happened.

"Now," he said to this general who had crossed half of Europe to see him, "you're going to Paris." A city, he added, where it seemed "the only fighting going on is over the seats in the officers' mess." That, he told Choltitz, was a disgrace, and his first job would be to put an end to it. He was to turn Paris "into a frontline city." He wanted Paris to become a "terror" for the "backsliders" of its rear echelons.

That, Hitler made clear, was the first step to the larger task ahead of him.

He was, he told Choltitz, naming him a *Befehlshaber*, making him the fortress commander of Paris and the bearer of his personal orders. That title meant Choltitz would have the widest range of powers a commander of a German city garrison could have. He would command Paris as though it were a besieged fortress.

"You will," Hitler told him, "stamp out without pity" any uprising by the civilian population, any act of terrorism, any act of sabotage against the German armed forces. "For that," Hitler rasped, "rest assured, Herr General, you will receive from me all the support you need."

It was clear the interview was over. Choltitz saluted, turned, and walked back across the bunker. As he marched to the door, it seemed to Choltitz that Hitler's eyes remained fixed on his retreating back.

Outside, Choltitz looked at Burgdorf for a sign of reassurance. He found none.

For this little Prussian officer, the few minutes he had just lived had been one of the most jarring experiences of his life.

He had crossed half a continent to find a leader in this bunker, to reawaken his faith in German arms. Instead of a leader, Dietrich von Choltitz had found a sick man; instead of faith, doubt. Much, in the days ahead, would depend on the disillusionments of this August morn.

8

NINE HUNDRED MILES AWAY, in the city whose destiny had now been consigned to Dietrich von Choltitz's care, another German general sat down to a candlelit dinner. Above General Walter Warlimont's white-coated shoulders glittered the Renaissance chandelier of the Palais du Luxembourg, the same sparkling crystal that had lit the dinners of Marie de Médicis, Louis XVI and Napoleon. Beside Warlimont, the chest of his white dress tunic jangling with his decorations, sat his host Generalfeldmarschall Hugo Sperrle, Commander in Chief of the Luftwaffe on the western front.

To Warlimont, Deputy Chief of Staff of Operations at Hitler's headquarters, the fat field marshal beside him seemed to personify "the incredibly indifferent serenity" that reigned in the German headquarters staff in Paris that August, an indifference so starkly in contrast to the inferno of the Normandy front barely 200 miles away. Warlimont had had a chance to measure for himself the magnitude of the disaster building on that front. He had been sent from Rastenburg to the west to oversee Germany's counterattack at Avranches, an attack designed to cut the thin neck of land through which the tanks of Lieutenant General George S. Patton's Third Army were spilling into Brittany. It had failed—largely, Warlimont thought, because the planes of the Luftwaffe field marshal beside him had been absent from the skies of Normandy. Looking at the heavy silverware and the porcelain before him, Warlimont thought sadly that in this calamitous summer of 1944, Paris was perhaps the only city in the world where German officers could still put on their white dress tunics for a candlelit dinner. He watched in silent astonishment as the red-faced Sperrle explained the history of this building, pointed out the room where David had sketched the "Rape of the Sabines," and the French Republic had installed its Conseil des Sages—wise men's assembly.

Then Sperrle raised his Baccarat goblet and started the toasts. Among them, one in particular struck Warlimont. It seemed to him to sum up all the gulf of unreality that lay between this elegant dinner and the hell he had seen in Normandy.

It was "To this city of Paris where the flag of Germany shall fly for a thousand years."

It was not just the officers of Sperrle's general staff who might hope in those early days of August that the Swastika would fly undisturbed in the skies of Paris for a thousand years. For hundreds of minor officers, and for many ordinary soldiers, the war in Paris had been the best years in their lives.

Music lover Sonderführer Alfred Schlenker, the interpreter at the military tribunal which each day sent a growing number of Parisians to the firing squad, had not missed a single performance at the Paris Opéra in three years. For Berliner Schlenker, it was a soothing way to put from his mind the cries of the court victims whose executions he was forced to witness at Mont Valérien. That evening, in the softly lit modern dining room of his headquarters in the Hotel de Crillon, he would eat his favorite dish, tripes à la Königsberg.

A few miles from the Crillon, in his requisitioned villa in suburban Neuilly, Colonel Hans Jay, a prewar international riding champion, would study himself in his mirror. Perhaps, as he twisted his monocle into its socket, he would think of the young lady he hoped to seduce that evening in the obligingly discreet shadows of the Shéhérazade cabaret. Since he had arrived in Paris in 1943, this precise little man had been a familiar figure of occupied Paris by night. Nothing, in those opening days of August, was going to interrupt his pleasant routine.

Across the Bois de Boulogne, at 26 Avenue Raphaël in the middle of the residential area of Passy, a pretty twenty-four-year-old blond girl would, just as she had done every evening for four years, light the massive heavy silver candelabra of the town house of the French perfume king, François Coty.

Annabella Waldner had for those four years been the official hostess at this sumptuous building which was the residence of the military governor of the city of Paris. Through its salons she had watched the flower of the Third Reich, of Fascist Italy, of Vichy France drift by. The wine cellars and pantries over which she presided had housed the rarest wines of France, caviar from Russia, the rich *foie gras* of Périgord—every delicacy, in short, that occupied Europe had been able to furnish its conquerors. For this pretty young girl, these four years had been a Cinderella existence. She had her own car and driver, a dressmaker, and, as the final accolade, a box at the Opéra, that of a general.

There were not only Germans like Annabella Waldner and Hans Jay who could hope that night that the Swastika would fly for a thousand years over the capital of France. Some Parisians shared their hopes. To brunette Antoinette Charbonnier, twenty-five, the daughter of a respected Parisian industrialist who had lost his arm at Verdun, nothing in the world could seem more horrible than the prospect of the liberation of Paris.

Antoinette Charbonnier was in love with a German officer. For her, the victors of 1940 "with their stern regard, their boots, their swelling chests and blond hair" had embodied, she later recalled, "a world in which suddenly I wanted to live, a world of force, of beauty, of virility."

For four years she had lived in that world. On the arm of her German, Captain Hans Werner, she had defied everybody: her parents, her friends, the world in which she had grown up. Together they had shared the Third Reich's *belle époque* in Paris. Arm in arm they had marched to the movies, restaurants, nightclubs, theaters. As she passed, her countrymen would sometimes spit on the pavement before her. Lately she had begun to receive threatening letters.

But in love with Hans Werner and intoxicated with his nation's propaganda, Antoinette believed in Hitler's miracles. She could not imagine that this life might end. That night she and Hans Werner would dance at Monseigneur. As she fastened the bodice of her dress in their apartment on the avenue Mozart, she laughingly wondered if, as it usually did, it would catch on the points of her handsome captain's Iron Cross.

But, of all those Germans preparing to savor one more of the few evenings left them in occupied Paris, none, perhaps,

looked forward to his evening more than Corporal Helmut
Mayer. Mayer was Dietrich von Choltitz's orderly. Choltitz
had left him behind to wait for him. That night Mayer would
see his first movie in ten months. It was the first episode of
The Buchholz Family, a German comedy at the Vendôme
cinema on the avenue de l'Opéra. He hoped von Choltitz
would not return too soon: the second episode would not run
until next week. Mayer did not want to miss it.

9

MAYER'S HOPES were in vain. Dietrich von
Choltitz was already rolling back toward the city whose future
now lay in his hands. He had left Rastenburg at eight o'clock
this evening of August 7, in the same yellow-and-blue *Schalf-
wagen* that had brought him to OKW. The same black
Mercedes staff car that picked him up at the unmarked siding
in the morning had delivered him back to the train. This
time, Choltitz's escort had been a young SS Sturmführer of
the "Gross Deutschland" Division. As Choltitz had prepared to
climb up the iron steps of the sleeping car, the young officer
had grabbed his hand.

"Herr General," he murmured, "good luck. How much I
envy you going to Paris!"

Now, alone in his compartment, Choltitz thought of that
young officer. His eager words seemed almost comforting. After
the day he had just spent at Rastenburg, it did not seem possible that anybody in the world could envy him for going to
Paris. In the afternoon he had been summoned to the office of
Generaloberst Alfred Jodl, the chief of the General Staff. Jodl
had handed him the five-point order assigning him to Paris. It
confirmed what Hitler had told him. He was going to Paris
with powers no Nazi general had ever been formally assigned
before, in Paris or in any other city in the Reich. He was
going as the commander of a besieged fortress. It was, Jodl
had told him, only the first of the orders OKW would have

for him. Crucial days were at hand and much would be asked of him in Paris.

Sitting in the gathering darkness of his compartment, Choltitz had the first intimations of what it might be that OKW would expect of him in Paris. He was, he began to suspect, going to be asked to immortalize his name and his family honor by razing a city of three and a half million people. Moodily Choltitz stared at the forest of Rastenburg slowly receding past the train. Soon night would fall, and the "Führer Sonderzug" would veer southwest across the flat and dull wheatlands of Prussia for the long run into Berlin.

In the melancholy silence, watching the ghostly firs of Rastenburg fly past, Choltitz felt "a heavy gloom" settling over him. He had come here looking for hope. He was leaving shaken, heading for an assignment about which he had already begun to have misgivings. He reached into his tunic and pulled out a cigar. Generalfeldmarschall Wilhelm Keitel had given it to him at lunch. He methodically bit a small hole in its tip and searched his pockets for a match. He had none. He got up, slid open the door of his compartment and looked into the corridor. Two doors away, leaning against an open window, he saw another man smoking a cigar.

Choltitz approached him. He recognized the man's graying temples and the red, black and white enamel pin of an SS Reichsleiter stuck in his lapel. He had sat next to this man at lunch. His name was Robert Ley.

Ley obligingly lit his cigar, and the two men began to talk. Between short puffs on his cigar, Choltitz confided to Ley that he had had an interview, his first, with the Führer that morning. He had, he told him, been assigned to Paris. Ley congratulated him. He was in an excellent humor. He recalled his own visits to Paris during the war. Alas, he told Choltitz, it would be a different city that awaited him. Paris now, he said, needed the strong hand of a field soldier.

Sensing perhaps the heavy mood that was on Choltitz, Ley suggested a drink. The OKW mess steward, he told the little Prussian, had given him a bottle of prewar Bordeaux. Nothing would seem more appropriate to Ley than to be able to share it with the new commander of Gross Paris.

Ley brought the bottle into Choltitz's compartment and the two men began to drink. They toasted Choltitz's success and the Führer. Then, as their conversation rambled on, Ley

revealed that he, too, had seen Hitler that day. The subject
of his meeting, he said, had been the text of a new law which
he had drafted himself. After several revisions, it had received
that afternoon the Führer's final approval. The law, he said,
would be promulgated from Berlin in a few days.

Its name, he told Choltitz, was the *Sippenhaft.* [*]

In his precise Hanoverian accents, Ley explained to Choltitz what its terms were. It was designed to meet the particularly difficult times in which Germany found herself. As they
both knew, he said, the Reich was going to need the un-
swerving devotion of all her soldiers if she was to win the war.
The law had been prompted by the unhappy fact that some
of her general officers had failed her recently. Some had surrendered, or proved incapable of meeting the tasks assigned
them. There had been, he said, the plot against the Führer.

The Sippenhaft Law was designed to prevent all that, he
told Choltitz. Under its terms, the families of German generals
would, from now on, be held responsible for a general's
failings. In a sense, they would become the hostages of the
state, the guarantors of a general's good conduct.

Inhaling deeply on his cigar, he admitted it was an extreme
measure. Unhappily, he said, its provisions, in order to make
the law meaningful, had to be very strict. In a few cases, where
a general's failings were grave and he had escaped German
justice by being taken a prisoner, the law provided the death
penalty for the man's family.

In the silence that followed Ley's words, Choltitz suddenly
felt sick. He stared into the last red dregs of his Bordeaux
and grasped for something to say. Finally, he stammered that
if Germany used practices like that, she was returning to the
Middle Ages.

Ley sighed. "Yes, perhaps," he said, slowly twisting out the
stub of his cigar in the ashtray between them. But he repeated
to Choltitz the phrase he had used several times before. "These
are exceptional times," he said.

The conversation died, and a few moments later Ley left.
Choltitz stood in the half-open door of his compartment and
watched Ley's back disappear down the darkened corridor.
He would never see him again. Then he slid the door shut
and locked it. Outside, the train had already settled into its

[*] Literally, the "apprehension and arrest of kin."

long flat run into Berlin. The next morning Choltitz would catch another train, this one to Baden-Baden. There he would say goodbye to his wife, his daughters Maria Angelika, fourteen, and Anna Barbara, eight, and the gift this seemingly emotionless Prussian had waited a lifetime for, his four-month-old son, Timo.

Choltitz undressed and climbed into bed. Then he did something he had never done before in his life. He reached over and shook out not one but three pink sleeping pills from the tube on his night table. He swallowed them one by one.

10

WRAPPED IN A MANTLE of fog, the little town stretched reluctantly into wakefulness at the bottom of the Oos River valley. At the end of Viktoriastrasse, behind the bulbous cupolas of the Russian Orthodox church, an old woman opened up her shop. She was Frau Gerber, the baker. Once, at this early hour, a Duesenberg, a Rolls or a Bugatti would stop in front of her shopwindow. For the glittering café society of a prewar Baden-Baden, it had been a tradition to finish the night with Frau Gerber's big, puffy breakfast pretzels. But in Baden-Baden, in this fifth year of war, there was no café society, and only a few signs remained of that distant era. At the end of its green lawn, behind its white pillars, the casino from which the sound of revelry by night had once so gaily drifted was locked shut. Frau Gerber's first client this day would be the maid of a family of Prussian refugees living nearby. For Dietrich von Choltitz, the pretzels that his maid Johanna Fischer would buy this morning would be his last of the war.

Between Rastenburg and Baden-Baden von Choltitz had stopped only briefly in Berlin. A cable had been waiting for him when he got off the "OKW Zug." Signed by Burgdorf, it announced to the commander of Gross Paris that he had been promoted to General der Infanterie "by the Führer's special order."

All night, en route to Baden-Baden, Choltitz wondered what lay behind that sudden promotion. He knew that OKW had never given the command of a city, even a capital, to a lieutenant general. In Paris itself, no military governor had ever exceeded the rank of major general.

When he finally reached the outskirts of Baden-Baden, Dietrich von Choltitz resolved to stop tormenting himself. For his wife, Uberta, the daughter of an officer, the granddaughter of a general, he knew there could be no greater joy this morning than the sight of the two new general's pips he carried on his shoulders.

Maria Angelika and Anna Barbara still remember the fantastic breakfast which marked their father's visit that morning. He had brought back from Rastenburg a big parcel called a "Führer Paket." It was the present Hitler gave to visitors to the Wolf's Lair. It contained pumpernickel, jam, chocolate, cans of pâté, candy and even a Stollen, the ginger spice cake the girls loved.

But Maria Angelika and Anna Barbara were to catch only a glimpse of their father that morning. Around ten o'clock, freshly shaved, General von Choltitz embraced his family and climbed back into his car. He wanted to reach Paris by nightfall. No outward emotion had marked his departure. For generations, the von Choltitzes had served the flag of Germany; discipline and training had taught them to mute the pangs of separation. And Paris, for Uberta von Choltitz, was just another post in her husband's career. If she felt any special apprehension at this parting, it was a strictly feminine foreboding which reflected her own ideas about Paris. A few minutes before the black Horch started her husband toward the west, Uberta von Choltitz had noticed his valet suddenly run back to the general's room and bring out a heavy suitcase. That suitcase, Uberta knew, contained her husband's civilian suits.

11

IN THE CITY toward which Dietrich von Choltitz now sped bearing Hitler's fateful order, a young man hummed softly to himself as he rode down the rue Saint-Martin. Yvon Morandat had, after all, every reason to be happy this morning. He was in love. And he was passionately devoted to a cause whose hour he knew was at hand, the Resistance.

The son of a farmer, twenty-six-year-old Morandat had come a long way since the June morning in 1940 when, with five other members of his battalion of Chasseurs Alpins, he stepped out of a formation in Manchester's Trentham Park and volunteered to join a general named de Gaulle. His instinctive faith had been rewarded. Now, pedaling down this half-empty street, he was one of the handful of men in Paris in whom de Gaulle had implicit confidence. With Jacques Chaban-Delmas, he belonged to the tiny band of men who were de Gaulle's chosen agents in the city.

Ahead of Morandat, the rue Saint-Martin dipped into a short trough. Along its side ran a shoulder-high concrete embankment supporting the sidewalk. As Morandat rode into that little dip, he heard the panting of a cyclist behind him coming up to overtake him. At the moment the cyclist's rear wheel drew alongside Morandat's front tire, his foot suddenly lashed out. With a vicious kick, he jammed Morandat's front wheel against the concrete embankment. Morandat buckled and started to tumble forward over his handlebars.

As he fell, Morandat heard the noise behind him. It was the sound of a car, and it was accelerating very fast. In that frozen second, Morandat could hear the squeal of its tires fighting for traction on the pavement. He dug at the concrete embankment with his fingertips, fighting to hold himself erect. His bicycle tumbled out from under him. Half pressed against the wall, Morandat saw the black mass hurtle toward him. Its wheels swept over the spot on the pavement where Morandat should have been lying, smashing the tires of his bike.

Morandat felt its fenders brush him as the car swept by. It did not stop. Instead the car built up speed, wheeled left down the boulevard Saint-Denis, and disappeared.

Morandat was still trembling when the first passerby helped him to his feet. "My God!" the man cried. "They tried to kill you!"

Morandat abandoned his smashed bicycle and proceeded on foot to his meeting with three young men. As he drew up to them, they fell silent, and in their astonished faces Morandat read the confirmation of what he had suspected. They looked at him as though "they were looking at a man back from the dead." Those three men were the only men in the city of Paris who knew that that morning, at this precise hour, a Gaullist leader named Yvon Morandat would be riding a bicycle down the rue Saint-Martin. All three were Communists. They had, Morandat believed, just tried to kill him.°

Halfway across Paris, in a metalworker's dowdy apartment in Montrouge, another Communist was preparing for the most momentous event of his thirty-six-year life. His name was Henri Tanguy, "Colonel Rol," and he was preparing the insurrection Charles de Gaulle had forbidden. When that insurrection came, this soft-spoken son of a Breton seaman would lead it. Since the day two months earlier, when he had received from the Communist-dominated COMAC the command of all the FFI in the Paris region, Rol had spared neither himself nor his men in preparing for it.

In a sense, Rol had been preparing for it all his life. Forced out of school to work at thirteen, he had educated himself at night, and at twenty-one had joined the Communist party. In the turbulent days of the Popular Front, union organizer Rol had been chased successively out of the Renault, Citroën and

---

° Morandat was also convinced he knew why. A few days earlier, on the pont Mirabeau, he had been asked by the party to serve as an informer. He had brusquely refused. The bid came through a Communist friend who introduced him to a stranger whose French had a heavy Slavic accent. To prewar union organizer Morandat, the stranger explained that the Communist party had long regarded him as a man it could work with. Then he told the astonished Morandat that the party wanted him to work for it. All that would be asked, he explained, was that Morandat keep a party liaison agent informed of all the instructions the Gaullists in Paris received from London. In return, he said, Morandat could count on the party for unqualified backing in any political career he undertook after the war. Shocked and angry, Morandat walked away. A few days later, he learned who his interlocutor was. His name was Kaganovich. He was a cousin of Lazar Kaganovich, and he made frequent trips into occupied France from Switzerland to bring the French party instructions from Moscow.

Bréguet plants for his trade union activities. He had fought in Spain, and the *nom de guerre* he carried this morning came from a comrade killed in the Sierra de Caballos. In 1940 he had been wounded fighting with a Senegalese infantry regiment. He had joined the Resistance as soon as his wounds had healed, and had fought without hesitation ever since. He was a devoted and disciplined Communist, a patriotic Frenchman, and a brave leader. Even his political foes, and he was to have many, admitted the courage of this precise Breton. None of these foes posed a graver menace to Rol's ambitions than the city's Gaullist command represented by men like Yvon Morandat, the cyclist of the rue Saint-Martin. That Gaullist Morandat could suspect the Communists of trying to kill him and that Rol could consider the Gaullists his political rivals were that day signs of the political divisions threatening to tear the Resistance apart as its finest hour approached.

The heart of that dissension was the Communists' determination to force the situation in Paris themselves. To Roger Villon, Paris depended "not on the Gaullists but on the masses of the city and our capacity to mobilize them." Those masses were by no means all Communists. The majority of them were patriotic Frenchmen who asked no reward other than the privilege of fighting Germans. Already Paris tossed restlessly under its occupiers' feet, anxious to cleanse the shame of the past four years, to find again its tradition of revolutions past. The Communists needed little besides an intelligent plan to bring the city to the edge of an uprising.

They had that plan. Soon a lone Communist organizer with a pistol and thirty brave men would launch a strike in the railroad marshaling yards of Villeneuve-Saint-Georges. It would be the first of a series of strikes that would cripple the city and bring it to the brink of the insurrection the Communists—and many patriotic Frenchmen—wanted.

It was a plan full of incalculable risks for Paris, its inhabitants, even France itself. Its price might be the destruction of Paris. But those who wanted that insurrection were prepared to pay a heavy price.

Soon this stolid Breton Communist called Rol would thump his fist on a table and vow, "Paris is worth 200,000 dead."

12

On the granite steps of his elegant town house at 26 avenue Raphaël, General Hans von Boineburg-Lengsfeld waited in the warm August twilight for his dinner guest. As he waited, he chatted quietly with the young lieutenant beside him, his aide-de-camp Count Dankvart von Arnim. Many bonds, forged during their eighteen months together in Paris, joined the old general, horribly mutilated by a tank in front of Stalingrad, and the young Brandenburg nobleman beside him. During those eighteen months, no parcel of the Third Reich had been easier to administer than the 30 square miles of the French capital assigned to Boineburg as the commander of Gross Paris.

Only two events had jarred the tranquillity of his stay. The first was the arrival, on March 14, 1944, of an officer from General Staff headquarters in Berlin. From Boineburg he demanded a file that had lain unattended in his office since it had originally been put together, just after the Dieppe raid in August, 1942. Its title was "Defensive Measures for the Paris Region in the Event of an Enemy Airborne Assault on the City." The officer took it to Berlin. Ten days later it arrived back in Boineburg's office. OKW had found the plan "grossly insufficient." Boineburg was ordered to prepare another, much more extensive, to include plans for "the widest destruction possible in the Paris area" in case of an enemy assault.

The other event was, for Boineburg, much more serious. It was the July 20 plot. Although Boineburg had not been an original member of the plotters' group, he had, when the code word *Übung* arrived at the headquarters of General von Stülpnagel, ordered his troops to arrest the 1,200 men of the SS and Gestapo in Paris. Since the moment, later that evening, when he had heard Hitler's harsh voice carried by the loudspeakers of the Hotel Raphaël, Boineburg had been waiting for his own punishment.

It had arrived on August 3 in a brief telegram from OB West (Headquarters of the Commander in Chief of the Wehrmacht in the West) announcing simply that he had been "suspended from his functions as military governor of Paris and replaced by General Dietrich von Choltitz." Boineburg knew nothing of this man who was to succeed him except the reputation that had preceded him to Paris. To Boineburg, von Arnim, and the handful of others who had survived July 20, Choltitz was known "as a devoted Nazi, and an unshakably obedient Prussian." In the hushed gossip of their mess, three names hung over his head: Warsaw, Rotterdam and Sebastopol.°

For von Boineburg, the stocky Prussian barking "Heil Hitler" at the sentry box below him this evening of August 9, 1944, could be only one thing—an unconditional Nazi. As he watched him march primly up the steps to his residence, he murmured to von Arnim, "He's a *ganz harter*." †

Inside, on the green velvet Louis XV chairs of Boineburg's salon, half-a-dozen anxious senior officers waited to study this little man. To von Arnim, it was "a pathetic instant." Cold and aloof, Choltitz felt ill at ease among them. There was little in the sight of these garrison officers around him to please this general who had spent most of his war in the mud of Russia.

Between the ortolans and the profiteroles au chocolat of Boineburg's Bulgarian chef, Choltitz dryly described his visit to Rastenburg. As he watched these silent men listening to him around the table, Choltitz felt folding over him the solitude that was to surround him during his stay in Paris. Between Choltitz, the new commander, and these men now at his orders a sense of mutual suspicion was already slowly arising at this dinner table.

For von Arnim, after listening to Choltitz, there was no longer any question of what Hitler's intentions were for Paris. Only one question remained in the young count's mind: Would this solemn man who just arrived in their midst help Hitler realize those intentions?

Alone with Choltitz and Boineburg over coffee and brandy,

° It was characteristic of the reputation that had preceded Choltitz into Paris that Warsaw was so often mentioned in connection with his name. In fact, he was nowhere near the city during the brutal German assault of the Polish capital in September, 1939.

† *ganz harter*: hard-boiled guy.

Arnim feared he had a hint. Boineburg's answer to Berlin's
harsh reaction to his plans had been to propose a defensive
line in front of the capital. It was already called the "Boineburg Line," and, with 25,000 men and adequate artillery,
it would form a solid barrier on the road to Paris. And it
would draw Paris's defenders away from the capital itself.
Further, Boineburg had done nothing to prepare for any
heavy demolition in the capital.

Now, haunted by his own memories of Stalingrad, Boineburg urged Choltitz to follow his plan and avoid fighting in
the city itself. He begged Choltitz to do "nothing that could
bring irreparable destruction to Paris." Von Arnim watched
the reaction of Choltitz, stiffly perched on his chair, holding
his coffee cup between his pudgy fingers. His face, it seemed
to von Arnim, was "as expressionless as the fat Buddha" on
the black marble fireplace behind him, just under a portrait
of the Führer.

A few minutes later Choltitz left. In the vestibule, he found
his orderly, Corporal Helmut Mayer, waiting for him. Choltitz
gave him the first order of his command. "Mayer," he ordered,
"prepare for me a bedroom at the Meurice." Then, turning
to Boineburg, he added with a very faint trace of sarcasm,
"For the days ahead, Herr General, I shall need a headquarters, not a residence."

As the two men stood on the doorstep, watching Choltitz's
Horch disappear past the full-leafed chestnut trees of the
Ranelagh Gardens down toward the Bois de Boulogne, Boine-
burg grasped his young aide's arm.

"Believe me, Arnim," he murmured, "the good days of Paris
are over forever."

13

For PIERRE LEFAUCHEUX, the good days had
ended in the splintering crash of the door to a fourth-floor
apartment at 88 rue Lecourbe, just after six o'clock on the
evening of June 7. There, in one swoop that night, the Gestapo

had arrested Lefaucheux, head of the Paris Resistance, and most of his aides. It was their biggest catch in four years.*

Now, his body spent and broken by days of torture, Pierre Lefaucheux lay on a straw sack in a dark prison cell and listened for a sound in the night. It was the metallic clanking of an iron-wheeled coffee cart. The sound of that cart, scraping over the brick gallery four flights below, had a special meaning to Pierre and the 2,980 other inmates of Fresnes prison.

It would be the Germans' announcement that another convoy of prisoners would leave Fresnes that day for the concentration camps of Germany. Pierre would stiffen if he heard it; then off in the blackness he would hear doors bang open one by one: the cell doors of the men who had been chosen to leave with the convoy. There in the predawn darkness, the guards would give each of them the last cup of coffee they would drink on French soil. Pierre could not relax those mornings until he had heard the cart roll safely past his own locked cell door.

Pierre saw the first soft grays beginning to lighten the night sky outside. He could breathe easier. It was dawn. Now he could be sure that that day, August 10, the coffee cart would not come. He knew he would pass another day, his sixty-fourth in Fresnes prison, another day in which he would not be deported to Buchenwald or Dachau, another day in which the Allied armies would draw closer to Paris, bringing with them the hope that somehow they might liberate him before another train, his train, would leave for Germany.

Just as it did to Pierre Lefaucheux, each of those August mornings brought to all the prisoners of the Gestapo in Paris that same special agony, that same mixture of hope and fear. Over 7,000 of them, the cream of the French Resistance, waited in Paris's prisons. In the gray stone fort of Romainville, 250 women prisoners waited, following each day the progress of the advancing Allies on a sliver of toilet paper tucked into the one jar of jam their guardians allowed into their prison each day. A few miles away, in a wooden army barracks at Drancy, 1,532 Jews, the last of the thousands who had passed there on their way to the gas chambers of Auschwitz and

---

* It had also led to Communist Rol's control of the Paris FFI. Rol replaced Lefaucheux who, days before his capture, had complained that he was "being drowned by the Communists."

Dachau, watched for the sign that would herald their departure. It was the arrival of a line of yellow-green buses, the same Paris city buses many of them had ridden to work each morning before the war.

Yet, strangely, to some of the Gestapo's prisoners, deportation to Germany would seem a relief. There were many who believed like Yvonne Pagniez, a Breton newspaperwoman at Fresnes, that anybody staying behind after the last convoy would be shot. To men like Captain Philippe Keun and Louis Armand, anything would seem better than the daily menace of new tortures at the Gestapo's rue des Saussaies headquarters. Keun, the deputy of the intelligence service's "Jade Amicol," and Armand, a railroad executive who had organized a Resistance network in the French railroads, were newcomers to Fresnes. The Gestapo had not yet finished trying to squeeze the last ration of information from their tortured bodies. For them, each new day meant the possibility they would be taken from their cells and delivered to the torture chambers of the rue des Saussaies.

From his cell, Armand could hear a faint shout drifting across the prison from the streets outside. It was the cry of a handful of brave Parisians yelling encouragement to the prisoners. "You shall not leave," they cried.

To the miserable Louis Armand, it was not a consoling thought. Nothing that morning could have made him happier than the knowledge that he might leave Fresnes.

●   ●   ●

A few miles—and light years—away from Fresnes, a fat man in monogrammed silk pajamas stood at the full-length windows of his apartment at 1 rue Montrosier. As he did, he made a mental inventory of all the Germans he knew in Paris. Raoul Nordling, Sweden's consul general, knew many. For four years, the SKF factories he directed had made ball bearings for the Wehrmacht. As dean of the city's consular corps, he had been a regular guest at their official functions. Standing under his collection of impressionist paintings, Nordling methodically thought through the people he knew who might lead him to the one German he was looking for this particular day. He knew that man only by the name "Bobby." He had met him only once, in 1942, on the terrace of the café Chez

Francis, at the Place de l'Alma. They had been introduced by one of the few Germans Nordling trusted, a Berlin businessman who, the Swede suspected, was connected with the Abwehr, the German military intelligence organization.

After they walked away from the meeting, his friend had told him, "If you ever want to open any doors in Paris, see Bobby."

It was to do just that that Raoul Nordling was this morning ransacking his brain for someone who could lead him to "Bobby." The doors he wanted to open were the cell doors of Pierre Lefaucheux, Louis Armand and the rest of the political prisoners in Paris. Nordling knew that, in Caen and Rennes, the departing SS had massacred their prisoners. The same thing, he was sure, would happen in Paris. To date he had made no progress. Now Nordling had decided to approach the city's new commander. But he wanted someone to prepare the way for him. He was sure that "Bobby," if he could find him, would be the man.

Emil "Bobby" Bender was at that instant already closing his last suitcases in his requisitioned apartment at 6 rue Euler. In a few hours he would leave Paris. He had been ordered by his chief, Colonel Friedrich Garthe, the head of the Abwehr for France, to report to Sainte-Menehould by nightfall. Bender, however, had other plans. Using his Abwehr pass, he intended to drive to Switzerland that day, join his mistress in Zurich and retire from the war.

It would be a sad departure for this graying forty-five-year-old World War I pilot. "Covered" as the representative of a Swiss paper pulp firm, he had circulated in Paris as an Abwehr agent since June 18, 1940. His first assignment had been to penetrate and report on the French business community. Later he had been assigned the delicate job of locating and requisitioning the precious objects whose sale in Switzerland provided hard currency to meet the demands of the Abwehr's worldwide espionage program. But these were not Bender's only activities. Since 1941, he had been a key member of an anti-Nazi network inside the Abwehr.

Nordling's telephone call reached him only a few moments before he planned to leave the apartment. The Swede had finally obtained his number from another German officer, Erich Posch-Pastor von Camperfeld, an Austrian secretly working with the Resistance. Bender did not want to stay. It was only

after long urgings by the Swede that he agreed to remain behind for "a few days" until he had made every effort he could
to get the prisoners released. He would, Bender reasoned, still
have time to get across the border into Switzerland.

It was a major miscalculation on his part. In two weeks he
would be a prisoner of the French. But during those two
weeks he would have in large measure repaid this city, which
knew him only as a middle-aged playboy, for the objects he
had gleaned from its treasure chests.

14

To GENERAL WALTER WARLIMONT, alone in
the Führer's conference room, the blacked-out headquarters
of the Oberkommando der Wehrmacht had always seemed like
a ghost town. Outside, the forest was still. Wolves and jackals
no longer disturbed the Rastenburg night with their cries;
the minefields and belts of electrified barbed wire that circled
OKW had long ago driven them to more distant retreats. A
new set of sounds had replaced their howls: the whir of
ventilating machinery, the clacking of teleprinters and, above
all, the jangling of telephones that, twenty-four hours a day,
wore away the nerves of Walter Warlimont and the hundreds
of other men like him whose lives revolved around the moment, twice a day, when, at his strategy conferences, the
Master of the Third Reich uttered the decisions which set the
course of the war.

As he did for each of those conferences, Warlimont had
arrived for this one half an hour early. Warlimont, just back
from his visit to the Normandy front, was responsible for
preparing each conference. Under his left arm he had carried
a sheaf of working papers, and in his right hand the rolls
of General Staff maps on which, in a few moments, Hitler
would study the latest situation reports. Since July 22, Warlimont had given up carrying these papers in his calfskin
briefcase; he was too proud to submit to the humiliating

searches of Hitler's gray-uniformed SS guard posted at the door.

Now Warlimont spread out on the conference table the huge 1/1,000,000 general situation map, and the sector-by-sector 1/200,000 cards on whose celluloid surfaces the OKW Ic (G3) had traced the latest frontline information.

One thing was to set this conference indelibly apart from all the others Warlimont had attended at OKW. That night, for the first time since June 21, 1941, Hitler swept aside the eastern-front maps Generaloberst Jodl set before him, and turned his attention first to the situation in the west. To Warlimont, the Führer seemed like "a nervous beast" as, for a long moment, he leaned over the maps spread out before him. Then he drew one 1/200,000 map apart from the others.

At its center was a huge black configuration capping three wide folds of the Seine. From it, like the lines of a spider web, flowed all the highways marked on the map. That black mass formed the outlines of Paris and its suburbs. Hitler took out his grease crayon and swiftly slashed at the map in front of him. Then he raised his head and announced that the time had come to prepare the defense of Paris.

"If we are to hold the Seine," he said, his voice rising, "we must hold Paris. We will hold in front of Paris, we will hold in Paris, we will hold Paris!" he declared.

To lose Paris, he told the generals around him, would have a disastrous effect on the morale of the Wehrmacht, on the population of Germany, on the world. Then, while at his side Jodl frantically took notes, Hitler issued his first direct orders for the defense of the city. First, he announced, "I want all the Seine bridges in the Paris area mined and prepared for destruction." Second, he declared, the city's industry "must be paralyzed." Last, he told Jodl, "all available reinforcements" were to be ordered to the city's commander.

"Paris is to be defended to the last man," he declared, "without regard for the destruction the fighting may cause."

He paused for a long moment and then he added a final phrase.

"Why should we care if Paris is destroyed?" he asked. "The Allies at this very moment, are destroying cities all over Germany with their bombs."

15

IT WAS ONE of those breathless summer days God reserves to Paris and poets. Already the first fishermen drowsed along the quais of the Seine in the early morning sunshine. Their bamboo poles, stuck into the gravel under them, leaned lazily over its muddy waters. Beyond, lost in a world of his own, a lone artist stroked his canvas at the end of the Vert Galant where its prowlike granite banks divide the Seine at the very tip of the Ile de la Cité. In a few hours, those riverbanks would come alive with the beach umbrellas and folding canvas chairs of thousands of Parisians looking for a place in the August sun. War, this peaceful summer Sunday morning, seemed far away.

For the city's millions, this Sunday, August 13, marked the beginning of a three-day Assumption holiday, and everywhere Parisians prepared to savor the promise of its cloudless blue skies. By the thousands they set out to picnic, to play, to love, and most of all to forget the risks of the coming battle for the liberation of their city.

Not a few of their occupiers decided to join the holidaying Parisians. At the Hotel de Crillon, Eugen Hommens wrapped a picnic lunch with the two greasy bratwurst sausages the hotel mess steward had given him. This Sunday, as they had done every Sunday that summer, Hommens and his French mistress planned to swim at the sandy beach of Nogent-sur-Marne just outside the capital.

In his elegant town house on the rue de la Manutention, the Marquis Louis de Fraquier hung his binoculars around his neck, put on his green race commissioner's badge, his white gloves and his gray top hat. Then this symbol of an ageless France stepped outside, climbed into his waiting red-and-black sulky and pranced off to the Sunday races at Auteuil.

But to no Parisian was this Sunday holiday a more welcome relief than it was to a gangling six-foot-three-inch giant in *bleu de travail* (French work clothes) that barely reached down to his bony ankles. Standing on the pont de Nanterre spanning the Seine just west of the capital, he looked down at the gun crew of a German antiaircraft battery sprawling in the sunshine on the grassy shore of the Ile de Chatou. Only his slim companion and the child between them could see the look of hatred on the big man's face.

Two and a half months earlier, at 11:15 on May 28, that very gun crew had shot Lieutenant Bob Woodrum's B-26 out of the Paris skies. This Sunday, dressed as a mason, Woodrum was on an outing, his first since he had been picked up by the Resistance. With him was the courageous Nanterre pork butcher who was hiding him, and the butcher's seven-year-old son. The three turned away from the scene, got back on their bicycles, and rode away. Proud Louis Berty, the butcher, had decided that on this Sunday afternoon he would give his American guest a tourist's tour of Paris.

• • •

So peaceful had this Sunday seemed to Paris's new German commander that he had set out for his meeting at OB West alone in his open Horch. Not a single Resistance bullet, not a single Allied plane, had disturbed his trip. The only discordant note was supplied by the man he had come to see, General-feldmarschall Günther von Kluge, the Commander in Chief of the western front. In his sunless underground bunker at Saint-Germain-en-Laye just outside the capital, Kluge defined for Choltitz the job expected of him in Paris.

It was Hitler's and his intention, he declared, to defend Paris. There was no question, he said, of turning Paris into an open city. "It will be defended," he told von Choltitz with finality, "and you will defend it."

OB West's intelligence estimates, Kluge informed him, predicted the Allies would try to outflank the city. By standing in Paris, Choltitz would, Kluge believed, "draw off the enemy's armor," force him to fight in a city where his mechanized force would be less effective, and "slow down his rush across France." The counterattack at Mortain, which Kluge had violently resisted, had caught his Seventh Army in the Falaise pocket now clanking shut. But Kluge still had available most of the nineteen divisions of the Fifteenth Army, the largest in France, which OKW had held immobilized in the Pas-de-Calais until early August in anticipation of a second landing. From those troops, Kluge promised Choltitz the reinforcements he would need to defend Paris when the time came. With three divisions, both men agreed, the city could be held in a wasting street battle for at least three weeks. Choltitz asked for the troops immediately. Kluge refused. The situation in Paris, he said, was not yet critical enough to warrant tying up troops there so soon.

After the briefing ended, Kluge invited Choltitz to lunch. It was a frosty meal. As it ended, Kluge repeated what he had told him earlier. "I'm afraid, my dear Choltitz," he concluded, "Paris may become a rather disagreeable assignment for you. It has the air of a burial place about it."

Choltitz was silent for a moment. Finally he replied. "At least," he said, "it will be a first-class burial."

• • •

Lieutenant Bob Woodrum felt the hand of Louis Berty's seven-year-old son slip into his. Never had Woodrum looked so hard at a painting as he did at this one by Claude Joseph Vernet in the French Naval Museum at the place du Trocadéro. Next to him a German officer pondered his blond hair, his blue eyes, his square American face—and his very long, very American frame. To keep himself from showing any emotion to the inquisitive German, Woodrum had fixed his eyes on the tricolor on the stern of one of the ships in the painting. Terrified, Woodrum heard the German beside him ask him a question. Out of the corner of his eye, the big American saw Berty's seven-year-old son turn and look up at the German.

"My father is deaf and dumb," he said.

• • •

High up in the judge's tribune of the Auteuil racetrack, the Marquis de Fraquier surveyed the crowd below through his binoculars. Suddenly he stiffened and lowered his glasses. A discordant sound had just jarred the almost perfect beauty of the marquis's summer day, just as it would mar this day for many of his fellow Parisians. Very faint and very far to the south, he had just heard the distant echo of cannon, the first Paris had heard since June, 1940.

•   •   •

Racing back to Paris in his Horch, von Choltitz could not even pause to breathe the fresh air of the Bois de Boulogne. Waiting for him back at the Meurice was a report on a delicate operation he had launched that morning, his first since arriving in Paris. It was the disarmament of Paris's 20,000-man police force. Kluge had ordered all the police in France disarmed in a "surprise move" that day.

It had begun, on Choltitz's orders, in the police commissariat of the tough industrial suburb of Saint-Denis, and spread as rapidly as possible through the rest of the city.

By the time he reached the Meurice, his aide, the young Count von Arnim, had a full report ready for him. The operation had gone off without incident. Over 5,000 arms had been seized. Choltitz was pleased. This peaceful city, now this unopposed accomplishment, augured well. He could focus his attention on the second piece of paper von Arnim handed him. It was a telexed copy of the oral order Kluge had given him before lunch. "Paris," it repeated, "will be defended at all costs."

•   •   •

The sands of the little beach at Nogent-sur-Marne were cooling in the last rays of late afternoon sunshine when Eugen Hommens decided to take a final swim. He handed his pistol in its leather holster to his mistress Annick and swam out to the middle of the Marne. He was lazily floating on its cool water when he heard her screams.

Here, on this quiet riverside beach, the French had just taken a first small revenge for Choltitz's disarming of the Paris police. Two FFI had stolen Eugen Hommens's pistol.

16

Sergeant Werner Nix, of the 190th Sicherungsregiment, cursed the new commander of Gross Paris. Instead of relaxing, as he did each Monday afternoon, in the
Soldatenkino—Soldiers' Cinema—of the place Clichy, Nix,
for the second time in an hour, was riding through the place
de l'Opéra in an armored car. Like every other available German soldier in Paris that afternoon, Nix was on parade.

The parade was Choltitz's idea. Since noon, in a long and
menacing flow of tanks, armored cars and trucks, his troops
had been tramping through the city in combat dress. To reinforce the impression he was trying to create, von Choltitz
had ordered his troops to double back over their tracks, leaving, he hoped, the illusion of far greater force than he had
actually put on parade.

It was an irony of history of which Choltitz probably was
unaware, but his hasty demonstration was the largest parade
the Germans had ever staged in Paris. In a sense, he was
honoring a rain check for another, grander parade Hitler had
planned for Paris on July 28, 1940. It was to have been the
most massive demonstration in the history of Nazi Germany,
an orgy of triumph to enshrine the Third Reich in Paris for
a thousand years.* Von Choltitz's aim was more modest: he
wanted his intimidating little display to cow the city into ac-
cepting the Third Reich just a bit longer.

Neither Nix, nor any of his comrades, nor any of the Parisians watching the Germans flow through the place de l'Opéra
had any reason to notice a fat little man in a gray suit pre-
tending to read a paper on the street corner in front of the
Café de la Paix. Beside him, three girls in summer dresses
were shrieking with laughter at the passing troops, and the

---

* The parade was postponed for a month, until August 28, and then can-
celled because, according to General Warlimont, Göring admitted he could
not guarantee the parade against a sneak attack by the RAF. Three days
earlier, the RAF had launched its first raid of the war on Berlin.

little man's face reddened in discomfiture. It was understandable that it should. The man in the gray suit was General von Choltitz. He had slipped into civilian clothes and melted into the crowd to test for himself the city's reaction to his show of force.

Choltitz could not speak French but he understood laughter, and he realized a scornful remark had set these girls beside him laughing. He saw that same scorn on all the faces around him. There, in the middle of this knot of Parisian passersby, Paris's German commander had obtained the information he had come for. His demonstration had failed. He would have to do something more than just show his force to keep Paris quiet.

• • •

The harsh, impatient voice of the Führer interrupted Generaloberst Alfred Jodl in the midst of the daily situation report at the first of OKW's strategy conferences that August 14. Once again Hitler's thoughts had turned to the defense of Paris. He cut Jodl short with a wave of his hand, and turned to General Buhle, OKW's ordnance officer.

"Where," he asked, "is the 600-millimeter mortar we built for the attack on Brest-Litovsk and Sebastopol?" He had, he announced, decided to send it to General von Choltitz.

Taken completely by surprise, Buhle turned toward Keitel, who turned toward Jodl, who turned toward Warlimont. None of them had any idea where the mortar was. In fact, Warlimont did not even know it existed. Furious at their embarrassed silence, Hitler began to bang the table with his fist. In an angry shout, he told Buhle to find the mortar and send it to Paris immediately. He demanded a report twice a day on its whereabouts until it reached the city.

Warlimont drew up a memo and tiptoed out of the conference room with Buhle to find out "where—and what—the Führer's mysterious mortar was."

Eight hours later, Warlimont's aide, Major Helmut Perponcher, brought him the answer. The mortar had been found in a Berlin warehouse. Specially designed for city warfare, it had been used at Brest-Litovsk, at Sebastopol and at Stalingrad. Von Choltitz himself had used it to batter apart Sebastopol's defenses. It was the most powerful single artillery piece developed by preatomic man. Baptized the "Karl" after its designer, General Karl Becker, the tractor-mounted mortar could lob a two-and-a-half-ton shell two feet thick more than three miles. That enormous charge could penetrate eight feet of reinforced concrete, and a few well-placed shells were enough to reduce an entire city block to rubble. It would provide a far more intimidating menace to a restive Paris than the parade the city's new commander had staged in its streets that morning.

That evening, at the Führer's second strategy conference of the day, Warlimont announced to Hitler that the "Karl," mounted on its own railroad flatcar, was on its way to Paris. It would be there, he said, in eight days.

• • •

At the end of the landing strip in southern England, General Jacques Chaban-Delmas studied the canvas suitcase at his feet. He had kept his rendezvous with the Lysander in a Mâcon cow pasture. In that suitcase was the disguise Chaban would now use for his return trip to Paris—a pair of worn sneakers, a soiled pair of slacks and an old tennis sweater. Chaban had hoped to parachute back. But his superior, General Pierre Koenig, Chief of the FFI, had ruled a jump too risky without a full moon. Instead, Chaban was going to ride into Paris on a bicycle, with a tennis racket in one hand and a dead chicken packed into his bike basket. To any inquisitive German along his way, he would just be a young father bringing home a meal to his family after a friendly game of tennis in the country.

A few yards away, taking on fuel, was the American fighter plane that would fly Chaban to Normandy. There an American escort would take him to the edge of the Allied lines where he would begin his bicycle ride home. In his hands, as he paced this landing field, Chaban clasped a piece of paper. Typed onto it were the instructions and code words he was taking back with him to Paris.

Chaban had failed to persuade the Allies to change their plans. He had pleaded his cause as desperately as he knew how to anyone who would listen. He had even spoken to Churchill's right-hand man, General Sir Hastings Ismay, in his underground war room at the Admiralty. From Ismay, as from everyone else he had spoken to, Chaban received the same answer: There would be no change in the Allies' carefully laid plans to accommodate Paris's political problems. But Chaban felt he had still achieved something of great importance. He had at least alerted de Gaulle and his Free French headquarters in London and Algiers to the situation in Paris. His orders were still to prevent an insurrection until the Allies were at the gates of the city. Then he might allow a short upheaval of no more than twenty-four hours to give the people of the city some sense of participation in their own liberation.

But if the Communists escaped his control and forced an insurrection, Chaban was now prepared for them. Typed onto this list he had already memorized were the outlines of a series of contingency plans to maintain control of Paris until the Allies could arrive.

The last line typed onto the thin paper in his hands was a five-word phrase. It was the code sign that would launch a last, desperate operation which Chaban himself had conceived. So bold and so potentially dangerous was that operation that this man who had planned it hoped he would never hear the words in front of him flickering over the BBC. They were: "As-tu bien déjeuné, Jacquot?"

Chaban studied them one last time. Then he handed the paper back to the escort officer beside him, picked up his suitcase, and walked to his waiting plane.

• • •

In Paris, in the dingy back room of a café on the rue de la Paix in the working-class suburb of Levallois-Perret, two perfect strangers sat down over a bottle of *vin ordinaire*. In the next room, behind the door separating the pair from the café itself, sat the two men who had introduced them after they themselves had matched up the two ends of a torn métro ticket. "Colonel Rol," the Communist leader of the Paris FFI, raised his glass to the man opposite him in the back room. That man was the leader of the Communist Resistance network in the Paris police. He had, that day, forced the strike of the Paris police.

From him Rol wanted to know one thing. Would the striking police follow his orders in an uprising? Soon, Rol knew, the

Allies would reach the Seine at Mantes and Melun downstream and upstream from Paris. The insurrection Chaban
was supposed to prevent was, Rol felt sure, only days, perhaps hours, away. When it came, he wanted one force in the
city above all under his orders, its 20,000-man police force.
He had come to this café to make sure of that.

•   •   •

Just as it did each year, the altar of the church in the little
village on the main highway between Paris and Calais would
have the most beautiful floral decorations in all Picardy for
the Feast of the Virgin. On this vigil of the Assumption, a tall,
poised woman and her six children left the gray-roofed Louis
XIII château they shared with sixty-five Germans, and pedaled
together toward the neighboring village of Warlus. There,
their arms spilling over with flowers, the de Hautecloque family entered the town church and began to decorate its altar
for the feast the next day, August 15.

Thérèse de Hautecloque felt a special devotion to the Virgin
Mary. Four years earlier, on July 3, 1940, she had confided
to her protection the well-being of the person closest to her in
the world, her husband Philippe. At six o'clock that morning,
perched on a red bicycle, Philippe had left the retreat in the
vineyards of Bordeaux to which the family had fled. He was
off to find, wherever he could, arms with which to continue the
war against France's invaders.

Their six children had been still sleeping that morning when
Philippe spoke his last words to his wife. "Courage, Thérèse,"
he had said. "Our separation may be long."

For almost four years, Thérèse de Hautecloque had not
known whether her husband was alive or dead. Then, one
night in March, 1944, huddled over the earphones of her
crystal set, separated only by a locked door from the Germans
occupying the room next to hers, she had started as she listened to the nightly broadcast of the BBC. For a moment
Thérèse thought "the earth was opening" under her feet. One
of the personal messages she had just heard was: "Philippe,
born November 22, 1902, sends to his wife and his half-dozen
dear ones a warm embrace." The man to whom Thérèse de
Hautecloque was married was born November 22, 1902.

As Thérèse and her six children fitted their treasure of roses, lilies and gladiolas onto the altar of the little church that afternoon, a voice broke into its cool confines. "Madame de Hautecloque, come quickly, come quickly!" called Mme. Dumont, the owner of the Café de la Place across the village square from the church. Thérèse de Hautecloque ran down the aisle, across the square, and into the back room of Mme. Dumont's bistro. From the wide, old-fashioned speaker of Mme. Dumont's radio, she heard a voice. For the first time since France's defeat, Thérèse de Hautecloque felt tears slipping down her cheeks. In the same quiet, reassuring tone in which he had said to her, "Courage, Thérèse," Philippe de Hautecloque, now known as General Jacques Leclerc, was announcing, this time to all France, that he had come back to French soil at the head of a French armored division to join the fight for his country's liberation. "Soon," he promised, "the tricolor will fly again over Paris." *

• • •

No one interrupted Yvonne Baratte that evening as she decorated another altar on this vigil of the Feast of the Assumption. One by one she fitted her tiny bouquet of violets into the tin cup before her and placed them at the base of the homemade crucifix in the middle of the wooden camp table that served as an altar for the prison of Romainville. Yvonne Baratte was one of the Gestapo's 250 women prisoners guarded in the decaying fortress. She had picked those few scrawny flowers herself that afternoon during her exercise period in the prison courtyard.

---

* Philippe François Marie Leclerc de Hautecloque took the name Jacques Philippe Leclerc as soon as he joined General de Gaulle in London, to protect his family. On March 10, 1941, Thérèse de Hautecloque, still unaware of the fact her husband had changed his name, picked a tract dropped by an English plane out of a bush on the family estate. It described "A Great French Victory," the capture of Koufra on March 1 "by French troops commanded by Colonel Leclerc." Those troops, the tract added, had marched all the way from their bases in Chad and Cameroun, a distance of 420 miles.

That night at dinner, she told her six children, "I don't know who this Colonel Leclerc is, but he's a fine man. That is how your father would act." Months later she learned from a Vichy functionary who arrived to sequester the family château and all her belongings that "Philippe Leclerc, born Hautecloque," had been deprived of his French citizenship for fighting with General de Gaulle.

Yvonne Baratte looked approvingly at her work. Then she tiptoed back to her cell. There, by the light of a stolen candle, she wrote a letter to her parents. The camp chaplain had promised to carry it out after Mass in the morning.

"I am full of hope," she began. "They will not have time to take us from here." She asked her mother to send her a nail file, a scarf and, if she could find a way to get it to her, a copy of Charles Péguy's *The Genius of France.* "I love you all, and I'm sure we'll meet again soon," she concluded. Then she blew out her candle and lay still.

Perhaps, in the silence of Romainville prison that night, Yvonne Baratte and the other women around her thought of Paris lying so near the walls of the prison. She could not know that she would not walk again the streets of that city. In a few hours, Yvonne Baratte had a rendezvous with a train that would carry her to a place called Ravensbrück. There, on a cold winter's morning in March, 1945, she would die of dysentery.

• • •

At Fresnes, Louis Armand, the Resistance organizer who so desperately wanted to be deported, lay on his straw sack curling and uncurling his toes. For the first time since his arrest, Armand was happy. With each twist of his ankle he could feel, almost sensuously, the cause of his happiness, the heavy winter boots wrapping his feet. That night the prison chaplain had brought them to him in a package from his family. Their reassuring presence, warm and secure on his feet, ended the one fear deportation had held for Armand. He had been afraid the thin summer shoes in which he was arrested would not survive the ordeal.

In the blackness of another cell across the silent prison, Pierre Lefaucheux tried to force himself to sleep. He had survived deportation another day. That day had brought encouraging news. Just before sundown, the tapping of a spoon striking a message in Morse code on a cell door had spread the word that the Allies were in Chartres. Only a few more days, he thought, and for his captors it would be too late.

Next to him, Pierre heard the crackling of the straw sack on which his cellmate was tossing. Then, in the darkness,

Pierre suddenly heard his voice, thin and despairing, reach out to him.

"*Je te parie que nous partons demain*—I'll bet we leave to-morrow," he said.

• • •

The terrifying summons of a telephone in the night filled the darkened apartment. Marie-Hélène Lefaucheux woke, reached for her dressing gown, and stumbled past the book-cases to the telephone in her library. From it the wife of the man lying on the straw prison mat at Fresnes heard the voice of an FFI friend.

"Something is going on at Fresnes," he said.

17

CLEAR, UNMISTAKABLE, Pierre Lefaucheux heard the metallic screech split the predawn silence with the suddenness of a piece of chalk rasping down a blackboard. Four floors below his cell, the unoiled wheels of Fresnes's coffee cart had just begun their last noisy journey through the corridors of the prison. One by one, Pierre could hear the doors below him clanging open. Never had there been so many. Finally the metallic scraping of the cart's wheels grew louder. Pierre heard the cart bang around the corner off to his left and start down the humid hallway leading toward his own cell. The noise stopped. Pierre Lefaucheux heard the rattle of the warden's key ring and then, as his own cell door swung open, he saw, outlined before him, the waiting coffee cart. In the semidarkness he heard, for the first time that morning, the voice of his cellmate.

"*Tu vois*," he said, "I won."

In the women's section of Fresnes, the day had begun with a predawn visit of a German officer. Twenty-year-old Jeannie Rousseau, the prettiest girl in the prison, screamed when she saw that German officer standing over her. Then she recognized the tip of chaplain Abbé Steinert's crucifix hanging out from under his tunic.

"Ladies," he announced to the five girls crowded side by side into Jeannie's windowless cell, "I have come to give you communion for the ordeal that awaits you in a few hours."

It was 4 A.M.

To the millions of Parisians still sleeping in the silent city beyond Fresnes's gray stone walls, this slowly dawning morning would open one last holiday to be snatched from their uncertain world. But to Pierre Lefaucheux, his cellmate, and 2,500 other prisoners at Fresnes as well as Romainville and Drancy, where 1,500 Jewish prisoners were held by the SS, this Feast of the Assumption would have another meaning. For them, in this gray day now dawning, a long calvary was beginning.

By sunrise the operation was well under way. At Fresnes, the women were herded away first. They were jammed into buses. In one a sympathetic driver told them to tuck their last messages to their families under the seats of the bus. He promised to deliver them. At Romainville, among the last prisoners to leave was a tubercular Polish singer named Nora. Never would the handful of prisoners left behind forget the image of the little Pole riding through the gate of the barbed-wire fence, singing proudly from the open rear end of the last bus:

Attends-moi dans ce pays de France,
Je serai bientôt de retour, garde confiance.

At Drancy, the 1,500 Jews scheduled for deportation got an unexpected reprieve. Not a single one of the buses assigned to carry them off would start. Someone had stolen their generators.

At Fresnes, the 2,000 men picked for the convoy were driven from their cells as soon as the women's buses had left. Captain Philippe Keun, the aide of the intelligence service's "Jade Amicol," thanked God he had been chosen. His tortures were over, and wherever the Germans might take him, he could go with a tranquil conscience. He had not betrayed his trust.

Louis Armand, in the very first packet of prisoners formed in the courtyard, made no effort to conceal his satisfaction. He could feel his heavy shoes snuggly wrapping his feet. And now, next to him in this group of departing prisoners whose names began with "A," he had found an old friend and college classmate, Pierre Angot. Angot was sick with despair. In a few days, just a few more days, he whispered to Armand, he would have been freed. Vichy's Minister of Production, Gaston Bichelonne, one of his close friends, had promised to get him out of Fresnes. Now, on his way to Germany, he was slipping out of Bichelonne's grasp.

From his own new reserve of optimism, Armand tried to find the words to cheer his despairing friend. The surest chance of survival, he told Angot, was in this mass of shuffling prisoners in Fresnes's courtyard. Those left behind, he whispered to Angot, "will be slaughtered when the Allies are in front of the prison." So intently was he whispering his encouragement to Angot, that Armand failed to hear the guard shout his name. Someone next to him nudged him. "They're calling you," he said.

The only trip this man so anxious to leave would make that day was the one to which a prison guard now summoned him, a walk back up the five flights of stairs to his prison cell. The Germans had taken his name from the list of departing prisoners. Numb with fear and disappointment, Armand stumbled back into the foul-smelling stone hall he had left just an hour before.

For one prisoner, the sight of the Frenchmen massed in the courtyard below his window seemed the most cruelly unjust sight he had ever seen. Funker (Signalman) Willi Wagenknecht had spent all but two days of his Paris assignment in this cell serving a six-month sentence for striking an officer in the telephone center at OB West. He shook his head in dismay. Willi Wagenknecht could not understand the injustice of it. Nothing would ever seem more illogical to him than watching that line of Frenchmen filing out of the prison gates toward Germany, while he, Willi Wagenknecht, stayed behind in their loathsome Paris jail.

Outside, Marie-Hélène Lefaucheux's nervous hands tightened over the grips of her handlebars as she watched the gates of Fresnes prison splitting apart. Since six o'clock, shunted onto a tiny patch of sidewalk by the prison's SS guards, Marie-Hélène Lefaucheux had waited in uncomplaining silence to see those gates swing open. Now she studied each of the prisoners as, one by one, they dragged themselves past the machine guns of their SS guards and up the steps to the waiting buses.

Then she saw him. A tight little cry escaped Marie-Hélène's mouth as she caught her first glimpse of her husband's drawn and pain-worn face. "My God, how thin he is," she said to herself. A wild exulting filled her young body. "He's alive, he's alive," she thought. It was only a few instants later that the awful reality of the scene she was watching struck Marie-Hélène Lefaucheux. Pierre, she suddenly understood, was being deported. In agony, she followed each of his painful steps up to the bus that would carry him away from her. Just as he stepped on, she was sure Pierre tossed his head in the cocky little gesture of affection that had always been a silent greeting between them. "He saw me," she said out loud. She could no longer hold back her tears. Through her blurred eyes, she saw Abbé Steinert's familiar figure in the group of German officers behind the open back platform of Pierre's bus. She darted past the SS guard in front of her and ran to him.

"My child," he whispered, "it's a blessing he's leaving. There'll be a massacre in the prison."

The buses' engines started, and the long line of green-and-yellow vehicles started to move forward. Marie-Hélène ran back to her bicycle. Without knowing why, she got on and pedaled after the convoy.

18

DIETRICH VON CHOLTITZ sat in the unreal light of OB West's underground command bunker and listened impassively to the dry voice of von Kluge's chief of staff, Generalleutnant Günther Blumentritt. Blumentritt was outlining a proposal for a "limited scorched-earth policy" * for the Paris region. His voice lightly counterpointed by the whirring of the bunker's ventilating equipment, Blumentritt outlined its details from a typewritten memorandum clasped in his left hand. Occasionally he looked up from the paper to gesture with his finger at one of the red tracings marked on the 1/10,000 map spread before him on Kluge's mahogany conference table. Those red grease-crayon lines on the map's celluloid overlay pinpointed every gas plant, power station, and reservoir serving the five million people of the Paris area.

Blumentritt's proposal was, like every staff study that came out of his G3 section, a precise, careful document. It broke down into two phases. The first, which he urged Kluge to begin immediately, entailed the systematic destruction of the city's gas, electric power and water facilities.† The second was the "selective sabotage" of the city's industrial plants. The Germans realized they had neither the time nor the manpower to devastate completely all the factories in the huge industrial belt ringing Paris. Blumentritt's plan called for a logical compromise. It was the destruction of the vital machinery in those plants whose loss would render them useless to the advancing Allies.‡

The "limited scorched-earth policy" he was proposing, Blumentritt told the conference, was "strategically essential." If Paris's industry was not crippled, it would, he pointed out, be turned against Germany by the Allies in a matter of weeks. "Setting the population into turmoil and paralyzing the city" by destroying its utilities would, he argued, help slow the

---

* The Germans had not used scorched-earth tactics in France. It was not, however, out of any special consideration for their French neighbors. In southern Italy, on the soil of their Allies, Eisenhower recalled, "they shot every cow and chicken they couldn't carry off." In France, since Avranches, they had simply been moving backward too fast to apply the strategy.

† To cut off the water supply, the Germans proposed destroying large segments of the four aqueducts that brought 97 per cent of the city's water to Paris. Contrary to rumors in Paris at the time, the Germans at no time considered poisoning the city water supply. Two alternative tactics were recommended for the power plants, either boring the 25 major turbines in the area and placing charges in the cores of the turbines, or destroying their distributing and regulating equipment. The first tactic would have, according to the senior Siemens engineer in the ctiy, deprived Paris of full industrial power "for two years." The second, less time-consuming and much less complex, would have cut Paris's power for "at least six months."

‡ At one point, Blumentritt used the phrase "blow up Paris." Next to him, Choltitz heard Generalleutnant Hans Speidel, Chief of Staff of Army Group B, growl, "Blow up Paris—what the hell does he mean? Has he found a power plant in Notre-Dame?"

enemy advance by forcing the Allies to divert part of their military resources to the distressed capital.

Blumentritt stressed the need of putting the first phase of the plan into operation at once. He handed Choltitz a list of naval depots where he could requisition additional explosives from the stores of the Kriegsmarine to supplement the Wehrmacht's stocks. If the program was not started right away, he argued, there was a risk it would not be finished before the Allies came within striking distance of the city.

To Choltitz, Blumentritt's presentation was "very dry, very professional, and very convincing." Nothing in his proposal surprised Choltitz. The day before, he had received his first direct OKW order since taking the Paris command. It ordered the "destruction or total paralysis" of the entire Paris industrial establishment. The order, he knew, had passed through OB West. As soon as he had received his summons to this early-morning conference, Choltitz had had no doubt it was to hear Blumentritt's recommendations on how to put Hitler's order into effect.

Nor did Choltitz find anything unusual in the order. The concept behind it seemed to him "perfectly sound." It was, after all, only an extension of the tactics used on the eastern front. And, at a time when Allied bombers were nightly leveling German cities, nothing seemed more reasonable to the men around Kluge's conference table than that the same tactic should be applied from the ground to Paris.

Choltitz did, however, object to one thing in Blumentritt's plan. It was its timing. For the moment, he was interested in defending Paris, not destroying it. The time to put Blumentritt's program into action, he argued that morning, was when they were preparing to abandon the city. Evidently, he pointed out, they had no intention of doing that for some time. Launching Blumentritt's plan prematurely would, he argued, throw thousands of factory workers into the hands of the Resistance, and "put the population into open warfare" against his troops. Besides, he added laconically, German soldiers drank water, too.

Impassively, Generalfeldmarschall von Kluge listened to the two men argue. Then without warning he held up his hand to indicate their discussion had gone on long enough. Both of them, he said, had made sound points. He told them he would "issue final orders later." The meeting was over. Choltitz nodded to Kluge and left. Fifty-six hours later, en route back to Germany after having been relieved of his command and replaced by one of the most savagely effective of Hitler's field marshals, von Kluge would commit suicide.

But before leaving, he would order Choltitz to start the systematic destruction Blumentritt proposed that morning.

• • •

Four men were waiting in the anteroom to his office in the Meurice when von Choltitz returned. On the orders they had brought with them from Berlin, Choltitz saw the signature of Generaloberst Jodl. As engineers, they had been sent to Paris by OKW "to prepare and supervise the demolition of all the major industrial installations in the Paris region." They had brought with them their working tools. In the anteroom of Choltitz's office were a dozen round black map cases. They contained the blueprints of every major factory in the Paris area.

Their leader, a graying, quiet man, explained to Choltitz that, by carefully siting a reasonable number of charges, they could "paralyze Paris's industry for at least six months."

Choltitz gave them a suite of rooms in the fourth floor of his hotel and ordered two staff cars put at their disposal so they could inspect the city's plants themselves. Two hours later, when he first visited their rooms, they were "awash in maps and blueprints." If Paris fell, one of them promised him, "the Allies won't find a single factory working in the city."

19

THE AUGUST SUN beat down on the rusting sheet-iron roofs of the cattle cars strung together on a siding of the Pantin freight station just behind the Paris stockyards. Inside that line of cars, packed together more tightly than the most jammed rush-hour métro crowd, the human freight the SS had selected for deportation to Germany gasped for breath in the unbearable heat. The cream of the French Resistance movement—2,104 men and 400 women, eight out of every ten prisoners at Fresnes and Romainville—waited in misery for the train to start.

Jeannie Rousseau was in a car jammed with 92 women. Its one window, crossed with barbed wire, was too high to allow even the tallest woman in the car a glimpse of the world outside. Never would this pretty girl forget the heat of that car, the rasping lungs gulping for its fetid air. One by one, the women took off everything but their underclothes. In one corner of the car, next to the tin bucket that served as the toilet, the women cleared a little space where three prisoners at a time could squat knee to shoulder blade and rest. The others had to stand up, and in the fierce heat their sweating bodies slipped and slid against each other.

In the next car there was more room. There Yvonne Pagniez and the other women were able to squat and link themselves into human chains. But, one after another, they fainted in the heat. A half dozen of them would soon be dead.

Yvonne Pagniez suddenly noticed a man in the doorway, his fat face glistening with sweat. She recognized the bulging silhouette of the Ukrainian SS guard who had supervised her torture sessions at the Gestapo's avenue Foch headquarters. It seemed to her that he had come to wish "*bon voyage* to this herd of cattle, on which he had stamped his brand, now being shipped to the slaughterhouse."

For the men, the conditions were even worse. Stripped half nude, packed more than 100 to a car, they had only one desperate desire. It was that this train they had hoped to miss would leave.

Pierre Lefaucheux stood in his car, dizzy with hunger, thirst and heat, praying that the train would move. Standing behind him, a desperately thirsty prisoner licked with his parched tongue at the sweat running down the small of Pierre's back.

•   •   •

His head bowed, his massive shoulders slack, a dejected man walked out of the Pantin station and into a nearby café. Emil "Bobby" Bender, the middle-aged playboy of the Abwehr, had just tried to stop the prisoners' train by bluffing its SS commander. He had failed.

Since Nordling had contacted him, the two men had tried desperately to transfer the political prisoners around Paris into Red Cross custody. None of their efforts had succeeded. Nordling had seen Pierre Laval, the Vichy prime minister; Otto Abetz, Germany's ambassador; Karl Oberg, head of the Gestapo in France. None of them had shown any interest in his idea. Von Choltitz had been too busy to see them.

Other men were trying that morning to stop the train of cattle cars lined up in the Pantin station. Their tactics were different. While the prisoners agonized in their sweltering cattle cars, a teen-age boy pedaled frantically out of Paris toward the little village of Nanteuil-Saacy. He carried an urgent oral message from the Paris FFI to the leader of the Resistance network in the village. It was a simple and direct order: At any cost, by any means, cut the main rail line from Paris to Nancy. It was the line over which the train waiting in the Pantin station would have to pass to get to Germany.

And, from a hidden transmitter in a Paris attic, a coded radio message went to London at midday. It read: "For urgent relay all FFI chiefs. Germans organized evacuation detainees Paris prisons particularly Fresnes by rail via Metz Nancy. Fear general massacre during trip. Take all measures possible sabotage transport."

20

THE TRAGEDY OPENING in the hot sunlight of the Pantin freight station would pass almost unnoticed in Paris this Assumption Day. Most of the city's inhabitants were preoccupied only by an increasingly desperate food situation. The dominant problem of the day for them was how to scavenge the ingredients of one more meal. Paris, declared *Paris-Soir* that evening, "is almost a besieged city, with its food shortage worsening every day, and the specter of famine beginning to appear." A M. Chevalier of the Academy of Science advised the city in *Le Petit Parisien* that, "in a desperate situation," the leaves of its elm, linden and ash trees were all edible.

For Paris's youngest citizens, the dominant event of this feast day was to have been a pilgrimage of all the schoolchildren of Paris to the Cathedral of Notre-Dame to ask the Virgin Mary, the patroness of France, to protect Paris, its capital. It was canceled at the last moment by von Choltitz.

At the western outskirts of that capital, at about the time the first of the city's schoolchildren should have opened their march toward Notre-Dame, a thirty-six-year-old German captain ordered his foliage-covered Kübelwagen to stop in the middle of the pont de Neuilly. Werner Ebernach waved the men of his 813th Pionierkompanie (Engineer Company) to a stop, and walked over to the bridge's concrete parapet. There the blue-eyed officer, who had lost three fingers of his left hand booby-trapping a peasant's cottage on the eastern front, lit a cigarette and stared down at the muddy waters of the Seine. He was surprised by its width. The Spree of his native Berlin seemed small by comparison. In front of him, stretching out of the green borders of the Bois de Boulogne, Ebernach could see the majestic arches of the pont de Puteaux. Behind him, downstream, the pont de la Jatte leaped the river in two spans, pausing in the middle on a little island covered with gray stone houses. Ebernach took a map out of his pocket and unfolded it on the parapet below him. With his finger, he began to count slowly along its surface.

Across Paris, from the suburb of Le Pecq in the west, to Choisy in the southeast, forty-five bridges like those on which Captain Ebernach stood spanned the Seine. Those forty-five bridges were the arteries that tied Paris together. Without them, Paris's long loops of the Seine would become again what they had been when the city was founded 2,000 years earlier on an island in the river, a formidable obstacle. Although Ebernach might not know it, some of those bridges were held by the French to be art treasures in themselves. The pont Alexandre III, so named by Czar Nicholas II, was a national monument. The pont de la Concorde contained the stones of the Bastille, and the original beams of the pont de la Tournelle dated to 1369.

Now, on the pont de Neuilly, Captain Werner Ebernach carried in his tunic pocket, under his Iron Cross First Class, a piece of blue paper which, in a few moments, he would hand to General von Choltitz. It was signed by Generaloberst Jodl, and carried the stamp "KR Blitz—top priority." It was an order to destroy the forty-five bridges crossing the Seine in Paris.

Werner Ebernach had no idea why Hitler wanted these forty-five bridges destroyed. He neither had access to OKW's strategy nor cared about it. He was only a thorough and workmanlike technician. Ebernach had blown up dozens of bridges in his career, and, standing on the pont de Neuilly, he did not think that these in Paris would present any more problems than those that he had destroyed in Kiev and Dnepropetrovsk. In a few moments he would remark to Paris's commanding general that when he was finished and "all the masonry of Paris's bridges has toppled into the river, the Seine will be dammed from one end of Paris to the other."

Before getting back into his Kübelwagen, Ebernach had one vital inspection to make of the pont de Neuilly's foundations. With the head of his explosives section, Master Sergeant Hegger, Ebernach walked down the riverbank and peered up at the bridge's superstructure. The gleam of his flashlight caught the reflection of the strip of metal he was looking for. There, fastened to the base of the bridge, just as Ebernach had hoped, was a rusting mining pan. By law, those mining pans had been fixed to every bridge in France for over seventy years. They had been placed there by the French so those bridges could be swiftly destroyed in an emergency.

• • •

Sunlight filtered through the grove of oak trees, and for the first time in months, General Jacques Chaban-Delmas heard the sound of birds singing. Two miles behind this little glen, down a dirt road, was the *pâté*-producing village of Connerré. One hundred miles straight ahead was Paris. The two American officers who had brought him to this farthermost point of the Allied advance in France handed him his cardboard suitcase. Next to him, with a plucked chicken, a slab of butter, and a bundle of cauliflower strapped to its handlebars, was the bicycle he would ride back to Paris. Chaban picked his tennis sneakers, shorts and sweater out of the suitcase and began to put them on.

When he had changed, he folded the uniform he had worn

for only four days into the cardboard case. One of his American escorts stopped him. Hesitant and faintly embarrassed, he asked Chaban for some souvenir of their few moments together. "You know," he told Chaban, "you're the first French general we've met." And he added, "You're going to ride a bike into Paris before our tanks get there."

Chaban stopped, and with his fingers shaking very slightly he picked the two stars off his shoulder boards and gave one to each of the two American officers who had brought him to this tiny glade. Then they shook hands, Chaban waved, and pedaled off down the dirt road to Paris.

• • •

For Dietrich von Choltitz, the order Captain Werner Ebernach carried in his hand as he walked into his Hotel Meurice office was no surprise; he had already received a copy of it himself directly from OKW. But Ebernach's presence in his office was. Von Choltitz had known this young officer before the war. At Gimma, in Saxony, he had already had a chance to admire his prowess in carrying out just the kind of assignment he had been sent to Paris to handle. There, during maneuvers in 1936, he had blown two old bridges over the River Mulde before von Choltitz's appreciative eyes.

The mature, determined look in Ebernach's face told Choltitz that August day that the officer before him had kept the promise of his youth. There was in the general's mind no doubt that Ebernach was capable, as he now pledged to do, of choking the Seine with the ruins of Paris's bridges. Von Choltitz, however, was determined to keep absolute control of the operation. He told Ebernach to "go ahead with all his preparations." But he added that he did not want any demolition carried out in Paris without his "personal approval." Then he told the high-spirited captain before him, "The Seine, Ebernach, is not the Mulde, and Paris is not Gimma. We have the whole world watching us here, not just a handful of generals."

Ebernach had been gone only a few moments when von Choltitz's chief of staff, Colonel Friedrich von Unger, entered his office with two reports. The first von Choltitz almost ignored; it was a report on the Paris police strike. But the second disturbed him. Eight German soldiers had been killed in an

ambush in a suburb called Aubervilliers. It was the first serious outbreak in the city.

Von Choltitz walked to the huge map of the city on his
wall, carrying the report in his hand. His fingers slid over it
until he located Aubervilliers. He sighed and murmured, "Today they are in the suburbs. Tomorrow they will be in Paris."

• • •

All along the line of cattle cars, couplings banged together
like the links in a long chain. Slowly the creaking wooden cars
began to slide down the siding of the Pantin station. For the
2,500 miserable human beings inside, the sounds of this long-
dreaded departure were now a blessed relief. From behind
the wooden slats of one car came, lightly at first, the sound
of singing. Then car after car picked up the song, until finally
it came in a defiant chorus from all these overloaded cattle
cars, and its proud notes filled the darkened Pantin station.
It was the "Marseillaise."

Outside the station, the Gothic figures on its worn clock
tower approached midnight. A railroad worker, his own eyes
red with tears, walked up to the lonely figure standing beside
her bicycle.

"C'est fini," he said as gently as he knew how. "They've
left." Marie-Hélène Lefaucheux got back on her bicycle and
pedaled home. There she set her alarm for three o'clock and
fell into bed. Without knowing why or how, she was determined to follow her husband's prison train as far as she could.

• • •

At Fresnes and Romainville, a lonely silence now filled the
corridors of the half-empty prisons. At Fresnes, a despairing
Louis Armand could not sleep. He listened in vain for a sound:
the clinking spoons of the inmates' telegraph that each night
tapped out on the prison bars the latest news smuggled into
Fresnes's walls. The only sound Louis Armand could hear that
night came from inside his own soul. It told him that, like the
rest of the prisoners left behind in Fresnes, he "would be
massacred" before the Germans retreated.

21

SERGEANT HERMANN PLUMPFRANCK, forty-three, emptied the last of the contents of his bureau drawers into the two cardboard valises on his bed, and knotted them shut with a length of string. In one of the suitcases was the hard currency Plumpfranck was taking with him as a precaution against what he feared were difficult days ahead: fifty pairs of silk stockings. Then the sergeant stepped down into the lobby of this Hotel Continental in which he had passed four years of his life, told the concierge he would "be back for Christmas," and, his suitcases in his hands, walked away.

Just as it had been every day during his four happy years as an occupation soldier in Paris, Plumpfranck's first stop that morning was at a newspaper kiosk at the Palais Royal opposite his office in the Ministry of Finance. There, from the kiosk's shrill-tongued *vendeuse*, he asked for his daily copy of the *Pariser Zeitung*, the city's German newspaper.

"*Petit boche,*" she told him, "there is none."

The previous day's edition of the paper, its 221st, had been its last. During the night its staff had left for Brussels. Plumpfranck picked up his valises again, and as he did, he noticed, smiling to him, the squat little woman with the tight mass of gray curls he had seen so often buying her morning paper at this newsstand. Her name was Colette, he knew, and she was a writer.

"*Alors,*" she said to Plumpfranck, "you're jilting us?"

Indeed Plumpfranck, just like thousands of other noncombatant German soldiers, was, that August 16, jilting Paris. The day before, General Warlimont had informed OB West that Hitler had authorized the SS, the Gestapo, the SD and the city's administrative staffs to evacuate Paris and leave the city to combat troops. The steady chain of their trucks flowing eastward that morning caused the first traffic jams the streets of Paris had known since the war.

Parisians watched impassively from their sidewalk cafés

as the first of their occupiers left. Some shouted, "We'll be back for Christmas," or sang *"Ce n'est qu'un au revoir"* as their trucks filed past. A few *"Souris Grises"*—gray mice, the Parisian nickname for the Wehrmacht's drab women soldiers—wept and waved their handkerchiefs. But the most astonishing sight of all was the stream of loot flowing out with the departing occupiers. Paris was being emptied by the truckload. Bathtubs, bidets, rugs, furniture, radios, cases and cases of wine—all rode past the angry eyes of Paris that morning. At the square Lamartine, in front of their disappointed neighbors, a group of German signalmen even carted off the little herd of pigs they had been raising in their garden.

Transport Officer Walter Neuling noticed a fellow officer at the Hotel Majestic yank down the draperies and stuff them into his suitcase. He explained to Neuling he was "going to make a dress with them later." At the Hotel Florida, Corporal Erwin Hesse saw his superior First Lieutenant Thierling tie up his sheets in a telephone cord, and then, as an afterthought, pack up the telephone itself.

Some Germans left like gentlemen. On the boulevard Victor-Hugo in Neuilly, an SS Standartenführer that morning wrote a thank-you note "to my unknown host for his unwilling hospitality."

He had, he wrote, "left the apartment as I found it. The gas, electricity and telephone bills have been paid, and the concierge tipped." He told his host he had admired "the three volumes of Voltaire which I have put back in their place." Then he left a bill along with the note to "replace the two crystal champagne goblets unfortunately broken during my stay." [*]

This moment posed a grave moral crisis for some Germans. For Captain Hans Werner of the Supply Service at the rue La Pérouse, the time had come to choose between the Wehrmacht and his mistress Antoinette Charbonnier. He chose Antoinette. At noon that day, dressed in civilian clothing and carrying a small suitcase, he left their apartment on the avenue Mozart and walked to the drab hotel on the rue Henri-Rochefort where Antoinette had prepared a hideaway for this conquering hero

---

[*] On Liberation Day, August 25, the note was found by United States Air Corps Major Bob Richardson. The night before, Richardson had met the owner of the apartment in his country home in the Valley of Chevreuse. The Frenchman gave Richardson a key to the apartment and invited him to use it.

of 1940. There they planned to take refuge until "things got back to normal again." Then they would get married.

Eugen Hommens, the man whose pistol had been stolen by the FFI three days earlier, chose duty over his mistress Annick. Besides, the thirty-eight-year-old Hommens "didn't want to be at the mercy of a jealous woman."

For some of the Germans scheduled to leave that day, luck rather than passion or patriotism would decide their destiny. Just before her truck was due to leave, secretary Maria Fuhs remembered she had left a watch at a repair shop on the boulevard Haussmann. When he saw her arrive, the repairman told her, "Haven't you left yet? You must get away as quickly as you can!"

But for Maria Fuhs it was too late. Her broken watch had cost her her seat in the departing convoy. Instead, she would stay behind with the thousands of combat soldiers now preparing to defend Paris.

• • •

Like every other resident of the Paris suburb of Saint-Cloud, Thérèse Jarillon knew that the 800-yard-long auto tunnel opening onto a superhighway just below her gray stone cottage was stuffed with explosives. Now this high-school teacher was in a state of near panic. She had just received from her charwoman, Mme. Capitaine, a source of unshakably accurate reports, an alarming piece of news. The Germans, according to Mme. Capitaine, were preparing to blow up the tunnel. If they did, Thérèse Jarillon knew her own little house, "Mon Rêve," and the hundreds of others like it in this hillside town would disappear along with it.

Thérèse Jarillon did the only thing possible. She took the pieces of crockery out of her Breton cupboard, wrapped them in old newspapers, and hid them under her bed. Then she lowered the cupboard onto the floor, opened all the windows, and fled.

Given the code name Pilz (mushroom) by the Germans, this auto tunnel depot was in fact a torpedo factory. Until the end of 1943, it had provided the torpedoes for most of Germany's Atlantic U-boat fleet. When, with Germany's growing U-boat losses, the undersea war slowed down, Pilz had gone right on turning out its torpedoes. They were stocked in endless underground caves next to the cramped living quarters where Pilz's requisitioned factory laborers lived.

There was only one way to destroy it; it had to be blown up from inside. That was exactly what its Kriegsmarine guards were preparing to do when Captain Werner Ebernach, the demolitions expert of the 813th Pionierkompanie, arrived. Ebernach had come to Pilz to see if he could find here the explosives with which to carry out the mission he had been assigned in Paris.

The captain was actually dizzied by the sight before him in the well-lit underground chambers of Pilz. There, in long neat lines, their black casings glistening in the light, were over 300 torpedoes charged and packed for shipping. Beyond them were hundreds more, all carefully stacked and packed with explosives, waiting only to be fitted with detonators from the cases of detonating equipment stored alongside them.*

In hushed respect, Ebernach mumbled *"Donnerwetter!"* To Master Sergeant Hegger beside him, he exclaimed, "My God, we can blow up half the bridges in the world with this!"

Then Captain Ebernach turned to the officer of the Kriegsmarine guiding him through the tunnel. In a dry, professional voice, he said, "I requisition all the material in this tunnel in the name of the commanding general of Gross Paris."

• • •

A few hundred yards from the tunnel entrance, the black Horch of the commanding general of Gross Paris twisted up a side street and stopped with a screech of its tires in front of a handsome hilltop villa on the rue Pozzo di Borgo. Waiting there for von Choltitz was his most important subordinate, Lt. Colonel Hubertus von Aulock, the man responsible for the defense of the approaches to the city. In the oak-paneled study of von Aulock's villa, before a huge map spread over the top of a handsome Bechstein grand piano, the two men

---

* Joachim von Knesebeck, the wartime director of the giant Siemens electric company in Paris and a distant cousin of von Choltitz, was a regular visitor to Pilz where he had installed the factory's electric machinery. During an interview in New York in 1963, he expressed understanding of Ebernach's astonishment at what he saw in the tunnel. There were in Pilz, in August, 1944, "enough torpedoes to shoot two wars through," in von Knesebeck's estimation.

roughed out that morning their first concrete plans for the defense of the French capital.

Von Choltitz adjusted his monocle and with a pencil sketched a line along the map in front of him. When he finished, he turned to von Aulock. "Here," he said, "is where you will stand."

Von Aulock looked down. He was astonished to see that the line von Choltitz had drafted swept over a 60-mile-long arc well in advance of the line his predecessor General von Boineburg had proposed. From the Seine west of Poissy, it swung all along the western, southern and southeastern approaches to the city to the Marne River village of La Varenne-Saint-Hilaire, passing through Saint-Germain-en-Laye, Versailles, Palaiseau, Orly and Villeneuve-Saint-Georges on its way.

Von Choltitz knew von Aulock could not hold that line without substantial reinforcements. But he had been promised those reinforcements. Until they arrived, Aulock's 10,000 men would provide a screen to the approaches of the city. To reinforce them, Choltitz accepted a suggestion put forward by Colonel Fritz Meise, the commander of the 11th Paratroop Regiment. He suggested they take down all the 88 antiaircraft pieces in the city and use them as antitank guns. The guns, Meise pointed out, "have no value in the city because the Allies are never going to bomb Paris."

Their conference over, von Aulock offered his new commander a glass of champagne. His devoted adjutant, Captain Theo Wulff, poured it for them in the crystal goblets belonging to the villa's owner, a Jewish industrialist named Stern, who had been living in New York since 1939. Von Choltitz raised his glass and toasted "the hard days that lie ahead of us."

Then, from behind him, Captain Wulff heard the nostalgic notes of an air by Lützow coming from the Bechstein grand piano. It was Colonel Seidel, of Dresden, the chief of one of von Aulock's three combat groups, playing. The little group of men fell silent. For a long moment they stood there listening, champagne glasses in their hands, looking through the wide bay window at the spectacle spread before their feet: the rooftops of Paris basking in the summer sun.

22

AHEAD OF MARIE-HÉLÈNE Lefaucheux, the medieval towers of the Cathedral of Saint-Étienne, soaring above the Marne River town of Meaux, reddened in the rising sun. Two hours and twenty-six miles now lay behind her in her pursuit of the wooden cattle car carrying her husband up the valley of the Marne to Nancy and the Rhine. But as she pedaled, her hopes of catching that train had already begun to fade. At each wayside station where she had stopped along her route, she had been given the same information: the train had passed two hours ahead of her. No matter how fast she had ridden, she had not been able to shorten that interval. She was, it seemed, condemned to chase this disappearing train across the faces of France, stumbling along two hours in its wake.

At that moment Pierre was twenty miles away, fighting to stay alive in a smoke-filled railroad tunnel. The bicycled Resistance message rushed north from Paris had arrived on time. Just beyond the tunnel of Nanteuil-Saacy, by a rocky cut on the eastern shoulder of the Marne, 46 miles from Paris, an FFI commando had blown apart sixty-five yards of the rail line to Nancy. The train was stuck.

To repair the ruined rail line would take the Germans most of the day. Rather than risk an attack, the SS guards had backed the train into the tunnel. In their cattle cars, behind their sealed doors, the 2,453 prisoners had long since forgotten the first burst of ecstasy that had swept the train when they realized the FFI had sabotaged the track. For two hours the SS had kept the locomotive pouring coils of black smoke into the cramped tunnel. Sick, hysterical, near suffocation, the prisoners could now only gasp for breath in the rancid black air settling around them. The floor of Yvonne Pagniez's car was already slick with vomit. In the car behind her, the women in pretty Jeannie Rousseau's wagon were certain the Germans were trying to asphyxiate them. They could hear the clump of their boots in the blackness as they ran along the tracks beside the train shouting orders at each other.

Yet each moment of misery passed in the rancid air of the tunnel brought the convoy's prisoners a step closer to freedom. Tucked behind a cluster of rocks in a grove of poplars on a hillside fronting the tunnel mouth, five men watched and waited. They had blown the rail line. And they knew that all across the Marne Valley, singly and in small groups, other FFI men were trying to find their way to this hillock. When enough arrived, they would attack the convoy's 200-man escort.

• • •

Those reinforcements would arrive too late. Through a cruel stroke of luck, the convoy's SS guards had, just three miles away, stumbled on the only train within 30 miles of Nanteuil-Saacy. It was a real cattle train, backed onto a siding at Nanteuil-sur-Marne with a load of beef for the Wehrmacht. They drove the cattle out of the train and requisitioned it for their prisoners. A few moments later the Germans backed the train out of the tunnel to march their prisoners along the torn-up track to their new train. As it nosed into the sunlight, a young woman came pedaling down the winding river road alongside the track. Marie-Hélène Lefaucheux had caught up with the train. Among the black and coughing figures lurching out of its wagons, she recognized Pierre. At that instant "nothing in the world, not even the SS" could keep her from talking to her husband. Still holding her bicycle, she bounded across the little field of daisies that separated them. Then, seeing his frail figure before her, she performed the first gesture that came to her mind: she took a white handkerchief from her pocket and wiped the soot from his eyes.

By some dispensation she would never understand, the guard behind Pierre shrugged his shoulders in indifference, and allowed Marie-Hélène to walk beside this pale, stumbling man who was her husband. Her skirt rustling lightly against his shredded trousers, her hand clasped in his, she savored two hours beside him. She would have ridden her bicycle to hell that morning for half as much as that. Of all the mumbled phrases they exchanged in that cruel walk, one would stay forever in her mind. When she heard it, Marie-Hélène knew that the tortures of the Gestapo had not broken the soul of this strong man. He still had his sense of humor.

"I'll promise you one thing," Pierre told her. "After this trip, I'll never argue with you again about the price of a sleeping car."

• • •

From a hilltop across an irregular loop of the Marne from Nanteuil-Saccy, five weeping men watched the prisoners, packed into their new cattle train, disappear down the green folds of the river valley toward Nancy. Their plan to ambush this convoy had failed. Although they could not know it, it had been the only chance the FFI would have to stop the train by force.

As the train rounded the last bend in the tip of the valley, the five men could see a tiny white figure following behind. It was Marie-Hélène Lefaucheux. For her, her journey had just begun.

23

LIEUTENANT ERNST VON BRESSENSDORF, the twenty-seven-year-old executive officer of the 550th Signal Company, started at the sight of the red lamp flashing on the switchboard in front of him on the third floor of the Hotel Meurice. That light meant Berlin, or Rastenburg was calling on the direct line linking them with Paris's military governor.

It was OKW, and immediately Bressensdorf recognized the dry, imperious voice of Generaloberst Alfred Jodl. It was "as clear as if he were calling from the Louvre." Bressensdorf switched the call to General von Choltitz's extension. Then, switching another peg into his relay box, he risked a court-martial and eavesdropped on the communication.

Bressensdorf started at the first words he heard Jodl speak. What, he asked von Choltitz, was the state of "the destruction we ordered for Paris"? Jodl told von Choltitz the Führer had asked that a report on his progress be drafted for submission at his midday strategy conference less than an hour away. There was a silence; then von Choltitz answered.

He told Jodl that "unfortunately" he had not been able to start them. The preparations were still going on, he explained; the demolition experts had arrived only twenty-four hours earlier. Jodl was "extremely disappointed." The Führer, he told von Choltitz, "was very impatient."

Then von Choltitz advanced to Jodl the same arguments he had used at OB West the day before. To actually carry out the proposed demolition would, he told Jodl, "set the city up in arms." He proposed that they proceed with all the preparations, but hold off the actual destruction for a few days. Jodl told von Choltitz he would present his recommendation to the Führer and call him back. But he warned him not to expect a change in plans. He was to go ahead as rapidly as possible with the preparations.

The conversation ended with a reassuring phrase from von Choltitz. The city was calm, he told the OKW chief of staff, and "the Parisians haven't dared to move."

●   ●   ●

The afternoon thundershower splashed savagely down on the red clay tennis courts beyond the clubhouse window. Martin, the groundskeeper at the Jean Bouin Tennis Club, knew he would have no customers this afternoon. He was wrong by one. As he mused, a knock sounded at the clubhouse's back door. There, dripping wet, clutching a dead chicken in his hands, was one of his best customers, Jacques Chaban-Delmas. Barely a week had passed since Martin had last seen the young man now standing in his clubhouse doorway.

"Where have you been?" he asked the drenched Chaban.

"In Versailles, getting this damned chicken," Chaban answered.

●   ●   ●

In the torrid heat of Algiers, acting partially on the information Chaban had brought out of Paris, Charles de Gaulle had made a decision: he was going to France. Now, under the lazily circling blades of his desert fan, de Gaulle was performing what would be the most distasteful act of that trip. He was requesting permission for it from General Sir Henry Maitland Wilson, the senior Allied commander in Algiers. It was Wilson's responsibility to pass along de Gaulle's request to SHAEF for clearance. Even now, de Gaulle had to go through the formality of getting clearance from his Allies to visit France.

To those Allies de Gaulle simply stated he would make a routine inspection of that part of France now liberated by the Allies. What he actually had in mind was a more ambitious move: He was going to transfer first himself, then his government, to France, and specifically to Paris. Whether the Allies liked it or not, whether Roosevelt recognized him or not, de Gaulle was determined to install himself and his government in France's capital. He deliberately did not reveal his intentions to SHAEF for two reasons. First, he did not consider it any of SHAEF's business. Second, from a practical standpoint, he was convinced that if his American allies realized what he was up to, they would try to freeze him in Algiers. This he was not going to allow. One way or another, the proud chieftain of Free France was determined to enter France and Paris. He would get there with or without the help of his Allies, by his own means, and at the risk of his life if necessary.

•   •   •

In his comfortable command caravan at Shellburst, General Eisenhower counted with satisfaction the mounting toll of German troops locked inside the Falaise gap. Already his mind was on the next phase of the battle for France, the dash to the Seine and beyond. In analyzing his preparations for that phase, he felt no particular concern about the situation in Paris. No one had bothered to inform the Supreme Allied Commander that an insurrection was about to break out in the city. The warning in Chaban's message had not reached the commander whose plans he wanted to change.

•   •   •

On the plateau above the gray stone houses of the village of Tousson 40 miles south of Paris, an imperceptible beam of light flashed skyward. Then, 600 yards east, a second flashed on, and finally, this time 600 yards to the south, a third. Scattered around the plateau, hidden in clumps of gorse and high grass, dozens of armed men waited as the lights blinked out their code—two longs and a short.

Those men belonged to the hand-picked commando of a thirty-year-old giant called "Fabri." * Now, in an aviator's old jacket and ski pants, Fabri watched with satisfaction as his men went through this nightly drill once again. A few hundred yards away, in the dense woods of Darvaux, Fabri had his command post: one tent, two tables and a radio powered by an automobile battery. Scattered around this plateau, in carefully selected hiding places, were arms for over 5,000 men. The men in his commando, hidden in these thick forests of Fontainebleau, once the hunting preserves of the kings of France, were a highly trained unit. They led in these woods—where a refugee Thomas à Becket had once found shelter—a military and spartan life.

They were their chief's pride, for the mission Fabri had been assigned was so extraordinary that only perfectly trained and disciplined men could carry it out. Since May his men had rehearsed it almost nightly. They were to receive a small plane on this plateau, bundle its passenger into one of the two stolen Wehrmacht Horchs hidden nearby, and then smuggle him to a destination in Paris. Part of Fabri's commandos were to form a suicide squad to seal off the road behind the departing cars.

This evening Fabri was specially gratified by the performance of his men. He had just returned from Paris, from a meeting with the man who had assigned him this mission. In the conspiratorial darkness of the Church of Saint-Sulpice, Jacques Chaban-Delmas had that afternoon given Fabri the code word that would launch his operation. From now on, Chaban told him, he was to be on permanent alert.

After the night's drill ended, Fabri brought his two top aides into his command tent beside the commando's radio. He ordered them to mount a twenty-four-hour watch on that

---

* Fabri's real name was Paul Delouvrier. Later, from 1958 to 1960, he served as France's Delegate General in Algeria during the height of the Algerian crisis.

radio. They would listen for a five-word sentence. It was "*As-tu bien déjeuné, Jacquot?*" If it arrived, six hours later a small plane would circle in for a landing on the plateau nearby and deliver the important visitor they had been preparing for two and a half months to receive.

Fabri looked at the two men with him in his small tent. "Gentlemen," he said, "I can now tell you that if that plane arrives, the man who will be on board will be General de Gaulle."

24

As HE DID EVERY day at this same early hour, the short man in the black homburg walked past the two German sentries into the archway under the eight-faced cupola of the Palais du Luxembourg. Marcel Macary, the conservator of the palace, was the only Frenchman allowed free access to this storied building that had, since August 25, 1940, headquartered Generalfeldmarschall Hugo Sperrle and his Third Luftwaffe staff. This morning Macary's stride was quicker than usual; he knew that the day before, August 16, Sperrle and his staff had left for Reims, leaving the palace to its newly arrived SS defenders.

To Macary, their passing marked only the end of a brief and soon-to-be-forgotten chapter in the four-century history of this building he loved so well; but it foretold another event he knew was at hand, the liberation of Paris. Soon Macary would be able to return intact to his capital this building which he had guarded for the past four years as though it were his own.

This massive gray palace had become for him almost a living thing. Every time a German jackboot had ground a cigarette into its parquet floors, Macary had noticed it and almost felt it sting his own pale skin.

This morning as on every morning for the last four years, his workday began with a tour of the palace treasures. The routine never varied: first, its 300,000-book library; then, over the main entry, Delacroix's "Alexander after the battle of Arbelles Deposits the Poems of Homer in Darius's Golden Safe." Each time Macary looked at that painting, it was with a special sense of relief. Only by his most persuasive efforts had he kept it from a place of honor among the treasures of that noted art collector, Hermann Göring.

Finally, he wandered through the Gold Room where Marie de Médicis once reigned, into the grand salon, past the huge canvas from which an imperious Napoleon had looked down at the banqueting usurpers of this palace he had once shared with Josephine. As his last stop on his morning's tour, Macary decided to pass by the Court of Honor where, he knew, the Germans were finishing work on a new underground shelter.

There, to his astonishment, this man who had always had free access to every corner of the Palais du Luxembourg found the way barred by a young SS trooper's machine gun. In the fleeting instant he stood at the entry to the court, Macary saw why. Lined up inside were a dozen Wehrmacht trucks from which workers of the TODT organization were unloading heavy wooden cases. On each case were stamped two words: ACHTUNG ECRASIT—and a large black skull and crossbones. Stacked beside the trucks, Macary saw a pile of pneumatic drills and a coil of air hoses. He understood.

The Germans were getting ready to mine this palace which he had jealously guarded for four years. Desperate, Macary debated what he might do to save it. He had an idea. There was one man, he thought, who might be able to thwart the Germans. He was an electrician named François Dalby. He knew every inch of electric wire in the palace, the wire the Germans would need to fire their explosives.

The Palais du Luxembourg was not the only place in Paris that morning where the preparations ordered by Hitler had suddenly and secretly started to go forward. Nor was it only factories and power stations that were affected.

The Chamber of Deputies and the Quai d'Orsay, home of the French Foreign Office—forming between them one side of the incomparably beautiful place de la Concorde—were being mined with truckloads of TNT. Elsewhere the Panhard factory at 19 avenue d'Ivry, turning out parts for the V-2 rocket, the giant Siemens-Westinghouse complex in Fontainebleau, the city's telephone centers, its railroad stations, its bridges—all were being readied for destruction.

On the rue Saint-Amand, near the Paris municipal slaughterhouses, Sergeants Bernhardt Blache and Max Schneider, of the 112th Signal Regiment, started to plant the ton of dynamite and the 200 explosive caps with which they would blow up the central telephone installations of Paris. For four years its trunk lines and 132 teletypewriters had been the military communications center of occupied France, receiving and distributing messages for the entire western front from Norway to Spain. Blache's superior, First Lieutenant von Berlipsch, planned to trigger the explosion from a *"Sprengkommando"* ("plunger") in a parked car tucked around the corner. At the same time, his colleague Lieutenant Daub would be blowing up the city's second telephone center under Napoleon's Tomb at Les Invalides.

At the Hotel Meurice, the man whose headquarters had set into motion those widely scattered preparations was that morning making his second inspection trip of the offices in which he had installed the demolition experts sent him from Berlin. They had inspected five major factories before noon. Among them were the Renault auto works and the aircraft factory of air pioneer Louis Blériot. As they visited each, they marked red x's on their blueprints at the spots where explosive charges should be sited. They showed those blueprints to von Choltitz. For each factory, he remembers, "there was a little sea of red crosses."

Waiting for him when he returned to his office, was his chief of staff, Colonel von Unger. Wordlessly von Unger handed him a blue OB West cableform. It was from von Kluge and it was marked "Urgent and Top Secret." One sentence at the bottom of the fourth paragraph of this order No. 6232/44 caught von Choltitz's immediate attention. It read: "I give the order for the neutralizations and destructions envisaged for Paris."

●　●　●

In the debris and chaos of the empty Hotel Majestic, two men ran desperately after a signature. But in those abandoned and disordered corridors it seemed that morning that there was no one left to give it. The Militärbefehlshaber Frankreich, the occupation authority for France, had retreated to a more distant corner of its fast-shrinking Frankreich. Sweden's

Raoul Nordling and his faithful ally, "Bobby" Bender, had, it seemed, arrived too late.

Here they had hoped to consummate four days of efforts, drawing under their protective custody the 3,633 political prisoners left in Paris and saving them from the massacre they were sure awaited them. Thirty minutes earlier von Choltitz had told the two men he "didn't give a damn about the political prisoners." He would, he said, enforce an agreement to release them, "provided it was approved by a signature of an officer of the Militärbefehlshaber Frankreich" on whom he depended. It had been the first encouragement Nordling and Bender had had in four days.

The two men started; they had just heard a sharp metallic bang echoing through these empty corridors. It was Major Josef Huhm, the Militärbefehlshaber's Chief of Staff, angrily slamming shut the top drawer of his metal filing cabinet. The last of the papers it contained were burning in the fireplace beside him. Huhm was probably the last officer left in this huge hotel. In a few minutes, he too would get into the staff car waiting for him on the avenue Kléber and start east to join his fellow staff officers.

When Nordling and Bender burst into his office, the German listened to their first explanations with evident impatience. Finally he told them that without the authorization of his superior, General Kitzinger, who was already in Nancy, there was nothing he could do. The Swede was not to be thrust off so easily. He told Huhm he was in a position to promise him "five German soldiers for every French political prisoner released by the Militärbefehlshaber." Huhm's attitude changed. What guarantee could Nordling give of such an offer? he asked.

Nordling solemnly assured him that he had "full authorization from the very highest Allied authorities" for his proposition.° Huhm now became interested. He would, he told Nordling, be ready to study such an agreement if it were drawn up in proper legal form. Then he looked at his watch. It was noon. "In one hour," he warned Nordling, "I must leave."

° Nordling, of course, had neither the intention nor the authority of giving Huhm or anyone else a single German prisoner. His sole aim was to force Huhm's signature at any price onto a piece of paper that would serve as cover for von Choltitz, who, he had sensed, was ready to release the prisoners.

The Swede and Bender raced out of the building and found a lawyer to put this traffic in human bodies into Teutonically acceptable legal form. Then Huhm, perhaps convinced he was winning 15,000 soldiers back for the Reich, put his name on a twelve-paragraph document ordering the German prison authorities to hand over all the political detainees in five prisons, three camps and three hospitals into Nordling's custody. As Huhm signed, Nordling looked at his watch. It was just one o'clock. In the past hour and fifteen minutes he had talked the Germans into an agreement which was to save the lives of hundreds of Frenchmen.

• • •

Since the last convoy left Fresnes, Louis Armand, the railroad executive who wanted to leave with it, had had one piece of food set before him. It was a moldy slab of Roquefort cheese. Never in his life had Armand eaten a piece of cheese. He had not been able to eat that one. Dizzy with hunger, he heard the regular, metallic clanging of cell doors opening one after another, and first thought it was his imagination. Then Armand realized those doors were not being shut. He recited a silent Act of Contrition and prepared to face the firing squad that he felt sure was waiting in the courtyard below.

In the courtyard, Swedish Consul General Raoul Nordling watched the prisoners file down to be counted. There were 532, including three men condemned to death. The next day, Nordling had been promised, they would be released.

Nordling watched the scene with impatience. He had much to do. Before him lay visits to the Jewish refugees at Drancy, the prison of Romainville, and a camp outside the Paris area at Compiègne. Then he hoped to stop the train carrying Pierre Lefaucheux, Yvonne Pagniez and 2,451 others to Germany.

• • •

Dietrich von Choltitz asked for a map of Paris. His hand waved across it; then, in a random gesture, he jabbed his fat forefinger into its surface. "Suppose," he said, turning to the spot at which his finger had fallen, "a bullet is fired at one of my soldiers, here, on the avenue de l'Opéra. I would burn down every building in the block, and shoot all their inhabitants."

For such a task, he assured his visitor, he had ample resources. He had at his disposition, he said, "22,000 troops, mostly SS, a hundred Tiger tanks, and ninety aircraft."

Pierre Charles Taittinger, the Vichy mayor of Paris, shuddered. An anonymous telephone call had brought him here. "The Germans," an unidentified voice had warned, "have started to evacuate the buildings around the bridges of Paris. They're going to blow them up." Now, in this dour Prussian so casually threatening to wipe out whole sections of Paris, Taittinger could detect nothing but "somber resolution." He had come to his office hoping to find a man with whom he could reason; in front of him was a martinet.

Turning back to his map, von Choltitz slid his finger along the spiraling loops of the Seine. "As an officer, Mr. Taittinger, you will understand," he said, "there are certain measures which I shall have to take in Paris. It is my duty to slow up as much as possible the advance of the Allies."

In a dry, hoarse voice von Choltitz specified just what he contemplated doing: destroying the city bridges, power plants, railroads, communications.

Taittinger sat stunned in his chair. This man, he thought, "was preparing to destroy Paris as indifferently as if it were a crossroads village in the Ukraine."

The Vichy-appointed mayor had no illusions about the authority left in his hands. He could do only one thing this August morning: try somehow to communicate to this unsympathetic soldier in front of him some hint of the emotional attachment he felt for Paris. The cold wrath of von Choltitz suddenly and unexpectedly gave Taittinger his opportunity. The little general, caught up by his emotions, broke into a fit of asthmatic coughing. Taittinger suggested they go out onto his balcony overlooking the sculptured garden of the Tuileries.

There, looking down on the peaceful scene spread before their eyes, Taittinger found the argument he was looking for. Below them, on the rue de Rivoli, a pretty girl in a flowered dress pushed down her billowing skirts as she rode past on her bicycle. Further on, amid the green lawns of the Tuileries, the hopeful sailors of a future age sent their sailboats dashing out into Le Nôtre's circular pond. Across the river, sparkling in the noonday sun, was the golden dome of Les Invalides, and beyond it, climbing to a cloudless sky, the Eiffel Tower.

Gesturing at that sight sprawling before them, Taittinger made a desperate emotional appeal to this seemingly emotionless soldier. To his left, he pointed to the gray wings of the Louvre holding its green gardens between them in their cold stone embrace; to the right, the flawless symmetry of the place de la Concorde.

"Often," Taittinger said, "it is given to a general to destroy, rarely to preserve. Imagine that one day it may be given to you to stand on this balcony again, as a tourist, to look once more on these monuments to our joys, our sufferings, and to be able to say, 'One day I could have destroyed all this, and I preserved it as a gift for humanity.' General, is not that worth all a conqueror's glory?"

Von Choltitz was silent. Then he turned to Taittinger, his voice softer now. "You are a good advocate for Paris, Mr. Taittinger," he said. "You have done your duty well. And likewise I, as a German general, must do mine."

•   •   •

Brigadier General Julius Holmes had to shout into the static-charged line in his office at SHAEF headquarters in London to make himself heard. It was understandable. The other end of his scrambled telephone line was 3,670 miles away in the State Department office of Assistant Secretary of War John J. McCloy. For Holmes, SHAEF's Civil Affairs head, this Washington call had been a fortunate coincidence. It would give him a chance to discuss directly with Washington the most important problem on his desk, Charles de Gaulle's proposed trip to France.

"Now," he said when McCloy had unburdened himself of the other problems on his mind, "about this de Gaulle visit to France, we want to be sure there's no governmental reason back there he shouldn't come."

"Where does he want to go and why?" McCloy asked.

Holmes explained the French leader wanted to visit the liberated areas of France and perhaps "hold himself available to go to Paris if he's able to in the fairly near future."

"How long does he want to stay?" McCloy and his military aide Major General William Hilldring demanded. Holmes admitted he did not know.

"That probably means he wants to stay," the Washington listeners quickly deducted. "It's not really a visit at all. There's a much more important question here. Don't you think you'd better ask him whether he intends to stay or whether it's just a visit? The decision back here would hinge on that." *

Washington warned Holmes, "We'll tackle this thing only if it's a visit. If you find out it's something else, let us know right away." Otherwise Holmes was authorized to clear the trip on his own "as another visit like his trip to Bayeux."

Holmes hung up and cabled General Sir Henry Maitland Wilson for further information. Within a few hours he received from Algiers the reassuring reply that de Gaulle planned only a visit to France. He had not indicated any intention of establishing himself on the Continent, SHAEF was told. Acting on that information, Holmes forwarded SHAEF's clearance for de Gaulle's visit. It was to prove to be of a much longer duration than SHAEF, and certainly Washington, had intended.

25

A LIGHT SUMMER BREEZE carried the high shrieks of the children playing in the Tuileries garden up to the Hotel Meurice balcony where von Choltitz, alone now, pondered moodily on the words he had heard from Pierre Taittinger a few moments before. He did not have long to meditate. He heard behind him von Unger's hurried call, and

---

* The answer to what F.D.R. would have done, had he known what de Gaulle's real intentions were, must remain a matter for conjecture. It was, however, the opinion of three members of the State Department who worked on French affairs at the time, that F.D.R. would have at least tried to delay de Gaulle's return. But they also point out that, however reluctant F.D.R. was to accept de Gaulle as the head of the French government, there was by late summer in 1944 no realistic alternative course open to him.

then, before the chief of staff could announce him, a man in a long leather coat burst into his office.

"Field Marshal Model," announced von Unger. Choltitz started at that name and the sight of this dust-covered man whose mocking little smile he knew so well. What, he wondered, was the commander of the Ukrainian Army Group doing in his office? Waving his field marshal's baton, Walther Model answered his unformed question for him. He had come, he told von Choltitz, to replace von Kluge as the commander in chief of the west. His orders, he added, were to hold Paris and the Seine "at all costs." Acidly he observed that his general mission was to restore order from the chaos on this western front—something, he told von Choltitz, that, judging by the stragglers he had seen on the road from Metz to Paris, seemed to need doing.

Like every other soldier in the German Army, von Choltitz knew Model's reputation. He was a devoted Nazi, a man of unbending will and great personal courage. He was also tempestuous and given to rash, quick decisions. Of him, an Allied intelligence officer would write in a SHAEF report in a few days, "He is known to be personally devoted to Hitler and likes nothing better than being asked to do the impossible."

His arrival was an unpleasant shock to von Choltitz, who had little faith in his judgment. And he was sure Model would not hesitate to assign him the honor of scorching the earth of Paris behind him; Model, von Choltitz knew, was a man with "an eastern front mentality."

His arrival did, however, offer one respite. Von Choltitz would be able to postpone the demolition work ordered by von Kluge earlier in the morning. He told Model it would be a hasty action. It might, he pointed out, serve only to stir up the civilian population. It could even hamper his own preparations for the city's defense. Model agreed. He told him to take no new action until he had had time to review his new command.

Von Choltitz's respite was, however, to be short-lived. As he took Model to the Horch which would deliver the field marshal to his new headquarters, the imperious little man turned to Paris's commander. Beside von Choltitz stood his young aide, Count von Arnim who, that night, would record Model's words for posterity in his green leather diary.

"Believe me, Choltitz," said Model, "what took us forty minutes in Kovel will take us forty hours in Paris. But when we are finished, this city will be destroyed." °

•   •   •

On the huge Louis XVI desk, "requisitioned" from the head of Jewish charities for France, Raoul Nordling found a half-eaten bowl of soup and a dish of chocolate pudding—the remains of the SS commandant's last lunch at Drancy internment camp. Just a few moments before the Swede's arrival, the commandant and his staff had fled to Nancy.

Nordling walked into the courtyard between the camp's three prison blocks where its 1,482 inmates were assembled. Trying to shout above their excited cries, he announced to them they were now free and under his custody. The prisoners swept over the chubby little Swede in a wild, happy mob.

"The stars, the stars!" someone cried. One by one, some not able to believe what they were doing, the 1,482 Jews left in camp ripped off the yellow stars that for years had been the badge of their misery. As Nordling left, the torn yellow stars littered the courtyard "like a carpet of dead autumn leaves."

•   •   •

Across the blacked-out streets of Paris, in the eighteenth-century splendor of the Hôtel de Matignon, the residence of the prime ministers of France, a lonely man splashed in a marble bathtub.

Pierre Laval had lost his last gamble. He had brought Édouard Herriot, president of France's defunct Chamber of Deputies, out of Nazi captivity to convene that Chamber. To that body Laval had planned to hand over his powers—and perhaps his skin—for safekeeping. But Heinrich Himmler had reclaimed Herriot and now Laval's world was coming down around him. Only one thing was left to Laval now—to flee. Downstairs in the graveled courtyard of the Hôtel de Matignon, the black SS Hotchkiss which would carry him north to Germany waited.

A few moments earlier, by the light of a pair of candles, he

_____
° Kovel was a small town in Poland obliterated by Model's troops.

had sat down at the desk from which he had governed France and, one by one, emptied its drawers. Soon he would knot his white tie, pick up his hat and cane, and go downstairs to the library to shake hands with the few faithful friends who had come to bid him goodbye. There, in that high-ceilinged room, lit like some ghostly funeral parlor by a pair of candles, were gathered a few sad survivors of the legion who had followed this man in his policy of collaboration with France's enemies.

At the doorsteps of the residence he would kiss his daughter Josie farewell, and walk down into the waiting Hotchkiss. Then, in a pathetic parting gesture, he would leap from the Hotchkiss, bound back up the steps, and—murmuring *"Toi encore une fois"*—give one last kiss to his only child. She would not see him again until he sat in the prisoners' dock in a Paris courtroom on trial for his life.

● ● ●

The black Hotchkiss grated over the graveled court and faded into the dark streets beyond. With a sharp, dry crash, the great gates of the Hôtel de Matignon swung shut. The House of Vichy was empty; a sad chapter in France's history had closed in the snap of those gates. But already, in the darkness of the blacked-out city, around the Hôtel de Matignon, the forces that would lead a different France were stirring.

26

FOR THE EARLY MORNING crowds swirling through the rue de Sèvres around the Bon Marché department store, they were just another young couple in love. Their foreheads almost touching, they leaned over the two bicycles pressed tightly between them on the curb and whispered to each other. Tenderly the girl drew him to her and ran her hands through his hair. As she did, the man's deft fingers slipped his tiny bicycle pump from his bike into hers.

The girl rode quietly home and walked up the three flights of stairs to her apartment on the rue Sédillot. With the door carefully locked behind her, she took a red leather-bound volume on Flemish painting from her bookcase, riffled through it to a color print of an obscure Brueghel and, pinching the page between her thumb and forefinger, slipped a piece of tissue paper out from under the color plate. Then she unscrewed the base of the little bicycle pump her lover had passed her, reached in with her finger, and drew out another piece of paper. She smoothed out the two pieces of paper on her desk and set to work.

The girl's name was Jocelyne. She was one of the two Resistance code girls in Paris. Printed on the paper hidden in her bookcase shelves was information for which the Gestapo would pay a king's ransom in blood or gold: the code for the headquarters of the Gaullist underground in France. Jocelyne was part of a complex chain which relayed all messages from Paris to Free French headquarters in London. There were three transmitters—Pleyel Violet, Montparnasse Black, and Apollo Black—in Paris, and three more in the suburbs. The Paris radios transmitted on even-numbered days; the suburban sets on odd days. This afternoon, after her coding was done, Jocelyne would pass the message she had received at the Bon Marché to another man on a bicycle on the quai Voltaire. He in turn would deliver it to a maid's room under the eaves of 8 rue Vaneau. There, in a niche over a rusting toilet, was Apollo Black.*

Long trained not to read the messages she coded, Jocelyne ignored this one carefully smoothed out in front of her. It was Chaban's first report to London since his return. But at the last of its five-character word blocks, she started in spite of herself. She drew back and, against instructions, read the full text:

. PARIS SITUATION EXTREMELY TOUCHY. STRIKES OF POLICE, RAILROADS, POSTS AND DEVELOPING TENDENCIES TO GENERAL STRIKE. ALL CONDITIONS NECESSARY FOR AN INSURRECTION

---

* The radio's antenna was rolled into the gutter for transmissions. While the radioman sent, a second man, armed with two fragmentation grenades, stood guard at the head of the stairway. In principle, broadcasts lasted only twenty minutes, to avoid detection by the Gestapo's radio-fixing equipment which prowled the streets in delivery vans. All the transmissions were on the 19-meter band, and each set could move to any one of four frequencies.

HAVE BEEN REALIZED. LOCAL INCIDENTS, WHETHER SPONTANE-
OUS, PROVOKED BY ENEMY, OR EVEN IMPATIENT RESISTANCE
GROUPS, WILL BE ENOUGH TO LEAD TO GRAVEST TROUBLES WITH
BLOODY REPRISALS FOR WHICH GERMANS SEEM TO HAVE AL-
READY TAKEN DECISIONS AND ASSEMBLED NECESSARY MEANS.
SITUATION WORSENING WITH PARALYSIS PUBLIC UTILITIES: NO
GAS, HOUR AND HALF ELECTRICITY DAILY, WATER LACKING IN
SOME PARTS OF TOWN, FOOD SITUATION DISASTROUS. NECESSARY
YOU INTERVENE WITH ALLIES TO DEMAND RAPID OCCUPATION
PARIS. OFFICIALLY WARN POPULATION IN SHARPEST MOST PRE-
CISE TERMS POSSIBLE VIA BBC TO AVOID NEW WARSAW.

"Warsaw," thought Jocelyne. Had it really come to that?
Beyond her window she saw the soft green line of treetops
stretching down the Champs-de-Mars to the base of the
Eiffel Tower. Was this, after all, she asked herself, not to be
spared?

●　　●　　●

The warning signs to justify Chaban's pessimistic predictions
were everywhere evident this sunny morning of Friday,
August 18, 1944. Vichy's ministers had fled. Behind them they
had left a beckoning political vacuum. The civil authority
that remained was rotted and waiting only to topple under
the first bold hand. The collaborationist press had disappeared.
The railroads, the subways, the mail and telegraph systems,
the police, even the Bank of France, had gone on strike. Above
all, the city itself was ready for revolt. Hurt by the humilia-
tion of four years of occupation, hungry, on the streets, with
no civil authority to hold it in check, the population of Paris
sensed the moment of revenge was at hand. The stage was
indeed set for the insurrection Chaban had been instructed
to prevent. Only one thing was needed to launch it—a strong
voice shouting the war cry "Aux Barricades!" That voice the
Communist party was now prepared to provide.

●　　●　　●

The traffic circle of Petit-Clamart, seven miles south of
Notre-Dame Cathedral, lay empty in the noonday sun—
except for the lone figure fretting over his bicycle under a

rusting billboard advertising Cadum soap. "Colonel Rol" pedaled down the blacktopped Paris road, turned into the circle, then swung lazily around its traffic island to the stranded cyclist. The two men nodded to each other. Rol asked if he could help. They talked for a moment. Then the man who had been repairing his bicycle got up and rode off. Rol followed him.

Six times in three hours, Raymond Bocquet, a coal miner from Lille, had enacted the little scene he had just finished under the rusting portrait of Baby Cadum. Each time he had taken in tow a different passerby and, as he was about to do with Rol, delivered each of his benefactors to a tin-roofed shanty at 9 rue d'Alsace in Clamart. There, beyond a scraggly vegetable patch bordered by a weathered slat fence, packed into a room the size of a monk's cell, sat the five members of the Comité Parisien de la Libération. In the stifling heat of the little room their sweating shirts stuck together.

André Tollet, the quick-tempered little Communist who ran the committee, made his first decision of the day: There would be no smoking. Tollet wanted to make sure nothing would give away their position that afternoon.

He could not afford to have this meeting interrupted. He had called these men to this abandoned shanty to take the most important decision his committee had been asked to make. It was, Tollet was fully aware, a decision that could lead to the devastation of the most beautiful city in the world and cost, perhaps, the lives of thousands of its inhabitants. In this scabrous hut at the end of a country road, André Tollet asked the four others to agree to an armed uprising in the streets of Paris.

It was, even the determined Tollet would later recall, "a wild chance." He expected his decision would bring down "massive reprisals" on Paris. But Tollet had received his orders from the party hierarchy forty-eight hours earlier. He was not to come out of this meeting without a stamp of approval to give political legitimacy to the movement they would, whatever the cost, launch the next day. Even the posters to call the city to arms had already been printed and carefully stored in a factory loft in Montrouge.

The party's plan was simple. Once set in motion, they were sure, their insurrection could not be stopped. In this secret meeting of a committee they controlled, they would get just enough political cover to justify their actions. Then they would launch the insurrection, confident they would carry along with them thousands of patriotic, non-Communist FFI who were burning to fight the Germans. By the time the Gaullists learned of their decision, they would be faced with a *fait accompli*. The insurrection would be already under way under Communist leadership. One thing was essential in that plan: Chaban, Parodi, and the other senior Gaullists in the city had to be kept ignorant of their plan until it was too late for them to stop the insurrection.

Two hours later, one by one, the five men slipped away from the little hut. Tollet was the last to leave. He was determined and happy. He had won. He and the party he represented would have their insurrection, the insurrection Charles de Gaulle and the Allies had forbidden. It would begin, without Chaban's and the Gaullist command's knowledge, the next morning.

•   •   •

In the courtyard of Fresnes prison, Louis Armand watched the guards walk up to his group of twenty-one prisoners. They said only one word: *"Raus."* Louis Armand walked out the prison gates a free man. He was the last of the 532 political prisoners freed that morning.

From his barred window, Willi Wagenknecht, the German soldier jailed for striking an officer, watched Armand go, just as he had watched the convoy prisoners march off three days earlier. Another example of the imbecility of the German Army, Wagenknecht thought. Soon, it seemed to him, Fresnes prison would have only one kind of inmate: German.

•   •   •

At the back end of the quai, in the corner of the Nancy railroad station a friendly railwayman had saved for her, Marie-Hélène Lefaucheux resumed the vigil that had already brought her 183 miles, three-quarters of the way to Germany, through two and a half days without sleep or rest. She did it with a heavy heart. This was as far as she could go.

As it had on Assumption Day, a hot sun hammered down on the train through the wattled tin roofing spanning the train shed. Marie-Hélène could hear the thin, despairing voices of the men inside begging for a drink. Occasionally she heard a more terrifying sound: the wild shriek of a prisoner lost in hysteria.

Her hands folded over her prewar Lanvin handbag, her lips moving very slightly in an occasional prayer, Marie-Hélène stood erect and dignified; and in the privacy of her soul, she suffered at every anguished cry that slipped through the wooden slats of the cattle cars before her.

After a time—she could not remember how long—she saw a scurrying of guards and railway workers alongside the convoy. The efforts of Consul General Nordling and "Bobby" Bender had been successful in Paris, but they had failed to stop this last convoy. The Gestapo would not yield up this wagon train of human misery.

There was a quick, echoing bang as the cattle wagons smashed together under the first lurch forward. Then, very slowly, the long line of cars slid out of the station. From behind the sealed doors of the departing train, Marie-Hélène heard again, as she had at the Pantin station, the proud, defiant words of the "Marseillaise." Gathering speed now, the train disappeared down the quai, out from under the shadows of the train shed into the sunshine beyond. She did not move until she could see its receding form no more, until its last creaking echo had died in the stillness of the empty station.

By the time she turned away, the train was already climbing through the rolling vineyards of Alsace toward Strasbourg and the Rhine. It would not stop again until it had delivered its 2,453 passengers to the gates of Ravensbrück and Buchenwald. Of those 2,453 proud men and women, fewer than 300 would come home again to France.°

• • •

The man on the balcony watched the white blouse and striped skirt of the girl disappear around the corner of the

---

° Pierre Angot died working in a salt mine; Philippe Keun, the aide of "Jade Amicol," was hanged. Yvonne Baratte died of dysentery in March, 1945. Both Yvonne Pagniez and Jeannie Rousseau, although broken in health, survived.

None had a more extraordinary experience than Pierre Lefaucheux. After the liberation of Paris, Marie-Hélène went back to Nancy, crossing both the American and German lines in a Red Cross ambulance. There she contacted a Gestapo officer known to friends in Paris. Through a series of pressures rue Montmartre. As the girl passed out of view, thirty-four-year-old Yves Bayet drew a corn-silk cigarette from his packet, lit it, and breathed a relieved lungful of tobacco. "This time," thought Bayet, "it will work." Bayet was the head of the Gaullist Resistance network in the Paris police force, one of the three struggling for control of those 20,000 men Rol wanted under his command. On her rusting Peugeot bicycle, Suzanne, his liaison agent, carried toward the Porte de Châtillon three envelopes hidden in the lining of the moleskin handbag slung over her shoulder. In them were three identical written messages, one to each of the police Resistance groups. They were, Bayet knew, the most important messages he had ever been ordered to send.

It was almost eight o'clock. In one hour the curfew ordered by the military governor of Gross Paris would lock the city shut for another night. Yves Bayet knew that Suzanne would have just enough time to deliver her three envelopes to their destination, the café that served as Bayet's message drop, and return. With an ironic smile he realized that this night the curfew of General von Choltitz would serve the cause of General de Gaulle. It would prevent one of the three envelopes Suzanne carried from reaching its goal before morning. That was exactly what Bayet wanted. The message which would not reach its destination this night was addressed to the largest and the most powerful of the Resistance movements in the police, the network controlled by the Communist Party. This night, the Communists would be the victims of their own obsession with security. Unlike the other two networks, their messages had to pass through not one, but two, letter drops before it reached its goal. The message Suzanne carried for them would spend the night frozen in their second mailbox.

Suzanne felt her bicycle slowing under her. Leaning over its handlebars, she understood why; her front tire was losing air. In a few minutes it was flat. Suzanne was half an hour from her destination. Cursing, she tried to inflate the tire. The

brought on him by Frenchmen with whom he had had black-market dealings, she was able to persuade him to take her in a German staff car across Germany into the very confines of Buchenwald, where he took Pierre into his custody. Then the trio drove back to Nancy, and Marie-Hélène Lefaucheux brought her husband home to Paris in early September. Tragedy, however, was to continue to stalk their lives. Pierre, the postwar director of the Renault auto works, was killed in an automobile accident in 1956. Marie-Hélène, a member of France's UN delegation, died in an airplane crash in Lake Pontchartrain, Louisiana, in February, 1964.

air swished out of the broken tire as fast as she pumped it in.
Behind her she heard another set of tires drawing to a stop.
She turned and saw a German staff car pull up beside her.
With a quick gesture, its driver jumped out and bent over her.
In impeccable French, the young Wehrmacht officer offered
his assistance to the pretty Parisienne. Suzanne scornfully
passed him her bicycle pump. The energetic German was no
more successful than she had been. He offered another answer.
He asked her if he might drive her to her destination. After a
second's hesitation she accepted and climbed into his B.M.W.
beside him.

Rarely would Teutonic gallantry be repaid with such
Gallic ingratitude. In the moleskin handbag Suzanne clutched
on her knees in this gracious young German's B.M.W. was a
veritable declaration of war on Paris's occupiers.

Alexandre Parodi, the political head of the Gaullist Resistance for France, had been informed by a Gaullist secretly
planted on André Tollet's committee that the Communists
would launch their insurrection the next day. Faced with that
stark news, Parodi had made a bold decision.

If the Communists had decided to move, he too would
move. Only he would move faster. He would deprive them
of the most important public building in Paris, the massive
city within a city that was its Prefecture of Police. The
messages Suzanne carried in her moleskin handbag ordered
the police of Paris to assemble the next day, August 19, at
seven o'clock, in the streets around that great brownstone
fortress only a few yards from Notre-Dame. There, under
Bayet's direction, they would seize the Prefecture of Police.

Suzanne smiled thinly at the German, slammed the door
of his B.M.W. and walked into a café. In the toilet, she slid
the three messages out of her handbag. A few minutes later
she passed them to the owner's son under the round wooden
tray from which he served her an ersatz lemonade. It was
8:30. Bayet's timing could not have been better. Tomorrow,
under the 800-year-old stones of Notre-Dame, the Paris police
would keep the first appointment of the insurrection the Communists had so carefully prepared. The Communist Party
would not be present at that rendezvous.

● ● ●

Ten thousand feet below, Captain Claude Guy could see the Atlas Mountains of Morocco, splashed purple in the setting sun, slipping steadily under the wings of the Lockheed Lodestar *France*. Opposite him, firmly buckled into his seat, a defiant cigar jammed into his mouth, Charles de Gaulle stared straight ahead. De Gaulle, Guy knew, loathed flying. Rarely did he speak aboard a plane. And the general had scarcely spoken three words since they left Algiers three hours earlier on this first leg of perhaps the most important flight de Gaulle had made since he flew out of France in June, 1940. He was lost in his own silent world.

Already the first of the incidents that were to plague their trip had delayed their departure from Algiers for Casablanca by several hours. Concerned that de Gaulle's Lodestar had neither the range nor fuel capacity it would need for the long flight from Gibraltar to Cherbourg, the United States Command in Algiers had put a B-17 with an American crew at his disposal. De Gaulle had accepted the gesture with reluctance. Then, landing at Maison Blanche airfield in Algiers to pick up de Gaulle, the B-17 had overshot its runway and torn out its undercarriage. The accident, de Gaulle was persuaded, was part of a deliberate American plan to delay his return to France. Looking at the disabled plane, he remarked, "You don't think it's just out of good will that they want to give me these planes of theirs, do you?"

For the moment those problems, Guy was sure, were forgotten. Another B-17 was meeting them in Casablanca. The mind of the man sitting opposite him was now deep in the far more difficult questions that lay just ahead. For de Gaulle, this was the beginning of the end of the long road that had begun in the lonely call of June 18, 1940. At the end of the road lay Paris, the city de Gaulle had left as an unknown brigadier general four years earlier. To get there, de Gaulle was prepared to defy his Allies, to stifle his political foes, even to risk his own life. It was there, and there alone, that the proposition inherent in his bold move four years before would find its answer.

Later it would seem strange that he should not have known what that answer would be. But Guy, flying through the African sunset, knew de Gaulle's mind was still assailed by doubts and questions. Above all, he still did not know whether the people of France were prepared to accept him as their leader. There was only one place, de Gaulle realized, where he could learn the answer to that question: in the streets of Paris.

In those streets in just one week's time, the melancholy passenger of the Lodestar *France* had a rendezvous with history.

PART TWO

THE STRUGGLE

1

[AUGUST 19]

THE AIR WAS DAMP and heavy. From the north, great gray ridges of cloud rolled down over the Butte of Montmartre, bringing with them a promise of rain. In the city's silent streets, the last German patrols hurried back to their barracks. Curfew was over. Soon the capital's housewives, in drab and hungry lines, would begin their daily vigil for a slab of black bread. With the tired and practiced routine of four years, Paris was awakening to another day of occupation. It would be a very special one. Never again after this gray morning would the soldiers of the Wehrmacht be able to claim the streets of Paris as truly theirs.

Yet for most of the 20,000 soldiers of the German garrison, nothing in the bleak dawn seemed to set this Saturday, August 19, 1944, apart from any of the other 1,518 days on which the people of Paris had peacefully, if unwillingly accepted their presence. At the Hotel Meurice, Sergeant Werner Nix, the reluctant parader, was angry again. He had just inspected his sentries in the garden of the Tuileries and, to his utter disgust, found them poking through its boxwood hedges looking for a little old lady's cat.

Above him, a tired and sorrowing Count Dankvart von Arnim stretched on his balcony. Three hours before, von Arnim's best friend had announced in a telephone call from the Hôpital de la Pitié that he had been wounded in Normandy, and his right leg had just been amputated. To his profound regret, von Arnim had found nothing more con-

soling to say to his weeping comrade than the trite phrase:
"At least for you the war is over." The young Count von
Arnim did not know it yet, but for him the war was beginning
this morning.

In apartments and hotels scattered across Paris, in hundreds
of homes and hideouts of the policemen summoned by the
messages in Suzanne's handbag, hundreds of determined men
had already begun to move. With a sleepy kiss and a loathsome cup of ersatz coffee, they left their homes and, alone or
in small groups, on foot or on bicycle, began to filter through
the streets of Paris toward Notre-Dame. There, in a few moments, these policemen would perform the first bold act in the
liberation of Paris, and reveal to its occupiers for the first time
the vengeful reality lying under the city's peaceful exterior.

To many ordinary Parisians, too, this Saturday would be a
memorable day.

Before the empty stalls of his Nanterre butchershop, Louis
Berty, the Frenchman hiding American pilot Bob Woodrum,
waited for his regular Saturday visitors, a group of guards from
the nearby prison of Mont Valérien. Faithfully each Saturday
they sliced up a week's supply of sausage on his meat-cutting
machine. He hated them. From his shop, Berty could hear
the daily volleys of Mont Valérien's firing squad executing his
countrymen.°

Before the guards arrived. Berty received another—unexpected—visitor, a man "from Zadig." It was the code word
that meant the Resistance network to which Berty belonged
was rousing to open action. Berty took for his weapon the Colt
.45 his American guest had carried on thirty-five missions over
German territory. He called his eighteen-year-old neighbor,
Pierre Le Guen, burning to join the men "from Zadig," and
gave him the 6.35-millimeter pistol his wife kept hidden in her
cashbox. Then, slipping on an armband stamped VIVRE LIBRE
OU MOURIR—Live Free or Die—Berty left to take up arms
against his country's occupiers.

At the other end of Paris from Berty's butchershop, a jovial
fat man in a blue beret gulped an early morning cognac and
climbed into a wood-burning Citroën P-45 truck. He was a
hijacker. His was a legitimate operation. Since August 1, Paul
Pardou, armed with false papers, had cleaned out twenty-
three of the thirty secret food depots of Vichy's hated militia,

_____
° Since 1941, they had executed 4,500 of them.

the Milice, and delivered to the Resistance 180 of the 250 tons of supplies the Milice had carefully set aside for just the kind of emergency about to occur in Paris.

Today Pardou had agreed to a last and special mission. He was going to hijack arms. He would haul them out of a Milice depot and deliver them to the FFI planning to seize the suburban Mairie of Le Perreux. Starting his *gazogène*, Pardou promised himself this trip would be his last.

For some of its citizens, unaware of the events about to overtake Paris, this would be a special day in their lives. Lysiane Thill, in her one-room apartment, sprinkled a few drops of water on the white silk dress she would wear in a few hours to her marriage in the Mairie of the First Arrondissement. Then she painstakingly pressed out its folds with an iron, which she warmed over a paper-burning stove. The man Lysiane Thill was marrying, salesman Narcisse Fétiveau, would never see it. He was in a German prisoner-of-war camp. Lysiane was being married by proxy.

● ● ●

The lone figure in the black cassock walked with slow, deliberate strides over the Pont-au-Double. The eyes of Abbé Robert Lepoutre, thirty-five, as they were every morning at this hour, were plunged into the breviary cradled in his hands before him. Rarely did his routine vary. By the time he had finished his last verses, Abbé Lepoutre would be at the wrought-iron gate of Sainte Anne at the Cathedral of Notre-Dame where he would say his morning Mass. At that moment the clock tower of the hospital of the Hôtel-Dieu would strike seven.

This morning the quiet priest would not finish his breviary. As he reached the square before Notre-Dame, usually empty at this early hour, the priest saw before him an unforgettable sight. In berets or hats or bareheaded; in suit jackets, sweaters or shirt-sleeves; hundreds of silent men were moving toward the gates of the Prefecture of Police. Seconds later, in the sky over its grim, gray roofs, Abbé Lepoutre saw a piece of cloth burst open in the breeze. For the first time in four years, two months and four days, the French tricolor floated officially from a building in the capital of France. Abbé Lepoutre closed his breviary and slipped it into the folds of his cassock. Caught up with curiosity, he joined the wave of men flowing into the Prefecture. During the seven hectic and heroic days about to begin, this besieged building giving birth to an insurrection would have a chaplain.

* * *

Daylight poured through the wooden shutters of his windows as Amédée Bussière, the prefect of the Paris police, awoke. For the last four days Bussière had been the captain of an empty ship. His striking policemen had abandoned him.

Stretching his hand to the night table beside him, the prefect rang for his valet. Five minutes later, erect and dignified as an English butler, his valet Georges brought Bussière his breakfast.

"Anything new, Georges?" Bussière asked.

"Yes, M. le Préfet," answered Georges with no hint of emotion, "there is something new. They have come back."

Bussière pulled on his slippers and rushed into the corridor toward the nearest window giving onto the huge enclosed courtyard of the Prefecture. Astonished by the sight below, he nervously grasped the lapels of his dressing gown. There, in the court, he saw hundreds of men—armed with pistols, rifles, grenades and their bare hands—gathered around a black Citroën, listening to a lanky blond man in a checked suit, his arm circled by a tricolor armband.

In a voice that carried up to Bussière's window, Yves Bayet proclaimed, "In the name of the Republic and Charles de Gaulle, I take possession of the Prefecture of Police."

As the cheers that followed his words faded, from somewhere a trumpet began to play, and up from the packed courtyard Bussière heard the strong and stirring words of the "Marseillaise."

The lone cyclist passing under the windows of the Prefecture of Police at that moment heard them too. He stopped to listen. Nothing was to surprise Communist leader Rol more that morning than "the sound of that full-bellied 'Marseillaise'" coming from the Prefecture. None of the careful orders folded inside the sleeping bag tied to Rol's bicycle envisaged a seizure of this imposing building. Surprised and angry, Rol tried to enter the Prefecture and was turned away. That gesture confirmed his suspicion: someone was trying to undermine his control of the insurrection.

He rode to a nearby garage, unrolled his sleeping bag and put on the leggings and high-necked tunic of the uniform he had last worn on the train that carried the International Brigades out of a doomed Barcelona. In that symbol of office, Rol marched into the Prefecture of Police determined to impose his authority on these rebels without orders, who threatened to compromise his direction of this carefully prepared insurrection.

Rol had arrived an hour too late. Yves Bayet was, at about the same moment, climbing out of a black police car and approaching a pale man reading a newspaper on the terrace of the Café des Deux Magots.

"M. le Préfet," Bayet said, "the Prefecture has been taken. It is yours."

The man smiled, got up, put on his felt hat and horn-rimmed glasses, and followed Bayet to the car. Seven days earlier, on the orders of Charles de Gaulle, Charles Luizet had parachuted into the south of France. He had been sent on a special mission. He was to be de Gaulle's Prefect of Police. His job was to make sure that Paris's vital police force remained in Gaullist and not Communist hands. In a few moments this quietly capable man would become the first public official named by de Gaulle to exercise his office in Paris. The Gaullists had won the first round. The building which was to become the symbol of the insurrection the Communists had prepared was in their hands. It would be the firm rock to which they would cling in the days ahead.

• • •

As Luizet entered his Prefecture, a shy man carrying two valises walked in by a side door and stepped into the police laboratory. From his bags he took out eight bottles of sulfuric acid and several pounds of potassium chlorate. Rolling up his sleeves, Frédéric Joliot-Curie took these bottles, borrowed from the laboratory in which his mother-in-law had discovered radium, and began to manufacture Molotov cocktails for the defense of the Prefecture.

2

APART FROM THE UNEXPECTED setback at the
Prefecture of Police, Rol's carefully prepared insurrection
had spread rapidly and effectively across the capital. The
orders being put into effect this morning had, during the last
four days, already been carefully drafted and distributed.
Rol's deputy for Paris proper, a slight schoolmaster who had
taken the Resistance name of "Dufresne," had spent the night
preparing the last ones in a hot bedroom off the avenue Foch,
listening as he worked to the footfalls of the Gestapo's sentries
around the corner. At seven o'clock he had passed them out to
his liaison agents on the quai de Conti, almost under the noses
of the Germans. Since dawn the Communists had been plaster-
ing the walls of the city with their posters calling for a
"Mobilisation générale."

For Rol and his hierarchy, the first problems of this morning
were complex: establishing their liaison and contacts, setting
up headquarters, bringing their arms out of hiding and distributing them to their FFI commandos. In the city's telephone
exchanges, the Resistance networks performed a first and
vital task that was to greatly facilitate the insurrection. They
destroyed the Germans' wiretapping equipment.

But for Rol's footsoldiers in this guerrilla battle the job was
simple. It was summed up in the phrase coined by Rol which
was to become the byword of this insurrection: "A chacun son
boche." Beginning at seven o'clock, all across Paris, the FFI
had begun to put that order into effect. FFI commandos in
small groups began to hunt down and attack isolated German
soldiers and vehicles wherever they found them. Above all,
their aim was to arm themselves by disarming the city's German occupiers.

By nine o'clock firing had broken out in isolated pockets
all across Paris. The first report of the insurrection stunned and
angered von Choltitz. It caught him completely by surprise.
None of his intelligence services had given him any warning of

it beyond a few generalities about "unrest" in the civilian population. His own morning report to Army Group B and OB West, minutes before the first reports began to come in, had reassuringly declared the city was "perfectly calm." So widespread and so well concerted did the first attacks seem that it was immediately clear to von Choltitz they "were being directed by a central authority."

In those first two hours, the face of the city had changed. Now a menacing and sullen air hung over its empty streets. The few passersby ducked nervously from door to door. Bicyclists rode along the sidewalks, and, occasionally, a car bearing the proud and rudely whitewashed letters FFI on its flanks sped past the city's stunned concierges. But, more than anything else, a new sound characterized the morning, a sound foreign to the streets of Paris since 1871. It was the sound of gunfire.

To a small band of men huddled in an empire salon on the rue de Bellechasse, a few blocks from the Seine, the sound of that gunfire was an unpleasant reminder of a phrase of Jean Paul Sartre: "While we debate, the dice are cast." The members of the Comité National de la Résistance (CNR), the highest political authority of the Resistance, had been summoned to this salon to give their approval to the insurrection decreed at Clamart the afternoon before by the Comité Parisien de la Libération, a body in theory subordinated to the CNR. At the instant their president, Georges Bidault, told them, "We are here to discuss the proposal to launch an insurrection," a burst of rifle fire of that insurrection echoed in the streets just under them. The tough Communist union leader, André Tollet, had, as he had planned, presented his colleagues with a *fait accompli*. The insurrection would go on, he told the men around him, whether it received their support or not.

To the quiet schoolmasterish man who represented the authority of Charles de Gaulle in the room, Tollet's words posed a sharp dilemma. Alexandre Parodi was convinced "the insurrection was as much a political gesture by the Communists as it was an effort to help defeat the Germans." Yet, in authorizing the seizure of the Prefecture of Police, he had in a sense already accepted its inevitability. If he refused to go ahead now, he would leave its direction to the Communists and open a public breach in the Resistance. He was haunted by one thought: The price of this Communist political gesture would be the destruction of Paris. In a few hours, agonizing over his decision, he would say, "If I have made a mistake, I shall have a lifetime to regret it in the ruins of Paris."

Now there seemed to be no choice. Two hours after its birth, the insurrection had grown so fast that Parodi realized there was no chance of stopping it. All that was left was to try to control it. Turning to Bidault, Parodi gave the blessing of Charles de Gaulle to the insurrection the leader of Free France had told him to prevent.

In the streets outside the rue de Bellechasse, the insurrection was already moving into its second phase. Organized bands of FFI, armed with whatever weapons they could find, had begun to move against public buildings all across the city. Following a carefully set-out plan, they moved to take over the mairies (town halls) of Paris's twenty arrondissements, police stations, public buildings, the post office, even the slaughterhouse, the morgue, and the Comédie Française. Everywhere, the first defiant gesture was the same. From windows and rooftops the forbidden flag of France—dusty from months in hiding, or improvised from bed sheets and silk dresses—came back to the skyline of its capital.

• • •

Colonel Paul Massebiau carefully brushed off the faded jacket he had not worn for so long and slipped it over his shoulders. Then, in the oval mirror of his bedroom, he gave himself a long and satisfied look. He smiled with pleasure at the five gold stripes on his sleeves and three rows of colored ribbon over his left pocket. Like hundreds of other reserve officers, Colonel Massebiau, a member of a military Resistance network, was going back on active service this morning.

A few minutes later, with the six men of his command, Colonel Massebiau stood under the Renaissance portico of the Church of Saint-Germain-l'Auxerrois, and proudly studied the objective which was to be his this insurrection day. There, a few yards away, opposite the high iron gates of the Louvre, was the Mairie of the First Arrondissement of the first city of France. Massebiau's aide Marcel Dupuy, the prompter of the Comédie Française, stood beside him, carrying the little commando's unique weapon, an old spin-barrel pistol. But in his pocket the proud prompter bore a more important weapon, a slip of paper stamped with the seal of the Liberation Committee of the First Arrondissement. Marcel the prompter was the new mayor of this gray building in which, at that moment, a traditional Saturday-morning ceremony had just begun.

Lysiane Thill, the young bride who had earlier pressed her new white dress, looked sadly at the empty red velvet chair beside her. For three years she had looked forward to this moment in which she would become the wife of Narcisse Fétiveau, the prisoner of war for whom she had waited so long. In a few moments her dream would be realized. His tricolor sash of office knotted around his waist, the debonair butcher-mayor, Henri Chadeville, prepared—under the eyes of Marshal Pétain, gazing benevolently down from a portrait—to unite Lysiane Thill in marriage with her absent salesman.

As Chadeville began to read the ceremony, the door to the Salle des Mariages burst open. Waving his pistol in his hand, Marcel the prompter sprang into the room. Behind him, proud and resolute, strode Colonel Massebiau followed by the four other members of the commando. They announced to the dumbfounded Vichy mayor that he was stripped of his office and under arrest.

The young bride on her red velvet chair broke into sobs. Colonel Massebiau solemnly announced that "in the name of the Committee of Liberation" he was taking possession of the Mairie of the First Arrondissement of Paris. Then, in a voice equally stern, he announced the ceremony would continue. Marcel the prompter took the tricolor sash of office from his deposed predecessor and wrapped it around his own waist. Then he took down the portrait of Marshal Pétain, and, "by virtue of the powers conferred on me by the Resistance," Marcel the prompter performed his first official act of office as the new mayor of the First Arrondissement of the capital of France. He joined Lysiane Thill and Narcisse Fétiveau in marriage.

*   *   *

There were no marriages to be interrupted that morning in the Mairie of Neuilly. Of all the sections of Paris, none had been more tranquil during the four years of the occupation than the collection of elegant villas bordering the Bois de

Boulogne that was the commune of Neuilly. Block for block,
its eighteenth-century town houses probably lodged more
collaborators, more Vichyites, more German agents, and more
Germans than any other part of Paris. Since 1940 it had
been the quietest corner of occupied Paris, a model of
disciplined acceptance of France's conquerors.

Like the rest of the 5,000 troops quartered in the commune,
the two German soldiers sipping a cognac in the café on the
rue de Chézy, around the corner from the town hall of Neuilly,
felt perfectly at home. At the sound of the door opening behind them, the two Germans exchanged a concupiscent smile.
It would be Janine, the pretty blond nursemaid they had come
to see. They turned, and saw instead Louis Berty, the Nanterre
pork butcher, pointing a gun at a German soldier for the first
time in his life. Berty disarmed his prisoners and marched them
to the Mairie. On the way he drove off three angry Parisians
who ran up to spit at their faces. "They're prisoners," he said.
One of the Germans turned, wiped his face, and nodded to
Berty. "*Danke schön,*" he said.

From his third-floor office window opposite the Mairie,
Émile Marion stared aghast at the sight below, first Berty and
his two prisoners, now the tricolor, proud and defiant, climbing into the sky over the town hall. With the formality of a
Clemenceau addressing the Chamber of Deputies, this fifty-
two-year-old veteran of Verdun turned to his elderly secretary.
"The Republic is saved," he proclaimed. Then he took his hat
and left to join the new occupants of the Mairie.

Another pair of eyes, equally aghast, watched that scene.
Janine, the nursemaid the two Germans had come to see, ran
for her bicycle to warn the German headquarters.

In the occupied Mairie, André Caillette, the factory owner
commanding Louis Berty and the sixty-five other men "from
Zadig" who had seized the town hall, scattered his men over
its three floors. The graying Caillette had barely finished
when a Wehrmacht truck summoned by Janine scraped to
a stop in the town hall square below. Crouched behind the
gray-green panels of its open rear end, half a dozen German
soldiers waved their rifles toward the Mairie's open windows.

An officer stepped out of the cab, jammed his fists onto his
hips, and stared up at the building. "Surrender and come
out!" he shouted.

From his perch above in the white-and-gold Salle des

Fêtes, under a painting of Henri IV falling into the Lake of Neuilly, Caillette stared back at this image of the conquerors of 1940. With the passionate pride of this, his first open act of resistance, and a pardonable overstatement of his strength, he answered, "Surrender yourself! This is the Army of Liberation."

The German flicked open his brown leather holster, drew out his pistol, and fired wildly toward the window from which Caillette had shouted. At that gesture, a vengeful fire swept down on the Germans from every window of the Mairie. The arrogant officer, Caillette saw, collapsed slowly onto the sidewalk "like a child's balloon with the air leaking out."

Finally the firing stopped. The town hall square was silent. Not a sound, not a single dying cry, came from the Germans. Only one, not quite dead, twitched. The rest lay still. Appalled and awestruck, the men "from Zadig" contemplated what they had just done. Then, in all the streets around them, they heard the rumbling trucks beginning to surround the Mairie.

● ● ●

Its top folded down, the gray Mercedes glided quietly under the reddening leaves of the plane trees lining the quai des Tuileries. Beside the driver, Count Dankvart von Arnim admired once again the finely chiseled façade of the Louvre sweeping past his eyes. The young lieutenant could not imagine Paris offering any other image than that of this peaceful and deserted quai fading behind him. Only his own car reminded Count von Arnim of the war. On the rear seat, two helmeted sergeants trained their machine guns on the windows above them.

Von Arnim gestured to the driver, and the car started over the Pont-au-Change toward Notre-Dame and the Prefecture of Police. Beyond the twin gray towers of the Conciergerie dominating this Ile de la Cité on which von Arnim had so often strolled, the young count could see the spire of Sainte-Chapelle stretching like a graceful sword into the morning sky. On his left, at the head of the quai aux Fleurs, he caught a glimpse of a few bouquets of flowers splashing their color against the pavement. At the top of the horloge

tower abutting on the Conciergerie, the gold needles of its
enormous open clock marked eleven.

The first burst of fire shook the empty street "like the
clash of a cymbal." Half a dozen of the rounds fired from
the Prefecture of Police struck the Mercedes. Behind him,
von Arnim saw one of the two sergeants drop his machine
gun and buckle forward. He was dead. Terrified, the young
count shrieked at the driver, "Faster, faster!" With two of
its tires shot out, the car screeched protestingly forward on
its rims. Then the helmet of the second sergeant clanged onto
the floor of the car and its owner slumped backward. Von
Arnim turned and saw blood squirting from a gaping hole in
his forehead. How, he wondered, could this have happened
in Paris?

That night, von Arnim would call his family château "Gross
Sperrenwalde" near Prenzlau. "Mother," he would murmur,
Paris has become hell."

• • •

Inside the Prefecture of Police, law student Edgar Pisani
stroked his black beard. On the inclined panel next to his
desk, twenty-four red lights blinked on and off. From all
over Paris, the police commissariats were calling the Prefecture. But this new director of the cabinet of Prefect of
Police Charles Luizet did not know how to answer them.
Pisani had not yet learned how to run the switchboard by
his side. Finally, punching haphazardly at the panel before
him, Pisani pushed a button and listened into his phone. At
the other end of the line he heard a frantic voice crying,
"Les boches are trying to storm the Mairie of Neuilly." The
rest of his caller's message was lost in a violent explosion
outside Pisani's window. On the boulevard du Palais, the
firing in which Count von Arnim had been caught a few
moments earlier had resumed. Pisani hung up and ran to
the window. In the middle of the pavement, a German truck,
hit by an incendiary bullet, blazed like a torch. "It was like
a shooting gallery," Pisani recalled later. One by one, the
Germans fleeing the burning truck were flipped over like little
tin targets.

None of the Germans caught in the deadly trap around the
Prefecture that morning was determined to resist more fero-

ciously than the man who had just finished mining the Saint-Amand Telephone Exchange, Sergeant Bernhard Blache, of the 112th Signal Regiment.

Clinging to the back of his open truck, Blache saw the two men folded over its front fenders scream and tumble to the pavement in the first cross fire from the Prefecture and the Palais de Justice next door. The driver had been hit on the right foot by a bullet and had lost control of the truck. Lurching wildly, it spun into a tree under the windows of the Prefecture. Someone screamed, "Everybody out," and the sergeant vaulted out of the open platform and crouched alongside the vehicle. In the van above him, his hands tearing at his chest, a soldier wounded in the lungs screamed, "Bernhard, Bernhard, help me!" Behind him, Blache saw an officer race across the street, firing his revolver wildly at the brownstone walls of the Prefecture as he ran. Halfway across, an explosive bullet hit his forehead. Blache watched the man's head "literally explode" and his body tumble to the asphalt. In the windows of the Prefecture above, the French were so close Blache could hear their voices when the firing slackened. Sliding along the truck, Blache worked his way to its cab. Peering up, he saw the driver slumped over the steering wheel. He was dead. Looking past the dead man's helmet up at the Prefecture through the open truck window above him, Blache suddenly saw a naked arm swing out over a stone windowsill. Clutched at the end of that arm, wrapped in a dirty towel, was a dark-green bottle.

Terrified, Blache sprang up and raced across the pavement toward the Pont-au-Change a hundred yards away. The sprinting German could see around him impacting bullets tearing little puffs of black out of the asphalt of the boulevard du Palais. Then he felt the pavement tremble under his feet. Fired by the Molotov cocktail dropped from the Prefecture, Blache's truck had just burst into flames.

At the edge of the bridge, Blache hurtled the parapet and lay gasping on the other side. Looking up, he saw, marching over the bridge, a spectacle which he found hard to believe: a little old man with a black hat and cane walking peacefully through the bullets flying around him as though he were on an afternoon stroll. For a second, in an unreasoning rage, Blache wanted to shoot down this incongruously peaceful figure.

Peering over the parapet, Blache saw a knot of civilians at the far end of the bridge in the place du Châtelet. Grabbing a "potato masher" hand grenade in each hand and howling madly, Blache raced across the bridge. At the sight of Blache waving his hand grenades, his face streaming with blood and sweat, the civilians scattered like a covey of terrified pigeons. In the now deserted square, a civilian car approached the sergeant. He waved it to a stop and, brandishing his grenades, forced its French doctor driver to take him to the Hotel Meurice.

Still waving those grenades, the half-mad Blache ran into the lobby of the Meurice and up the flight of stairs ahead of him. He threw open the first door he found, and burst into the room behind it. "My God, my God!" he cried. "What are you waiting for, to send the tanks? They're cooking my men like sausages!"

3

THE TANKS, three of them, had already arrived at the Mairie of Neuilly. Two had twisted into position in the square below its chipped and blackened façade; the third had circled toward the garden in its rear. Surrounded, under fire for three hours, their ammunition almost spent, the men "from Zadig" inside despaired. The parquet floor of the Salle des Fêtes was a littered mass of grenade fragments, cartridges, glass and plaster. Its paintings hung in shreds. The white-and-gold embossed woodwork of the room was charred and splintered. Next door, at the head of the Mairie's marble staircase, on a row of wooden desks assembled from the mayor's office, the dead and dying lay side by side. In those exhilarating moments a few hours earlier when these men "from Zadig" had seized the Mairie, no one had remembered to bring along as much as a roll of adhesive tape. Now, without medicine, anesthetic or bandages, their wounded bled to death in this sticky common bed.

Never would André Caillette forget the frightened eyes

of one man, his stomach shot away, who pleaded with him for help. With desperate logic, Caillette did the only thing that seemed possible; using his belt, he tried to strap the man's dangling intestinal tubes back into his abdomen.

From his window in the Salle des Fêtes, Caillette's brother Charles spotted a German crawling out of an oval window on the rooftop opposite him. The German started to sprint up its gray slate tiles toward the cover of a stubby yellow chimney. Charles fired once. The German fell and, bouncing gently, slid down the dark slate tiles, leaving behind him a bright swath of blood. For a second he clawed at the gutter with his fingers, lost his grip and dropped screaming to the pavement five floors below. Charles was the best shot in Neuilly.

His brother had another assignment for him. Behind the Mairie, at the junction of two little moss-covered garden walls, a machine-gun nest dominated the windows of one side of the besieged building. Charles took a World War I Lebel rifle, and, leaning it from a window ledge opposite the machine gun, fired. The gunner, almost hidden behind a stack of sandbags, slumped forward. From behind the little moss-covered garden wall, Charles saw two pairs of hands reach out and drag the gunner to cover by his boots. Another gunner took his place. This one had spotted Charles. He put his first burst into the window right over his head, flicking off the Frenchman's blue beret. Charles crawled to another window, sighted his Lebel and fired again. The new gunner leaped up, threw his arms wide over his head, and fell to the ground. From behind the little moss-covered garden wall, Charles saw one pair of hands reach out and drag the gunner's body out of sight. A third man took the machine gun. Charles moved to a new window ledge and fired his third shot. The new gunner rolled over beside the gun he had not yet fired. This time there were no hands to reach out from behind the garden wall. The gun remained silent.

Through the noisy clatter of gunfire all around him, André Caillette heard a discordant sound. It was the high-pitched tinkle of the mayor's telephone. Caillette crawled through the broken glass and plaster littering the mayor's office to the heap of upended furniture on which the phone rested. Picking up the receiver, he heard, across the static of a bad connection, an excited voice yelling at him from fifty miles away.

It was a policeman calling from the commissariat of the city of Chartres. The unknown policeman described the spectacle flowing past the window of his commissariat: the liberators of Chartres streaming by in an unending flood of tanks and armored cars. "My God," he told Caillette, "the Americans even have a truck so big they can put three tanks on it!" As Caillette listened, too numb to respond to this description of a sight he feared he would never see, a roar shook his own besieged building. The German tanks outside his window had begun to fire high-explosive shells at the Mairie.

Caillette hung up and, weeping with emotion, stumbled back into the Salle des Fêtes. "*Les gars,*" he rasped in a voice raw and hoarse from strain, "the Americans are in Chartres!" The exhausted and beaten men looked at each other, then back at Caillette. He was standing at attention, tears rolling down his face, singing the "Marseillaise." For a moment they stood still; then they too began to sing. As the sound of their song, rising defiantly over the firing, drifted from the building, hundreds of men and women, watching the fight from windows and balconies, joined in. For a poignant moment, the singing of the Frenchmen inside and outside the surrounded Mairie blended together in a strange communion, stifling for an instant the angry crash of rifle fire. Edging to a window, Caillette looked out and saw on the balcony of his own apartment three blocks away a familiar figure singing with them. Behind a pot of geraniums was the wife he had not seen in three months of hiding from the Gestapo. She did not even know he was in this building.

Their situation was desperate. By now there were ten dead and three dozen wounded inside the Mairie. Outside, a German officer with a loudspeaker warned, "Surrender, or we'll destroy the Mairie over your heads." The men "from Zadig" answered with another burst of their dwindling ammunition supply.

In the square, a tank advanced. With one high-explosive shell, it tore apart the Mairie's iron door, and started slithering up its marble steps. The French were defenseless. Medicine was not the only thing they had forgotten to bring into the building; they had no Molotov cocktails. From behind the marble staircase in the lobby, choked by dust and smoke, Caillette and his men fired rifles at the gray form menacing them. It was hopeless.

Caillette ordered the men with him on the first floor to retreat into the basement. There, under a cement manhole cover two feet wide, was a cylindrical hole dropping down to an antechamber the size of a big closet. Beyond that antechamber, on the other side of a bricked-up wall, was a canal of the Paris sewer system, and safety. It was the only way out. While the Germans swarmed after them, Caillette and a handful of his men ran into the basement and scrambled down the hole. An hour earlier, two men had started to smash an opening in the wall dividing the dark chamber from the sewers. Now Caillette and his men, packed into a sweating mass, without light, in rigid silence, waited for them to finish the job. They gagged the wounded to stifle their cries. To muffle the sound of their blows, the two men chopping the hole wrapped their pickaxes in their shirts.

At the top of the rusty iron ladder leading into the hole, Caillette hunched under the closed cement manhole cover and listened. Above him, inches away, he could hear the scraping feet of the Germans running through the basement looking for them, driving out the stragglers. Then he heard one pair of boots stop right over his head. He heard the German's feet rubbing against the grains of sand and dust on top of the lid, almost as though he was grinding them into his balding skull. The German yelled to someone. A trembling Caillette waited for him to lift the lid and drop in the half-dozen hand grenades that would be enough to kill him and all the other Frenchmen huddled in this dark pit.

• • •

At the Prefecture of Police, the first shell tore open the building's heavy iron main gate. The shock spun law student Edgar Pisani around and hurled him into a corner of his room under a shower of plaster chips. As he groped through the dusty pile of rubble looking for his glasses, the black-bearded Pisani heard a panicky voice cry, "The tanks are here!"

The tanks, two Panthers and a Renault of the 5th Sicherungsregiment, circled the wide square between Notre-Dame and the Prefecture. It was 3:30 P.M. Trapped behind their flimsy sandbag barricades, armed with pistols, World War I

bolt-action rifles, and a few slow Hotchkiss machine guns, the
police watched them in awe. There, before the bulky outlines of Notre-Dame was the price of their bold gesture.
Panic overtook them. First in handfuls, then by the dozens,
they abandoned their barricades and stampeded toward the
building's only safety valve, the internal subway station
whose underground passage led to the Left Bank of the Seine.

One determined man stopped them. Police Sergeant Armand Fournet, chief of one of the two Resistance networks
in the Police Department, tore through the retreating mob,
elbowing his way to the head of the stairs. Tearing his pistol
from its holster, Fournet promised to shoot the first man who
tried to walk past him. "Our only chance of survival," he
shouted, "is to win!" Stunned and ashamed, the men halted.

Above them, law student Pisani, back on his feet, dictated
an urgent appeal to the teletype operator before him. "A
German attack on the Prefecture is imminent," he said. "All
FFI forces available needed to attack Germans from the
rear." As he dictated, the operator punched his message directly onto the printer that would carry it into every police
station in the city. When he had tapped out the last words,
he reached over and pushed a button marked "A.G." It was
the general alarm button for the Paris police force.

In the dimly lit cellar of the Prefecture itself, three men,
barechested and sweating, assembled the building's most
potent weapon. Stacked in the walls before them were the
champagne bottles of Vichy's police prefect. One after another, their corks were popped, and, without a look, the team
assembled by Frédéric Joliot-Curie poured the precious liquid
onto the floor until it sloshed over the soles of their shoes.
As fast as they could replace it with gas and sulfuric acid,
they recorked the bottles and wrapped them with paper
soaked in potassium chlorate. A waiting relay team of policemen ran the bottles to the upper stories of the building.

On the square in front of Notre-Dame, tanker Willi Linke
of the 5th Sicherungsregiment saw one of Joliot-Curie's deadly
bottles go wavering through the air and plop into the im-
prudently open turret of the tank beside him "like a basket-
ball in a basket." A great burst of yellow flame shot out of
the turret. In seconds the whole tank was a mass of flames.
Buttoned up inside his own tank, Linke could hear the jubi-

lant cries of the policemen in the Prefecture ringing over his head. Furious, Linke ordered another shell into his own 88 and sent it smashing against the Prefecture.

Just before five o'clock, a chilling rumor swept the embattled building. Their ammunition was almost gone. Sergeant Fournet, who had stopped the panicky stampede of the police earlier, walked glumly into Pisani's office to confirm it. Some of the men, he told Pisani, "already have barely two minutes of fire left."

The young law student picked up his telephone and dialed a number. It was the home of his sister Laurence. "We're not going to get out of it alive," he told her. "Our ammunition is almost gone. The only thing that can save us now," he said, "is if the Americans get here in an awful hurry." He asked her to kiss his two children for him. Then he hung up.

●   ●   ●

But for the score of Americans 175 miles away, in a paneled map van half the size of a railroad car, Paris that day was "nothing more than an inkspot on our maps to be bypassed as we headed toward the Rhine." * Their maps were the maps of Eagletac, the advance headquarters of the U.S. Twelfth Army Group settled in an apple orchard on the banks of the Mayenne River near the cotton-milling town of Laval, and it was on those maps that the destiny of Paris would soon be charted. To the Twelfth Army Group commander, Lieutenant General Omar N. Bradley, to the men of his staff around him, it was a place to be avoided at all costs.

For this gentle Missourian with the steel-rimmed glasses and balding head, there was just one goal. It was to drive his men forward as fast and as far as possible, to punch a hole in the Siegfried Line, and roll up to the Rhine before the enemy stumbling backward before him could reorganize his forces. He had only one worry now: it was gasoline.

Two days before, SHAEF had informed him his daily fuel allocation would be cut by 67,000 gallons on Paris's liberation to haul supplies to the city's population. He had been shocked and appalled by the figure. It was enough to move an entire corps 25 miles a day. He believed that "if we could

rush on to the Siegfried Line with the tonnage destined for
Paris," the city might be repaid "by an earlier end to the
war." *

Now in his caravan, in the midst of his daily staff conference, Bradley listened as his G4 ticked off the vital figures
of the fuel situation on which so much depended: the number
of gallons landed the day before on the beaches, the number
trucked forward over their lengthening supply routes, the
number left in reserve in his divisions' forward depots. To
the man just behind him, his aide Major Chester Bayard Hansen, watching the slow daily erosion of those last two figures
was "like watching a man dying of a terminal illness."

Bradley did not notice the runner slip into the end of the
caravan and deliver a handwritten note to his G2, Brigadier
General Edwin Sibert. It was a routine radio intercept of a
German communication. Sibert mentioned it in passing in
his own report. "It seems," he said, "that there are some kind
of civil disturbances in Paris."

Bradley sat up.

"Dammit, Eddie," he ordered, "find out what's going on
there. We can't let Paris get in our way." Omar Bradley, at
the head of the army on which Edgar Pisani and his besieged
mates counted, was "determined we would not be dissuaded
from our plan for bypassing Paris."

Bradley had good reasons for his concern. André Tollet and
his fellow insurgents had chosen to launch their insurrection
on the very day the Allies had committed themselves to the
post-D-Day plan to bypass the capital. A few hours before
this Eagletac conference, after a long consultation with his
worried supply officers, Dwight Eisenhower had given his
forces the order to cross the Seine. That night, while the
embattled men of the Prefecture of Police were watching
their last rounds of ammunition dribble away, the troops of
the 313th U.S. Infantry Regiment would thread across the
river on a dam at Mantes-Gassicourt to set into motion the
plan for bypassing Paris.

*   *   *

Paris that afternoon was the preoccupation of another military conference half a continent away from the Norman apple

---

* *Ibid.*

orchard folding over Eagletac. Adolf Hitler did not yet know of the insurrection spilling into the streets of the French capital. All he knew about any trouble in Paris was the information, received from OB West twenty-four hours before, that there had been a few scattered clashes between "terrorists" and German troops. Still, General Walter Warlimont had considered it unusual enough to order it typed up in the special large character designed to spare the Führer's eyes and taken to his bunker. "Just another reason not to declare Paris an open city," Hitler had growled.

Now, in the opening OKW conference this Saturday, the meticulous General Warlimont jotted down the first angry question of an angry Hitler.

"Where," he asked, "is the mortar?"

Embarrassed, General Buhle had to admit the "Karl" with its special freight train of high-explosive ammunition had not yet crossed the frontier. The Allied air attacks ravaging Germany's railways had slowed its progress west. Furious, Hitler reminded Buhle that he had been promised the Karl would be in Paris by August 22. Turning to Jodl, he demanded "absolute priority" for its movements.

Then, once again, he abruptly pushed aside his chief of staff's traditional opening presentation on the east.

"The west," he demanded.

The 1/200,000 map card of the Paris region, which Hitler had seized six days earlier at a similar conference, now enclosed the focal point on which his whole western front pivoted. To the angry Führer, the uneven black splotch spreading over the center of that map was an inkspot to be defended at all costs; on it depended all his slim hopes of checking the onrushing Allies at the Seine, and slowing their snowballing rush to the Ruhr. With every bridge over the Seine except those in Paris destroyed by Allied air power, Paris had become the funnel through which all the German troops south of the Seine had to be supplied. Von Choltitz's military objections to the premature destruction of the Paris bridges were amply vindicated. Beyond that, the Paris bridges, Hitler now realized, bore charmed lives; the Allies would never bomb them.

To the men around him in his Rastenburg bunker Hitler repeated, this time in quiet, considered tones, what he had said earlier. Holding Paris was "indispensable." He ordered "all available reinforcements put at the disposition of the commander of Gross Paris." Then he went beyond even that. He personally canvassed the forces available to bolster the Paris defenses. First, he considered transferring some of Generalfeldmarschall Kesselring's reserves from the Alps across France to Paris. Then he found another, faster solution. He ordered, in a KR Blitz (top priority) wire, the 26th and 27th Panzer Divisions to march out of Denmark and move south to Paris. The forward elements of those divisions, moving by night to avoid Allied air attacks, could reach the Paris area by August 25 or 26, Warlimont, his operations chief, assured him.

In clear categoric terms, Hitler dictated his first order to Generalfeldmarschall Model, the man he had chosen to restore in the west. He was, he told him, "to join the First Army and the Fifth Panzer Army into a fortified belt in front of Paris," then to reinforce it further with the Nineteenth Army retreating from the southwest.

To the man of whom he expected miracles, Hitler now defined the terms of what the first miracle should be. "The most urgent mission of the commander in chief of the west," he told Model, "is to assemble his units in front of Paris—he must remain above all the master of the situation in front of Paris." For Hitler, there could be no compromise with his conquered prize, this city in which, although he did not know it yet, the soldiers of the Wehrmacht had been "cooking like sausages" for the past eight hours.

4

THE ELEGANT COLONEL HANS Jay whitened at the sight of his dead soldiers folded around their truck in front of the Mairie of Neuilly. Looking at the prisoners lined up against the wall opposite him with their hands over their heads, Jay decided to "shoot them all on the spot."

Louis Berty, his kidneys throbbing from the clubbing he had received as the Germans chased them from the Mairie, and his young Nanterre neighbor Pierre Le Guen, were in that sorry line. They had both been trapped on the third floor of the building when the Germans swarmed inside.

Neuilly's Vichy mayor, Max Roger, convinced Jay that some of the men lined up against the wall were his employees. Jay let him pick them out. By the time he had finished, the little colonel's temper had cooled. He would not, he decided, shoot the others. He ordered them marched off, hands in the air, to his Kommandantur on the avenue de Madrid. As their miserable column stumbled away, people cheered from the windows along their route. On the curb, women wept and twisted rosary beads as they passed.

In the black hole underneath the Mairie, the two men stealthily cutting at the brick sealing them off from escape could now hear the sloshing of the sewer waters, and smell the vile air in the dank canal beside them. Finally they pushed open a hole. One by one, twenty yards apart, the surviving men "from Zadig" squirmed through the hole and started to follow the waist-deep sewage flowing down the canal.

Charles Caillette, the sharpshooter, carried Henri Guérin, a World War I veteran whose wooden leg had been shot away by a fragment from a tank shell. Looking at it, Guérin had remarked, "Thank God, they always shoot the same one." Above him, André Caillette could still hear the Germans' boots pounding back and forth over the thin concrete cap hiding them.

At the Neuilly Kommandantur, Louis Berty and the twenty men captured with him had been ordered into a circle. A German soldier pushed into it, and he started, one by one, to march past the prisoners. He was one of the two men Berty had so proudly captured six hours before in the café around the corner from the Mairie. Obviously, he had been told to identify his captors. As the soldier circled toward him, Berty, weak with fear, felt he could not hold his hands up any longer. The German stepped opposite him and looked straight into the slender Berty's eyes. He made a gesture as though he was "wiping a lump of spit from his cheek" as he studied Berty. Then, without a sign of recognition, he stepped past him and turned to the next man.

• • •

From a window of a room in the Palais du Luxembourg another Frenchman watched three other FFI prisoners march off to their deaths, carrying on their shoulders the picks and shovels with which they would dig their own graves. It was Paul Pardou, the self-effacing truck driver in a blue beret who had systematically hijacked the food hoards of Vichy's Milice for the Resistance. Pardou's mission on this Saturday, the one he had vowed would be his last, had ended in disaster. He had been caught in a German roadblock. Pardou had had one instinctive gesture. He had swallowed the fake Milice identity papers he had used to pillage Vichy's food supplies. At no price, he had decided, would he take the chance of being handed over to the Milice.

With his own photo sticking in his throat, Pardou had been arrested for not having any identity papers and taken to this room in the Palais du Luxembourg. Behind him now, the door opened and a corpulent German sergeant, rolls of sweating fat spilling over his collar, beckoned to him. His name was Franz. He was the palace mess sergeant. He pushed Pardou down the corridor to his kitchen.

There he gestured to a mass of greasy pans. "Tomorrow," Franz announced, "you shot. Tonight you make kitchen clean."

•   •   •

His face closed and hard, Dietrich von Choltitz climbed up the stairs to his Hotel Meurice office. Like Colonel Hans Jay, von Choltitz had just seen the bodies of some of the first soldiers of his command killed in the suddenly hostile streets of Paris. Across the Seine, in front of the Gare d'Orsay, Choltitz had a few moments earlier looked on the burned and bloody bodies of six Germans killed in an FFI ambush.

He was determined to strike back. As he walked into his office, his chief of staff, Colonel von Unger, handed him a slip of paper. It spoke with less eloquence but more precision than the sight Choltitz had just seen. It was the day's casualty figures, and they showed Choltitz had already lost over fifty men killed and a hundred wounded.

The angry general ordered his key aides into his office. His voice firm and quiet, Choltitz reviewed the different possibilities open to him. They came down to a simple choice.

Either he put into effect the threat he had made to Paris's mayor three days earlier and use massive reprisals against a part of the city, or he could smash the Prefecture of Police which seemed to be the insurrection's heart, with a "bloody gesture that would kill their insurrection once and for all." Von Choltitz polled his aides for advice, then thought a minute himself. From the open windows of his office they could hear the sounds of firing in the area around the Prefecture.

Von Choltitz decided to attack the Prefecture. To do it, he proposed to put together the core of his strike forces, the 190th Sicherungsregiment, the tanks of his 5th Sicherungsregiment, and the SS tanks of the Prince Eugène barracks in the place de la République. In addition, he decided he would call on the Luftwaffe to bomb the building before he attacked.

In fact, he considered the air support essential. He planned to send his tanks over two exposed bridges—pont Saint-Michel and the Pont-Neuf—so they could attack the Prefecture from its most exposed point. But before sending his tanks across those open bridges, he wanted the building dive-bombed into submission, so his tanks would have only to "roll over the rubble." Since the Luftwaffe would not put its planes into the sky in daylight, his plan meant he had to attack at dusk or dawn.

At the same time he was attacking the Prefecture, he decided, he would send tank and armored car assaults against a few other pockets of resistance. He would, he was convinced, be able in one brutal lesson to shock the city back to calm. Looking at the faces around him in his office, Choltitz saw nothing but approbation for his plan. To the men of his staff on this August afternoon, a Paris in arms could be addressed in only one language, the language of force.

The only problem that remained to be resolved was when to attack. Colonel Hagen, his G2, wanted to strike that evening. Choltitz remembers looking at his watch. It was already 5:30 and he was against the idea of a dusk attack. When the planes had finished, his tanks would be attacking in darkness, and under its cover the men in the Prefecture might get away.

The attack, he ordered, would take place the next day, half

an hour after sunrise. He told von Unger to alert the Luftwaffe, and fix the time of the attack.

Sunrise, August 20, 1944, was at 5:51 Paris time.

• • •

In front of the Kommandantur of Neuilly the Germans loaded Louis Berty and twenty of his comrades, seized at the Neuilly Mairie, into an open Wehrmacht truck. One of the prisoners taken in the town hall was missing. It was Pierre Le Guen, the eighteen-year-old to whom Berty's wife had lent a pistol that morning so he could join the men setting out for the Mairie. Le Guen had kept it with him so he could return it, and that gesture had just cost him his life. Of all the prisoners taken in the Mairie, he was the only one caught with a weapon. He was shot.

Berty, hands clasped behind his head, his knees jammed under his chin by the back of the prisoner ahead of him, failed for a moment to notice that the truck had turned off the avenue du President-Wilson in Suresnes and was heading down a dusty side road. Berty looked up. At the end of the road, rising from the summit of a wooded hill, he recognized a hexagon-shaped fortress. For three years he had heard the echoes of its firing squad in his butchershop only a mile away. It was Mont Valérien, the most-feared German prison in Paris.

5

FROM THE BALCONY OF the Hotel Meurice, two men watched a young girl in a red dress ride her bicycle through the Tuileries, her blond hair flying in the breeze. "I like those pretty Parisiennes," General von Choltitz told the man beside him. "It would be a tragedy to have to kill them and destroy their city."

Swedish Consul General Raoul Nordling started at that phrase so casually flowing from the lips of the coughing German beside him. Was this somber Prussian, he asked himself in dismay, really preparing to commit an act as wanton as the destruction of Paris? Raze Paris, he solemnly warned Choltitz, and he would commit a crime history would never pardon.

The German shrugged his shoulders. "I am a soldier," he answered. "I get orders. I execute them."

As they talked, a burst of gunfire rang out from behind the gray masses of the Louvre to their left, and the area around the besieged Prefecture. Choltitz's square face hardened at the sound. The little general felt a sharp surge of anger well up inside him.

"I'll get them out of their Prefecture," he promised. "I'll bomb them out of it."

Startled, Nordling turned to him. He did not know that Choltitz planned in just a few hours to smash that Prefecture into ruins. "Do you realize," he asked, "your near misses will fall on Notre-Dame and the Sainte-Chapelle?"

Von Choltitz shrugged. The fact that Notre-Dame was only 200 yards away and Sainte-Chapelle just across the street from the building which he proposed to reduce to rubble at dawn was not his concern. "You know the situation," he told the Swede. "Put yourself in my place. What alternative do I have?"

It was precisely to offer the commander of Gross Paris an alternative that the Swede had come to this room at sunset.

A few moments before, a telephone had rung in his Consulate a few blocks away on the rue d'Anjou. It was the Prefecture of Police. At the other end of the line, Nordling had heard an anguished voice pleading: "Our situation is desperate. We've only got a few minutes of ammunition left. Can't you do something?"

As soon as he had hung up, Nordling had called Choltitz for an appointment. On his way to the Meurice, an idea had occurred to him. He now proposed it to the German beside him. It was a temporary cease-fire "to pick up the dead and wounded." If it worked, he said, it might be extended.

Von Choltitz started at the Swede's suggestion. In his thirty years as a soldier, he had never given or asked for a cease-fire. But after his initial surprise had worn off, Choltitz began to see several advantages in the Swede's bold suggestion. Choltitz's main interest that night was keeping Paris quiet. If a cease-fire could do it for him, it would, he reasoned, have its merits. His troops would no longer be tied down fighting the insurrection. They would be free for more important jobs. If it was effective, it would mean he would not have to use extra police forces to keep his lines of communication through the city open.

But, above all, if it worked, it would allow him to postpone the attack on the Prefecture he had scheduled for dawn. That attack would be, he knew, an irrevocable step, a declaration of war on the city. Once he had ordered the Luftwaffe into the skies of Paris, there would be no turning back. It was a major decision, and Dietrich von Choltitz did not like making major decisions.

The autonomy this Paris command gave him was a new experience for von Choltitz. Until now, he had always been firmly locked inside Germany's impersonal military machine. His decisions, with the exception of minor tactical ones, had always been made for him. Now, at the very moment at which his visit to Rastenburg had jarred his confidence in the Third Reich and its leader, circumstances had placed von Choltitz in a command in which he had to make decisions. He preferred to postpone them. Nordling's suggestion offered him that chance.

If, he told Nordling, the commanders at the Prefecture of Police could demonstrate in an hour's trial that they could control their men, he would agree to discuss a cease-fire for the city.

Yet one thing disturbed von Choltitz about what he was doing. It was "against the spirit of the orders" he had received for Paris. He did not want Model to find out about it.

In a lowered tone, he said to Nordling, "I have one thing to ask you. Don't associate my name with your truce."

He escorted Nordling to the door, shook hands with the Swede, and then summoned von Unger. He curtly told him the attack on the Prefecture was "postponed for the moment." Then he marched up to his room to ponder what he had just done.

• • •

The insistent red light on the switchboard at the Prefecture of Police flared on again. Law student Edgar Pisani picked it up. Behind him, one of his despairing aides remarked, "The

Allies are going to let us go to hell. They're going to bypass Paris." On the phone, Pisani heard Nordling's voice. The Germans, he told him, had agreed to a truce.

Pisani turned and fell into the arms of Armand Fournet, the tough sergeant who had halted the panicking police in the courtyard.

"Thank God," he murmured, "we've saved Paris."

6

TWELVE HUNDRED MILES FROM Paris, the tail of a plane sat almost in the wavelets lapping at the end of a darkened runway alongside the rocky fortress of Gibraltar. In its blacked-out cabin, the fluorescent needles of its instrument panel bounced under the pilot's worried gaze. Ahead of the pilot 1,200 yards away was the Mediterranean, a black and menacing stillness at the end of the brief runway. The plane was crammed with 950 gallons of gas, more than it had ever carried before. The pilot, Colonel Lionel de Marmier, knew that the plane was more than half a ton overweight.

He drove up the power on his two engines until the flickering needle in front of him stood at 2,700 rpm. The plane shook, and behind him de Marmier could feel its tail twitching lightly. Slowly his engine temperature rose to 104, 113, 122 degrees. Still de Marmier held his plane back, thrusting his rpm as high as he dared.

"Ready?" he said to the man beside him.

"Ready," he answered.

De Marmier flipped off his brake. The overloaded plane shivered an instant, then lurched down the runway. De Marmier felt the reluctance of the overloaded plane. The black runway swept past his eyes, pulling him closer and closer to the chopping waters of the Mediterranean; 600, 800, 900 yards and still the plane refused to be coaxed into the air. Now de Marmier could see the bobbing whitecaps of the phosphorescent sea rushing up at him: 1,100 yards. He teased his plane one last time. He felt it, slowly, protesting, lift a few feet off the ground. Slipping over the waves just below his wings, de Marmier held his plane horizontal, building its airspeed. Then, slowly, he eased up his flaps and started to climb. Over his shoulder he saw in a relieved glance the towering black mass of Gibraltar fall away behind him. Lionel de Marmier sighed. He had just made the most difficult takeoff in his 15,000 hours of flying time.

In the compartment behind him, Charles de Gaulle unsnapped his safety belt and reached into his tunic for a cigar. In silent defiance of de Marmier's regulations, he put it into his mouth and lit it.

De Gaulle himself had ordered the takeoff against the advice of his aides and his English hosts. The Flying Fortress, the second assigned to take him to France, had bruised a tire landing in Gibraltar. It would have taken twenty-four hours to fly in a new tire. Informed of the delay, de Gaulle had told his protesting hosts, "I shall leave at eleven o'clock as scheduled, and I shall leave in my own plane."

Nursing his precious fuel for this, the longest trip the Lockheed Lodestar *France* would ever make, de Marmier pivoted north around Cape St. Vincent's light in southern Portugal and up the Portuguese coast. Ahead the city of Lisbon beckoned, a miracle of light in a blacked-out world. Farther on, on the northwest tip of Spain, lay his last beacon, the light of Cape Finisterre. From there he would fly almost due north, on a course of 357°, along the black and menacing coast of occupied France, until he found a waiting RAF escort off the southern tip of England.

In the dark and silent passengers' compartment de Gaulle's aide, Claude Guy, stared at the little orange light burning opposite him and thought how strange it was that all the destiny of his country should now hang "on a glowing cigar stub in a blacked-out airplane."

7

THE FIRST SHAFTS OF daylight broke a sky still cluttered with the clouds of a night of storm. A new stillness muffled the city. Dazed and bruised, Paris seemed to pause in the early hours of this Sunday, August 20, to count her wounds.

For the awakening capital, this humid Sunday would bring chaos, contrast and confusion. For a few Parisians, it was just another Sunday. On the banks of the Seine below Notre-Dame, at the site of the heaviest fighting in the city the day before, half a dozen fishermen were already testing the muddy waters of the river. In the Bois de Boulogne, not even an insurrection could stay a few elegant Sunday riders from a brisk morning trot through its shaded bridle paths.

For the moment, in these early Sunday hours, the tenuous truce concluded by Swedish Consul General Raoul Nordling at three o'clock in the morning had tamped down the violence of the day before. For occupier and occupied alike, it brought a brief pause, an instant of reckoning to measure the portent of Saturday's upheaval.

To many a man in the bewildered German garrison, which had been startled by the fury suddenly shown by a city dormant through four years of occupation, these few hours of calm offered a chance to write a last letter home. From his window in the Hotel de Crillon, watching the TODT organization's workers drive antitank spikes into the pavement of the place de la Concorde, Sergeant Erich Vandamm, forty-two, wrote his wife in another capital, Berlin. "Dear Ursula," he began, "it may be you will not hear from me for a long time. I have the feeling things are going to get bad here fast." Warrant Officer Otto Kirschner, a few blocks away, chose to pen a macabre joke. On the back of a postcard of the Invalides, he wrote to his wife Friedl, "This is where the French

buried Napoleon. Take a good look at it. By the time you
get this card, it probably won't exist any more." Sergeant
Paul Schallück, of the 1st Flak Brigade, had not had time
to finish his letter before going out on patrol. It started, "Dear
Mama, I'm afraid this city I like so much is going to be
turned into a dump heap." Schallück folded it up and put
it into his wallet. It arrived two years later. Minutes after
putting it away, Schallück was seriously wounded by the
FFI near the pont des Arts, and taken prisoner.

With Germanic thoroughness, Captain Otto Nietzki, of the
Military Police, made his regular morning round of the city's
bars and brothels. Lying on his back in the bed of a brothel
on the rue de Provence, before the terrorized eyes of its
madam, Nietzki found a major, the only German left that
morning in these usually well-patronized precincts. He was
shooting out the lights of a chandelier overhead with his
pistol. "What are they waiting for to get us out of here?" he
asked over and over again in a drunken gibberish.

None of the Germans in the city, however, had a task any
stranger than that assigned to MP Sergeant Rudolf Reis,
thirty-two, of the Platzkommandantur.

Reis had spent the day before huddled behind a parapet
of the quai de Montebello, firing at the besieged policemen
in the Prefecture of Police. This morning he was riding
through the streets in a Paris police car, flanked by two of
the policemen he had been trying to kill the day before.
They were announcing Nordling's cease-fire. All across the
city, Parisians in summer dresses and shirt-sleeves rushed to
what had become their newspapers, the city's walls, to read
the first of the mass of contradictory *affiches* announcing and
denouncing this truce. At the corner of the avenue de l'Opéra
and the rue des Pyramides, an astonished Reis saw the owner
of a café rush toward their car with a bottle of red wine
and three glasses. Then, before the stupefied regard of a
handful of passersby, the German soldier and the two policemen clinked glasses and drank to the success of the cease-
fire they were announcing to Paris.

8

For Alexandre Parodi and his devoted band of Gaullists, haunted by the image of a ravaged Warsaw, the precarious peace being promised by MP Rudolf Reis and the two policemen beside him had offered a chance—their last, perhaps—to save Paris. To these men, it presented an unhoped-for way to control the insurrection they had been unable to prevent. With the energy of apostles of a new faith, they sought to impose it on the city. They spared no tactic. Parodi himself summed up all their desperate aspirations in one passionate phrase that Sunday morning: "Time. We must gain time."

All across the city, a flood of mysterious telephone calls poured into FFI headquarters, ordering the cease-fire, often citing the authority of the FFI's Communist chief, "Colonel Rol." One of his aides picked up a phone and, amazed, heard an unknown caller order a cease-fire—in his own name. From London, in grave and measured tones, General Pierre Koenig addressed the city over the BBC. "There would be no greater danger to the city of Paris," he warned, "than if the population were to listen to a call for an uprising."

Charles Luizet, installed in his Prefecture of Police less than twenty-four hours, ordered his men "not to fire unless attacked or provoked." He placed his police cars at Nordling's disposition to announce the truce to the city. Before a group of Rol's own officers, Jacques Chaban-Delmas, the man who had flown to London to warn the Allies of this insurrection, shouted, "Rol and the men around him are leading Paris to a massacre!"

With the same skill and astuteness with which Communist trade union leader André Tollet had forced the decision to launch an insurrection forty-eight hours earlier, Parodi now jammed the truce past the same political body, the Conseil National de la Résistance. To these worried men who, the day before, had had no alternative but to endorse the Com-

135

munists' *fait accompli*, Parodi presented the truce as a German request. It covered four points negotiated by Nordling serving as an intermediary between Choltitz's and Parodi's headquarters. The FFI were recognized as regular troops to be treated as prisoners of war; the Germans accepted the presence of the FFI in the public buildings they occupied; the FFI agreed not to attack German strongpoints in the city; the Germans would have free access to a series of defined major arteries for their troop movements. Paraphrasing his treasurer Alexandre de Saint-Phalle, Parodi told the man before him, "If you sign a truce between, on the one hand, an army that, whether you like it or not, was once the most powerful in the world, and an unorganized group of FFI who've barely opened fire, *eh bien*, it's the Germans who are disgracing themselves in signing the truce, not us."

To second him, Chaban-Delmas outlined a harsh military reality: Half a German army—enough troops and armor to produce in the streets of Paris all the rubble the demented mind of Adolf Hitler could demand—waited to withdraw through the city. And although Chaban and the men with him could not know it, at about the same time he was addressing the CNR, Lieutenant General George Patton was making his first angry comment on their premature uprising to his staff: "They started their goddamned insurrection," he said. "Now let them finish it."

Acting with speed and coordination, Parodi and the men around him seemed to be winning. It appeared to them that they were about to put "in the icebox" this insurrection they had not been able to stop. Caught off balance by the rapidity of their attack, the Communists were still reacting. Soon they would counterattack with violence.

But in these early hours of a summer Sunday, as timid and uncertain as a child taking its first steps, their truce began to spread over the city. Relieved and excited, Parisians poured into the streets of the city so empty the day before. To thousands of its ordinary citizens, horrified by Saturday's sudden violence, it was a moment to breathe easily once again. It seemed to many on this humid morning that Paris had been saved.

●   ●   ●

Second Lieutenant Aimé Bully's anguished eyes once again swept over the four fuel gauges on the instrument panel before him. There was one for each of his four fuel tanks. Three were empty. Bully had sucked the last drops from each of them with his hand pump. Now the white needle on the fourth had started its slide down to zero. The thirty-three-year-old flight engineer realized there was not even half an hour's flying time left in that last tank. For more than an hour, lost in fog and rain, pitched by storm winds, the Lockheed Lodestar *France* had wandered through this piece of sky somewhere over the English coast, looking for the RAF fighter escort that would guide it to safety in Normandy. A voice cut through Bully's worried reflections.

"Fuel?" asked the man ahead of him.

"We're emptying our last tank," the flight engineer replied to pilot Lionel de Marmier. "You can't go on playing much longer."

His hand sweating nervously, de Marmier realized he would have to find land. He would have to do it alone, without instruments, without using his radio, with no idea of his ceiling, with his gas running out—and with the man who carried the destiny of France on his shoulders smoking a cigar in his cabin. De Marmier throttled back his engines and set the plane into a slow descent. Watching the altimeter descend toward ground level, Bully silently prayed that they were over the Channel and not land. In the cabin behind them, silent and impassive, Charles de Gaulle glared at the bleak world outside his window.

"Fuel?" asked de Marmier.

"A few more minutes, Colonel."

Now, below the plane, Bully could see the churning white-caps of the Channel. Then, ahead of them, out of the mist, loomed the gray outline of the English coast. The cabin door opened. De Gaulle's aide, Claude Guy, stepped in.

"What's happening?" Guy demanded.

"We've been left in the lurch," answered Marmier. "There's no escort." He told Guy they would have to land in England.

The young aide went back to the cabin. To the imperturbable man before him, he announced the fighter escort had failed to show up.

De Gaulle sighed. "What is it this time?" he asked Guy. "The English? The Americans? Or both?"

Then Guy announced they were almost out of fuel and would have to land in England.

De Gaulle sat up. "England?" he said. "Never! Tell Marmier I will land only in France."

"Fuel?" Marmier asked his flight engineer.

This time Bully swallowed as he answered. "Almost empty."

Skimming over the choppy waters of the Channel, with less than a hundred yards of visibility, the Lodestar bucketed dead south toward the coast of France. Bully stroked the hand pump with which he would suck the last drops of gas out of their last fuel tank. De Marmier licked nervously at his lips. Never, it seemed to Bully, had he lived minutes as long as these in this cabin. Then, rising ahead of them, was the long, low coast of France. Quickly the plane swept over an abandoned beach studded with blockhouses and rubble. De Marmier stared blankly at the sight. He recognized nothing. He knew he had no time to gallivant over the countryside below him trying to find out where he was.

"Bully," he ordered, "take this map back to *le patron* and see if he can recognize where we are."

De Gaulle put on his glasses, squinted at the map, peered outside for a long moment; then he turned back, jabbed his finger at a bump of land at the tip of Normandy, and announced, "We're here, just east of Cherbourg." Bully scurried forward.

De Marmier, meanwhile, had found their bearings. They were indeed just east of Cherbourg, at the precise spot de Gaulle had indicated. Already de Marmier was sloping down to land on an improvised fighter strip below.

As the plane slid down the waffled prefabricated runway, a small red light on Bully's instrument panel started to blink on and off. It was the warning light of the last reserve tank of the Lodestar *France*. It meant that the plane had exactly 120 seconds of fuel left on board. By that margin of just two minutes, Charles de Gaulle had come safely home to France —and not to a tragic end in the waters of the English Channel.

No one was at this tiny landing strip of Maupertus to greet him. There was no fanfare, no crowd, only mud and a fine Norman drizzle. His aide Claude Guy walked toward a barn that had been turned into the landing field's administration building. A bored noncommissioned officer stepped out and fixed Guy with the snout of his submachine gun. "What," he asked, "are you doing here? And who have you got on that plane?"

"You can put away your machine gun," Guy told him. The man he had on the plane, he announced, "is General de Gaulle."

De Gaulle and his party drove into Cherbourg in a puffing *gazogène*. In that battered seaport, the exhausted and dirty party could find only one razor blade with which to shave. De Gaulle was honored with its first use. The other members of his party passed it around in order of their seniority. Then de Gaulle asked Guy to do two things: get him some paper on which he could write a speech, and arrange an appointment with Eisenhower as soon as possible.

A few minutes later in the prefecture of Cherbourg, General Koenig told de Gaulle, "There's been an uprising in Paris." The general reacted with a rare display of emotion. His political foes had thrown down the challenge he had suspected was coming. The die was now cast. Before nightfall, he was determined he must have Eisenhower's decision to march on Paris.

* * *

Alexandre Parodi was late. He pushed aside his half-eaten lunch, meticulously prepared by his Paris headquarters' sole prisoner, a German mess steward locked between meals into Saint-Phalle's greenhouse. Gesturing to two of his aides, Roland Pré and Émile Laffon, Parodi got up from the table, picked up a black briefcase full of documents, and left for a meeting with his military counterpart, Jacques Chaban-Delmas. He, too, had an objective to achieve by nightfall. He hoped to preserve Paris for de Gaulle, for history, with the only thing that seemed capable, that midday, of saving it from destruction—Nordling's truce.

Waiting for him outside was a black Citroën driven by a pretty girl in a blue uniform. Around her shirt-sleeve was an armband with the Croix de Lorraine. Saint-Phalle watched them from a window as they drove away. "How wonderful," he mused. "Liberation is so close we can drive around now in chauffeur-driven cars."

9

AT THE BOTTOM OF an underground fortress 210 miles from the rainy landing strip on which Charles de Gaulle had come home to France, Generalleutnant Hans Speidel, forty-one, waited for the return of his new commander in chief, Generalfeldmarschall Walther Model. "WII" was the code name of this new headquarters of Army Group B, buried in an abandoned rock quarry outside the village of Margival, a few miles from Soissons 60 miles north of Paris. Four years earlier, from this underground labyrinth of corridors, conference rooms and communications centers, Adolf Hitler himself had planned to command the invasion of England. Now, in the neon-lit sterility of its rooms, Generalfeldmarschall Model was condemned to supervise a less glorious endeavor, the Wehrmacht's retreat from France. In the forty-eight hours since Model had left to inspect his new command, the imperious orders of OKW had accumulated on Speidel's desk. Those orders had left, in the mind of this mild-mannered man who was Model's chief of staff, no illusions about the fate Hitler had ordained for the capital of France. There would be little that he could do to prevent it. Deeply compromised in the July 20 plot, Speidel already suspected his own days in this headquarters were numbered.

When his door opened and Model burst in unannounced, a surprised Hans Speidel closed the thick leather book before him. This morning, this doctor of philosophy from the University of Tübingen was reading the third volume of the *Essais* of Montaigne.

The usually energetic little field marshal, Speidel remembers, was exhausted. His face was unshaven, his features drawn. An uncharacteristic depression clouded over him. Model slumped into a chair. The inspection trip he had just finished, he told Speidel, had been a nightmare to rival his worst ordeals on the eastern front. He had been stunned to find that the situation was far worse than he had expected.

Everywhere, his men were exhausted and disheartened. The Front, if indeed it was a front, was in shambles. That trip had shown Hitler's man of miracles what his first miracle would have to be. Somehow, Model would have to bring order back to the chaos of the western front. Somewhere on that overstretched and disintegrating front, Model would have to gamble for the time to regroup his battered forces. Despite his categoric orders from a man to whom he was almost blindly loyal, despite the pile of formal communications Speidel had handed him, Model made his choice. He chose to gamble on Paris.

Two elements led him to that decision. The first was Choltitz. From the moment the insurrection had broken out, Choltitz had deliberately and systematically understated the extent of the troubles in Paris. The morning report from Gross Paris, sent at 8:20 this Sunday, August 20, announced "a quiet night. Only isolated and minor skirmishes in the morning." The reports for Saturday had been equally reassuring. From the reports before him that morning, Model had no reason to believe that there was any problem in Paris beyond a few "terrorist" actions.°

The second was the carefully considered weekly intelligence report of OB West's G2, Lt. Colonel I. G. Staubwasser. It had been completed the night before, and, as always, the heart of the report was its estimate of enemy intentions. "The Allies," the report declared, "with 53 divisions,† were preparing to push east along the Caen-Lisieux road and north and northwest from Dreux to try to encircle the German troops west of the Seine below Paris." At the same time, the report predicted, they would "strike east from Orléans, south of Paris."

It concluded: "There is no immediate danger of a major attack against Paris." And, as a final corroboration, the morning reports before Model indicated only "reconnaissance" activity on the sweep of front before the capital of France. Everything, he told Speidel, confirmed what he already be-

° Twenty years later, in Baden-Baden, von Choltitz revealed why he deliberately understated the troubles in Paris to his commander. Like most German generals, he was wary of Model's fast and impetuous temper. He did not want to draw his attention to him and to Paris.

† As was consistently the case, the German generals overestimated the size of the Allied forces facing them. In fact, there were only 39 Allied divisions in Normandy that day.

lieved: the Allies were not going to attack Paris directly. Thus
reassured there was no immediate threat to the city, Model
decided his first effort would be to extricate his menaced
troops west of the Seine below Paris. Before the Allies could
trap them, he would pull them back across the Seine. Then he
would work on the "fortified belt" Hitler had assigned him as
a first task. When the reinforcements promised in OKW's
orders—the 26th and 27th SS Panzer Divisions—arrived, they
and any spare elements of the Seventh Army he had available
could be moved through the city to a tight defensive position
on its outskirts. To Army Group B's G3, Colonel Hans von
Tempelhof, Model dictated the series of orders that would
put his first decisions as commander in the west into effect.
He neglected one thing. He did not tell his commander in
Gross Paris that two Panzer divisions had been earmarked for
him by OKW. It was an oversight that would have grave
consequences.

When Model left, Speidel stood pensively in the center of
his office. On its walls were the three engravings he had
bought as a young student at the Sorbonne fourteen years
earlier. Through all these years they had followed him everywhere he went, even down to this underground fortress.
Drawn in the eighteenth century, they showed the Tuileries,
Versailles and Notre-Dame. For a moment the bespectacled
Speidel wondered if they, too, would go down to destruction
as a part of the mad disaster into which Hitler had led Europe.

• • •

No engravings decorated the Hotel Meurice headquarters
of Dietrich von Choltitz. Behind his desk, opposite his map of
Paris, Count von Arnim had hung a huge map of the Normandy front. On it von Choltitz could follow the same Allied
double thrust around Paris that had been so evident to
Model's intelligence chief 60 miles away. He had expected it.
His estimates that day were that the Allied attack on the city
itself "wouldn't come before early September."

When that attack came, von Choltitz expected to defend
Paris. It would be, this dour little Prussian now realized, a
thoroughly disagreeable task. But he expected to do it; his
mission in Paris was still defined in the words of von Kluge

shortly after his arrival: "Paris will be defended and you will defend it."

Hitler's idea, he realized, was to turn the city into a *Festung Paris* and fight for it house by house. It would mean incalculable damage to the city. But it was, and Choltitz himself had to admit it, "a sound military idea." To do it as Hitler expected it to be done would require five divisions. He knew he would never get that many from the battered armies of the west. But with three divisions, von Choltitz knew he could turn Paris into a murderous battlefield that would tie up the enemy for several weeks—and turn the city into a slag heap. It would be an inglorious way to end his military career. But von Choltitz was aware that once those troops were assigned to his command, he would have no choice but to do it, and do it he would.

The little Prussian's moody reflections were interrupted by the imperious summons of the faceless black telephone on his desk. It was the phone which, through von Bressensdorf's switchboard above, linked him directly to OKW and Berlin. For the third time, Generaloberst Jodl was calling him. The rasping tone of his voice told von Choltitz that the Führer's chief of staff was in a state of high indignation.

The Führer, he said, wanted his personal explanation why OKW had not yet received a single report on the demolition he had been ordered to carry out in the Paris area. Von Choltitz was worried and embarrassed by his question. The four experts furnished by Berlin had finished their work that morning. Deposited in his office was the result of their work, the carefully prepared plans for the destruction of well over 200 industrial plants, including, Choltitz had noted with ironic amusement, two bicycle factories. Soon those men would be back in Berlin. He could no longer cover his failure in starting the destruction he had been ordered to carry out by claiming their preliminary work was not completed. Trapped by the impatient man on the other end of the line, Choltitz gave an explanation. It was the only one available, and one he quickly regretted. He had not been able to start the demolition, he told Jodl, because his men had been occupied fighting "terrorist" outbreaks all across the capital.

Jodl, Choltitz recalled later, was "flabbergasted." These words were the first indication OKW had had of how serious the situation in Paris had become. Jodl was silent for a long,

shocked moment. He had just left Hitler's first daily conference. Hitler's orders were still scrawled in his shorthand
note pad. Again he had stressed "the greatest importance was
to be assigned to the defense of Paris, and, as a result, every
measure must be taken for its defense."

The Führer, Jodl told von Choltitz, would be furious to
learn trouble had broken out in Paris. He warned his Paris
commander that he must take every measure possible to restore order in the city.

Then, carefully choosing his words, speaking in a dry,
measured voice to force on von Choltitz the full impact of
what he was saying, Jodl declared, "Whatever happens, the
Führer expects you to carry out the widest destruction possible in the area assigned to your command."

            •   •   •

Listening to the soft Norman rain splash the trees outside,
the Supreme Commander paced the wooden floors of the map
tent at his Shellburst advance headquarters at Granville, at
the base of the Cotentin Peninsula. Dwight Eisenhower was
waiting, patient and determined, for his visitor. He thought he
knew exactly what Charles de Gaulle wanted this rainy August
day: Paris. He was determined he should not have it yet.

Like de Gaulle, Eisenhower had learned a few hours earlier
of the outbreak of fighting in the city. He had been "damned
mad" when he found out about it. In his view, the Paris uprising posed "just the kind of a situation I didn't want, a situation that wasn't under our control, that might force us to
change our plans before we were ready for it." It was to
force a change in those plans, Eisenhower was sure, that de
Gaulle was coming to his Shellburst headquarters. He resented
it. He saw it as another example of de Gaulle's annoying
habit of "trying to get us to change our plans to accommodate his political needs." For this American general at the
head of the Allied armies, "the political aspects of Paris
were secondary." He had only one concern: fighting Germans.
He would let nothing, not even Paris, slow him down. As
he heard the footfalls of his approaching visitor, he vowed
once more "not to let myself get committed to Paris."

Dour and moody, Charles de Gaulle stepped over the wet
grass leading to the Supreme Commander's tent. He had come

Under Napoleon's Arch—"Deutschland, Deutschland Über Alles"

Every day for four years, from the day of Paris's fall, June 14, 1940, to the day of its liberation, August 25, 1944, a Nazi band and a battalion of soldiers circled the Arc de Triomphe and at the stroke of noon marched down the Champs Elysées to the Place de la Concorde. Like some massive metronome, their footfalls tolled out to Paris and to all France the passage of another day of occupation. Above, under the stroke of a drum major's baton, the daily parade begins.

The Conquerors Rode First Class...

First-class carriages in the Paris métro were mainly occupied by the soldiers of the Wehrmacht [ABOVE]. In the city's streets, empty of civilian automobiles, others [RIGHT] used the occupation taxi, the velocab, here towed by a lady bicycle rider.

PHOTO ROGER SCHALL

...and Played Tourist in Their Captured Capital

Towed by a bicycle built for two, a pair of occupation newlyweds [LEFT] ride off to their wedding reception in a super velocab. Their wedding guests pedal along behind them.

"A Man Who Never Wavered in the Execution of an Order"

On the strength of that recommendation, on August 3, 1944, Adolf Hitler chose General Dietrich von Choltitz to defend—and destroy—the city of Paris. Above and lower left, Choltitz at the scene of his greatest triumph, the Siege of Sebastopol. Although wounded himself, Choltitz, at the head of the 347 survivors of his 4,800-man regiment, captured the Black Sea port on July 27, 1942. At lower right, Choltitz, his wife Uberta, and his daughters, Maria Angelika and Anna Barbara; missing is his son Timo, three months old in August 1944.

General von Choltitz's troops [ABOVE] parade past the windows of his Paris headquarters in the Hotel Meurice on the rue de Rivoli opposite the Tuileries. One of them, Private Fritz Gottschalk [WHITE ARROW] will parade down the same street again in a few days, this time as a prisoner.

Like trees, these signposts sprang from the streets of Paris in 1940, guiding German drivers across the city. In the summer of 1944 appeared a new sign, bringing hope to Parisians: "Zur Normandie Front."

To Ravage Paris—
Torpedoes and
Big Bertha's
Heir

Some of the tools General von Choltitz was to have used to accomplish the destruction of Paris. In the St. Cloud auto tunnel west of Paris [ABOVE], *Pilz,* the torpedo depot and factory of the Kriegsmarine. Stored there in 1944 were, in the words of one German, "enough torpedoes to shoot two wars through." The siege mortar KARL [BELOW]. First used to blow apart the defense of Sebastopol and Stalingrad, the KARL could hurl a 2½-ton shell four miles. One was enough to destroy the best part of a city block. It was the most destructive artillery piece invented by pre-atomic man, and on August 14, 1944, Hitler ordered it sent to Paris.

A Swede, a German— and 2,070 French Lives

Afraid the Gestapo would murder the political detainees left in their Paris prisons when the Allies aproached the city (as they had elsewhere in France), Swedish Consul General Raoul Nordling [ABOVE, RIGHT] set out to bargain for those prisoners' lives with the capital's German command. To smooth his way, he enlisted the aid of Emil "Bobby" Bender [RIGHT], deputy commander of German military intelligence in France and a dedicated anti-Nazi. Together, the two men saved 2,070 French Resistants in four Paris prisons from almost certain execution in the Gestapo's hidden death chambers, like the one below, found in the cellar of the Air Ministry only a few yards from the Eiffel Tower.

AGENCE FRANCE PRESSE

AGENCE FRANCE PRESSE

US ARMY PHOTO

The Communist — Colonel Henri "Rol" Tanguy, head of the Paris Resistance and artisan of the popular uprising de Gaulle and Eisenhower had proscribed. "Paris," he cried, defending his action, "is worth 200,000 dead!"

The Resistance Heroine — Marie Hélène Lefaucheux. Her husband commanded the Paris Resistance until he was arrested by the Gestapo, June 7, 1944. On August 15, Marie Hélène learned he was to be shipped to Buchenwald with the last convoy of prisoners to leave Paris. She followed him —on a bicycle—and later rescued him from the death camp.

The Gaullist—Jacques Chaban-Delmas, 29, a tennis champion, a general, and de Gaulle's senior military representative in France. Fearing a Communist-led insurrection that would reduce Paris to ruins, he made a clandestine trip to London, August 8, 1944, to warn the Allies of the danger growing in the city.

The Liberators—Lt. General Omar Bradley [WITHOUT CAP], commander of the 12th U.S. Army Group, and General Dwight Eisenhower, the Supreme Commander, outside Bradley's headquarters.

The Writer—Ernest "Papa" Hemingway [WITH HELMET] with some of the Germans captured by his band of FFI irregulars on the outskirts of Paris.

German Tank Traps and a Defiant Barricade

A dead German soldier [ABOVE] sprawls behind one of the hastily erected barbed wire and steel spike barriers with which the Wehrmacht surrounded its Paris strongpoints in the closing days of the insurrection. This one was near the Hotel Raphael, a few yards from the Etoile.

At right, a typical Paris barricade, a heap of bedsteads, sandbags, paving stones and even a car. Others were even more picturesque. On one, an enthusiastic antique dealer heaped up the treasures of his cellar; the bulwark of another was an enormous five-man *pissotière*. Some, like the one at the intersection of the boulevards St.-Michel and St.-Germain, nicknamed "Death's Crossroads," were masterpieces of improvised engineering. By the time the Allies arrived, over 400 barricades had been thrown up in the streets of Paris.

PHOTO PIERRE ROUGHOL

On the rue de la Huchette, opposite the besieged Prefecture of Police, Colette Briant [ABOVE], wearing the Croix de Lorraine and a helmet taken from a fallen member of the Wehrmacht, takes charge of the barricades.

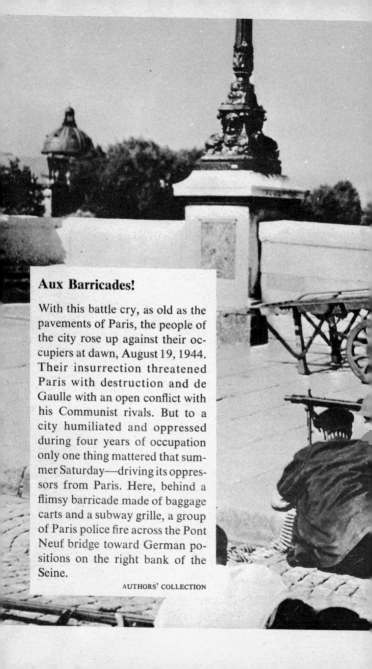

Aux Barricades!

With this battle cry, as old as the pavements of Paris, the people of the city rose up against their occupiers at dawn, August 19, 1944. Their insurrection threatened Paris with destruction and de Gaulle with an open conflict with his Communist rivals. But to a city humiliated and oppressed during four years of occupation only one thing mattered that summer Saturday—driving its oppressors from Paris. Here, behind a flimsy barricade made of baggage carts and a subway grille, a group of Paris police fire across the Pont Neuf bridge toward German positions on the right bank of the Seine.

Just Ahead for the 2nd French Armored Division—

To lead the advance on Paris, General Eisenhower chose the only French unit on his Normandy front, the 2nd French Armored Division. It was a gesture much appreciated by his often difficult ally Charles de Gaulle. Major Jacques Massu [WITH CIGARETTE], leads the advance elements of the division through the outskirts of the capital.

Paris, and a Promise Four Years in the Keeping

August 25, 1944—Through the morning mists still lying over the countryside, the tanks and men of the 2nd Division parade past their commander. General Jacques Philippe Leclerc [IN KEPI]. Just four years earlier to the day, crossing the Wouri River in the Cameroons with 17 men and three pirogues, the dour French general had vowed to come home one day to liberate the capital of his country.

An Occupation Ends as It Began—in the Clatter of Panzer Treads

home that morning—in a plane running out of gas, to an almost empty airstrip manned by an indifferent functionary, to a shave with a borrowed razor blade—in order to lead his country. It was a nation in which millions knew his voice, but did not know his face. He was a ghost to those millions, an ideal; and he had now to give himself flesh and blood, to embody the ideal which must now become a political reality. For him, the political aspects of Paris were supreme; with its Communists already clamoring for authority, the city was for de Gaulle a personal and a national imperative. As he stepped past the canvas flaps into the Supreme Commander's tent, de Gaulle, no less than Eisenhower, was determined that his will should prevail at this meeting.

• • •

Colonel Lionel de Marmier, from the cockpit of the Lodestar *France*, watched the three men tramping slowly through the ankle-deep grass toward the plane. Two paces ahead, hands clasped behind his back, de Gaulle walked alone. His head slightly bowed, his shoulders hunched, he seemed to his pilot "more melancholy, more distant" than he had ever seen him before. "All the weight of the world," thought de Marmier, seemed to be bearing down on de Gaulle's heavy shoulders.

Charles de Gaulle had failed: Eisenhower had not agreed to modify his plans and move immediately on Paris.

Their meeting had come right to the point. Moving from map to map, tapping his charts with his rubber-tipped pointer, Eisenhower had explained to de Gaulle "what we were up to, and what our plans were." Sweeping over his maps, Eisenhower sketched out the details of the planned double envelopment of the French capital outlined in his post-Neptune planning study. A final draft of that document had reached his desk just forty-eight hours earlier, twenty-four hours before the tricolor went up over the Prefecture of Police. With his fast-changing front, the Supreme Commander had set no timetable for the liberation of Paris. But to the experienced eyes of General de Gaulle, the message in Eisenhower's maps had held no mystery. Eisenhower's timetable was not his.

De Gaulle, Eisenhower was to recall, had "immediately

asked us to reconsider on Paris. He made no bones about it; he said there was a serious menace from the Communists in the city."

He had warned the Supreme Commander that if he delayed in moving in, he would risk finding "a disastrous political situation in the city, one that might be disruptive to the Allied war effort."

Despite his high regard for de Gaulle's judgment, Eisenhower had refused to change his plans. De Gaulle suspected his hesitation was political;° the Supreme Commander would later insist it had been "purely military." For Eisenhower, it was "too early." He was still concerned that "we might get ourselves in a helluva fight there." †

For the stooped and solemn man walking back to Marmier's plane, Eisenhower's answer now posed a cruel dilemma. It had faced de Gaulle with a terrible decision. A few moments before, he had hinted to the frowning American before him what it might be. Stiffly correct, de Gaulle had told Eisenhower the liberation of Paris was a matter of such prime national importance to France that, if he had to, he was prepared to withdraw the 2nd French Armored Division from the Allied Command and send it to Paris on his own authority. ‡ Paris, for de Gaulle, was so crucial he was prepared to tear asunder four years of Allied unity to get it.

° "I had the sentiment," de Gaulle wrote in the second volume of his *Memoirs*, page 296, "that Eisenhower shared my way of thinking but, for reasons which were not wholly strategic, he could not do anything about it yet." It was an allusion to his conviction Washington had endorsed Laval's last-minute maneuvers with Herriot.

† One of the reasons for his concern might have been a pair of messages awaiting analysis in his intelligence section. The first, dated August 19, read: "26th Panzer Division moving out of Denmark; destination unknown." The second, dated twenty-four hours later, read: "Ground sources indicate 26th SS Panzer Division scheduled for Paris area." Those messages indicated how quickly Hitler's orders had been carried out—and how effective Allied intelligence in the occupied countries was. They also tended to confirm Eisenhower's own suspicions that day: "that Model would stick two or three divisions in there for a wasting house-to-house fight . . . that he'd try to give us a good little battle for a while." Eisenhower's idea was "to avoid his little battle" and his own supply problem, and, by the time Model woke up, "we'd be up around Reims somewhere, and his troops would just drop into our laps."

‡ Eisenhower had smiled; he had not taken the polite threat seriously. He was convinced the 2nd Armored "couldn't have moved a mile if I didn't want it to, and wouldn't have." Later, at a tenser moment of the war, during the Battle of the Bulge, de Gaulle was to make a similar threat, this time about the divisions of the French First Army the Supreme Commander wanted to pull out of Strasbourg. Then an angry Eisenhower told him, "General, I'll keep those troops in Strasbourg as long as I can. But if you want to take

Turning to his young and worried aide, de Gaulle asked one question before climbing back into his Lodestar *France:* "Where is General Leclerc?"

10

FOR THE COMMUNIST CHIEF of the Paris FFI, Nordling's truce, beginning to take hold in the city, was an act of treason. Since learning of it in an early morning phone call, "Colonel Rol" had devoted all his efforts to breaking it. To this blunt Breton, it was a personal as well as a political betrayal. For four years, in lonely clandestine combat, he had waited for this moment when he would lead an open fight against his country's conquerors. No one was going to deprive him of that fight now.

Just as his Gaullist rivals were using every tactic available to impose the truce on the city, so Rol used every means he could find to smash it. By phone, by courier, in person, Rol reiterated his command of the day before: "The order is insurrection," he said. "As long as there is a single German left in the streets of Paris, we shall fight." To his disciplined Communist-led commandos, the FTP (Francs-Tireurs et Partisans), he issued an urgent order to attack the Germans wherever they could find them. He would not let the sound of gunfire disappear from the streets of Paris. Silence would indicate the truce had been accepted. By noon, to support him, the Communists began to plaster the walls of the city with thousands of posters denouncing the cease-fire as a trick to "exterminate the working classes of Paris," and allow "those stirred by hatred and fear of the people to work their dirty deals."

With all the obstinacy of his Breton blood, Rol sought to reforge the chains of his FFI command short-circuited by the

those divisions back, you go right ahead. Just remember one thing. You won't get one more cartridge, one more pound of supplies, or one more gallon of gasoline. But if you want those divisions back, General, you go right ahead and take them back."

Gaullists in their efforts to undercut him. No battle of the
liberation would be more venomous than this, no battlefield
more bizarre than those on which it was being fought. To
Yvon Morandat, the bicycle rider who believed the Communists had tried to kill him, it seemed as though "the Communists were ready for a new *Commune*, and we Gaullists
had been selected to play the role of the gentlemen of
Versailles." In André Tollet's mind, the Gaullists, with their
truce, had committed "treason," and Parodi was striving "to
neutralize the Resistance and hold the FFI in check until
de Gaulle was ready to liberate the city himself."

For both the Gaullists and their foes, the common battleground was the massive Prefecture of Police. Inside its
labyrinth of offices and corridors, the two factions fought for
its control. Their heated debates filled its corridors that afternoon with almost as much passion as the fight with the Germans had the day before. Maurice Kriegel-Valrimont, a
Communist planted in the Prefecture to swing its rank and file
away from Gaullist direction, urged the police to ignore their
leaders. During one fiery exchange, Alexandre de Saint-Phalle,
the Gaullist treasurer, grabbed the plump Communist's hand
in his. "If you go on with this insurrection of yours," he cried
angrily, "this hand will be covered with the blood of thousands
of slaughtered Parisians." Valrimont, Saint-Phalle recalled
later, stared quizzically at his hand.

A few doors away, in another meeting room, Lorrain Cruse,
a young aide of Jacques Chaban-Delmas, pleaded with the
unyielding man before him to accept the truce. He despaired
because the price of this Communist political move would be
200,000 dead and a blackened ruin of a city. The stolid man
opposite him stared disdainfully. Then, with a thump of his
open hand on the table before him, Rol answered in a voice
no less passionate than that of his interlocutor. Cruse would
never forget his words.

"Paris," Rol vowed, "is worth 200,000 dead."

• • •

Little by little, under Rol's relentless prodding, the insurrection regained the momentum it had lost in the early hours
of the day. The sound of gunfire, so conspicuously absent at
midmorning, gradually came back to the streets of Paris. In

disciplined bands all over the city, Rol's Communist FTP opened fire on passing German patrols. The Germans, many of whom scorned von Choltitz's truce, returned their fire with zest, or started the shooting themselves. Like a sweater unraveling, the truce began to fall apart.

Sunday strollers, brought out by curiosity or custom, found themselves caught in sudden cross fire.° Householders who had happily hoisted the tricolor from their windows a few hours earlier found they were now a target for roving German patrols.

In the tangle of twisting alleys between the Seine and Saint-Germain-des-Prés, on streets with names as quaint as the rue du Chat-qui-Pêche and rue Gît-le-Coeur,† hidden FFI squads trapped four truckloads of German soldiers. Some of them, their uniforms blazing from the splatterings of Molotov cocktails, ran screaming through those scenic little side streets, human torches in a thousand-year-old haven of human amusement.

And the city organized itself. In hidden presses, the men who had printed clandestine newspapers now rolled out handbills on how to make a Molotov cocktail or build a barricade. Paris's druggists, with their supplies of potassium chlorate, became the keepers of its arsenals. The hospitals, long and secretly organized, were now taken over by the Resistance. In apartments and stores, medical students and young girls organized emergency clinics. Volunteer stretcher-bearers, most of them teen-agers, posted themselves across the city. In Les Halles, FFI warehousemen seized all the food supplies they could find for a series of restaurants turned into soup kitchens. They offered hungry and food-short householders a *plat unique*, one plate of hot soup a day.

But in all the bustling city, nowhere was the work of Resistance organized with more flair than it was in a square gray building at the place du Palais-Royal. There, in the House of Molière, the men and women of the Comédie Française, the national theater troupe of France, turned this classical theater into a hospital and barricaded strongpoint. Marie Bell, the husky-voiced queen of the French theater, Lise Delamare and

---

° Despite the early promise of the truce, 106 Frenchmen were killed and 357 wounded this Sunday, a figure only slightly lower than that of the day before, when 125 had been killed and 479 wounded.

† Literally, the streets of "the fishing cat" and "where the heart lies."

Mony Dalmès, two of its prettiest young actresses, rummaged through their wardrobe trunks for the seventeenth-century sleeping gowns which served them as improvised nursing dresses. Among the volunteer stretcher-bearers was a quiet man with horn-rimmed glasses. He took the night duty because it would, he thought, be quieter. He wanted to record his impressions of these days on paper. His name was Jean Paul Sartre. The actors broke out a carefully nourished cache of arms from the boiler room. To supplement their meager hoard, they ransacked their prop trunks. Jacques Dacqmine put on the costume of his last film. He had played a French World War I army captain, and had kept the old Winchester rifle he had been assigned for the part. Another—Georges Marchal, the wavy-haired darling of the nation's young— armed himself with a rare vintage weapon. It was an eighteenth-century blunderbuss.

11

A CURL OF GRAY cloud along the horizon seemed, to the practiced eye of Dietrich von Choltitz, to promise new storms to the city before him. As he did each day after lunch, Choltitz stood on his little Hotel Meurice balcony and inhaled a quiet breath of the warm August air. Nothing in the world at that moment could have pleased the chunky little German general more than a prolongation of the midday torpor into which the city seemed to have sunk. But, already, he could hear the muffled snapping of small-arms fire bubbling up in little intermittent gasps of noise all along the horizon before him. Their echoes struck a disquieting response in Choltitz.

Just as it had done for his adversaries, the truce suggested by Consul General Nordling had brought an unexpected respite for Choltitz. Without it, he thought, looking toward the line of treetops shrouding the Seine, the Prefecture of Police—and with it, perhaps the whole Ile de la Cité—would already be a heap of rubble. It was not in itself a thought to chill Choltitz. His orders were, after all, to maintain order in the city at any cost. For the commander of Gross Paris, the truce had been, above all, a last chance to avoid a bloody showdown that would have put the city and his troops into irreversible conflict. There was little, to his mind, to be gained from that conflict if it could be avoided. He had better uses for his troops. Now, however, that last chance seemed to be slipping rapidly away.

As he listened to those spreading sounds of gunfire, von Choltitz thought back on the conversation he had had with Jodl barely an hour earlier. The admission he had been forced to make, the unwilling warning he had given OKW of the gravity of the Paris situation, had ended his hopes of diverting the Führer's eyes from his troubled command. Now, he knew, Hitler would give him no rest. The little German realized that if the Swedish diplomat could not restore order to the city with his truce, Hitler would compel him to do it with violence —or put someone in his place who would.

Once again, the tinkling of a telephone interrupted his thoughts. He walked back into his office and picked up his phone, this time the ordinary one. From it he heard the voice of a caller demanding to speak personally to the commander of Gross Paris.

"Speaking," rasped von Choltitz.

His caller identified himself. It was an officer of the Military Tribunal in Saint-Cloud. His voice inflated with pride, he announced to Choltitz that he had seized, in a car stuffed with arms and documents, three civilians who claimed they were "ministers of de Gaulle." It seemed, he said, the most important capture they had made in Paris in months. He asked von Choltitz whether the men should be summarily executed for carrying arms, or handed over to the SD who were claiming them. Von Choltitz's troops had the order to shoot on sight civilians carrying arms, and he followed his first instincts.

"Ja, natürlich," he said, "shoot them." Then he had a second thought. If indeed these men were what they pretended to be, General de Gaulle's representatives in this city, then, Choltitz realized, they might be men capable of bringing order back to the capital.

"Bring them to my office," von Choltitz ordered. "I want to see them before you execute them."

Shortly before their arrival, a breathless Consul General

Nordling and "Bobby" Bender appeared in his office. An extraordinary coincidence had brought them there. On the avenue Henri-Martin, in the middle of a casual Sunday stroll, a pretty Parisienne had seen three handcuffed men sweep past her in a Wehrmacht truck. Among them she had recognized her fiancé. Nordling begged von Choltitz to find these three men, to get them out of the hands of the SS before they were executed. They were, he told the German, the men with whom he had negotiated the truce the night before. Without them, the leadership of the city would surely pass to the Communists. One of them was even a minister of Charles de Gaulle. His name, Nordling told von Choltitz, was Alexandre Parodi.

The general's face twisted into a rare smile. "Herr Consul," he said, "it seems those are the three gentlemen I'm waiting for now."

•   •   •

The commander of Gross Paris tugged lightly at his monocle and stared in curiosity at the three men being pushed toward him by two enormous German MPs. Von Choltitz had often wondered in the past twenty-four hours what the men leading this faceless uprising against him looked like. Would they be, as his intelligence service claimed, "hoodlums" or "Communists"? To his surprise, the German saw before him three timid men, little different from any of the thousands of clerks filling the streets of Paris after a working day.

He studied them. Then, unable to suppress a faint smile, he expressed his amazement that three chiefs of a secret Resistance could have been stupid enough to wander the streets in broad daylight in a chauffeur-driven car bulging with arms and compromising documents. "Do you take my soldiers for boy scouts?" he asked.

But von Choltitz had not brought them to his office to exercise his capacity for scorn. They were there to hear from his own mouth the dimensions of the disaster awaiting Paris if the truce which they had accepted should fall apart. All across the city, he said, firing had started up again. As military governor of Paris, responsible for order and for the safety of his own troops, he would have no choice but to answer violence with violence. He was absolutely determined, he warned the three men before him, to keep his communications in and through Paris open. If fighting broke out again, the consequences for the capital and its citizens could be tragic.

Von Choltitz saw Parodi pale sightly at his threat. He had taken an immediate dislike to this man. Stiff-necked and uncompromising, Parodi showed none of the humility it seemed to von Choltitz his position dictated. Now the Frenchman answered him. He told von Choltitz he, too, wanted order in the city. But he added, "You, General, command an army. You give orders and your men obey. The Resistance is made up of many movements. I do not control them all."

Von Choltitz looked at him for a long moment. A few minutes earlier he had had an intense desire to have this arrogant little Frenchman shot in the Tuileries garden outside his window. However, he still hoped something might come from this meeting. If indeed his warnings had reached those men, their authority might help maintain Nordling's truce. Turning to the Swede, he said, "Herr Consul, since these men were arrested after the cease-fire, I've decided to place them in your custody."

With those words, the German got up and came around his desk. He asked Parodi if he was an officer. The Frenchman replied he was, in the reserve. "Then," said von Choltitz, "between officers, this gesture is allowed." The Prussian general extended his hand to the man whose life he had just spared.

Parodi refused to take it.

Nordling saw the color flare in von Choltitz's proud and injured face. It was a gesture von Choltitz, twenty years later, would still recall with bitterness. But his anger was no greater than that of the furious officer of the Feldgendarmerie from whom he had taken the three prisoners. As the officer marched the men down the stairs of the Meurice, the alert ear of another officer heard him mumble, "We'll get them." "Bobby" Bender pushed ahead of the little group and into the street. On his left, at the curb of the rue de Rivoli, he saw a black Packard with its motor idling. Beside the driver, a man in civilian clothes watched the group. In front of him, at the tip of the dashboard, Bender caught the black glint of a submachine gun.

The Abwehr agent walked over to the open window of

Nordling's car. He told the Swede and the three Frenchmen with him not to leave until he had started his own car.

"Bobby" pressed the ignition of his Citroën coupé a few yards away. Under its hood was a secret which would, in a few seconds, save the lives of Nordling and the three Gaullist leaders with him. Bender, a prewar Citroën agent, had had installed in his car a triple-carburetor racing engine that made it the fastest vehicle in Paris. He saw Nordling's car start. Then, as he expected, the black Packard slid away right behind it. Bender bore down on his accelerator.

The screeching of the tires brought von Choltitz rushing to his balcony. At the end of the rue de Rivoli, at the mouth of the place de la Concorde, he saw Bender's Citroën coupé cut at right angles in front of the black Packard, barring its path. Disappearing across the square, its little Swedish flag flapping as it went, was Nordling's black Citroën. Von Choltitz understood. The predatory men of the SD, a law unto themselves, had tried to reclaim these Gaullists he had just freed. They had been prepared to machine-gun them, and Sweden's consul general along with them, almost on his own doorstep.

"*Mein Gott,*" thought von Choltitz, "they were lucky."

* * *

For dinner, the two men peeled pears by candlelight. In the aging villa of the village of Saint-Nom-la-Bretèche where they had taken refuge for the night, that handful of overripe fruit was the only thing they had found to eat. Beyond the villa's rusting seventeenth-century gates, they could hear rain splashing the cobbled streets and, more ominous, the passing footfalls of the SS battalion occupying the little town. Major Roger Gallois, and his guide, Dr. Robert Monod, were dejected. In half a day of trying, they had been able to get no farther than this village, only 18 miles from Paris, well within the German lines.

Gallois, chief of staff of Rol's Paris FFI, had been ordered to follow Monod through the German lines on the most important mission he had ever undertaken for the Resistance. He had been sent by Rol to ask the Allies for a massive parachute drop of arms, the arms with which Rol hoped to finish his insurrection, and install his triumphant Communist-led Resistance in Paris.

Gallois and Monod were old friends; but it was through purest coincidence they were together in this damp villa. Inspector of health for the area around Paris, and at the same time head of the area's medical activities for the Resistance, Dr. Monod had a car and enough German passes to get himself to Berlin if he wanted to. It was from this rare privilege that the idea for this mission had been born.

For weeks Monod had watched the Communists plant party agents in every one of his Resistance chains, infiltrating even his own office. Monod saw the insurrection as the first step toward a Communist *coup d'état.* He was determined to thwart them if he could. Saturday night he had discovered through one of his agents a hole in the German lines through which an emissary could be slipped to the Allies. To Rol, he proposed to guide a man through it to "establish a liaison with the Allies and ask for arms." As he hoped he would, Rol grabbed at the idea.

In this damp and dreary villa, in the quiet and reasoned voice of his profession, Monod told Gallois that to ask for an arms drop on Paris would be a cruel and reckless folly. To ask the Americans to drop so much as a "single cartridge" on Paris would serve only one end, to prepare a Communist *coup d'état.* Instead of arms, the doctor pleaded, the goal of the mission should be to get the Allies, and above all de Gaulle, into Paris as quickly as possible.

Gallois knew Rol was in no hurry to see the Allies' Shermans, with their great white stars stamped on their armor plate, roll into the streets of Paris. What the Communist FFI leader wanted was Eisenhower's machine guns, not his soldiers. To get those arms, Rol had committed the tactical error of sending on this mission perhaps the only man on his staff who would be receptive to the pressing plea of surgeon Monod.

The one candle lighting the room sputtered out in its own wax and a long silence filled the darkened villa. Finally Gallois spoke. "Robert," he said, "I think you're right."

As the rain lashed the gray tiles above them, the two men fell asleep. In a few hours, Roger Gallois, an unknown French Resistant, disguised as a male nurse, would achieve what even Charles de Gaulle had failed to do. He would persuade Dwight Eisenhower to change his plans and send his troops on Paris.

12

It was a night for conspiracy. The Norman apple orchard was black and silent under a moonless sky. Low and scattered among the trees, the peaked outlines of the tents were almost invisible. Dawn was still an hour away. At the edge of the narrow road leading out of the orchard toward the little hamlet of Écouché, a command car waited. Its lights were out; its motor idled gently. The tall figure stepping noiselessly over the dew-slicked grass got into the car and sat down beside its driver. With him, he carried a briefcase made from the skin of a katambouru, an antelope of Chad. In that briefcase was a slip of white paper and a 1/100,000 map stamped with the serial number 10G. At its center was a large, irregular black splotch, the city of Paris.

As the command car started to glide softly forward, another figure, striking at the wet grass with a cane, loomed out of the blackness. To the passenger in the car, he murmured three words: "You are lucky."

The man with the cane was General Jacques Philippe Leclerc, commander of the 2nd French Armored Division whose headquarters tents lay hidden in this orchard. Without authority, on his own responsibility, he had given the order for this stealthy departure.

For Lieutenant Colonel Jacques de Guillebon, thirty-four, the man to whom Leclerc had just murmured that brief au revoir, the road past Écouché led to the black splotch on his map. Of all the soldiers of the armies of liberation, he was the first to march on the capital of France. With 17 light tanks, 10 armored cars and two platoons of infantry, he was to "represent the French Army in a free capital," and become the first French military governor of Paris.

As Guillebon left, the other men of his select contingent softly into their vehicles and began to drive toward their assembly point just outside the village of Écouché. They had been picked from all the encampments of the armored division tucked into the Norman countryside so that their absence would be difficult to notice. Their canteens, their packs, their gas tanks bulged with enough ammunition, C rations and fuel to carry them to Strasbourg. Each officer, before leaving, had received a slip of yellow paper on which Guillebon himself had written the word "Confidential" and the most important single instruction he had to give them for the 122-mile trip ahead. It came down to one succinct phrase: "Avoid the Americans at all costs."

Alone and pensive on the steps of his command caravan, Leclerc listened to the sounds of Guillebon's command car fading away in the night, and reflected on this bold action he had just taken. He knew it was an act of open insubordination to the Allied Command on which he depended. But Leclerc had a pledge to honor, a pledge he had made to himself three years earlier at the first enemy position he had captured, a fort called Koufra, in the Libyan Desert. There, 1,800 miles from the capital of France, he had sworn he would one day liberate Paris.

Already other divisions of the Allied Command were striking close to the city while he and his men of the only French division on the Normandy front were impatiently biding their time in an apple orchard. He was afraid the Allies would move on to the city without him. Six days earlier he had written to General Patton, stating his desire to be relieved of his command if his division did not participate in the liberation of Paris. To be sure that honor did not entirely escape him, he had sent Guillebon driving down the road to Écouché.

Three days before Charles de Gaulle had threatened to extract the 2nd French Armored Division from Allied Command, Leclerc himself had independently prepared the division for just such a move. Dwight Eisenhower was wrong; the 2nd Armored Division could move without Allied help. It could move as far as Paris. For four days, on Leclerc's orders, his fuel trucks had charged a double ration, taking on four tons daily instead of two. His regimental commanders had not reported their vehicle losses, so they could go on claiming the fuel and ammunition rations for their destroyed machines. And, for the past three nights, distracting their United States sentries, the men of the division had requisitioned by moonlight the rest of the fuel and munitions they needed from Allied supply dumps. On this dark morning, the 2,000 vehicles and 16,000 men of the 2nd French Armored Division were ready to follow the tracks of Jacques de Guillebon's command car to Paris if Leclerc—or de Gaulle—gave them the order. But, despite all his frantic appeals to his United States superiors, Leclerc had received no order except "Sit still and be patient."

Now, on the steps of his caravan, Leclerc was content. Commanded by a Picardian like himself, a symbolic detachment of his division at least was on the high road to Paris. It was the road he himself would soon follow. He had only one preoccupation: that his American superiors not find out about his gesture until it was too late to stop it.

Before going back to sleep, he took a last precaution. He woke up Captain Alain de Boissieu, the commanding officer of his escort section. Gesturing with his cane toward a jeep and a tent just beyond him, Leclerc told de Boissieu to politely kidnap the two men in that tent for a day. "Take them on a little sightseeing trip," Leclerc ordered. Of all the 16,000 men in his division, Lieutenant Dick Rifkind and Captain Bob Hoye were the only individuals who might report Guillebon's disappearance to Leclerc's United States V Corps superiors. They were his American liaison officers.

• • •

The only sound in the room was the raw scratching of Dietrich von Choltitz's pen. Outside silence shrouded the darkened streets of Paris. At the center of the black splotch on map 10G, dawn was still an hour away.

Beside von Choltitz's elbow, wrapped in brown paper, was the most precious gift the mess of a Wehrmacht general could offer this summer, a sack of coffee. His aide, Corporal Helmut Mayer, had "requisitioned" it from the kitchen of the Hotel Meurice the night before. Unshaven, in his flannel dressing gown, von Choltitz finished the letter that would accompany that gift, the last he was to send for three and a half years, to his wife in Baden-Baden,

"Our task is hard," he wrote, "and our days grow difficult. I try always to do my duty, and must often ask God to help me find the paths on which it lies." Then he asked his wife if his four-month-old son, Timo, had started to cut his teeth, and told her to kiss their daughters Maria Angelika and Anna Barbara for him. "They must be proud of their father, no matter what the future holds," he said. When he heard the soft knock on his bedroom door, he had almost finished.

Standing in his darkened doorway, waiting to carry this last letter to Baden-Baden, was the only man in the city of Paris Dietrich von Choltitz trusted. Adolf von Carlowitz was his cousin, his confidant and adviser. Von Choltitz had brought him with him to Paris from the Hermann Göring airframe factory he directed in Berlin. Now Paris was in arms, and, under the protective mantle of this last hour of darkness, Adolf von Carlowitz was going home to Germany.

The two men embraced. *"Mach's gut, Dietz,"* von Carlowitz whispered to the unkempt little general in his flannel dressing gown. Then he turned quickly and was gone. Watching the door click shut behind him, von Choltitz wondered if he would ever see that man—or the woman to whom he carried a letter—again. He listened as the sound of his cousin's clacking leather heels faded down the hotel corridor. When they had died, a thought came to Dietrich von Choltitz. In this city of three and a half million people, he realized, he was now alone, totally, overwhelmingly, alone.

* * *

At the opposite end of Paris, another group of men slipped through the predawn darkness. Among the figures dropping noiselessly through an open trapdoor in the basement of the headquarters of the Paris Waters and Sewers Administration, was Dietrich von Choltitz's most implacable enemy, "Colonel Rol." Rol walked softly down the 138 stone steps to his new underground command post. At the bottom of the last step, an armor-plated metal door creaked open. Here, on the foundations of Paris among the skulls and skeletons of forty generations of Parisians, was the secret fortress from which he would now direct the battle for the streets of the city 90 feet above his head. Its code name was Duroc, for another French soldier, a marshal of Napoleon's armies. Its door led to a city under a city, the 300 miles of tunnels threading the foundations of Paris for its sewers, its métros and its cata-combs.

Stepping inside Duroc, throwing the beam of his flashlight over the room in a first satisfied inspection, Rol started with a surprise he could recall twenty years later. On the ventilating machine above his head, his flashlight had fallen on the plate bearing the name of its manufacturer. He knew that name—and the machine, made on a special order—well. Eight years earlier, before leaving to fight in Spain, Henri Tanguy, a simple metalworker at Nessi Frères, had riveted together the seams of this ventilator which would today filter the air he would breathe during the most glorious hours of his life.

It was not the only surprise he would have this morning. Here in this secret hideout was a telephone, a special telephone that, independent of the Paris phone system, communicated with the 250 posts of the Paris Waters and Sewers Administration. It was a network free of German wiretapping and eavesdropping, with which Rol would soon command his insurrection. Now that telephone rang. The men with Rol froze at the sound in the darkened chamber. Their guide, the regular watchman of this underground chamber, picked it up. From the receiver Rol heard two words, clear and guttural, filling the little room. They were *"Alles gut?"*

"Ja, ja," answered Rol's escort. *"Alles gut."*

Two miles away, in room 347 at the Crillon, a reassured Lieutenant Otto Dummler of the Platzkommandantur—the only German who knew of Duroc's existence—hung up his phone. Dummler knew the sewers of Paris as well as he knew the streets of his native Stuttgart. He was the German officer responsible for their upkeep, their security and their defense. Every morning for two years, with the faithful regularity of an automaton, he had telephoned Duroc's guardian to ask that question. Every day, for the rest of the week, he would go on making his call at this fixed morning hour and receive from the headquarters of the insurrection his countrymen were fighting the same reassuring reply, *"Alles gut."*

A messenger bounded down the steps to Duroc and, stepping across its threshold, threw a hastily wrapped bundle on a table. There, still smelling of fresh printer's ink, were the first newspapers of a new era. Their names announced it: *Le Parisien Libéré, Libération, Défense de la France*. Rol spread them out with ferocious haste. Spread across the front pages of these papers was a war cry as old as the paving stones of Paris. Rol himself had launched it. With it he hoped to infuse his insurrection with new movement, to galvanize the people of the capital to whom he could now speak directly through this new medium. On the first pages of these newspapers of Monday, August 21, in headlines as big as a house, were the words "AUX BARRICADES!"

13

FROM THE BANKS of the Seine in Saint-Cloud to the grimy industrial slums of Pantin and Saint-Denis, from the slopes of Montmartre, past the crooked alleys of the Latin Quarter to the far reaches of Montparnasse and beyond, Rol's barricades sprouted from the pavements of Paris like daffodils after an April rain. By sunset there would be dozens; by the time the Allies arrived, over 400 in a diversity of shape and size as great as that of the people who built them.

At the corner of the rue Saint-Jacques, his pipe in his mouth, his cassock rolled above his knees, the parish priest, an ex-engineer, showed his parishioners how to build theirs; they capped it with enormous portraits of Hitler and Göring. On the rue de la Huchette, just a block from the Seine, opposite the besieged Prefecture of Police, it was a woman, Colette Briant, her energetic head lost in a huge Wehrmacht helmet, who led the work.

Everything that could be moved or carried was heaped onto the barricades. Women and children passed paving stones from hand to hand as they were ripped from the streets. The sandbags of the Civil Defense, sewer gratings, trees, burned-out German trucks, a massive grand piano, mattresses, furniture, old signs reading LOTTERIE NATIONALE TIRAGE CE SOIR and DÉFENSE D'URINER—all were used to flesh them out. At the rue Dauphine and the Pont-Neuf at the tip of the Ile de la Cité, a rusty green *pissoir*, proud and imposing, formed the core of a barricade. On the rue de Buci, an antique dealer emptied his cellar to buttress the one before his door.

Most imposing, perhaps, of all the barricades in the city was the stonework of a group of engineering students at the corner of the boulevard Saint-Germain and boulevard Saint-Michel in the heart of the Latin Quarter. Made entirely of paving stones, six feet thick, it dominated a key crossroads in the city, soon to be known as the Carrefour de la Mort—the Crossroads of Death.

In front of the Café de l'Univers, opposite the Comédie Française, the actors of the theater built their own barricade, swelling its girth with the leftovers from their scenery storeroom. They found it skinny and unprepossessing. To fend off German tanks, they decided to use psychology. They set a ring of canning jars around it. On each they wrote the words "*Achtung! Minen!*" All week long not a single German tank ventured within striking distance of their frail fortress.

For Rol, the prompt flowering of the barricades was an enormous satisfaction. Now he had another concern, arms. From Lorrain Cruse—the young aide of Chaban-Dalmas to whom he had, the day before, vowed Paris was worth 200,000 dead—Rol demanded the means to make certain a fair proportion of those dead would be Germans. Unsure of the fate of Gallois and his mission, he asked for a massive parachuting of Allied arms on the city. From Cruse, in a drafted list, he asked for 10,000 Gammon grenades, five tons of plastic and thousands of feet of Bickford fuse cord as well as arms and ammunition. He asked it with distaste and suspicion. Chaban-Delmas controlled the radio over which that demand would have to pass, and Rol suspected it would never reach London, or that if it did, it would be ignored.

• • •

The stocky young man banged down the receiver of the telephone with a jolt. Yvon Morandat needed in a hurry 30 FFI loyal to de Gaulle. In all armed Paris he had not been able to find one. This trade unionist, who believed the Communists had tried to kill him ten days earlier, was going to play the key role in a bold Gaullist gamble called "Opération Prise du Pouvoir." He realized he was going to have to play it alone, or almost alone. He was to seize the Hôtel de Matignon, the residence of the prime ministers of France, and only one person was ready to help him do it: his dimpled blond secretary and fiancée, Claire.

In this modest apartment on the rue Saint-Augustin in which

Morandat and Claire stood, Alexandre Parodi had decided a few minutes earlier to launch the operation. Long and carefully prepared, approved by London, Opération Prise du Pouvoir was, both Parodi and Morandat were later to admit, "an enormous psychological bluff."

Parodi had realized that Dietrich von Choltitz's gesture of the night before had saved his life, perhaps, but it risked compromising his authority. The truce with which he had hoped to save Paris was disintegrating; the insurrection he had wanted to freeze was moving forward again. There remained, it seemed to him, only a last fragment—a few hours, perhaps—of the time he had wanted to win with the truce. While his rivals' attention remained riveted to that truce, Parodi resolved to use those last hours not to conserve the present but to assure the future.

In one swift gesture Parodi would attempt to publicly install the government of Charles de Gaulle in a Paris in arms. He would, with Opération Prise du Pouvoir, beat the Communists to seats of power in Paris.

For every minister in the de Gaulle Cabinet, there existed in the capital a carefully selected stand-in, a deputy who was to fill the Minister's functions until he could arrive. Under Opération Prise du Pouvoir, Parodi was to place them in their Ministries wherever possible. Then, he had resolved to convoke them to a symbolic Cabinet meeting at the prime minister's residence, the Hôtel de Matignon. There, in a defiant gesture, he would publicly proclaim to the capital that the government of de Gaulle had come to the surface and was functioning. If the Communists wanted to usurp those offices of power, they would then have to displace Parodi's men first and publicly disavow the skeletal authority he had put in place.

To support him, from the plateau above Tousson where Fabri's commandos waited for the code word "*As-tu bien déjeuné, Jacquot?*" the Gaullists of Parodi's Delégation Générale had begun to smuggle hundreds of arms into Paris from their carefully hidden caches. They would use them to arm their own Praetorian Guard, a group called the "Force Gouvernementale." It was made up of devout Gaullists and the dependable elements of the police, gendarmerie and Garde Mobile. In the days ahead, these men ordered to hold the capital of France for the arrival of Charles de Gaulle knew they might have to defend the buildings they were occupying.

And, they feared, their assailants might not be limited to the
gray-green soldiers of the Wehrmacht.

Now Morandat, the twenty-six-year-old trade unionist
chosen to begin this game of political power, slid aside the
curtains of the rue Saint-Augustin apartment, and, with the
reflex action of the Resistance, checked the street below. To
his dismay, it was full of Germans. The building was surrounded. The meeting, he thought in despair, had been betrayed. Days before the Liberation, he was to fall into the
hands of the Gestapo.

Incredulous and relieved, Morandat saw he was mistaken.
The German soldiers beneath his window were raiding a
brothel next door.

Morandat went downstairs. With Claire on the handlebars,
he set off on a bicycle to take over the residence of the prime
ministers of France. A fine Cartesian sense of logic directed
him straight to the avenue Matignon at the foot of the
Champs-Élysées. To his surprise, the sole public building on
the avenue Matignon flew the Swastika and was guarded by
German soldiers. Morandat pedaled up to the only other
Frenchman on the empty street, an elderly man in a derby
hat walking his poodle. Embarrassed, Morandat had to ask
him directions. The young Gaullist sent to seize the residence
of the prime ministers of France had just realized that he did
not know where it was.

14

RAILROAD WORKER HEINRICH HAUSER, thirty-
nine, of the Eisenbahnbezirksdirektion Nord, the headquarters of the northern portion of the occupied French railways,
did not have to ask directions on this sunny August morning.
The fat and contented Hauser and his forty-eight comrades
knew exactly where they wanted to go. They wanted to go
home to Germany.

In the eight months that he had spent in Paris as the chief
switchman of the Batignolles station, Hauser had divided his

life between the station and the Soldatenheim of the place Clichy where he lived. The night before, in its enormous restaurant, Hauser and his comrades had celebrated their last evening in Paris. Enriching their plain spaghetti goulash with a generous ration of champagne, they had drunk themselves into a morose and melancholy haze. Tears in his eyes, his champagne glass swinging in grand arcs before him, Hauser had led the group singing "On the Rhine, on the beautiful Rhine" while the Soldatenheim's women's orchestra, playing for the last time, trailed along after his lugubrious voice. All night in his room Hauser and his friends had continued their farewell feast, washing away their last occupation marks in a proliferation of cognac and champagne.

Now, his head heavy with a memorable hangover, Hauser waited for the truck that his chief, Oberinspektor der Reichsbahn Wacker, had promised to send to evacuate the railway workers of the Batignolles station. Since dawn, the men of the 813th Pionierkompanie of Captain Werner Ebernach had been frantically mining the station and all the installations around it. Hauser realized it would blow up in a few hours, which, if they had not left, would place them at the mercy of the French "terrorists" already filling the neighborhood.

The truck did not arrive. That did not bother Heinrich Hauser. During all the war he had performed only one task, one that did not call for an Iron Cross. He had run a railroad. He would use this railroad to run himself out of Paris. On one of the tracks of the huge empty station was an old locomotive with one freight car behind it. Hauser and his comrades would use it to head for the Rhine, their beautiful Rhine. It would be an easy task. They knew the Paris railroad network as well as the lines of their own hands. Hauser climbed up into his switch tower and performed a maneuver he could have conducted with his eyes shut: he threw the switches that would shunt their locomotive out past Le Bourget airport to Strasbourg and Germany.

In a hiss of steam, like any band of railroad workers heading home after a day's work, the forty-nine men rolled slowly out of the station, leaving behind them all the menacing air of Paris. For Hauser and his comrades there was now only one fear left—Allied airplanes. For a long moment Hauser, from the little rear window of the freight car, watched the white dome of Sacré-Coeur sparkling in the sunlight fade behind him. Then he dozed into a light sleep.

When he woke a few moments later, Hauser looked out the same window. He rubbed his eyes in wonder. The sun had somehow changed direction. Now it was shining from the front of the locomotive instead of behind it. He leaped to his feet and, in a burst of fury, began to pound his comrades. "Those swine!" he screamed. "They reversed the switches. We're heading back to Paris!"

• • •

Yvon Morandat had arrived where he wanted to go. He had found the Hôtel de Matignon. It was on the rue de Varenne, across the Seine from the Champs-Élysées, deep in the Left Bank. Now, his bicycle resting inconspicuously against its yellow stone walls, he and Claire approached the great green gates which, four days earlier, had snapped shut behind Pierre Laval. Morandat rapped firmly. The Judas grille slid open. To the face pressed flush against it, Morandat announced he had come to see the commander. In respectful reply, the wooden gate creaked open.

The sight upon which it opened made Morandat gape in dismay. There, on the graveled court, arms stacked in ritual regularity, grenades buckled to the belts of their black uniforms, were over a hundred men of Laval's bodyguard. In what he hoped was discreet and respectful silence, Morandat, taking Claire by the arm, posted himself in a corner of the courtyard. "Here, Yvon," Claire whispered, "put this on," and she passed Morandat his tricolor armband. Then, with fluttering fingers, she twisted her own up the sleeve of her dress. The commander of the guard, short and pompous, crunched across the white gravel toward them. Morandat wondered what to do. "If there is opposition," Parodi had told him, "leave." "If there is opposition," Morandat thought, "I'll leave in a coffin."

"I am the commander," rasped the little man before him. "What do you want?"

At that instant Morandat decided what to do. In a voice of stentorian splendor, in a rich authoritative tone that even surprised him, he announced, "I have come to occupy these premises in the name of the provisional government of the French Republic."

The little man who for four years had given his allegiance to the government of Vichy braced to attention. "At your orders," he said. "I have always been a firm republican."

He called his guard to attention, and Claire in her summer dress and Morandat in his shirt-sleeves marched past them to the marble steps of the handsome residence. There at the top, waiting for them in his white bow tie, his black tails, his heavy silver seal of office hanging from a chain around his neck, was the maître d'hôtel.

With a dignified nod and a gracious wave of his white-gloved hand he welcomed them to the premises. Then he took them on an inspection tour. He showed them Laval's empty office, the drawers of its desk still hanging open. He guided them upstairs to its living quarters, past its elegant suites and the marble-decked bathroom in which, by candlelight, Pierre Laval had taken a last bath four nights before. Morandat, he suggested, might want to take the Green Room next to it for his personal use.

What, asked Morandat, was the Green Room? With only the barest trace of his surprise, the white-gloved maître d'hôtel told the new occupant of this chamber, "It is the bedroom of the Prime Minister of France."

* * *

Flat on his stomach behind the parapet running along the rue de Crimée over the mouth of the Buttes-Chaumont railroad tunnel, machinist Germain Berton looked at his watch. In seven minutes the old locomotive of the Batignolles station would appear in the sights of his rifle. Fifteen minutes earlier, in a kindergarten classroom turned into an FFI headquarters, Berton had been warned a German freight train heading toward the suburb of Ivry would pass through the Buttes-Chaumont tunnel in a quarter of an hour. Berton and his men had sprung into position to ambush this unhoped-for prize.

For the past hour, each click of their wheels had taken Heinrich Hauser and his forty-eight comrades farther away from their goal. Their locomotive with its sole freight car was puffing steadily toward the suburb of Ivry. Soon, trapped in this maze of derouted switches, they would have crossed all Paris from north to south. Instead of the banks of their beautiful Rhine. Heinrich Hauser and his hung-over comrades were heading straight toward the American lines.

Suddenly darkness settled over their car. They had plunged into the Buttes-Chaumont tunnel. At its other end, on the bridge of the rue de Crimée, Germain Berton peered forward, squinting down the sights of his Lebel rifle.

At the first sight of the locomotive, his men opened fire. With a brutal gesture, the engineer reversed his steam and managed to back into the tunnel. Inside, Hauser jumped to the ground. In the darkness he noticed a second train was pulled up on the next track. He struck a match and walked up to it. By the shaking light of that match, he saw an enormous stack of wooden crates and, on each, a white sticker that made him hurl the burning splinter to the ground. It was a skull and crossbones and, under it, the words ACHTUNG—LEBENSGE-FÄHRLICH (Attention—Danger). Hauser and his forty-eight comrades were trapped in this tunnel next to a train packed full of explosives.

The last trip Heinrich Hauser would organize for many years was over. Hands over his aching and hung-over head, the disheartened railway man started down the tunnel toward the waiting men of Germain Berton.

•   •   •

For Roger Gallois, the emissary sent by Rol to ask the Allies for arms, a trip was about to end too. Squatting behind a ragged haystack, looking straight at the exhausted Frenchman, was a German soldier, the last man separating Roger Gallois from the small group of Americans just 500 yards away. For hours Gallois had maneuvered to get to this crossroads town of Pussay, 56 miles west of Paris, from the villa in which he and his surgeon escort had spent a rainy night.

Alone now, he took a calculated risk. The German, he told himself, would not fire at a single civilian and expose his position to the Americans. Gallois set out past the German, his heart tripping under his crumpled suit, and the champagne to which he had treated himself at lunch bitter in his dry and nervous mouth. As he had hoped, the soldier watched him go with no gesture more menacing than a sullen stare.

It had worked! He had crossed the German lines! Exultant, almost delirious with his sense of triumph, the dirty, unshaven

Frenchman rushed up to these, the first American soldiers he had ever seen.

The first GI he reached was squatting in a roadside ditch, eating something from a green can. To him, Gallois jubilantly announced, "I come from Paris with a message for General Eisenhower!"

The GI spooned out another mouthful of the gooey mass in his can and looked up at Gallois. "Yeah?" he said. "So what?"

15

ONCE, ON AUGUST DAYS like this, the planes of the German Luftflotte No. 3, which the ruddy major beside Dietrich von Choltitz represented, had filled the skies of France in awesome assembly, shuttling endlessly over the Channel to London and all England. But that had been four years earlier, in another summer. Now the core of that air fleet in France was 150 bombers stationed at Le Bourget airport, seven miles from the Hotel Meurice room in which the two men talked. Soon even those planes would have to flee north or risk destruction. But before they left, their new commander proposed to add another laurel to an air force whose escutcheon already bore the names of Rotterdam, London and Coventry.

Generaloberst Otto Dessloch had relieved the fat and ineffective Generalfeldmarschall Hugo Sperrle as commander of Luftflotte No. 3 at noon, August 18, with orders to get it back into the skies over the western front. As one of his first gestures, he had sent this major to von Choltitz "to offer the assistance of the Luftwaffe in suppressing the troubles in Paris." Von Choltitz's first reaction had been to resuggest his canceled attack on the Prefecture of Police. But the major had had another suggestion. It could be carried out at night against a wider target area. No ground fire or Allied fighters could disturb it. It was a simple, safe, although somewhat savage, way to end the uprising on the territory of the commander of Gross Paris. He proposed to raze the northeastern corner of the city in one long night of shuttle-bombing.

With a pudgy finger the major traced out on von Choltitz's map the slice of working-class Paris he had in mind. It ran from the slopes of Montmartre east to the dreary suburb of Pantin, from the Buttes-Chaumont north to the empty stock-yards of the porte de la Villette. He had picked it because Le Bourget was just five miles away. From that airfield, he proposed to fly his planes in relays into this undefended area of 800,000 people. Each plane, he estimated, could make a minimum of ten bombing runs, thus draining the underground storage depots of Le Bourget, which were bulging with explosives a retreating Luftwaffe would otherwise never be able to use or carry away.

After a night of low-altitude bombing against a clearly defined target, with no opposition, "not a cat or dog" would be moving in northeast Paris, the major promised. It would be, he said, "a little Hamburg." The comparison was one von Choltitz would always remember. The officer before him was a native of the Hanseatic seaport. He had lost his wife and two children in the July, 1943, "fire raid" on the city.

All the plan required of von Choltitz's men was that they get out of the area, mark it clearly with flares, break its water mains so the fires started by the attack could spread unchecked, and—if they chose—give the population a few minutes' warning of the attack.

Von Choltitz was, this morning, looking for some weapon "to humble the population." His gesture the evening before, in releasing Alexandre Parodi and his two aides, had borne no fruit. Instead of checking the insurrection, it seemed to have helped spread it. Barricades had leaped from the pavement all across the city. On his desk was the most painful and persuasive measurement he had yet received of the insurrection's vigor: his casualty lists. Sunday, the day on which he had supposedly concluded a truce with the insurrection, he had lost over 75 killed, more than he had on Saturday, the day the uprising had begun.

It was clear where his first duty lay. It was to his soldiers. The major's proposal was "brutal and bloody." But, von Choltitz reasoned, "it would show the population I could reach out and defend myself." He owed his soldiers as much. He told the major he would order his staff to draw up a plan for the attack.

• • •

Amid the litter of cables on the varnished surface of the Louis XVI desk was a piece of plain white paper. In its upper left-hand corner, the President of the Provisional Government of the French Republic had had engraved a simple black letterhead, "Le Général de Gaulle." For the imperious figure erect and poised behind this desk, those four words sufficed to represent the sovereignty of France. Now, alone in the office of the Prefect of the Department of Rennes, in his neat, upward-slanting handwriting, Charles de Gaulle drafted on that sheet of stationery a last appeal to General Eisenhower.

All the night before, and all during the morning, "Pleyel Violet," "Apollo Noir" and "Montparnasse Noir"—the secret transmitters of Jacques Chaban-Delmas and Alexandre Parodi —had showered him with urgent appeals demanding "the immediate entry of the Allies" into Paris. The most urgent read: "Insurrection launched Saturday and held in check for two days by truce . . . cannot be contained beyond this evening. Battle tomorrow throughout Paris with a tragic imbalance of forces seems certain."

The deteriorating situation described in those messages seemed to de Gaulle so grave that nothing could be allowed to delay further his own and the Allies' entry into Paris. Each passing hour, he knew, benefited his political foes. The chaos and anarchy he felt they sought to provoke with the insurrection would soon be general; the disorder on which they hoped to build their political designs would be rampant. If it did not come quickly, his own entry into the capital might be too late. So imminent did he feel the danger was that, speaking with the sovereignty of France, Charles de Gaulle accepted a risk even his Allies were reluctant to run. So urgent was the occupation of the capital, he wrote, that it must be undertaken *"even if it should produce fighting and damage in the interior of the city."*

To hand-carry this letter to Eisenhower, de Gaulle selected the only man in France, outside of his own brothers, who had the right to speak to him in the familiar *"tu"* form of address.

Passing it to General Alphonse Juin, the proud conqueror of Monte Cassino, de Gaulle added a postscript for the Supreme Commander, to be delivered orally. If this last pressing appeal went unheeded, he said, he would feel compelled to withdraw the 2nd French Armored Division from Allied Command and send it to Paris on his own orders.

When the door closed behind Juin, de Gaulle took another sheet of paper and composed a second message, this one to Leclerc, the commander of the 2nd Armored Division. To the impatient young general whose first illegally dispatched detachment was already slipping past the spires of Chartres, de Gaulle addressed a formal warning. His threat to Eisenhower was not an idle gesture. Painful though the idea was, costly as its consequences might be, de Gaulle was ready to rip apart the Allied Command for Paris. He told Leclerc to be prepared to ignore the orders of his Allied commanders and consider himself directly under the orders of the French government. If Eisenhower did not intend to send Leclerc to Paris, de Gaulle did.

And in case the Allies should try to bar the road to Paris to Leclerc, there remained to Charles de Gaulle one last way to impose his presence on the French capital. In the dense undergrowth of the forest of Nemours, the commandos of Fabri listened with anxiety and impatience to their radio. On their improvised little landing field, everything was ready. For those men, only one thing remained now: to hear the crackling of the phrase "*As-tu bien déjeuné, Jacquot?*" filtering through the static of their radio.

•   •   •

The words jolting out of the telephone receiver pressed to Dietrich von Choltitz's ear were painfully clear. With the special arrogance he reserved for his generals, Generalfeldmarschall Walther Model was berating his Paris commander for his failure to maintain order in the capital. He had, he told von Choltitz, even heard rumors that he had been treating with the terrorists in the city.

Flushed and fearful, von Choltitz denied the accusation. Model accepted his denial; but he warned von Choltitz against "exceeding your authority in Paris." Model was irritated and impatient. What he wanted from von Choltitz, he said, was order in Paris, and he expected him "to use every means available to get it." Von Choltitz promised Model he would. But he warned the field marshal that if the troubles got out of hand, he would have to have reinforcements. Model erupted into a torrent of angry abuse. "Get along with what you have," he told his Paris commander. Finally, under von Choltitz's determined pleas, he agreed to give him part of the 48th Infantry Division being drawn down from the Low Countries.

Model's impatience and irritation were understandable. For almost forty-eight hours the little field marshal had been working at cross purposes with the man for whom he was supposed to be performing miracles. From a general who bore such unmeasured personal devotion to the Führer, it was inexplicable.*

Sunday, hours after he had decided in Speidel's presence to give first priority to getting his threatened troops back across the Seine, he had received a new order, this one stating in the most categoric terms that his primary mission was to defend the Paris bridgehead. It was signed with the personal seal of the master of the Third Reich: "*Gez:* Adolf Hitler." Model was told to "hold the Paris bridgehead at any price" and to cling to it "without any regard for the destruction" he would cause in Paris. No one knew any better than Model that "at any price" meant, to the man whose name was on the cable, a defense to the last man, a defense of the kind symbolized at Stalingrad, Smolensk and Monte Cassino.

The order, the first sent from the Führer's evening strategy conference, had arrived at OB West at 11:30 P.M. By the time it arrived, Model's earlier orders to his Fifth Panzer Army to begin preparations for a withdrawal across the Seine had already gone out. The field marshal had apparently decided it was too late to stop them. Now the Panzers Hitler wanted in Paris were literally caught in midstream.

So, in a sense, was Model. His only consolation could be the fact that his gamble for time in front of Paris was working. There his operations section reported "only limited enemy

---

* For Martin Blumenson, an official military historian of the U.S. Army, Model's attitude was, from a command standpoint, not only inexplicable; it was "inexcusable." (*Breakout and Pursuit, U.S. Army in World War II, European Theater of Operations,* vol. II, page 598)

reconnaissance." Perhaps because he felt himself too deeply committed along the Seine, perhaps because he doubted the strategic wisdom of a brawling fight for Paris, Model would, later this same day, suggest a defense of Paris north and east of the city. His reply from Jodl would be brutal and final. In words that deprived him of any choice, Jodl would tell him Paris was to be defended not from the north, not from the east, but in the city itself.

Now, concluding his angry telephone call with his Paris commander, Model, for the second time in twenty-four hours, neglected to inform von Choltitz of the vital fact that two Panzer divisions, earmarked by OKW for his command, were on their way south. For von Choltitz he had only one sharp parting phrase: "Restore order in the city at any price."

16

THE STREETS OF PARIS which, a few hours earlier, had rung with the proud words *"Aux Barricades!,"* now echoed a more anguished cry, rising up from those first flimsy fortifications. It was "The tanks are coming." Infuriated by the challenge in the defiant symbols rising from the city's pavements, the Wehrmacht command had taken the first steps to restore the order demanded by Model. From their tank parks across the city, the Panzers that had given Adolf Hitler the key to Paris in 1940 swarmed again into the streets of the capital.

To one resistant, their arrival was announced in a politely formal phone call. From the Palais du Luxembourg almost around the corner from FFI headquarters in the Fifth Arrondissement Police Commissariat, the SS commander told "Monsieur le FFI" that he must "remove the barricade" or else the tanks would do it for him. Dazed by the German's precise French and stiffly proper tone, young law student Raymond Sarran hesitated a moment; then, as dryly as he could, he replied, "You no longer give orders here, Colonel."

Ten minutes later, the tanks arrived. Roped to the turret of each tank, Sarran saw, were two Frenchmen in civilian clothes. To protect his tankers from Sarran's Molotov cocktails, the SS commander had decided to use a set of human shields. In perfect order, they set about destroying Sarran's barricades.

From the place de la République, two tanks from the Prince Eugène Barracks swept the boulevard Voltaire with intermittent fire. Two women, each tugging at one of the handles of a huge wicker laundry basket wrapped with a white tablecloth, ran for cover. The laundry basket was full of Molotov cocktails. Clara Bonté, the wife of a Communist deputy, and her daughter Marguerite had filled them themselves. They and the other women of the neighborhood had set up a Molotov cocktail factory in the Eleventh Arrondissement Ladies' Club a few doors away. Their husbands waited at a windowsill on the place de la République to hurl them onto these two tanks now firing at the two women scurrying for cover.

At the other end of Paris, the FFI pushed forward a scrap-iron Don Quixote to do battle with the Panzers. When their prewar Somua tank, captured in a factory in nearby Saint-Ouen, appeared, a triumphant crowd had decked its turret with a tricolor. That flag was, alas, to remain the only weapon of this, the only tank of the Paris Resistance. The FFI had no shell for its cannon.

But it was not just von Choltitz's tanks that menaced many Parisians this cloudy day. In his cell in the hexagonal fortress of Mont Valérien, Louis Berty, the pork butcher captured during the fighting at the Neuilly town hall, listened to a familiar sound. For almost every day for three years; the echo of that sound had drifted up to his little Nanterre shop barely a mile from his cell. It was the sound of Mont Valérien's hard-pressed firing squad. This little man who had left to fight his country's enemies with his armband "Live Free or Die" knew that soon that sound would echo for him.

At the foot of the little wooded slope leading up to Mont Valérien's walls a group of men listened to the pathetic entreaties of a woman. Lieutenant Bob Woodrum, the American pilot, hidden in Berty's house, two other aviators and the survivors of Berty's Resistance group had wanted to storm Mont Valérien. Lucille Berty pleaded with them not to: It would only end in their deaths and her husband's too, she said. Heartsick, the men abandoned their scheme.

In the center of Paris, at the Palais du Luxembourg from which the well-protected tanks of the SS colonel had made their exit, Paul Pardou, the Resistance hijacker, watched. For the second time, he saw a group of civilians, a pickax and a shovel on each shoulder, march past him. This time there were four men. A few minutes later Pardou heard a rapid burst of firing and understood they had been laid into their freshly dug graves. At that sound, Franz, the red-necked German mess sergeant under whose orders he worked, turned to him and, for what seemed like the hundredth time, repeated the only phrase he seemed capable of articulating in the French language: "Tomorrow you shot. Today you make kitchen clean."

In the same building, two stories above, another man heard the shots too. François Dalby, the electrician whom this building's caretaker had sought days earlier when he saw the Germans mining the palace, had done his work well. Thus far he had caused seventeen hours of breakdowns—seventeen hours in which the pneumatic drills chipping out mine emplacements in this palace had not been able to work. But thirty-six hours earlier Dalby had been given a blunt warning by the building's commander: Get the electric system working or else. Now Dalby wondered as he heard the shots how much longer it would be before he too would shoulder a pickax and shovel and march off to dig his own grave.

*   *   *

On the other side of the Seine, an impatient man paced the lobby of the Hotel Meurice. In six days of hard and determined work, the men of Captain Werner Ebernach's 813th Pionierkompanie had almost finished their job. With the torpedoes from Pilz, the underground storehouse of the Kriegsmarine, they had already planted over 12 tons of explosives around the city. The day before, two anguished policemen had rushed into the office of law student Edgar Pisani at the Prefecture of Police to announce that the Germans had even mined the two bridges leading toward Notre-Dame. The thoughtful Ebernach had also set aside a store of explosives to blow out the supports of the very symbol of Paris, the Eiffel Tower.

Now he wanted the order to start the first of his explosions. Irritated and impatient, he had waited two hours in the

Meurice for a meeting with von Choltitz. For his efforts he received only a short message, relayed from the commander of Gross Paris through his aide Count von Arnim. Ebernach, he said, was to go on with his preparations "and stand by for further orders."

That evening brought the first drops of a new rainstorm and, along with it, a wild and welcome rumor. It buoyed up the spirits of the entire population of Paris. In his apartment on the rue du Bac, playwright André Roussin set it down: "A day begun in fear ends in hope," he wrote. "It seems the Americans are in Rambouillet. Tomorrow they will be in Paris."

•   •   •

The Americans were indeed in Rambouillet, only 30 miles from Paris. Playwright André Roussin had, however, somewhat overestimated their number. There were three of them, and none of them had any real business being there. The first was a courtly Virginian named David Bruce,° a colonel, the head of the OSS for France, whose capture would have afforded untrammeled delight to the Germans. The second was a jeep driver, a taciturn GI named "Red" Pelkey, from West Virginia. The third was a war correspondent. True to a promise sworn long before, Ernest Hemingway was leading the United States press corps to Paris.

His first act had been to liberate the bar of the Hotel du Grand Veneur, a honeysuckle-covered inn favored by weekending Parisians and their ladies. In the bar he had installed a case of hand grenades, a carbine, a bottle of the grateful owner's best cognac and a prewar Michelin road map on which he had already begun to plot the German positions in the neighborhood. To the FFI who had started to drift into the hotel, Hemingway was "mon capitaine." By the time Paris was liberated, in one of the most rapid promotions in French military history, he would be "mon général."

Sole liberators of this hunting preserve of the kings and presidents of France, and forty-eight hours ahead of the rest of the Allied armies, the trio found themselves saddled with an embarrassing problem: too many Germans. "Every time we

° Later United States Ambassador to Germany and to Great Britain.

turned around," Bruce found, "one was crawling out of the
woodwork to surrender." Hemingway took away their pants
and put them to work in the kitchen peeling potatoes for his
growing band of FFI.

17

SMILING INCONGRUOUSLY, A RING of rosy-
cheeked abbots looked down from the tinted engravings on
the wall at the circle of angry men sitting side by side
in Alphonse Juge's humid apartment. Below them a soft
rain slapped the leafy treetops along the avenue du Parc-
Montsouris. In one corner of the room were the six votive
candles Juge had set aside to light this meeting if darkness
overtook it. He had, with an apologetic genuflexion, requisitioned those frail candles earlier in the day from the Altar of
the Virgin in the nearby Church of Saint-Dominique. Alone in
her kitchen, his wife listened to the angry mutter of the men
in the next room and regretted that on this sticky evening she
had not been able to find anything to offer them beyond a
few glasses of watery ersatz lemonade.

Those troubled men had graver matters on their minds,
however, than something to drink. Never, except in the prison
cells of the Gestapo, had so many leaders of the Resistance
been gathered in one room as were now huddled in Alphonse
Juge's third-floor apartment. And never would a meeting of
that Resistance unleash venom such as that now filling this
smoky salon. These men had come here to decide the fate of
Consul General Nordling's disintegrating truce.

Alexandre Parodi, so despairing earlier in the day, now believed he might save it. Beside him, General Jacques Chaban-
Delmas, the twenty-nine-year-old rugby player who had flown
to London two weeks before, defended the truce as though
it were a trench in Verdun. Concluding his arguments, he
said it was a "gentlemen's agreement" with von Choltitz.

At those words the room erupted in a howl of angry voices.

"You don't make gentlemen's agreements with murderers!" someone screamed.

"And you," Chaban shouted back at his accuser, "you want to massacre 150,000 people for nothing!"

Opposite Chaban, spitting out his words with fury, Roger Villon, the senior Communist in the room, snarled, "I've never seen such a gutless French general."

Whatever order had been left in the room disappeared. Chaban stood up, his heavy fists clenched. In her kitchen Mme. Juge clutched her cheeks in dismay. The Germans, she thought, will come. Suddenly, above the angry roar of voices in her living room, she heard the quick cracking of broken glass. Then there was silence.

In the salon the shamefaced men looked at each other. Gaullist author Jacques Debû-Bridel, using an old parliamentarian's trick, had smashed a windowpane and shocked the room to order.

As it settled down, a quiet soft-spoken non-Communist rose to rebut the arguments of Chaban-Delmas. He bore a name as old as France. For three years, Count Jean de Vogüé had lived in clandestinity in an industrial slum, a world away from the drawing rooms and polished elegance of the Paris into which he had been born. He had even avoided his own mother on a rainy street corner, pulling his old felt hat over his eyes so she would not recognize a son she had not seen in three years. Now, in a voice dry with fatigue, this aristocrat spoke for the thousands of ordinary Parisians who asked only to fight Germans, whatever the cost. "On the barricades," he pleaded, "we must wipe out the shame of 1940."

Villon followed to deliver the *coup de grâce* to the truce with which Parodi had hoped to save Paris from destruction. Paris, for Communist Villon, was "the best city in the world for guerrilla warfare." De Gaulle had refused to sign an armistice in 1940, he declared, and the Communists were "not going to sign one now just because he wants us to." Then, in what was little less than an open declaration of war on Parodi and the men around him, he promised that the Communist party would "plaster every wall in Paris with a poster accusing the Gaullists of stabbing the people of Paris in the back" if the truce was accepted. The posters, he told Parodi, were already being printed.

Overwhelmed, Parodi slumped in his chair.* He was being blackmailed. He could not, no matter what the price, let the Communists publicly divide the Resistance. His truce was going to be defeated. A few minutes later it was, by one vote, his own, defeated. So high a price did Parodi put on the unity of the Resistance that, in the face of Villon's threat, he had felt he must place that unity above even the safety of his country's capital.

This broken man felt they now had only to wait for the sound of Choltitz's cannon smashing apart the sacred stones of Paris. For the rest of the night, the secret transmitters of Chaban-Delmas would send a final anguished plea into the night air. With the ardor of despair, Chaban and Parodi would beg de Gaulle to get the Allies to Paris.

Now, in the narrow hall of Mme. Juge's apartment, Parodi, exhausted, struggled to pull his coat over his purple suspenders. Sobbing, he half collapsed against the man whose venomous threat had just ended his truce.

"My God," he wept to Roger Villon, "they're going to destroy Paris now. Our beautiful Notre-Dame will be bombed to ruins."

Arrogant, vindictive in his triumph, Villon snarled back, "So what if Paris is destroyed? We will be destroyed along with it. Better Paris be destroyed like Warsaw than that she live another 1940."

18

OF ALL THE NIGHTS in the life of Dietrich von Choltitz, this one, in a hot hotel room, was perhaps the loneliest he would ever spend. Twenty years later, even his orderly Corporal Helmut Mayer would remember it. It was the only time in their seven years of service together that von Choltitz had addressed him in an angry voice. "Get out and don't

---

* By a stroke of irony, while these men argued, General Koenig was once again pleading, over the BBC, that "nothing will be gained from an uprising —except useless sacrifice of French lives."

bother me!" he had shouted when the always cheerful corporal appeared in his doorway to fix his room for the night.

Now in that darkened room, sweating and naked to the waist, the little general who bore this humid evening more responsibility for the fate of Paris than Charles de Gaulle or all the generals of the American Army, sat and agonized alone at the stirrings of a Prussian conscience. The one man who might have eased his solitude had gone. His cousin Adolf von Carlowitz, Choltitz mused, would be in Baden-Baden by now.

From his windows von Choltitz watched the softly stirring treetops of the Tuileries garden and heard the sound of gunfire rising past those leafy sentinels, over the blacked-out skyline of Paris. In the damp heat, sweat dribbled down his stomach.

All his orderly world, it seemed that night, was collapsing around him. He had gambled on Nordling's truce and failed. He had only to listen a few minutes to measure by how much. Berlin and Model, he was afraid, knew about those negotiations with his enemy.

None of the orders he had received from OKW had been carried out. In the anteroom of his office, just where they had been left twenty-four hours earlier, were the neatly stacked blueprints of OKW's four demolition experts. Yet on this evening of August 21—four days after von Kluge had given him the order to start destroying the industries of Paris, more than twenty-four hours after Jodl had personally repeated it to him by telephone—von Choltitz had not given the order to destroy a single factory. He had even refused, in the afternoon, to receive Captain Ebernach. And tucked into the pocket of his tunic, tossed on the bed beside his high-backed easy chair, was the latest and shortest order he had received from OKW. It read: "Generaloberst Jodl orders that the destruction of the Paris bridges be prepared whatever the cost." His name, he was certain, "was under a shadow at OKW."

For the first time in twenty-nine years as a German officer, he was, he recognized, "in a state of insubordination." At this thought, he recalled the face of the Reichsleiter, Robert Ley, in the smoky sleeping compartment of his train from Rastenburg to Berlin. On his night table, on top of his *History of the Franco-Prussian War*, bordered by a simple leather frame, was a portrait of three of the human beings to whom the Reichleiter's admirably precise Sippenhaft Law applied: his

wife Uberta and his two daughters. Timo, his son, had not
been born when this picture he had carried through four years
of warfare was taken.

Lonely and depressed, he felt this evening "a sense of failure," a conviction he had badly handled his assignment in
Paris. To this insurrection spreading like a contagious disease,
to an OKW stirring with doubts about his role in the city, he
must, he thought, "make a bold assertion of authority, a demonstration of force." The proposal of the ruddy Luftwaffe
major came repeatedly to his mind. The suggestion of that
obscure officer had the merit of being simple and easy to
execute. Le Bourget airfield and the major were only as far
away, he knew, as the black telephone beside his bed.

He regretted now his decision to cancel his attack on the
Prefecture of Police. And twenty years later he could still
recall the bitterness he felt this night at his "mistake" in
releasing Alexandre Parodi and his two aides. He could
rectify both errors, he thought, with the major's plan. At one
point he sprang to his feet, cursing aloud and vowing to carry
out the plan. By now, in the breathless heat of the room, he
was stifling. He stripped down to his undershorts and walked
to his open window.

It was late. This city, in which a group of angry men in a
nondescript tenement two miles to the south had just vowed
a remorseless fight against him, was quiet once again. The
only sound he could hear, measured and reassuring, was the
clip-clop of the boots of his sentries pacing the pavement of
the rue de Rivoli below him. An improbable figure in sweaty
undershorts, this man who had cannonaded Sebastopol to
cinders, stared from his window at the darkened skyline of
Paris, and reckoned the cost in ruins of restoring order to
the city before him.

In his lonely debate, a new element preyed on his mind.
Never in his forty-nine years had Dietrich von Choltitz had
reason to question the verities of his Silesian upbringing, his
belief in Germany's destiny, his Prussian officer's code of discipline. Now he did.

Since the half hour he had spent two weeks earlier in the
windowless bunker of Rastenburg, von Choltitz had been
haunted by the thought that the man to whom he had sworn
blind obedience was mad. And from that day on, another
equally awful reality had begun to penetrate his mind. For

Germany, he feared, there would be no more miracles; the road from Danzig was leading to defeat.

In the past twenty-four hours his talks with Jodl and with Model had all confirmed the same nagging suspicion. It was that OKW had not placed him in Paris to play a military role. To defend Paris against an enemy, even at the cost of its destruction, was a militarily valid act. But wantonly to ravage the city for the sole satisfaction of wiping one of the wonders of Europe from the map was an act without military justification. It was this, he had begun to fear, that Hitler had sent him here to do. This madman, he suspected, wanted him to devastate the city, "and then sit in its ashes and accept the consequences."

Twenty years later, von Choltitz would still be haunted by his awful debate this August evening with his own conscience. Between his instinctive obedience to orders and the apocalypse to which they seemed to be leading him, he found himself caught in an appalling dilemma. That history would never forgive the man who destroyed Paris was a persuasive argument to von Choltitz; that the man who did it might be hanged in its ashes was more convincing. Von Choltitz was prepared to die as a soldier in Paris, but not as a criminal. That night, showing Jodl's latest order to Count von Arnim, he had laconically remarked, "And I will sit on the last bridge and blow myself up along with it because it will be the only thing left for me."

To the terrible dilemma in which he found himself, there seemed to be only one answer: the sweeping of the Allies into the city, which would relieve him of this ugly burden. Earlier in this day, he had learned a startling fact. General Kurt von der Chevallerie, the commander of the First Army, had informed him that, on Model's orders, he was sliding his army south from its position in front of Paris. That meant, he had realized, that the front door to Paris lay open and beckoning. The Allies had only to change their plans and they could rush into the city before he or anyone else could stop them.

The telephone cut into his thoughts. Von Choltitz closed the shutters of his window with a bang and stumbled to his telephone in the darkness. On the other end of the line, von Choltitz heard the voice of General Wilhelm Burgdorf at OKW, the man who had chosen him for this job. Once, in 1942, the cocky Burgdorf had told the hero of Sebastopol, "I have so

many generals I could use them to feed the pigs." Tonight he
was calling von Choltitz to tell him there were no generals
left at OKW. Instead of sending him, as Choltitz had asked, a
general officer to command the troops outside the city, Hitler,
Burgdorf told him, had decided to promote Hubertus von
Aulock, the man with whom von Choltitz had drunk champagne in a Saint-Cloud villa, from Lieutenant Colonel to
Brigadier General. Von Choltitz thanked Burgdorf for his
"solicitude" and hung up.

Then he stretched on his bed and stared up at the ceiling.
Finally, with the same indecision that had led him forty-eight
hours earlier to accept Nordling's truce, he decided he would
accord himself one last reprieve. He would wait twenty-four
hours before calling the red-faced major at Le Bourget. That
decision taken, he turned his mind to a simpler military
problem. Where, he wondered, would he find in this troubled
city the two general's pips of his new office for the shoulder
boards of Generalmajor Hubertus von Aulock?

19

FOR ROGER GALLOIS, the man who, despite the
orders of his Communist chief, had assigned himself the task
of getting the Allies into Paris, the name of the man he was
about to see was still a mystery. But he knew, from the attitude of the Americans with him in this camouflaged tent, that
he was important. For the exhausted but happy Frenchman,
the last few hours had been a hectic and overwhelming experience.

After the indifferent reception he had received from the
first GI he had seen, Gallois had been placed in a jeep. Its
boyish driver had had orders not to talk. For two painful
hours, astir with wonder and curiosity at his first sight of the
Allied armies, Gallois had heard no sound but the regular
snapping of his escort's chewing gum.

The jeep finally stopped in a grove of poplar trees filled with
tents. There his American hosts had verified his identity in a

fashion so startling that Gallois still wondered over it. In perfect French, with a sweeping knowledge of the Resistance, Colonel Robert I. Powell, a New York architect, had asked him dozens of questions in a manner as casual as if he were asking about the weather. Then, in what seemed to be just another routine question to cross-check his knowledge of the Resistance, Powell had asked Gallois if he had ever met a resistant named André de Brabois. Gallois had vaguely remembered he had met someone by that name on a Paris street corner ten days earlier. Powell asked if he had seen him again. Gallois thought, and recalled they had set another meeting but de Brabois had not shown up. Why? asked Powell. Gallois had admitted he did not know why.

"I'll show you why," Powell had replied. He turned and murmured something to an aide behind him.

An instant later, a lean, uniformed man stepped into the tent. For a few seconds Gallois had been so astonished he could not articulate the name of the man standing before him. It was André de Brabois.

Now, through the folds of this tent, another man appeared. His hair was unkempt and his khaki shirt only partially jammed into his trousers. "Excuse me," he said, "I've been sleeping." Then he added, "O.K., I'm listening. What's your story?"

Gallois told it with all the passion pent up in his Gallic soul. When he had finished, the American before him said, "You are a soldier, and I'm a soldier. I'm going to answer you as a soldier." He told Gallois the answer was no, for three reasons. The Allies were "destroying Germans, not capturing capitals." The Resistance had started the insurrection without orders and "would have to accept the consequences." The gas-short Allies could not "accept the moral responsibility of feeding the city." He offered his hand to Gallois. His words had been so brutally definitive and his tone so authoritative that, for Gallois, his answer seemed beyond appeal. Well it might have. The American general Gallois had aroused from a midnight sleep was George S. Patton.

For the dirty and unshaven Frenchman, sustained through all the risks of his trip by the belief that he would save Paris from the fate of Warsaw, this was the most depressing moment of his life. He was, as he reported later, "in a state of emotional collapse."

Patton left and returned a few moments later. He asked the Frenchman if he would mind making another trip to a town called Laval to see another American general.

* * *

In an apple orchard outside that Norman town, another Frenchman agonized that evening over the fate of the capital of France. He was sitting on the edge of a camp cot, writing by the uneven light of a kerosene lamp. For the first time in all his months of duty as a liaison officer with the United States Army, Colonel Albert Lebel was trying to change a decision of the men with whom he served. On a plain sheet of paper, in words no less concerned than those of Charles de Gaulle, Lebel concluded the personal plea of an obscure French officer for the capital of his country.

"If the American Army," he wrote, "seeing Paris in a state of insurrection, does not come to its aid, it will be an omission the people of France will never be able to forget."

He folded the paper and put it away. The next day his commander, General Omar Bradley, was flying to a conference with the Supreme Commander. Lebel was resolved to slide this personal appeal into the papers Bradley would carry with him to that meeting. He firmly believed that the conference would be of overwhelming importance to the history of his country. If Paris was to escape devastation, it was at that meeting a few hours away that the order to march on the capital would have to be given.

20

[AUGUST 22]

LIEUTENANT COLONEL CHUCK HEFLIN shivered in the damp English night and, for warmth, pressed his fingers against the thick coffee mug he clutched in his hands. Outside his Nissen hut, the silhouettes of the B-24s of his "Carpetbagger" Squadron stretched in a dark line toward the rise of hills before the town of Harrington in this northwestern corner of England. Already the enlisted men of Heflin's squadron were stuffing those planes with the 200-pound containers of arms and ammunition they would shortly parachute into occupied Europe.

Heflin and the 3,000 men of his squadron were a highly specialized unit. The "bombs" they dropped had a delayed-action fuse. With a companion squadron in the RAF, they supplied the Resistance of Europe with arms. Since January, 1943, the Carpetbaggers had flown over 300 missions, parachuting thousands of tons of arms and ammunition and hundreds of men to the Resistance forces of France, Belgium, Holland, Norway and Poland. Few of those missions had been as difficult as the one ahead of the Carpetbaggers this morning. Its code name was Operation Beggar. Heflin's men would fly it by daylight, at 400 feet, over an area ringed with German flak, onto targets some of which were little bigger than a football field.

"Colonel Rol" had won. His urgent radio messages for arms had, after all, gotten through. In a few hours, soon after the first gray streaks of dawn had softened the English sky, 130 planes of the Carpetbagger Squadron would, in a "maximum effort" operation, shower 200 tons of arms into the very heart of Paris, onto the Bois de Boulogne, the Auteuil and Longchamp racetracks, the Esplanade of the Invalides, the place de la République . . . and right into the courtyard of the besieged Prefecture of Police.

● ● ●

For Colonel Albert Lebel, the author of the midnight plea for Paris, the sight of his dirty, unshaven countryman climbing out of a jeep at the security tent of Eagletac, headquarters of General Bradley's Twelfth Army Group, was a providential coincidence. If ever, thought Lebel, there was a right man at the right place at the right time, it was the exhausted Parisian before him. In a few moments, at six o'clock, Lebel would have his last meeting with his superior, Brigadier General Edwin Sibert, Twelfth Army Group's intelligence chief. After their meeting, Sibert was scheduled to leave with General Bradley for Eisenhower's headquarters. There those three men would debate the fate of Paris.

For the past forty-eight hours, Sibert had resisted the idea of a change in Allied plans and an immediate march on the city. This meeting was Lebel's last chance to change his mind. In the red-eyed and unkempt Roger Gallois now standing before him, Lebel had an argument more direct, more persuasive, than any of the impassioned pleas he himself might utter.

Gallois, downcast after another jeep trip, his third in twelve hours with a rigorously silent GI driver, at once understood the importance of what was happening. The curt "no" of General Patton the night before was not, after all, final. He was going to get a second chance. "Last night," he told himself, "I wasn't convincing enough. This time I'll make it better."

He did. With a sincerity and conviction that stirred the American officers around him, Gallois begged not for their arms for which he had been sent, but for their soldiers.

"The people of Paris," he said, "wanted to liberate their capital themselves and present it to the Allies. But they cannot finish what they have started. You must come to our help," he pleaded, "or there is going to be a terrible slaughter. Hundreds of thousands of Frenchmen are going to be killed."

The room was silent when he concluded. General Sibert, coughing lightly, thanked Gallois and gathered up his papers. On his way out of the room, he gave Colonel Lebel a friendly pinch on the elbow. "Your impatient lion, Leclerc, is coming today," he said. "Take care of him. We may have some news for him tonight."

Then, his documents under his arm, his head bowed in thought, this New England Yankee walked to his waiting Piper Cub. Gallois's words had "profoundly impressed" Sibert. Strapping himself into his plane, he thought to himself, "If we don't get into Paris in a couple of days, there's going to be an awful massacre."

•   •   •

At the edge of a grove of trees near the Falaise battlefield, just outside the village of Grandchamp, Dwight Eisenhower, too, had been thinking of Paris in the early hours of this Tuesday morning. Before him, on the varnished desk of his command caravan, was a plain sheet of white stationery, the same piece of paper on which, twenty-four hours before, Charles de Gaulle had addressed his urgent demand for Paris's liberation. In his firm and neat handwriting, Eisenhower penned with little enthusiasm a reluctant postscript of his own to that message: "It looks," he wrote his chief of staff, General Walter Bedell Smith, "as though we shall be compelled to go into Paris."

It was a move Eisenhower would make, if he had to, with great reluctance. Already an angry George Patton was on the field telephone to his supply officer three times a day, demanding more gas.

Yet, despite the firmness of his reply to de Gaulle two days before, Eisenhower had, since their meeting, been brooding on what the Frenchman had told him. He held de Gaulle in high esteem. If de Gaulle was concerned about order in Paris, he would be too. Above all, two years of experience had taught Eisenhower to appreciate one hard reality about the man who led the Free French. De Gaulle, he knew, "was always determined to get where he wanted to go, and he wasn't about to let anybody stop him." If he was going to be "compelled" to go into Paris, it would be the stern Frenchman, and not the Wehrmacht, that would do the compelling.

Before starting off on his morning appointments, the Supreme Commander summed up his frustrations in a brief cable to his commander, General George Marshall, in Washington. "Because of the supply commitment in the liberation of Paris," he said, "it is desirable to delay the capture of the city until after the important matter of destroying the enemy forces up to and including those in the Pas-de-Calais has been accomplished."

But, he warned Marshall, this might not be possible. Should the liberation take place soon, he advised him that *some days thereafter, de Gaulle will be allowed to make his formal entry into the city.* Eisenhower's plan was that when the Allies had pushed the Germans back a suitable distance from the capital, de Gaulle would be allowed to come in "probably under some joint Allied setup." The London *Daily Herald* had even announced this August morning, citing high diplomatic sources, that F.D.R. and Winston Churchill would head a "triumphal Allied march into the capital" sometime after its liberation. "De Gaulle," the paper added, "would *probably* have the place of honor."

There was no question of his staying once he got there. The Supreme Commander had been informed de Gaulle was in France only for a temporary tour of inspection. The Franco-American Civil Affairs Agreement, accepted in principle in Washington in July, still had not been signed. As Eisenhower's Civil Affairs deputy, Brigadier General Julius Holmes, knew, none of the State Department planners working on that agreement had any intention of permitting de Gaulle to transfer the seat of his authority from Algiers to Paris for some time to come. They assumed de Gaulle would go peacefully back to Algiers. From there he would be allowed gradually to transfer his functions from Algiers to some large French city, and finally to Paris only after he had been given formal *de facto* recognition by Washington, and the Germans had been largely chased out of France.

His allies' reservations were well known to de Gaulle. In his temporary headquarters at the Prefecture of Le Mans this warm morning, he had no intention of letting Eisenhower or anybody else "allow" him to make a formal entry into Paris. He intended to go into Paris with the first Allied troops and to stay there. And, whether Eisenhower liked it or not, he had decided that the 2nd French Armored Division was going to be marching on the capital within hours on either the Supreme Commander's orders or his.

Never would Charles de Gaulle agree to enter the capital of his country under the auspices of his allies. He intended to make his entry alone, as Charles de Gaulle, the head of Free France. Then he would welcome the Allies into his capital. He had even ordered his aide-de-camp, Claude Guy, to find him a French car for the occasion. Guy had, the night before, requisitioned a magnificent Hotchkiss from a Swiss businessman in Rennes.

In that French car, driven by a French driver, guarded by French troops, de Gaulle intended to make his own entry into Paris. Just as he had deliberately neglected to inform his allies that his "visit" to France was going to be permanent, he neglected now to inform them of one other fact: He had no intention of leaving Paris once he got there. For de Gaulle, his own entry into Paris was just the first in a rapid series of steps that would plant his provisional government, recognition or no recognition, in Paris.*

Well aware of his allies' reluctance to accept such a move, de Gaulle resolved this morning to allow no last-minute United States diplomatic maneuver to thwart his plans. From this morning on, he told his aides, his exact whereabouts was to be "discreetly unavailable" to his allies.†

* * *

The high-pitched ring of the green scrambler telephone galvanized the men in the operations room of the Carpetbagger Squadron. That telephone linked their Harrington Air Force Base directly to OSS headquarters in London. Lieutenant Colonel Bob Sullivan picked it up. Over the static of the scrambler, the voice of his caller seem to be percolating through water. "Stand down Operation Beggar," Sullivan was told. The operation, London said, was reset for the next day, Wednesday, August 23.

Like Dietrich von Choltitz, General Pierre Koenig, the head of the FFI, had just decided to accord himself a twenty-four-hour respite. Koenig had ordered Operation Beggar, and just a few minutes before Sullivan's scrambler telephone rang, he had postponed it. To Koenig and the other men of his Free French headquarters at London's Bryanston Square, an arms drop on Paris was a terrifying risk. It could lead to a massacre of the Parisians rushing to recover them. Many of those weapons would fall into German hands. But, above all, most of them, they knew, would fall into the arms of de Gaulle's Communist rivals. In three years of operations, no edict had been more strictly applied by this headquarters than that against parachuting arms to cities and areas where substantial quantities of arms would fall into Communist hands. That edict would not be easily cast aside in the last weeks of France's liberation for an operation which would shower arms

---

* The day before, in a cable to Algiers, he told the members of his government he had named General Pierre Koenig military governor of Paris, in order to "fix immediately the conditions under which the authority of the government will be established from the moment the Allies enter the capital."

† How well he succeeded is indicated by the reply by Eisenhower's chief of staff twenty-four hours later to a question posed by the American major newly assigned to de Gaulle as a liaison officer. "How the hell should I know where he is?" asked Walter Bedell Smith. "Do you think he tells us?"

into one of the densest concentrations of Communists in
France.

Yet, as much as they disapproved of the insurrection and
hesitated to begin this operation, Koenig and the Free French
of London could not stand by and watch their fellow citizens
fight against German tanks in the streets of Paris with pistols
and old rifles. Beset with doubts and misgivings, Koenig had
decided on the drop, then decided to wait one more day. If
the fighting was not under control in twenty-four hours, he
vowed, he would, whatever the political consequences, rain
thousands of rifles onto the rooftops of Paris.

21

FOR PARIS, THERE WAS no twenty-four-hour
respite. The fighting resumed after dawn in growing intensity
all across the city. Shortly after eight, four tanks of the in-
genious SS Standartenführer appeared again outside the Police
Commissariat of Raymond Sarran, the law student who, the
day before, had told the colonel, "You no longer give orders
here." This time the Standartenführer's tankers had left behind their human shields. In two hours of furious combat they
drove Sarran and his men from the building. Before scampering across the neighborhood rooftops, Sarran's men exacted a
price. One of them, at the cost of his life, bolted out to a
German tank and smashed a Molotov cocktail against its
ventilator, leaving it a flaming wreck.

In the Seventeenth Arrondissement where the lone and
silent tank of the Resistance had made its appearance the day
before, the Germans shelled apart a group of apartment
houses, an apparent reply to their mute rival. On the Left
Bank, the FFI were now the masters of the crooked little
alleyways from the Seine to the boulevard Saint-Germain. No
Germans dared to move into those twisting streets too narrow
for a tank. At the "Carrefour de la Mort," at the intersection
of the boulevards Saint-Germain and Saint-Michel, excited
French student gunners piled up a line of flaming German

trucks. From one they took a dozen prisoners and a heavy machine gun which they quickly mounted on their neatly terraced barricade. At the Gare de Lyon, a truckload of German soldiers, caught in an ambush, retreated to a café. The dozen patrons inside started to laugh at their plight. The Germans shot them all. The courtyard of the Prefecture of Police was a junk pile of captured German vehicles, the white letters "FFI" painted over their blistered surfaces.

The small group of men around Alexandre Parodi had no time to savor the dramatic success of Opération Prise du Pouvoir the day before. Just as they had planned, they had the afternoon before held a full-fledged meeting of the government of Charles de Gaulle in the office of the Prime Minister. Yvon Morandat's fiancée Claire had faithfully taken the minutes of the extraordinary session. Then, sober and dignified as any press secretary of the Third Republic announcing a new ministerial crisis, she read those notes to the reporters of Paris's newspapers gathered outside. Now, while their foes remained concentrated on the problem of waging their insurrection, Parodi's men began to move into the key government ministries still left unoccupied. Yvon Morandat, who had the day before occupied the Prime Minister's residence, was demoted. This time he was assigned a simple ministry, the Ministry of the Interior.

At the Hôtel de Ville, the huge Renaissance city hall of Paris that had been occupied forty-eight hours earlier, Parodi's rivals had begun to create a citadel of their own, a counterweight to the Gaullist bastion that was the Prefecture of Police. It, too, was taken under attack by Choltitz's men. While André Tollet, the man who had forced the first decision for this insurrection, taught a group of sixteen-year-olds inside how to fire a pistol, four German tanks shelled the building from outside. Tollet slid to the window to fire himself. As he looked out, he saw a young girl crawl over the embankment of the Seine and, her red skirt swelling around her like a flower blossom, run to the nearest tank. In a quick movement she hoisted herself onto the flank of the tank. He saw her arm sweep up, clutching a green champagne bottle which she poised for a second in the air, then smashed down into the tank's turret. A geyser of flame spat out of the hole. The girl leaped down from the tank and ran back to the embankment. A few feet away she fell, shot, her red skirt spreading over the sidewalk "like a tulip flicked from its stalk by a knife stroke." The three remaining tanks left.

For the millions of Parisians, this fourth day of fighting brought a new, ugly menace, hunger. The bakers had neither wheat nor wood for their ovens. A few who still had a few sacks of wheat cut down the trees of the Bois de Boulogne to burn in their ovens. To an unhappy group of men around him, Parodi's temporary Minister of Food Supplies announced that if "trucks can't get out of Paris in a few days, there will be a famine by the end of the week."

None of Paris's hungry citizens was more surprised this Tuesday than Paul Pardou, the little Resistance hijacker being held prisoner in the Palais du Luxembourg. The fat mess sergeant Franz who had regularly announced Pardou's approaching execution offered him, before his forthcoming journey to a firing squad, a last meal, a plate of Rinderbraten, the specialty of his native Württemberg.

To another prisoner, the distant and distinguished Captain Wilhelm von Zigesar-Beines, the German baron who had kept Paris's racetracks open, the policemen of the commissariat of the Grand Palais just off the Champs-Élysées had nothing to offer but a specialty of the occupation, a plate of boiled and tasteless rutabagas. For the last twenty-four hours, the monocled cavalry officer had been locked in a cave of the Grand Palais. He knew the building well. Before the war, von Zigesar-Beines had lived a more glorious hour in this palace. He had been one of the stars of the German Army equestrian team and had, on countless occasions, galloped the tanbark of the ring over his head, the applause of thousands of admiring Frenchmen ringing in his ears. Now, from his window, von Zigesar-Beines saw a German soldier, like some comic-strip figure, leading a flock of rosy pigs down the Champs-Élysées. First Sergeant Heinrich Müller, head of the General Staff garage on the rue Marbeuf, had been ordered to bring those pigs to the Tuileries garden. That evening two of his wards, killed by FFI bullets, would turn on a spit to provide a last Parisian feast for First Sergeant Müller and his two dozen men.

The saddest individual in all a hungry Paris, perhaps, was an old man on the rue Racine dragging a little wooden cart. In it he had a treasure, four pounds of potatoes. A stray round from a machine gun had smashed his cart and its load to ruins. Looking at the pieces rolling in the gutter, the weeping old man murmured to a bystander, "At least, now there's a little wood to boil the potatoes that are left."

22

SWEDISH CONSUL GENERAL RAOUL Nordling wondered what Dietrich von Choltitz was fumbling for in the little cabinet behind his desk. He had never seen him open it before in his presence. With a clatter, the general took out a decanter and two glasses. Then, with a conspiratorial smile, he leaned across his desk. "Don't tell the English," he said, "but I'm going to have a whisky." He offered one to Nordling. Decidedly, thought the Swede, this little German, wearing what he thought was the first thin smile he had ever seen on his face, was a bizarre individual. Was it, he wondered, to offer him a drink that von Choltitz had invited him here, having proposed, even, to send an armored car to get him?

Von Choltitz poured their drinks. He raised his glass, murmured a polite "Prosit," and swallowed his whisky in one neat gulp.

Then he leaned back in his chair and, for a few seconds, looked quizzically at the diplomat. "Your truce, Herr Consul General," he observed, "doesn't seem to be working very well." Before Nordling could reply, he added, with a bitter note in his voice, that the three prisoners he had released Sunday had done nothing to justify his gesture. The insurrection, he remarked, was becoming more widespread every day.

Nordling sighed. There was only one man the FFI really obeyed, he pointed out. It was General de Gaulle, and he was not in Paris. He was probably somewhere in Normandy with the Allies.

Again Choltitz looked at Nordling for a fleeting moment. Then, in a quiet, direct voice, he said to the Swedish diplomat, "Why doesn't somebody go to see him?"

For a moment the Swede did not know what to reply. Was Choltitz joking? he wondered. Or was this little Parisian officer before him actually suggesting that someone go on a mission to the Allied Command?

Nordling asked Choltitz if he would authorize someone to pass through the German lines to see the Allies.

"Why not?" answered the German.

Nordling was taken aback. He slid his empty glass across the desk toward Choltitz. As a neutral diplomat, he told him, he was prepared to undertake a mission to the Allies if he had a valid *laissez-passer*.

Von Choltitz nodded, but he seemed indifferent. To Nordling, it was clear he had something else on his mind. The general rested his whisky glass on the table. Unfastening a button of his tunic with his thumb and forefinger, he drew out from his gray jacket a sheet of blue paper and spread it out on his desk.

He did not invite Nordling to look at it. It was, he told the Swede, an order, one of several orders he had received in the past few days. By now, he told him, he should have already begun the program of systematic destruction those orders called for. Despite constant pressure from OKW, despite Hitler's insistence he take brutal action to stamp out the insurrection even if it meant destroying large parts of the city, he had, he reminded Nordling, preferred to try his truce. It had failed, and now he was going to be forced to carry out those orders.

To the silent and slightly awed diplomat, Choltitz declared that "very soon" he was going to have to execute them or be relieved of his command. Speaking slowly, in a very sober tone, he leaned forward and told Nordling that the only thing that might prevent those orders from being carried out was the rapid arrival of the Allies in Paris.

Wheezing slightly with his asthma, he added, his voice faint, "You must realize that my behavior in telling you this could be interpreted as treason." For a few seconds the room was still and breathless in the warm August midday. Then, choosing his words very carefully, von Choltitz spoke a final phrase: "Because," he said, "what I am really doing is asking the Allies to help me."

Nordling felt the impact of each one of Choltitz's words. With the instinctive reaction of his long years of diplomacy he realized that his own words might not be enough to convince the Allies of what he had just heard. He asked Choltitz if he would give him a written document for the Allies.

The German looked at him, astonished. "I could not possibly put what I have just told you on paper," he said.

Then, with a few strokes of his pen, Choltitz scratched out for Nordling the only written warrant he was willing to give him. "The Commanding General of Gross Paris," he wrote, "authorizes the Consul General of Sweden R. Nordling to leave Paris and its line of defense." He passed the piece of paper across his desk to the chubby Swede. Nordling, sweating lightly in his nervous excitement, asked Choltitz for some further guarantee that would get him through the German lines.

Von Choltitz told Nordling to take "Bobby" Bender with him as far as the last German outposts. With great reluctance, he agreed that if they had trouble getting through, he would repeat his instruction orally, by telephone.

Von Choltitz got up and came around his desk to take Nordling to the door. He felt "a great load off his conscience." He had found a way to warn the Allies of the danger hanging over Paris, and he hoped to make them realize that, for the moment at least, the road to Paris was open. How long it would remain open he could not know. If the reinforcements he had been promised arrived before the Allies did, his soldier's honor would force him to try to close the door himself, and defend Paris in a wasting and destructive street battle. But the Allies had their warning. If they did not act on it in time, he thought, they, and not he, would bear before history the responsibility for the consequences.

With an affectionate gesture he took Nordling by the crook of his elbow. Puffing slightly, he guided him to the door. There he suddenly grasped his hand. "Go fast," he said. "Twenty-four, forty-eight hours are all you have. After that, I cannot promise you what will happen here."

23

RARELY IN HIS thirty-five-year diplomatic career had Consul General Raoul Nordling faced so complicated a task. To cross the German lines would be one thing; to convince de Gaulle and the Allies of the accuracy of his story, another. If he was going to have any chance of success, he reasoned, somebody was going to have to leave with him who was known to the Allies. Without informing von Choltitz of what he was doing, Nordling decided to add two men to his party: Alexandre de Saint-Phalle, the treasurer of the Gaullist Resistance in Paris, and Jean Laurent, a banker who had been a member of de Gaulle's staff at the Ministry of Defense in 1940. Their presence, he believed, would give the party validity in de Gaulle's eyes. The Swede was mistaken. He had no way of knowing it, but neither man was among the people who had access to the general.

They, however, were not to be the only additions to this strange party the Swede was frantically putting together. In midafternoon, while Nordling waited for a report from Saint-Phalle on the best route to the Allied lines, he heard the ringing of the Consulate doorbell. Waiting for him at the door was a balding giant with deep blue eyes. His name, he told Nordling, was Arnoux, and he represented the Red Cross. He wanted to leave with the party. His presence, he said, might help them through the German lines. The Swede was both angry and astonished. In the jealous little world of neutrals, he could see no reason for involving anybody from the Red Cross in his mission. More important, he was dismayed that the news of his trip had leaked out.

In curt and clear words, he told Arnoux there was neither a place nor a need for him on the trip. Saint-Phalle, who had just arrived, intervened. He insisted that Arnoux go. Reluctantly, Nordling agreed. Several weeks later he discovered who the curious M. Arnoux of the Red Cross was. The Swede had just assigned a place in the mission authorized by the

German commander of Gross Paris to the head of all British intelligence for France. Arnoux was Colonel Claude Ollivier, the "Jade Amicol" for whom Alain Perpezat had parachuted into a moonless night almost three weeks earlier.

Nordling did, at least, know the next uninvited guest who rang his doorbell: the tall young Austrian who had found "Bobby" Bender for him ten days earlier. The elegantly embroidered initials E.P.P. over the chest pocket of his shirt, Nordling knew, stood for Erich Posch-Pastor. The Swede suspected he was a German intelligence agent, and he suspected further that he had been, on von Choltitz's orders, assigned to watch him for the past week.

Nordling's estimate, this time, was partially correct. Posch-Pastor was an intelligence agent, but not for Germany. To the members of the Goelette Resistance net, the initials E.P.P. on Posch-Pastor's chest had another meaning. They stood for Étienne Paul Provost, the code name the twenty-nine-year old Austrian nobleman had borne since he joined the Resistance in October, 1943. During that time, Posch-Pastor, son of the Austro-Hungarian Empire's last ambassador to the Vatican, had furnished the Allies a notable store of military information, including some of the first stolen designs of the V-1 rocket. In his most recent assignment for the Wehrmacht, the young lieutenant had been the security officer of a factory making proximity fuzes in Niort, near the Atlantic Coast. There, through a careful reorganization of his security duties, he had supervised a reduction in the factory's rate of production from 13,000 fuzes a month to fewer than 1,000.

Now, to a disagreeably surprised Nordling, he announced von Choltitz had assigned him to accompany the mission to the Allies.* The Swede, sure he had been ordered on him

---

* The exact nature of von Choltitz's relations with Posch-Pastor, and the role of the Austrian himself, remain, unfortunately, unclear. Of all the hundreds of people the authors spoke to in preparing this book, Posch-Pastor, now an employee of the Zurich branch of a German metallurgical firm, was the only man who categorically refused to discuss his experiences during the liberation of Paris. Born June 15, 1915, in Innsbruck, Erich Posch-Pastor von Camperfeld was a lieutenant in the Austrian Army at the time of the Anschluss. His regiment was one of the few to oppose the Nazis, and he was interned at Dachau for a year thereafter. He arrived in France in February, 1942, after being wounded in Russia, and joined the French Resistance in October, 1943. He received the Médaille de la Résistance with a citation reading in part: "For eight months without letup, he passed economic and military information of the highest importance to the Allies, including some of the first designs of the V-1 rocket." In July, 1944, he was fired from his job in Niort for incompetence and ordered to an infantry unit in Italy. He

as a watchdog by Choltitz, accepted him with little grace.

For the chunky Nordling, spent by his efforts, there remained one last disagreeable surprise on this astonishing afternoon. As he charted the last arrangements for his trip, Nordling felt a band of pain tighten around his chest. He fell to his knees gasping for breath.

This man who had been chosen to carry the desperate warning of Dietrich von Choltitz to the Allies 60 miles away could barely drag himself the few feet across his office to a spare bed. He had just had a heart attack.

Half an hour after his collapse, while he lay half conscious in the Consulate, his black Citroën left for Versailles. Von Choltitz's message was on its way to Dwight Eisenhower.

In Nordling's black Citroën were two Gaullists Charles de Gaulle did not want to see, two Allied intelligence agents who did not know each other, and the wrong Swedish diplomat. Raoul Nordling had sent in his place the only other man in Paris who could fill this mission for him and answer to the name "R. Nordling," handwritten on von Choltitz's *laissez-passer*. It was his brother Rolf.

•   •   •

Forty-five minutes and three roadblocks later, Nordling's car, shepherded by the watchful "Bobby" Bender in his super-

---

deserted and came back to Paris. During the period of the liberation of Paris, both he and "Bobby" Bender, the Abwehr agent, had relatively free access to the Hotel Meurice. Von Choltitz angrily denied to the authors that he had ordered Posch-Pastor to leave with the Nordling mission; the Austrian, he claimed, forced himself on Nordling on his own initiative. Posch-Pastor would not discuss the matter. However, Daniel Klotz, the American OSS agent who interrogated him on his arrival behind the Allied lines, recalls Posch-Pastor was immediately recognized and requested by British intelligence. The day after the Liberation, Posch-Pastor was back in Paris, this time in Allied uniform.

The only comment Posch-Pastor made on his role in the liberation of Paris was the declaration that on Monday, August 21, while he was in Choltitz's outer office, he heard the German general "save his life." Through the walls of the office, Posch-Pastor says he heard three agents of the SD ask Choltitz if he had any idea where he was. With his own terrified ears, he heard the little general tell the three men he "had never heard of any Posch-Pastor." Von Choltitz recalled the incident. About it he would only say that "he wouldn't have turned a stray dog over to the SD."

In Paris, the only trace that now remains of the mysterious Etienne Paul Provost is a dusty dossier in a two-room apartment of the rue Royer-Collard. There, in the fading archives of the Goelette network, in a brown folder marked "CLAYREC RJ4570," are the record of Posch-Pastor's service with the network and a copy of his citations.

charged Citroën coupé, slipped through the village of Saint-Cyr and pointed past the green fields of the Ile de France toward the distant cathedral city of Chartres and the American lines.

Just outside the crossroads village of Trappes, a half-naked figure in a Wehrmacht helmet and a polka-dot bathing suit leaped from a roadside ditch and, with an angry wave of his submachine gun, flagged them to a halt. Jabbing the snout of his weapon through Saint-Phalle's opened window, he demanded, "Was ist das?" Saint-Phalle's only reaction was to stare dumbly at the silver medal dangling from a chain around the German's neck. It was the Iron Cross. Then, past his bare shoulders, Saint-Phalle saw the camouflaged forms of eight Tiger tanks in a pocket of trees just off the road. "We're lost," he thought. In his rearview mirror he caught a glimpse of the Red Cross's "M. Arnoux" twisting a string of black rosary beads through his fingers. Beside him, smoking a cornsilk cigarette with smiling unconcern, was Posch-Pastor. Later Saint-Phalle would learn that the only identification Posch-Pastor had with him that evening was a false French identity card in the name of Étienne Paul Provost tucked into the heel of his left sock.

Now Saint-Phalle could hear the angry Germanic tones of "Bobby" Bender shouting at their captor. From the tank park beside the road, an SS Hauptsturmführer in a camouflaged battle smock came over to the car. Bender shouted "Heil Hitler" to the advancing officer and handed him his Abwehr identity papers. Then, from Saint-Phalle, Bender took von Choltitz's *laissez-passer* for this curious caravan and handed it to the Hauptsturmführer. With a quick and brutal gesture, the SS captain pushed it back at Bender. "I don't give a damn what general signed it," he said. "Since the 20th of July, we don't obey Wehrmacht generals."

Bender was flustered for a moment; then he flew into a rage. The Hauptsturmführer, surprised at the vigor of his reaction, finally agreed to telephone the Gross Paris headquarters for instructions. With Bender at his side, he walked off, leaving Saint-Phalle and his companions in a shocked silence marred only by the soft Ave Marias rising from the Red Cross man on the back seat of their Citroën.

An hour later the two men came back. Bender had played his role well. He had succeeded in getting to the phone the only man in the headquarters of Gross Paris who knew of the existence of this mission. In an angry voice, Choltitz had told the obstinate SS officer that if he failed to clear the party through his lines, he would "come out and see it's done" himself.

With an indifferent shrug of his shoulders, the Hauptsturm-führer waved Saint-Phalle ahead. Behind them Bender, his job done, watched them go.

Saint-Phalle had just begun to accelerate when another German leaped at them from a roadside ditch and hurled himself at the hood of the Citroën. Saint-Phalle skidded to a stop. As he did, he heard the word the German had been frantically shouting: "*Minen.*" Just three feet from the Cit-roën's front wheels was the first emplacement of a carefully seeded minefield. Any one of those mines would have de-stroyed this handful of men and, with them, the plea on which the destiny of Paris seemed to depend.

The German took a piece of paper from his pocket and studied it in front of the car. Then, beckoning Saint-Phalle to follow him, the German, his eyes cautiously fixed on the asphalt, led the Citroën on a zigzag course. For thirty-five minutes, perspiring fiercely, the five men in the car twisted through the minefield in a terrifying slalom. At a final inter-section the German straightened up and tucked the paper back into his pocket. Then he pointed his hand west and proudly announced, "The Americans. Five hundred meters."

Saint-Phalle, with his carload of hope for three and a half million Parisians and a distressed Dietrich von Choltitz, turned down the fork in the road leading to Neauphle-le-Vieux to find those Americans. For the sandy-haired banker, it was an instinctive gesture. He had taken that same road almost every Sunday of his life. It led to his grandmother's house.

24

THE MAN CALLED THE "impatient lion" by his American superiors, General Jacques Philippe Leclerc, paced the grassy airstrip outside the headquarters of Eagletac, swatting at the stalks of grass along his route with quick, angry strokes of his cane. Behind him, in respectful silence, walked the shorter figure of Roger Gallois, the man sent from Paris by "Colonel Rol." General Omar Bradley had still not returned from his conference with General Eisenhower, and in a few minutes—fifteen or twenty, perhaps—Leclerc would have to leave this airstrip to fly back to his own division headquarters.

During the first of the fifty or sixty trips they had taken up and down this airstrip, Gallois had talked with Leclerc until the general's conversation had dropped to one insistent phrase: "I must have the orders tonight."

At the first faint sound of an airplane engine, Leclerc stood stock-still, scanning the skyline. A Piper Cub appeared and landed. Its propeller was still turning when Leclerc rushed up to it. Inside, General Edwin Sibert unbuckled his seat belt and yelled over the noise of the engine to his "impatient lion," "You win. They've decided to send you straight to Paris."

A short while earlier, in the Grandchamp conference tent in which the Supreme Commander had been briefing a visiting delegation of labor leaders, Sibert had filled in Bradley and Eisenhower on the information Gallois had supplied in the morning. Eisenhower had furrowed his forehead in his familiar frown. Then he had sighed and said to Bradley, "Well, what the hell, Brad. I guess we'll have to go in."

Behind them now, Bradley's Cub slid to a stop and the quiet Missourian stepped out and called Leclerc and Gallois to his side. "The decision has been made to enter Paris," he told them, "and the three of us share in the responsibility for it: I, because I have given the order; you, General Leclerc, because you are going to execute it; and you, Major Gallois, because it was largely on the basis of the information you brought us that the decision was made." This little messenger, persuaded in a rain-drenched villa two nights earlier to ignore the instructions of his Communist commander and ask the Allies for troops and not arms, had accomplished what even Charles de Gaulle had not been able to achieve. Thanks to Roger Gallois, Allied troops would be on their way to the menaced capital of France in a few hours.

Then Bradley turned to Leclerc and, in his high, twanging voice said, "I want you to remember one thing above all: I don't want any fighting in Paris itself. It's the only order I have for you—at no cost is there to be heavy fighting in Paris." ° Omar Bradley had seen Saint-Lô. The day he did, the onetime Missouri farmboy had vowed to himself he would not, if he could help it, let that tragedy repeat itself in a city he had admired from afar but never seen, Paris.

Leclerc ran to his own Piper Cub. As he did Bradley called after him, "Get your orders from your Corps commander." †

By the time Leclerc reached his own division headquarters, it was almost dark. With the leap of a schoolboy, he bolted from his plane. To his waiting G3, Major André Gribius, he yelled in one joyous shriek the phrase he had waited four years to pronounce: "Gribius, *mouvement immédiat sur Paris!*"

●　●　●

Of all units under the command of Dwight Eisenhower, none was a stranger or more heterogeneous group than this 2nd French Armored Division soon to be galvanized into action by the excited words of its young commander. It contained Frenchmen who had abandoned their families with-

---

° Those orders were spelled out in even greater detail in Bradley's Twelfth Army Group Field Order No. 21. "It must be emphasized," he wrote, "that the move on to Paris must not be made by heavy fighting. We don't want any bombing or artillery fire in the city if we can possibly avoid it."

† Those orders were already being drafted by an American colonel named John Hill, on the back of a piece of scrap paper in the headquarters of the First U.S. Army. To support the 2nd French Armored Division's entrance into the city, they called for the 4th U.S. Infantry Division to shoulder along the southern edge of the city and push across the Seine just below the capital. As Hill finished his draft, General Courtney H. Hodges, the commanding general of the First Army who on Sunday had told Leclerc that Paris was "a secondary objective," added a last phrase. "Hill," he said, "take a couple of artillery battalions away from those divisions. I don't want them to get the idea they can beat up Paris with a howitzer every time a machine gun gets in their way."

out a word to risk arrest and deportation, to walk hundreds of miles to the frozen Pyrenees, often to spend months in a Spanish concentration camp, for the sole satisfaction of serving in its ranks. It contained men who had crossed the English Channel in stolen rowboats and fishing boats; prisoners of 1940 who had escaped from their German stalags and walked east over Poland to Russia to enlist again in a fight they had lost once; men whose families did not know whether they were dead or alive; men whose families wished them dead for having broken faith with a different France, that of Vichy. There were Frenchmen who had never seen the soil of metropolitan France; Arabs who could barely speak French; Africans from the jungles of the Cameroun, Tuaregs from the Sahara; Spanish veterans of the Loyalist armies; Lebanese, Chileans, Mexicans who had kept faith with France. There were even Frenchmen who had fought and killed each other in Syria and Tunisia in the name of Charles de Gaulle and Henri Philippe Pétain. For these men, this war in Europe was indeed a crusade. Their Jerusalem was now just ahead, the city at the end of the four-word phrase a jubilant Jacques Philippe Leclerc had shouted to his operations officer.

Many of them had never been in Paris. For some who had, that city was a bitter memory: the image of a capital that was no longer theirs. It was a city they had thought of in the Libyan Desert, the Atlas Mountains of Morocco, in the wet green hills of England. Now the news that it was their next target swept them with the speed of sound, the sound of their own clamoring tongues, announcing the magic news that their next destination was the capital of their country.

To gunner Jean René Champion, a Frenchman from Mexico who had never lived in France, the thought of liberating Paris "was a dream too perfect in an imperfect world." Now, slumped on the flanks of his tank *Mort-Homme,* named for a World War I battlefield, Champion learned his dream was about to come true. Captain Raymond Dronne, of the Regiment of Chad, took the news calmly. He set his tank company to work, then took a small round glass from his command car. Hanging the mirror in the branches of an apple tree, Dronne trimmed his flourishing red beard. He wanted to look good to the Parisiennes on his arrival. In forty-eight hours, filthy, stinking of sweat and grease, an exhausted Dronne would see those Parisiennes, and to many of them he would be the most beautiful man they had ever seen. He would be the first French soldier to enter Paris.

For the crew of the tank destroyer *Simoun*, this evening of August 22 was already a special one. They were celebrating the thirty-sixth birthday of their commander, Second Mate Paul Quinion. To mark it they had a special treat, a duck that gunner's aide Guy Robin had procured from a nearby farm. Plucked and cleaned, the duck was ready for roasting when a breathless officer rushed up to their group and told them, "Pack it up, we're moving. This time, it's Paname." ° Robert Mady, the gunner, remembers the stunned silence of the crew. Then, in one voice, they murmured, "*Merde*—the duck!"

Captain Charles d'Orgeix, of the 12th Regiment of Cuirassiers, felt tears sting his eyes when he heard of their destination. Four years, two months and nine days earlier, on a motorcycle, Orgeix had been one of the last handful of men defending the approaches to his capital. Alone and helpless, the group had been swarmed over by Panzers of the Wehrmacht. Now Orgeix was going back for a rematch with those Panzers. This time he would have a tank instead of a motorcycle, the new Sherman against which he leaned in the Norman dusk. Its name was painted along its turret in white letters. It was the *Paris*.

• • •

With a sense of impatience only slightly less acute perhaps than that of Leclerc and the men of his 2nd French Armored Division, the correspondents with the liberating armies prepared for their own highly competitive march on Paris. Already scores were swarming over the road Ernest Hemingway had already taken toward the capital. In fact, in the whole massive press corps, only one man, it seemed, was not headed for Paris. He was heading in almost the opposite direction, for England. Yet CBS's Larry Lesueur had a very special reason for wanting to be on hand for the liberation of Paris. He had been the last American correspondent to broadcast from a free Paris, on his thirtieth birthday, June 10, 1940. He had vowed to be the first American to broadcast from a liberated capital.

° An affectionate slang title for Paris, popularized in song before the war by Edith Piaf.

Three days earlier, tragedy had overtaken Lesueur. He had bitten hard onto a bar of K rations, and this ration bar had bitten back. It had chipped off part of a front tooth. What to his fellow newsmen would have been only a minor discomfort was, to broadcaster Lesueur, a disabling wound. He whistled when he talked. He had done everything to repair it; he had stuffed the gap with bubble gum, with his finger, with his tongue, with a gluey flour paste that had dissolved as soon as it had entered his mouth. Nothing worked. Lesueur could not broadcast without sounding like a midday factory whistle.

Now he was doing the only thing that seemed possible. He was going back to London to a dentist. As he flew over the Channel, he had one reassuring thought to comfort him. Before deciding to leave, he had asked General Courtney Hodges, the Commander of the First U.S. Army, if there was any chance that Paris would be liberated in the next few days.

"Hell, no," Hodges told him. "We aren't going to be in Paris for at least two weeks."

As Lesueur flew back to London, the one competitor he feared more than any other was already announcing the liberation of Paris. Charles Collingwood, the second CBS man assigned to the Allied armies, had stumbled on a prized piece of information shortly after Lesueur's departure. He had run into General Bradley just after Bradley's return to Twelfth Army Group headquarters. In passing, Bradley had told him, "The FFI have risen in Paris. It looks as though the 2nd French Armored is going in to liberate the city."

Now, on one of the two experimental tape recorders CBS was using in the theater, Collingwood was taping a "canned" announcement of Paris's liberation. He knew SHAEF's capacity for communications foul-ups. He was not going to be caught in another one. When the first flash of the capital's liberation came, he might be stuck far from a transmitter, but this breathless and dramatic account of that moment would be sitting in London, ready for instant relay to all America.

"The 2nd French Armored Division," he dictated, "entered Paris today after the Parisians rose as one man to beat down the terrified German troops who had garrisoned the city."

Collingwood finished recording and, with great satisfaction, wrapped it up to be forwarded to SHAEF's censors. Nobody was going to beat Charles Collingwood with the news of Paris's liberation.

• • •

In his Hotel Meurice office, General von Choltitz started perceptibly in his chair. With his characteristic inscrutability, his chief of staff, Colonel Friedrich von Unger, had just announced to him that four SS officers were waiting in his anteroom to see him. The little general could deduce only one thing: they had found out about the Nordling mission, and he was being placed under arrest.

The four men tramped in, banged their heels ostentatiously together and braced into a noisy "Heil Hitler." One of them, a thin man with a long scar over his cheekbone, stepped to Choltitz's desk. He was an Obersturmbannführer, and von Choltitz saw on his tunic sleeve the insignia of one of the most celebrated units in the SS, the Panzer Division "Adolf Hitler Leibstandarte." He announced to Choltitz that he had received, 40 miles east of Paris, over the radio of his command car, a personal order from Heinrich Himmler. The mention of the name of the head of the SS and the Gestapo was to Choltitz the final confirmation of his fear; he was indeed about to be placed under arrest.

Instead, the Obersturmbannführer announced that Himmler had ordered him to report to Paris immediately to take possession of an art object in the Louvre, a tapestry that had been evacuated to Paris from the Museum of the Norman city of Bayeux. In no case, said the Obersturmbannführer, was the tapestry to be allowed to fall into Allied hands. He had formal orders to bring it back to Germany for safekeeping.

A relieved Choltitz had difficulty containing his desire to laugh. "Ach, Kinder," he said to the four SS men, "how wonderful of you to help save these valuable objects from destruction." He even suggested to the officer before him that he take advantage of his stay to take into his protective custody some of the other objects in the Louvre, such as the Winged Victory and the Mona Lisa.* No, no, the Obersturmbannführer answered, the only thing Himmler and the Führer wanted was the Bayeux tapestry.

Von Choltitz took his four visitors to the balcony. Leaning

---

* Von Choltitz, who had never been in the Louvre, did not know it, but the French had already removed most of its treasures to protect them from such solicitous gestures as this.

against its railing with his elbows, he gestured toward the outline of the Louvre to his left, solid and imposing in the evening darkness. At just about that instant, a furious burst of firing which seemed to be coming from the Louvre itself tore apart the night. "The terrorists have apparently occupied the building," Choltitz remarked. The slightly concerned SS officers agreed. However, Choltitz added, he was sure a band of French terrorists were no particular menace to four officers of the SS.

The SS Obersturmbannführer was silent for a few seconds. Then he asked von Choltitz if he did not believe the French would have already moved the tapestry to some other location. No, no, Choltitz answered, "Why would they have done that?" Again the firing broke out around the building, and once again the SS men expressed doubts that the tapestry would be in the Louvre. Von Choltitz—who by now was enjoying every moment of their visit—rang for an aging officer who bore, perhaps, the most euphemistic title on his staff. He was the captain in charge of the "Protection of French Monuments and Works of Art." He solemnly assured the SS officers that the tapestry was indeed in the Louvre.

To ease their burden, Choltitz offered to place at their disposal an armored car and a section of soldiers to "cover the building from the street" while the four officers went after the tapestry.

The scarred Obersturmbannführer seemed perplexed by the situation. He told Choltitz he would radio Berlin for further instructions and report back in an hour. With another sharp Hitlerian salute, he left.

Von Choltitz never saw the four men again. The precious tapestry which they had been ordered to save from the Allies, and which represented a unique moment in history, remained in the Louvre. On its 84 square yards of fabric, the ladies of the court of William the Conqueror had, nine centuries earlier, embroidered a scene the cameramen of Adolf Hitler had often been promised but never filmed: the invasion of England.

25

THE LITTLE APPLE ORCHARD before Écouché
was smothered in the same conspiratorial darkness that, forty-
four hours before, had covered the stealthy departure of Lieutenant Colonel Jacques de Guillebon. But this night, in the
tents tucked under its fruit-filled trees, there was neither
silence nor stealth. In the command caravan from which he
had watched de Guillebon's departure, General Jacques
Philippe Leclerc listened to the clacking typewriter of his
clerk finishing the last words of the formal eight-point order
he had just dictated. In just six and a half hours, at 6:30 in
the morning, Philippe Leclerc would start with the men of
his division the last 122 miles remaining in the journey he had
begun four years earlier: in a pirogue on a riverbank in
British Nigeria opposite French Cameroun. Leclerc reread
the order his clerk handed to him: "I demand, for this movement which will lead the Division to the capital of France," he
had written, "a supreme effort which I am sure to obtain from
you all." Leclerc looked at his watch, then signed and dated
the order. It was just midnight.

•   •   •

Eleven hundred miles to the east—in another grove of trees
four times as high as the apple trees of Écouché, the fir trees
of Rastenburg—the evening strategy conference of Adolf
Hitler had begun almost on the stroke of midnight this August
22. Around the Führer's conference table, Generalfeldmarschall Keitel, Generals Warlimont, Burgdorf, Fegelein, and
Hitler's SS aide, Hauptsturmführer Günsche, listened in sober
silence as Generaloberst Jodl, his hands stretched flat on the
table before him, presented the western front situation report.
Once again, Hitler had ordered that report ahead of the news
from the eastern front. The Führer, Warlimont was later to
note in his diary, was seated, and his right hand, spread over

the celluloid surface of a map before him, trembled lightly as he listened to Jodl's words.

When Jodl had finished, Hitler jerked up his head. In an angry, rasping voice he asked, "Where is the mortar?" This time General Warlimont had welcome news for him. The "Karl," with its wagon train of ammunition, had reached Soissons, less than 60 miles from Paris. In another twenty-four hours, Warlimont told Hitler, the "Karl" would be in the French capital.

At the thought that this cannon with all its destructive capacity would soon be in Paris, Hitler mumbled in satisfaction. Then he snapped, "Jodl, write." The words spilled from his mouth in a torrent so feverish the dignified Jodl's scribbling pencil could barely keep the pace.

"The defense of the Paris bridgehead," he declared, "is of capital importance in the military and political plans. The loss of the city would lead to the rupture of the whole coastal front north of the Seine and deprive us of our rocket-launching sites for the long-distance war against England.

"In all history," he said, "the loss of Paris has inevitably brought with it the loss of all France."

Hitler reminded his commander in chief in the west that he had designated two SS Panzer divisions for the defense of the city. He ordered the insurrection in Paris smashed with every brutal tactic available, including "the razing of entire city blocks," a task that the arrival of the "Karl" would facilitate, and "the public execution of ringleaders."

He concluded, "Paris must not fall into the hands of the enemy, or, if it does, *he must find there nothing but a field of ruins.*"

The bunker was silent when Hitler finished. The only sound was the steady whirring of its ventilating equipment and the frantic scribbling of Jodl trying to set down the last of the Führer's words.

•   •   •

In the blacked-out city of Metz, a bare 35 miles from the Franco-German frontier, the dark forms of the Panzers smashed noisily over the cobblestone streets, their slick surfaces tramped thin by three generations of German invaders along this highway to the heart of France. In the jouncing

vehicles the soldiers, wearied by their long trip south from
the Jutland Peninsula, dozed as best they could. These were
the men about whose arrival Dietrich von Choltitz had not
been informed, the reinforcements that would force him to
fight for his command. They were the first elements of the 26th
SS Panzer Division to arrive in France. Like the men of the
2nd Armored Division in the apple orchards of Écouché, they,
too, were headed for Paris. And they had just 188 miles to go.

26

[AUGUST 23]

WITH A BENIGN AND satisfied regard, the sun-
tanned man looked at the empty banks of seats climbing over
his head up to the domed glass roof of the enormous Grand
Palais. His name was Jean Houcke. He was a Swedish circus
owner and he was in Paris on business. For his circus he had
rented, at great expense, this sprawling building set between
the Seine and the Champs-Élysées, just across the river from
Napoleon's Tomb. It was one of the largest buildings in Paris.
Since 1900 its Ionic façade, two and a half times the length
of a football field, had beckoned Parisians to every major ex-
position the city had seen.
In a few days, Houcke thought, Paris would be liberated
and those same façades would beckon thousands of celebrating Frenchmen here to see his circus, the only *grand spectacle*
that would be functioning in the capital. It was the largest
circus left in Europe, and he had invested every krona he
could find to bring it here. Houcke had everything. In a hungry
Paris, his cages were full of lions, tigers, panthers. He had
clowns, horses and trapeze artists that rivaled Barnum's. He
even had a clown who would have a new act for the Liberation, one the Swede had asked him to prepare especially for
it. It was an imitation of Hitler. Everything Houcke owned
was in this building; even the little cash he still had left was
packed into a valise in his office downstairs. Standing in the

sawdust-filled arena on this muggy Wednesday morning, he could already envision the crowds pouring into the Grand Palais to fill these seats. The liberation of Paris, Jean Houcke was sure, was going to make him a rich man.

Underneath the arena, in the basement belonging to the police commissariat of the Eighth Arrondissement, which occupied one wing of the Grand Palais, policeman André Saumon watched a line of German trucks stopping under the trees along the Champs-Élysées. Twenty minutes earlier, Saumon's colleagues had ambushed a German car driving down that broad avenue, killing all its occupants. "Les boches," thought Saumon, "are going to pay us back." Suddenly Saumon saw a strange beetlelike vehicle start crawling toward the building. He turned to the prisoner he was guarding, Captain Wilhelm von Zigesar-Beines, the officer who before the war, as the captain of the German Army's equestrian team, had lived more glorious moments than this in this very building. "What," Saumon asked, "is that thing?"

Von Zigesar-Beines watched the squat-treaded vehicle coming straight for their window. It looked just like a little toy tank. With majestic calm, he turned to Saumon and remarked, "It's a special machine stuffed with explosives, and if we don't get out of here, we are going to be blown to bits."

Half of Paris heard the sound of Houcke's circus exploding. As the last vibrations of its echo fluttered out, a column of black smoke started seeping up from the Grand Palais. To finish the work started by the radio-guided, explosives-laden tank Saumon had seen, the German tanks outside started to fire incendiary shells into the building. Inside, smoke, screams, the sound of running feet, animal and human, produced a panic. The lions and tigers of Houcke's circus roared in terror. His horses stampeded through the burning building. In the commissariat, the police hastily opened their cellblocks, turning out the band of prostitutes they had rounded up the night before, and the shrieks of the frightened women mixed in the smoke and dust with the outcries of Houcke's frightened lions.

Outside, the tank company around the building shot out the hoses of the firemen trying to extinguish the blaze. Soon the palace was a mass of flames. One of Houcke's horses escaped and plunged into the bullet-swept streets. He was shot and fell neighing to the asphalt. From every building nearby, hungry Parisians with plates and knives in their hands swarmed toward the dying animal still harnessed in the red, white and blue ribbons Houcke had ordered for his Liberation show.

Trapped by the Germans, the fire, and Houcke's rampaging animals, the policemen of the Grand Palais realized their position was hopeless. A group of them turned to the commissariat's only German prisoner, the dignified little baron who, the evening before, had shared a plate of rutabagas with them, and asked him to arrange their surrender. Taking a long iron prod used by Houcke's lion tamer, von Zigesar-Beines tied a white handkerchief to it and marched out of the smoke and dust to surrender his captors to his countrymen.

As the flames finished their work on the shell of the Grand Palais, a sobbing man slumped alone against a tree and mumbled over and over again, "All is lost . . . all is lost." A sympathetic passerby came up to Jean Houcke to comfort him. He patted him on his drooping shoulders and said reassuringly, "Don't worry, the Allies will be here in a few days, you'll see." Circus owner Houcke stared at the man in dumb fury. Then, louder than ever, he started sobbing again.

• • •

All day, like some dark precursor of destruction, the black smoke pouring out of the Grand Palais splotched the gray sky of Paris. For a city which had not seen the work of a dozen robot tanks or a heavy air raid, the ease with which one robot tank and a few incendiary shells had gutted the huge building was a jolting experience. As the humid and depressing hours dragged by, the burning building became a constant reminder of the rumor sweeping the city: that the Wehrmacht was preparing to destroy it.

After four and a half days of fighting, the spirits of the FFI now sagged for the first time. Ammunition was running low. Casualties were high. The Germans were striking with more vengefulness. By nightfall on this bloody Wednesday the 500th Parisian would be killed in the streets of the city; 2,000 would have been wounded. And nowhere was there any sign of the help so many had expected within hours after the uprising had started.

In every part of the city, the tempo of the fighting increased. At La Villette, fighting with their backs to the empty stockyards, a band of FFI drove off repeated assaults by over 50 German soldiers. On the rue de Jessaint, on the flanks of Montmartre, a barricade manned by two dozen tough Communist railroad workers held out against a tank and two truckloads of German troops.

In his office at the Hotel Meurice, Warrant Officer Otto Vogel of the 650th Signal Company picked up an incoming call. He heard a pleading German cry, "Hypnose, help!" Hypnose was the new code name for the Hotel Meurice. "The terrorists are attacking us. Quick, help!" added the voice. Then Vogel heard over the open telephone line a burst of firing. "They are crossing the court!" cried his unknown caller. Another series of shots rang out. Vogel heard a gasp and, slow and sinking softly, the words *"Mutter, Mutter, Hilfe"* ("Mother, mother, help"). The telephone was silent. Then, faintly, Vogel heard a voice speaking in French. He hung up.

On both sides, acts of wanton viciousness spread. At the place de l'Opéra, a German leaped from a car, ran up to a Frenchman reading one of the city's new Liberation newspapers, and shot him.

Then he turned to the old lady who had sold it to him. She saved herself by claiming she could not read.

On the rue de la Harpe, in her aid station in a classroom of the school of Saint-Vincent-de-Paul, Mme. André Koch had no room for the slightly wounded eighteen-year-old German in her clinic. "Never mind," the FFI escorting him told her, "we shoot them all anyway." The German grabbed Mme. Koch's hands and, looking at her with a son's pleading eyes, mumbled something to her in German. She made his FFI guard promise not to shoot him. They left, and seconds later she heard firing. "They got him," one of her stretcher-bearers announced.

But as always there were acts of decency to balance them. At almost the same moment in the ward of the hospital Hôtel-Dieu where the stretcher-bearers of the FFI had carried him, Sonderführer Alfred Schlenker, the interpreter of the Military Tribunal which had kept the firing squads of Mont Valérien busy, saw above his bed the figure of a bloody French civilian. Berliner Schlenker, wounded three hours earlier near the "Carrefour de la Mort" in the boulevard Saint-

Michel, was sure the "terrorists" were about to finish him off. Schlenker watched the man reach into his pocket. "He's taking out his pistol," thought Schlenker, and he closed his eyes. When he opened them a few seconds later, he saw a hand stretching toward him. At the end of it was a cigarette. "You're lucky, Fritz," said the Frenchman, handing it to him. "For you the war is over."

• • •

Of all the menaces threatening the people of Paris, none was more pressing this Wednesday than the growing shortage of arms and ammunition. At the Prefecture of Police, despite the supplies smuggled in through its underground métro passages, only a few hours of fire were left. In his underground command post "Duroc," "Colonel Rol" was besieged with pleas for more arms and ammunition, the two items he lacked. Rol cursed his Gaullist rivals, certain that they had never delivered his urgent appeals for arms to London.

But this morning it was not the machinations of the Gaullists that had thwarted Rol. General Pierre Koenig had, as he had promised himself he would, ordered the massive arms drop on the city he had canceled at the last minute the day before. One hundred thirty planes of the Carpetbagger squadron, bulging with the thousands of arms and rounds of ammunition Rol so desperately wanted, were ready to take off for Paris. Only one thing held them up, an enemy more implacable than any political foe: fog; thick, impenetrable English fog. Since dawn it had nailed the planes of Colonel Heflin to their airfield in Harrington. Heflin despaired now of ever flying this mission.

The green scrambler telephone beside him rang. In London, General Pierre Koenig's headquarters had just learned that the 2nd Armored Division had been ordered to Paris. There was no longer any justification for the arms drop. On the orders of a relieved Pierre Koenig, Operation Beggar was canceled again, this time for good. In a few minutes Heflin's enlisted men would start unloading his 130 aircraft. The men of his Carpetbagger Squadron would indeed fly their unusual mission to Paris, three days later on August 26. But instead of the hand grenades and machine guns Rol so desperately wanted, they would fly sacks of coal and food.

27

SINCE DAWN, LIKE A pair of giant serpents thirteen miles long, the two columns of the 2nd Armored had twisted through the rolling farmlands of Normandy, racing in a driving rainstorm toward beleaguered Paris. Skidding and slithering on the wet and narrow roads, shaking the oaken beams of the Norman farmhouses as they went, the 4,000 vehicles and 16,000 men of the Division pressed toward their beckoning capital in a colorful and jubilant caravan.

From the open turrets of their tanks and armored cars bobbed the red garrison caps of Moroccan Spahis, the scarlet-tufted pompons of French marines, the jaunty black berets of the men of the Regiment of Chad. Along their route, in a never-ending funnel of humanity, the peasants of Normandy spurred them forward, cheering wildly at the tricolor and Cross of Lorraine they carried on their Shermans and GMCs, hailing the white letters along the turrets of their tanks, letters marking the names of other battles of France: *Marne, Verdun,* and *Austerlitz.*

Their eyes smarting in the stinging rain and exhaust fumes, the anxious drivers of the 2nd Armored tanks, armored cars, half-tracks and trucks fought to hold their sliding vehicles on the slippery roads, to keep their columns closed up, to force this cumbersome mass of armor over the miles separating them from Paris.

From the armored cars of the Spahis at the point of the columns to the bulky transports at their rear, the entire division was alive with an electric sense of anticipation, an almost hysterical joy at the idea that this time they were driving for Paris.

Jean René Champion, the Frenchman from Mexico going home to a capital he had never seen, moved his eyes back and forth between the treads of the tank ahead of him and the slowly sinking white needle of his oil-pressure gauge. Once that needle slid past its red danger line, Champion knew his "perfect dream" of liberating Paris would be ended. Like almost every other man in the column, he had just one fear this rainy Wednesday: being forced to drop out with a breakdown.

For many of these excited men pushing forward with frantic energy, this wet and hasty dash across the face of France was poignant with memories, or the promise of seeing a loved face just a few miles ahead. Lieutenant Henri Karcher tucked a photo into the windshield of his half-track. It was the picture of a little boy, the four-year-old son Karcher had never seen. Karcher wanted to be sure he recognized him the first time he saw him.

At the head of one of the division's two columns, gunner Robert Mady, of the tank destroyer "Simoun," started at the sight rising before him. "In a sea of yellow wheat," Mady saw beckoning ahead the majestic spires of Chartres. Then another thought occurred to Mady. "What's wrong with them?" he said to himself. "They haven't gotten the wheat in." °

For Captain Alain de Boissieu, thirty, the commander of Leclerc's escort squadron, the sight of Chartres's storied silhouette meant much more than history. For Boissieu, it was home. Behind the cathedral, on the banks of the River Eure, in the elegant town house he had not seen for five years, were Boissieu's parents. Tramping down on the accelerator of his jeep, Boissieu pushed onto the shoulder of the road and overtook the advancing column. He raced into the city, past the cathedral, down to the end of the boulevard Charles-Péguy. There he vaulted from his jeep and ran toward the riverbank and the bridge he would cross to his parents' house. Turning sharply, he saw before him the bridge, or what was left of it, a few broken strands of steel and dangling slabs of concrete. On the other side of the river was a building with its roof torn off, its sides blown out, only its broken façade, like the false front of a movie set, still standing. It was his home.

Grief-stricken, Boissieu ran to a neighbor nearby. The Germans, she told him, had evacuated everyone, including his parents, from the area; then they had blown up the bridges and with them most of the buildings along the river. On the

---

° The oversight of Chartres' farmers was deliberate: FFI Headquarters in London had ordered them to postpone their harvests so the Germans wouldn't get the crops.

bridge in front of his own home, she said, the German commander had placed an extra ration of torpedoes, "so Mme.
de Boissieu will understand what it means to have a son with
de Gaulle."

Looking numbly at the ruins all around him, Boissieu suddenly had an awful thought. "My God," he said to himself,
"if they do this in Paris, what a tragedy we're going to see
tomorrow!"

*   *   *

For twelve hours, the man who carried the desperate message that might spare Paris the destiny of Warsaw and Stalingrad had passed through the identical round of checks and
debriefings Roger Gallois had endured twenty-four hours
earlier. Now, on the same Normandy airstrip on which General Bradley had ordered Leclerc to Paris the evening before,
Rolf Nordling passed his message to the American general.

Helmet tilted back on his balding head, Bradley listened
to the Swede in silence. The German general commanding
Paris, Nordling told him, had "formal orders" to destroy as
much of the city as possible. He had not yet begun to carry
them out, but, Nordling warned, he was "being backed into
a corner," and if the situation went on much longer, he would
act on the orders. Already, Nordling said, the German felt
he was in some danger of being relieved of his command.
What he seemed to want was the arrival of the Allies in the
city before he was reinforced or had to begin executing his
orders.

Bradley reacted immediately. The operation he had ordered
the night before had suddenly taken on a desperate urgency.
Like Ike, Bradley knew the 26th and 27th Panzers and parts
of several other German divisions were moving into France.
Some of them, he realized, might be heading for Paris. If
the Allies failed to beat them to the city, Paris could become
a frightful battlefield. Above all, Bradley was worried about
Choltitz. "We can't," he thought, "take any chance on that
guy changing his mind." To General Sibert at his side, Bradley
said, "Tell Hodges to have the French division hurry the hell
in there." Then, remembering the long distance the 2nd
Armored had to move, Bradley made another decision. "Tell

him to have the 4th Division ready to get in there too. We
can't take any chances on that general changing his mind and
knocking hell out of the city."

28

DIETRICH VON CHOLTITZ wordlessly passed
the blue cable form to the little colonel beside him. Von Choltitz had known Hans Jay for twenty years, since the day they
had served together as junior officers in the same regiment.
Two years earlier, it was with Jay that von Choltitz had celebrated his first general's pips in the Hotel Adlon in Berlin. As
Jay read the cable, von Choltitz stared out at the Tuileries
garden below his window. No laughing children pushed the
white outlines of their sailboats into Lenôtre's graceful pools
this morning. The two-and-a-half-century-old hedgerows and
footpaths were deserted except for the somber and menacing
forms of the soldiers of von Choltitz's own command.

Jay folded up the cable and passed it back to von Choltitz.
In vain Choltitz searched his face for some flicker of emotion.
From his friend of twenty years he expected some word of
understanding, some comforting gesture, some hint that he
was not alone. For onto that blue cable form was pasted the
most brutal order Dietrich von Choltitz had ever received, the
savage command dictated by Hitler the night before. It
ordered the stubby general to turn this city spread before
his eyes "into a field of ruins."

Jay uttered one phrase: "It's too bad," he sighed.°

Ten minutes earlier, Dietrich von Choltitz had heard exactly the same resigned phrase of acceptance from the only

---

° Twenty years later, in his Dublin, Ireland, home, Colonel Jay revealed
that he had not had the courage that August morning to utter to von Choltitz
the words that formed in his mind as he read the cable: "Ignore it." He had
no way of knowing what had gone on in the mind of the tough hero of
Sebastopol since their lunch two years before in Berlin. And since July 20,
Jay and his fellow officers in Paris had found it wise to keep their own
counsel.

other man to whom he had shown this cable: his cold and distant chief of staff, Colonel Friedrich von Unger.

Von Choltitz turned away from the window and walked resolutely to his telephone. With an angry gesture he yanked up its receiver and demanded Army Group B.

In the artificial light of his underground bunker at Margival, 60 miles north of Paris, Generalleutnant Hans Speidel's skin had already taken on a waxy hue from five days without fresh air. Now, listening to the bitterness and brutality in the voice of Dietrich von Choltitz, the chief of staff of Army Group B paled still more.

"The Grand Palais, you'll be happy to know," began Choltitz, "is in flames." Then he "thanked" Speidel for the "nice" order he had sent him.

"What order?" asked Speidel.

"The order to reduce Paris to a field of ruins," Choltitz replied. Army Group B, Speidel protested, had only transmitted the order. "It came from the Führer," he told Choltitz. Ignoring him, Choltitz continued. He had, he told Speidel, already placed over a ton of explosives in the Chamber of Deputies, two tons in the basement of the Invalides and three tons in the crypt of Notre-Dame.

"I suppose, my dear Speidel," Choltitz said, "you agree with those measures?" There was an awkward moment of silence. Speidel looked up over his head at the engravings of Notre-Dame and the Tuileries. Then in a barely perceptible voice, Speidel replied, "Yes, yes, Herr General, I agree."

Choltitz continued. He was ready, he told Speidel, "to blow up the Madeleine and the Opéra in one stroke." Soon he planned to dynamite the Arc de Triomphe to clear a field of fire up the Champs-Élysées and "blow up the Eiffel Tower so its ruins will block the access to the bridges which will already have been blown up."

In his still underground room Speidel wondered if Choltitz had gone mad or was trying to be funny. Choltitz was neither. In his fury at this order Army Group B had passed him, he was only trying to "make Speidel understand the terrible situation of a soldier who gets such an order and is obligated to carry it out."

• • •

Across the Seine from von Choltitz's office, in the nearly empty Saint-Amand telephone exchange, the strokes of Sergeant Bernhard Blache's ax rang out like shots. Blache, whose men had been "cooking like sausages" four days earlier in front of the Prefecture of Police, was destroying one by one the 132 teleprinters in the building. His comrade, Max Schneider, unrolled the 600 feet of primer cord branched to the 25 explosive charges set throughout the three-story building. The cord stretched a block and a half away to the Peugeot 202 in which their commanding officer, Lieutenant Colonel von Berlipsch, had hidden his primer. Blache chopped through his last teleprinter and the six men ran out of the building. Behind them Blache heard the faint strains of a waltz. In their haste to get out of the telephone center, they had forgotten to turn off the radio.

A hundred yards away, behind a cordon of military police, Blache saw the stony faces of the residents of the neighborhood staring blankly back toward their homes. With a quick thrust of his hand, Lt. Colonel von Berlipsch downed the handle of his plunger. Seconds later the telephone exchange from which all the armies of the Reich from Norway to Spain had once received their orders disappeared in a cloud of dust and debris. It was 11:55 A.M. The first minuscule part of the destruction program ordered for the territory of Gross Paris by Adolf Hitler had been carried out.

In the cellar of Les Invalides, another officer, Lt. Colonel Daub, watched his men branch primer cord onto the two tons of explosives they had seeded through their underground communications center. In addition to the explosives, his men had set out dozens of steel cylinders of oxygen compressed at 180 atmospheres. When the charges fired, those cylinders would have the effect of dozens of incendiary bombs, spreading a raging fire through the communications center and, in all probability, through the entire 30-acre Hôtel des Invalides with its French Army Museum, military art gallery, four-century-old barracks, and its golden-domed tomb of an earlier conqueror of Europe, Napoleon Bonaparte.

In the Palais du Luxembourg, despite the 35 hours of electric power failure a courageous François Dalby had managed to provoke, the workmen of the TODT organization had almost finished drilling their mine emplacements. Already they had stuffed this palace, built in 1627 for Marie de Médicis, with seven tons of TNT, enough to scatter its eight-domed cupola and the shreds of its thirty-one Delacroix paintings over half the Left Bank.

On the beautiful place de la Concorde, behind the matchless Corinthian columns of Gabriel's palace over which for the last four years the emblem of the Kriegsmarine had floated, over five tons of Teller mines and munitions had been stored—enough to blow up the building, everything in the block behind it and the Hôtel de Talleyrand next door.

At the other end of Louis XV's place de la Concorde, across the Seine in the courtyard of the Chamber of Deputies, the men of Captain Werner Ebernach's 813th Pionierkompanie had received reinforcements, the 177th Pionierkompanie of the 77th Infantry Division. While Ebernach's men finished mining the forty-five bridges over the Seine for a series of explosions which, in the densely populated Paris area, would make the tragedy Alain de Boissieu had seen earlier in Chartres seem minor in dimension, the new company finished drilling the area around the Chamber of Deputies. They had already drilled and mined the Palais-Bourbon, France's Parliament, and the sprawling offices behind it bordering the beautiful place du Palais-Bourbon. Now their pneumatic drills were finishing emplacements for explosives in the elegant eighteenth-century palace that housed the offices of the President of the Chamber of Deputies and the columned Quai d'Orsay, the Foreign Office of France. In one sweep those twenty beautiful acres of priceless architecture along the Seine and the place de la Concorde would be wiped out, thus honoring the symmetry of the most beautiful square in the world. On either side there would be nothing left but a set of matching ruins.

And on this dreary morning, a Kübelwagen bristling with branches of camouflage pulled up in front of the southern pillar of the Eiffel Tower at the crest of the Champs-de-Mars. Four men got out and inspected, one by one, the four concrete-and-steel supports of the soaring tower. An hour before, they had received from Berlin the order to mine the "Symbol of Paris." For Untersturmführer Hans Schnett of Leipzig and his three comrades who were circling the exposed supports of this spindly skeleton, there had been no question. To them the symbol of Paris was the Eiffel Tower.

Everywhere in Paris—in its railroad stations, power plants,

telephone exchange, in the Palais du Luxembourg, the Chamber of Deputies, the Quai d'Orsay, the Kriegsmarine, under the Invalides, along the forty-five bridges—the preparations for the savaging of the territory of Gross Paris ordered by OKW neared completion. All that was needed now was a few more hours of work, and a command from the wavering Prussian general in the Hotel Meurice. There, stricken with indecision, Choltitz waited and wondered how much longer he could delay before ordering the action that would consign some of the most beautiful monuments of Paris to dust and debris.

29

THE RADIO WAS PLAYING a quiet selection of American dance tunes. Comfortably settled into the chair of a London dentist, the man who whistled when he talked saw the end of his troubles approaching. Dangling before Larry Lesueur's eyes was the new plastic jacket the dentist was preparing for his broken front tooth.

He had been lucky, Lesueur told himself. If this accident had happened a week later, he might well have missed the one event he would not miss for anything in the world, the liberation of Paris. As the dentist bent over his yawning mouth, the radio beside Lesueur stopped.

In the classic form with which he himself was so familiar, an announcer told his listeners to stand by for an "important announcement."

Then in a voice ringing with un-BBC-like emotion, a broadcaster declared, "Paris has been liberated. I repeat, Paris has been liberated."

Larry Lesueur was sick.

At the other end of London, in the offices of CBS, Lesueur's London colleague, Richard C. Hottelet, was at that moment one of the happiest men in the British capital. In his hands Hottelet held a circular metal box which contained a document of extraordinary value. It was the "canned" announcement of the liberation of Paris recorded the evening before by Lesueur's direct competitor and colleague, Charles Collingwood. SHAEF's field censors, unable to play back the experimental tape, had passed it to London. London's censors assumed it had been cleared in the field and passed it on to CBS. As soon as he heard the first flash over the BBC, the excited Hottelet passed it on to the world. Charles Collingwood had his scoop.

Within minutes, his dramatic description of the Liberation was ringing into millions of homes. Two New York papers made over their late editions to carry it verbatim under huge headlines. In Mexico City the newspaper *Excelsior* blinked the words PARIS ESTA LIBERTADA from its light tower, and all the city's papers published extras. In Perón's Buenos Aires 1,800 miles south, for the first time since 1939, cheering crowds dared to chant, *"Democracia, sí. Axis, no."* Quebec broke out the French tricolor, and Mayor Lucien Borne asked his fellow citizens to ignore their wartime "brown-out" and illuminate their homes at night. From Washington F.D.R. called the news "an ebullient passage of total victory," and from his hospital bed General John J. Pershing called it "a great step on the road to victory."

In New York, Lily Pons, in a USO uniform, sang the "Marseillaise" for 20,000 excited Americans at Rockefeller Center while 32 French sailors in pompons raised the tricolor. London went wild. People kissed and danced in the streets of Soho, on Picadilly Circus, around Nelson's column in Trafalgar Square. To hard-pressed London, the news was a happy prelude to V-E Day, which, it seemed, could not now be far off. Anthony Eden interrupted a banquet marking the Franco-English Civil Affairs Agreement to propose a joyous toast to his French counterpart, René Massigli. The king himself sent a warm cable of congratulations to de Gaulle.

In the general euphoria that followed the BBC flash, no one paid any attention to SHAEF's awkwardly phrased denials of the story. All day and night, the BBC announcement and Collingwood's broadcast, carried across the Atlantic by the Yankee Doodle Network, went on and on like a long-playing record.

And it was all a ghastly mistake.

In a distinctly unliberated Paris where the men of General von Choltitz, more menacing with each passing hour, were still very much present, the news was greeted with fury and stupefaction.

Lieutenant Bob Woodrum, the American pilot, heard it as he sat on the steps of Louis Berty's back porch wondering if his pork-butcher friend and host was still alive. On his radio, he heard a replay of Lily Pons in New York. He also heard a less appealing sound, the sound of German troops running through a nearby street, "shooting at everything in sight." One of their bullets chipped the tiles overhead, and Woodrum decided to go inside. "Someone," he thought, "sure didn't get the word." Yvon Morandat and his secretary Claire heard the announcement in the Green Room of the Prime Minister's residence. Morandat listened to the ponderous chimes of Big Ben announcing their liberation to London, and the rifle fire in the streets outside. He almost felt like crying. Claire was furious. "Those imbeciles," she said "they're really out of it."

•   •   •

For the first time in three days and nights, Colonel André Vernon looked with something approaching satisfaction at the dry sandwiches and chipped mug of cold tea on his desk in London's Bryanston Square headquarters of the FFI. This precise wavy-haired man was the author of the monumental hoax which had sent millions of people around the globe into ecstasy.

Six hours earlier in this same office, Vernon had decoded the latest desperate appeal from Jacques Chaban-Delmas in Paris, an urgent cry for Allied forces before the masacre they all sensed was coming fell on the city. Vernon did not know that the 2nd Armored Division had received the evening before the order to rush to the city's aid. Haunted by the Chaban-Delmas telegram, he sought some way to help the city to "break the log jam" and force SHAEF to march on the capital. Suddenly he had swept up a piece of paper and written out a wholly imaginary news bulletin announcing that the city had "liberated itself." Then he ordered his subordinates to pass it over to the BBC without clearing it through SHAEF censorship. If the BBC, he shrewdly reasoned, announced to the world that Paris was free, SHAEF would have no excuse for not moving its forces into the city he had prematurely liberated with a few strokes of his pen.

Just before noon, minutes before the opening of the BBC's daily French news broadcast, a young officer from the Free French information office telephoned Vernon's flash to the BBC. He assured the announcer the bulletin had been orally cleared with SHAEF's censor, a technique the two often resorted to for last-minute news flashes. Seconds later, jubilant and unconcerned, the announcer sent the false flash off on its journey around the world.

30

LIEUTENANT SAM BRIGHTMAN OF SHAEF's press section stared at the sodden mass of humanity packing the streets of Rambouillet, 30 miles from Paris. Tanks, jeeps, trucks, French soldiers, GI's, FFI, newsmen and plain Frenchmen jammed together outside his window in the restaurant of the Grand Veneur Hotel in Rambouillet. "The only thing they need is de Gaulle," Brightman thought, "and the Germans will have their best goddamned target since D Day."

Brightman at least had a smile on his face. At his elbow was a treasure rare in this town whose already spare cupboards had been stripped bare by its friendly invaders. It was a cold bottle of Riesling wine. Now the pretty waitress of the Grand Veneur was bringing him a plate of warmed-up C rations to go with it. At the moment she reached his table, she gasped and dropped the plate of C rations, knocking over Brightman's bottle. As Brightman watched his precious wine sloshing to the floor, she stood transfixed, staring out the window with tears in her eyes, repeating over and over again the words "de-Gaulle, de Gaulle, de Gaulle."

Charles de Gaulle had indeed just arrived in Rambouillet. Here, on the very doorstep of his nation's capital, in the vanguard of the army assigned to liberate it, this solitary figure had reached the next-to-last stop on the long road home from exile that had begun in June, 1940. For his aide, Claude Guy, one image would always remain of this August evening. Not all

the people in Rambouillet would, like the waitress in the
Grand Veneur, recognize de Gaulle's lonely figure. Hundreds
cheered de Gaulle's name but, in their ignorance of his face,
did not know whom to applaud as he passed.

De Gaulle's party went straight to the Château de Rambouillet, its doors, its sheets, even its silverware still stamped
with "État Français," symbol of its last Vichy occupants. Guy
watched de Gaulle choose from a bookcase the leather-bound
volume that would hold his impatient nerves in check in the
hours ahead. It was Molière's *Le Bourgeois Gentilhomme*. De
Gaulle tucked it under his arm and then their four-man party
went downstairs to the château's magnificent Salle des Fêtes.
There in the dark and imposing room where Charles X had
abdicated, where the kings, emperors, and presidents of
France from Louis XVI to Napoleon and Poincaré had ban-
queted, Charles de Gaulle and his three faithful aides sat
down and opened cans of cold C rations for dinner.

As soon as he had finished, de Gaulle called for Leclerc. He
was blazing with impatience to get into Paris. For him now
each hour counted.

Leclerc, after studying the intelligence supplied by Hemingway's private task force, and by the dozens of FFI agents
who had slipped through to his lines, had reached an important
decision. His orders from his American superiors were to slam
straight ahead over the shortest road to Paris, through Rambouillet and Versailles. In the last twenty-four hours, his reports showed, the Germans had slipped 60 new tanks into
that area and seeded it with mines. On his own, Leclerc had
decided to sideslip 17 miles east to Arpajon and Longjumeau
and enter the capital from the southeast by the porte d'Orleans.
He neglected to clear his plans with his superiors at V Corps,
an omission which was to cause a bitter and angry reaction in
a few hours.

Now, in the château, Leclerc outlined his assault plans to
de Gaulle. Both men knew time was pressing. The German
strength ahead of them was rising rapidly. What had appeared
twenty-four hours earlier as a walk-in was now going to be a
fight. Worse, if it was not swiftly resolved, Leclerc could bog
down on the road to Paris while the Germans in the capital
ravaged the insurrection and, alerted to his attack, drew up
reinforcements. With longing in his own eyes, de Gaulle

studied his young commander's plan. After a long and thoughtful pause, he gave it his blessing.°

Then he looked at Leclerc. De Gaulle bore a special affection for this outspoken and impetuous Picardian. To the aloof leader of Free France, Leclerc was almost a son. "You are lucky," he murmured. There was a long pause. Then he added, "Go fast. We cannot have another *Commune*."

31

THREE DAYS EARLIER, the German Feldkommandant of Rambouillet had spent his last night in this bed whose Wehrmacht sheets Corporal Louis Loustalot now folded away. He replaced them with a new set of his own, then carefully placed a chocolate bar on the night table beside the bed. "The boss," Corporal Loustalot knew, liked to eat a chocolate bar on the morning of an attack. Tomorrow morning Jacques Philippe Leclerc, the man being urged a few blocks away to "go fast," would with the 16,000 men of his division open the most memorable attack of his life, the assault on Paris.

Spent by their long and wearing rush to Rambouillet, eyes burning from fourteen hours in the open, soaked through by a drenching rain, Leclerc's men scattered through the forests and villages around Rambouillet and grabbed what little sleep they could. Stalking through the night, the division's GMCs dropped off jerricans of fuel to the tanks and armored cars, formed now into three assault groups for the dawn attack. Men planned, dreamed, reminisced of their last sight of Paris, prayed or simply dropped into a fatigue-deadened sleep. In his tent, by a kerosene lamp, Major Henri Mirambeau of the 40th Artillery Regiment laid down a fire plan with the American lieutenant colonel whose 155s would back him up the next day. Gunner Robert Mady and his mates of the tank destroyer

---

° It is probable that Leclerc's failure to notify his corps commander that he was changing his division's boundary and line of attack without authorization stemmed from a determination to show the world that the liberation of Paris was a purely French operation and that de Gaulle's approval of his plans was sufficient.

Simoun looked longingly at their still-uncooked duck sitting in their shell rack. They were too tired to roast it. Instead, they gulped cold C rations and fell asleep.

Lieutenant Henri Karcher, his eyes red from hours of exposure to exhaust fumes, looked once more at the photo of his son before him and fell asleep. Jacques de Guillebon, the thirty-four-year-old lieutenant colonel sent stealthily out ahead of the division forty-eight hours before, regarded the arrival of his mates with mixed emotions. For twenty-four hours he had wanted to stage a bold maneuver of his own, to slip into the besieged city and lend its insurgents the support of his little unit. But the youngest military governor in Paris's history had never received a clearance for the move from Leclerc. Leclerc's aide had not dared to wake him with Guillebon's request the night before. Dejected, Guillebon had waited at Rambouillet for the rest of the division to catch up with him.

No soldier in the 2nd Armored was more excited, perhaps, than Pfc. Paul Landrieux lying in a foxhole beside his Sherman *Marne* at the edge of the little village of Breis. Landrieux's tank company had just received its orders for the next day. Their destination was the suburb of Fresnes, 15 miles away. For Paul Landrieux, those 15 miles were all that was left of an 1,800-mile journey that had taken him through the concentration camps of Spain, the deserts of Chad and Libya into this foxhole. It had begun three years earlier on an evening such as this when, telling his wife, "I'm going out for a pack of Gauloises, I'll be back in ten minutes," Landrieux had walked out of his apartment in the town of Fresnes. Tomorrow those ten minutes would be up. In the streets of Fresnes, Landrieux would fight for the liberation of his own home, and a wife who did not know whether he was alive or dead. For a surprise, he had decided he would bring her the pack of cigarettes he had left to buy three years before. Instead of Gauloises, they would be C-rations Camels.

•   •   •

As the exhausted men of the 2nd Armored sprawled for the night in the forests around Rambouillet, another division began the same long march they had just completed. At Carrouges, 132 miles from Paris, in a driving rainstorm and a blackout, the 4th U.S. Infantry Division set out for the capital.

It was appropriate that General Bradley, alarmed at Rolf Nordling's message, had picked this division to back up the 2nd Armored. Since D Day, with the 1st and 29th Divisions, the 4th had formed the American Army's first team in Europe. It had landed at Utah Beach, taken Cherbourg, then held off three Panzer divisions at Mortain to turn back the desperate Normandy counterattack Walter Warlimont had been sent from OKW to supervise. For the element leading its overnight march, the 12th Infantry Regiment, this road to Paris had already been a bloody calvary. Behind the 3,000-man regiment, as it rolled through the rain, were 4,034 dead and wounded, their casualties in the seventy-eight days since June 6.

Now, crowded into their six-by-sixes, the GIs of the 4th Division shared the exhilarating sense of anticipation gripping the men of the 2nd Armored. Stirred by the exotic legends of the AEF, by the memories of forgotten textbooks, by history and Hollywood, Alexandre Dumas and *The Hunchback of Notre-Dame*, by Gay Paree and "Mademoiselle from Armentières," by visions of the Eiffel Tower and Notre-Dame, they rode through the rain with a fervor only slightly less than that of the homecoming soldiers of the French division.

"We got rain in our fatigues, rain in our coffee, rain in our rations, rain in our faces," Medic Joe Ganna, of Roxbury, Massachusetts, wrote in his illegal diary, "but the thrill that keeps us going is waiting to see Paris and we're getting closer." Beside him in his bouncing six-by-six, Pfc. "Davey" Davison told Ganna "he and the other guys could have the wine and women." What he wanted, Davison said, was "one night's sleep in a real bed."

To some Americans, Paris was the road home. Lieutenant Dan Hunter of the OSS had lived there most of his life. In the tent of the commander of the Paris Task Force, a unit ordered to go over intelligence targets in the city, Hunter's finger slid over a map of the approaches to the city. He had been asked to pick a forward base for the unit. With playful vengeance, his finger stopped at a familiar name, and Hunter made his choice. He chose his old school.

In Chartres, Colonel John Haskill of the OSS decided "just for the hell of it" to see if he could call Paris. He decided to call an old friend, Mimi Gielgud, sister-in-law of actor John Gielgud. She had spent the entire war in occupied Paris, and

Haskill wondered how—and if—she had survived. He placed his call, and to his amazement and relief he heard at the other end of the phone—50 miles away, in a city still swarming with German troops—the clear unruffled voice of this English-woman.

"Oh, John," she said, as unconcerned as if he had been calling to announce an invitation to a bridge game, "I was waiting for your call."

•   •   •

For all the exhilaration stirring the men of the 2nd Armored and the 4th Infantry Divisions, this coming liberation of Paris was going to exact its price. Everywhere, this August evening, the logistics officers of SHAEF prepared to meet it. Waiting in Bristol and Southampton were 53 tons of medical supplies, 23,338 tons of biscuits, tinned meat, margarine, soup, vitamin-ized chocolate and dried milk, which now had an urgent priority for transfer to the Continent and Paris. Three thou-sand tons of that would be delivered by air, by the Carpet-baggers. To move the rest, Britain's Twenty-first Army Group was stripped of 2,000 trucks and 300 heavy vehicles with three-ton trailers. Another 1,000 trucks were peeled off the American supply lines.

In addition, Montgomery's Twenty-first Army Group was ordered to deliver 5,000 tons of supplies a day to the city in military vehicles and the American 500 more. Seventy thou-sand precious gallons of gasoline a day was going to be the price of that effort, one million gallons during the next two vital weeks in the race across France.

In the tent in which forty-eight hours earlier he had said no to Gallois and Paris, General George Patton studied in fury and frustration an urgent report. It told him that on this day, August 23, his racing armored columns had, for the first time since the breakout at Avranches, consumed more fuel than they had received. The "terminal illness" seen four days earlier by Bradley's aide Major Chet Hansen was setting in. In just one week's time, in front of Metz, with the Rhine only 100 agonizingly short miles away and the German forces stumbling before them in full disarray, the tanks of Patton's Third Army would run out of gas.

There would be none left. They would need just one million

gallons, the amount that the premature liberation of Paris would cost, to reach the Rhine. By the time they got it in late September, the Germans before them would be reinforced and regrouped, waiting in the Siegfried Line. Patton would not reach the Rhine for seven long months, not until March 22, 1945.*

•   •   •

Its headlights out, the black B.M.W. slipped noiselessly through the night. Folded onto the back seat, "Mister," Generalmajor Hubertus von Aulock's French poodle, slept in uncomplaining silence. The general, as usual, was driving. This evening, for the first time in several days, von Aulock felt reassured. The reinforcements he had requested for his 10,000-man defense line screening the main approaches to Paris had finally begun to arrive. In less than six hours, he had received a regiment of tanks commanded by a one-legged veteran of the eastern front, Colonel Dietmar Pulovski, and for the western end of his line the Messerschmidt Sturm-Battallion. More important, von Aulock had heard reports all evening that elements of the Fifth Army would be reassigned to his command in the next two days.

Now, with his aide, Captain Theo Wulff, von Aulock was on his way back to his Saint-Cloud villa after an exhaustive inspection tour of his defenses, the defenses on which would fall in a few hours the full fury of the 2nd French Armored Division. Yet on this miserable and damp evening, neither von Aulock nor Wulff had any hint that less than 15 miles away, hidden in the forest of Rambouillet like an anxious wolf pack, the men of that division waited impatiently for the dawn.

In fact, for von Aulock, it had been a rather leisurely inspection. After hearing the report of his Versailles area com-

---

* The exact cost of the early liberation of Paris in the Allied drive to the Rhine can probably never be reckoned. In any event, with or without Paris, a fuel crisis was in the making for the Allies. Eisenhower says: "The key thing is this was the critical part of the campaign. These were the two vital weeks. It's hard to say exactly how far Patton would have gotten. He would certainly have taken Metz and much of the area beyond it." General Bradley says, "If we could have gotten to the Rhine, it wouldn't have been a giant's step. We needed just two more weeks of gasoline, I think, to do it. Those were my thoughts about Paris. I didn't want to lose those two weeks there, and perhaps we did."

mander, Colonel Seidel, he had even taken time for a glass of
Benedictine, and let the Dresden pianist play some music for
him. Satisfied with the state of his defense line, thinking of
the steel he could put in it if the Fifth Army reinforced him,
von Aulock whacked his aide on the knee with an enthusiastic
gesture.

"Believe me, Wulff," he said, "when they come, we'll make
them pay for their Paris."

In the city itself, in the bar of the Hotel Raphaël, Transport
Officer Walter Neuling watched the captain beside him start
his third bottle of champagne. It had, the captain confided to
Walter Neuling, been his desire in life to be an architect, but
instead he was a demolition expert, and he had just completed
the biggest job he had ever done. He had, Werner Ebernach
told Neuling, finished mining "half of Paris." Emptying his
champagne glass, Ebernach admitted to Neuling it had not
been a pleasant assignment, but when he got the order to fire
his charges, he would do so. "They'll hear the noise in
Berlin," he said.

● ● ●

It was midnight when the two silent figures stopped on the
little bridge over the Seine, to watch the smoke still rising
from the charred skeleton of the Grand Palais. It was one of
the bleakest sights Alexandre Parodi had ever looked on.
Paris was running out of arms, out of ammunition, out of food,
and out of hope. The insurrection begun so bravely four days
before could not sustain itself much longer without support
from outside. Yet no one in Paris knew help was finally on the
way. To Parodi, as to thousands of others in the city, Paris
this night seemed to have been abandoned to its fate, a fate
symbolized by the column of gray smoke drifting from the
wreckage of the Grand Palais.

Tears in his eyes, Parodi turned to Morandat and said softly,
"Ah, Yvon, now they are going to burn all Paris and it is I
history shall hold responsible."

32

FOR THE SECOND TIME in less than twenty-four hours, Generaloberst Alfred Jodl could not stay abreast of Adolf Hitler's angry torrent of words. All day the teleprinters of OKW had clacked out reports of a worsening situation in Paris. In his last bulletin, von Choltitz had finally been forced to admit that "terrorists" were engaging in "intense activity" all through the city. Those reports had provoked Hitler to a memorable display of temper. It had been compounded by the hapless General Buhle, his ordnance expert, who had had to announce that a series of savage Allied air attacks had paralyzed all rail traffic around Paris. The desperate pleas of Jacques Chaban-Delmas had served a timely end. The "Karl," Buhle had reluctantly had to admit to Hitler, had not moved an inch all day.

Screaming at Jodl, Hitler declared that if the Wehrmacht could not "crush the despicable rabble" of the streets of Paris, it would "cover itself with the worst shame and dishonor in its history." Model, he told Jodl, was to send every available tank and armored vehicle to the city. As for von Choltitz, Hitler ordered him to assemble his armor and artillery into special attack units to "pitilessly crush the centers of the insurrection." The Luftwaffe, he commanded, would follow with heavy bombing and incendiary attacks to "annihilate" the quarters of Paris which still threatened his forces.

To General Walter Warlimont, Hitler's display of uncontrolled fury this Wednesday evening would always stand out as one of the worst outbursts he had ever witnessed from the Führer in this bunker. Now, jotting down Hitler's words in his own notebook, Warlimont reflected in a quick instant a thought that had passed through the minds of so many Frenchmen. "Paris," he said to himself, "is going to be like Warsaw."

● ● ●

In his underground Army Group B command post at Margival, Generalfeldmarschall Walther Model studied the evening situation reports of the western front. They gave him no reason to suspect the blow that was about to fall on his screen of forces before the city, a blow his Paris commander had deliberately invited. As it had for the past four days, the OB West nightly report noted "only light armored probes" in front of the capital. It even optimistically added that the Allies would have to "bring up new units" before a major drive on the city could be mounted. No one in Model's headquarters had signaled the rapid move forward of the 2nd Armored or the stirrings of the 4th U.S. Infantry Division.

Nonetheless, Model had apparently decided twenty-four hours earlier that he had stalled for time in front of Paris as long as he dared. Instrumental, perhaps, was a polite but insistent call made by Warlimont on Hitler's order. Hitler, Warlimont had told him, wanted to know why more had not been done. "Tell the Führer," the angry Model had replied, "that I know what I am doing." But since then he had begun to use what scattered units he could round up to reinforce von Aulock's lines in front of the capital.

On this Wednesday evening—realizing that with Allied air attacks restricting their movements to darkness, the 26th and 27th Panzer Divisions would be slow in getting to Paris— Model looked for a temporary means to bolster his troops in front of the city. He made three moves. He ordered the 47th Infantry Division to assemble around the Méru-Neuilly region, just north of the capital, ready to take up a position on its northwestern flank. He ordered the First Army to assemble 47 tanks at Meaux, 26 miles from Paris, for immediate assignment to the city. Finally he ordered the 11th Brigade of Assault Cannons to the city. He expected those units to be ready for action in thirty-six to forty-eight hours: on August 25 and 26. In an emergency, they could tide von Choltitz over until the 26th and 27th Panzer Divisions arrived. Then, with better than three divisions under his orders, the hero of Sebastopol could, Model was sure, give Hitler as sanguine and tenacious a fight for the city as even his embittered mind could demand. All Model needed now was just a little more time, just enough to get these units he had shifted tonight into position. He needed, in fact, just forty-eight more hours.

33

War seemed faint and far away in the little German town gathered under the darkness of a soft summer night. In its empty streets there were few sounds besides the stirring of its linden trees and now the anxious tapping of a woman's leather heels. A worried Uberta von Choltitz was hurrying home. A few moments before, while she watched her favorite opera, Wagner's *Flying Dutchman*, in Baden-Baden's white-porticoed opera house, an usherette had whispered to her that she was wanted "urgently" at home.

Sure that something had happened to her four-month-old son Timo, Uberta von Choltitz hurried past the darkened Russian Orthodox Church and down Viktoriastrasse. Puffing from her climb up three flights of stairs, she burst through the door and clasped her hands on her breast in relief at the sight of the infant sleeping peacefully in his crib. Then her maid, Johanna Fischer, who three weeks earlier had fetched her husband his last breakfast pretzels, passed her a piece of paper. Her husband had called but he had not been able to hold open the telephone line. On this slip of paper was the message he had wanted to give to her. It was the last Uberta von Choltitz would receive for over a year.

"We are doing our duty," it said.

34

WITH DISCREET AND PRACTICED tread, Corporal Helmut Mayer glided down the long, red-carpeted hotel corridor. In one hand he balanced a breakfast tray, its contents fixed by seven years of habit: a pot of black coffee, a jar of English marmalade, and four slices of bread. In the other Mayer clutched a black folder. Count von Arnim had handed it to him a few minutes before. In it were the cables that had arrived for the commander of Gross Paris during the night. It was, Mayer noted, the thickest pouchful of messages he had carried down this hallway since his arrival in Paris.

At room 238, Mayer paused, opened the door, set down the tray, and parted the blackout curtains. As the first shafts of light pierced the darkness, Choltitz stirred in his bed. He opened his eyes and looked at Mayer. Then, as he had done almost every morning for the past seven years, Choltitz asked the genial corporal, "What's the weather like?"

It was dull and gray, and it was exactly seven o'clock, Thursday, August 24, the last day in his life Corporal Mayer would bring Dietrich von Choltitz his breakfast.

Von Choltitz reached for the monocle on the night table beside him and, one by one, leafed through the cables tucked into Mayer's black folder. The first was the brutal order Hitler had dictated to Jodl the night before, ordering Choltitz to "crush the centers of the insurrection . . . and annihilate any quarter of the city in which it persisted with bombing and incendiary attacks." Under it were copies of the orders Generalfeldmarschall Model had sent to the 47th Infantry Division, the First Army, and the 11th Brigade of Assault Cannons, ordering reinforcements to Paris. But above all, the black folder contained, in a cable from the G3 of Army Group B, the information Model had twice declined to furnish his Paris commander, the news that the 26th and 27th SS Panzer

Divisions had entered France and were on their way to Paris for assignment to his command.*

For a long moment the little general rested motionless on his bed. The dilemma that had haunted him for days was now resolved. Choltitz had hoped for another solution. But in the thirty-six hours that had elapsed since Rolf Nordling's departure, neither Choltitz nor anyone else in Paris had heard from the Swede. The Allies, it was clear to the commander of Gross Paris, either did not want to, or could not, take advantage of his gesture. They were not going to sweep through the beckoning gap in front of Paris before Model's reinforcements had slammed it shut. Instead, he was going to get his reinforcements, and be forced to defend the city. It would be a useless fight in a war already lost. It would gain Germany only a few days. Its cost would be a handsome pile of ruins the world would not quickly forget nor France forgive. But Choltitz had been backed into a corner. His sense of duty, his soldier's code, would give him no exit. He would have to fight.

It was the first time in his career that the conqueror of Rotterdam and Sebastopol envisioned the prospect of a fight with so little enthusiasm. But whatever were his own reservations about the wisdom of such a battle, he would wage it without weakness.

Saddened, but growing in resolve, Choltitz gulped his coffee in one swallow and walked barefooted to the bath Corporal Mayer had just drawn for him.

•   •   •

On the second floor of a building on the rue d'Anjou, barely 500 yards from the bathroom where, in a cloud of steam, the German general brooded over the messages he had just received, a young Frenchman listened in astonishment to the German seated before him. Sprawled comfortably in an armchair by the bed of ailing Swedish Consul General Raoul Nordling, Abwehr agent "Bobby" Bender was repeating to a representative of the French Resistance the substance of the secret cables the commander of Gross Paris had just read.

* Von Choltitz believes Model's oversight in regard to the two divisions was deliberate. It stemmed, he feels, from Model's own conviction that they could be better used elsewhere, and the field marshal's desire to avoid openly committing them to Paris as long as possible.

With the extraordinary freedom of movement he had enjoyed at the Hotel Meurice for the past ten days, Bender had visited the hotel before seven and carefully noted the contents of the cables waiting for the breakfast tray of the commander of Gross Paris; Bender knew that half an hour later he would have this rendezvous with Lorrain Cruse, the aide of General Jacques Chaban-Delmas.

The situation, Bender told Cruse, was worsening with each passing hour. He catalogued the list of reinforcements about to fall on the city, and the grim fact that two SS Divisions were now racing toward Paris. If they reached Paris before the Allies did, Bender declared, Choltitz would use them to carry out a brutal defensive action. Hitler's orders for demolition and reprisals in the city, Bender told Cruse, were becoming more savage every day. Choltitz was going to have to start carrying them out or risk arrest himself and possible execution for his family. In a voice that was strained—almost, it seemed to Cruse, pathetic—Bender warned that if "the Allies don't get to Paris within hours, there is going to be a disaster."

Hearing his words, Cruse got up, gave Bender and his Swedish host a hasty nod of thanks, and bolted to his bicycle. A few minutes later, a breathless Cruse burst into the hideout of Chaban-Delmas. "Quick," he told him, "we've got to get a warning to the Allies. Choltitz is going to get reinforcements. He's got orders to blow up Paris!"

35

SINCE DAWN THE VEHICLES of the 2nd Armored Division had been sliding past the hundred-year-old oaks of the rain-soaked forests of Rambouillet, pointing toward France's menaced capital now only 20 tantalizing miles away. On a ridge of high ground, just outside those ancient hunting preserves of the rulers of France, a captain's raincoat tossed over his shoulders, Jacques Philippe Leclerc watched his first troops move forward.

For his attack, Leclerc had split his forces into three

ROBERT CAPA—MAGNUM PHOTO

The Attack Opens

Arm upraised, a French officer waves his men forward as he runs into the Place du Palais Bourbon behind the Chamber of Deputies. The Chamber, and three dozen other major buildings, many of them artistic monuments, were turned into barricaded strongpoints by Paris's German defenders.

Mady

Bizien

Shermans vs. Panther
on the Place de la Concorde
AUTHORS' COLLECTION

The tank destroyer "Simoun" [ABOVE, LEFT] was the first French vehicle to reach the Etoile. There, its gunner, Second Mate Robert Mady [PORTRAIT, ABOVE], spotted a Panther tank [BELOW, LEFT] behind the obelisk in the Place de la Concorde. Remembering that he'd read in an almanac years before that the exact length of the Champs Elysées was 1,800 meters, Mady set his gun for that range and fired. His first shot blew one of the Panther's treads off. Seconds later, the Sherman "Douaumont" [ABOVE], commanded by Sgt. Marcel Bizien [PORTRAIT, ABOVE], spun into the Place de la Concorde and rammed the German tank, putting it out of action. In the confusion, the German crew escaped. Six months later, on a German autobahn, a sergeant stepped from a column of prisoners and hailed the passing "Douaumont." It was the commander of the panther destroyed in the Place de la Concorde on Liberation Day.

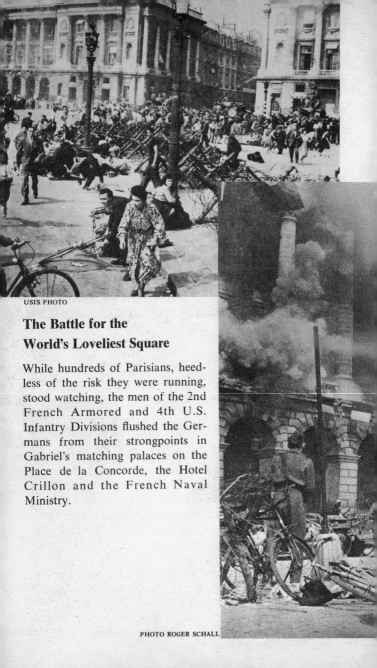

The Battle for the
World's Loveliest Square

While hundreds of Parisians, heedless of the risk they were running, stood watching, the men of the 2nd French Armored and 4th U.S. Infantry Divisions flushed the Germans from their strongpoints in Gabriel's matching palaces on the Place de la Concorde, the Hotel Crillon and the French Naval Ministry.

The battle's principal victim was one of Gabriel's massive Corinthian columns, the fifth from the left along the façade of the Hotel Crillon [BELOW, SHROUDED IN SMOKE]. According to legend, it was shot apart by the gunner of the tank destroyer "Filibuster" after he had been warned by his commander to "watch out for the fifth column." The commander was referring to collaborationist snipers.

USIS PHOTO

As armed FFI patrol the street, a German car [BELOW] burns in front of Notre-Dame.

PRESSE-LIBERATION PHOTO

The fighting in Paris was brief, but it was often savage. A group of German prisoners [LEFT] machine-gunned to death on the Place de l'Etoile, where the Wehrmacht had staged so many triumphant parades. Seconds before, one of them had thrown a hidden hand grenade at their French captors. Lt. Henri Karcher [RIGHT], captor of Gen. Dietrich von Choltitz and his staff at the Hotel Meurice. [BELOW] One of the French Shermans leading the assault on that hotel. A few seconds after the picture was taken, the tank was knocked out of action.

AUTHORS' COLLECTION

AUTHORS' COLLECTION

The Wounded and the Welcome

Civilian volunteer stretcher bearers [LEFT] rush a wounded French soldier out of the line of fire around the French Foreign Ministry, the Quai d'Orsay. German medics [BELOW, LEFT] tend their wounded in the courtyard of the French senate. For most of the city's liberators, however, like these lucky G.I.s [BELOW, RIGHT], liberation was a day of frenzy, flowers and fervent kisses of welcome from the women of Paris.

USIS PHOTO

USIS PHOTO

USIS PHOTO

ROBERT CAPA—MAGNUM PHOTO

The Prisoners

For many of the soldiers of the Wehrmacht taken prisoner in the fighting in Paris, the first steps on the road to captivity were painful ones. On these men, a vengeful population worked out the hatreds pent up during four years of occupation. The German with hands clasped [ABOVE] seems to be beseeching a crowd to spare him the punishment apparently handed out to his bleeding comrade being marched off between two French soldiers [BELOW].

USIS PHOTO

For the Once Proud
Wehrmacht Conquerors—
and Their French Collaborators—
the Hour of Reckoning

For those who had collaborated with the enemy or profited from his presence, the people of Paris reserved a particularly bloody and bitter vengeance. Women who had slept with the Germans had their heads shaved, then [LEFT, BELOW] were paraded half naked through the city's streets. Male collaborators fared worse. They were beaten bloody [TOP LEFT] or herded [ABOVE] in disgrace to some other, often violent, end.

AGENCE FRANCE PRESSE

General von Choltitz [ABOVE] rides in a French half-track from the Prefecture of Police to the Montparnasse railroad station, to return Paris to France. Behind him, in a beret, a smiling Colonel "Rol." Choltitz [BELOW] is interrogated in the presence of grinning G.I.s.

US ARMY PHOTO

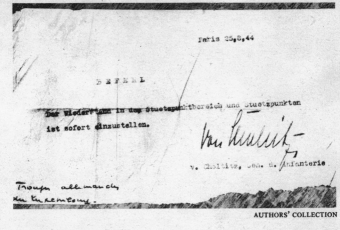

Paris 25.8.44

BEFEHL

Der Wiederkampf in den Stuetzpunktbereich und Stuetzpunkten
ist sofort einzustellen.

v. Choltitz, Gen. d. Infanterie

Troupes allemandes
du Luxembourg.

De Gaulle and Leclerc, seated in the baggage room of the
Montparnasse station [BELOW], read the text of Choltitz's surrender, a fragment of which is shown above. Leclerc, faithful
to de Gaulle's orders, accepted the surrender in the name of
the French Government instead of in the name of the Allied
Command as protocol demanded.

One Minute—and Sudden Death—
Separate These Photos

In the photo at the top, the members of von Choltitz's staff march off to captivity along the rue de Rivoli. In the circles, from left to right, are: Captain Otto Kayser, a prewar literature professor at Cologne University, Lieutenant Ernst von Bressendorf, von Choltitz's communications officer, and Lieutenant Dankvart von Arnim, his aide de camp. In the photo below, Kayser lies dying, shot through the head by an unknown Parisian who burst into the line of prisoners and fired his pistol at the first German that came before his eyes.

The Debris of Victory in the Birthplace
of the Insurrection

Burned-out Wehrmacht trucks, cars and buses litter the courtyard of the Prefecture of Police. They had been captured by
the FFI during the week-long insurrection that began with the
raising of the tricolor in the courtyard.

For de Gaulle a Grateful Kiss and a Hero's Welcome

On August 26, 1944, de Gaulle and his principal aides marked Paris's deliverance with a triumphant march [MIDDLE PHOTO] down the Champs Elysées. Visible with him, from left to right: Joseph Laniel, André Le Trocquer, René Mayer, Georges Bidault and Alexandre Parodi (over Bidault's left shoulder). In the bottom photo, a group of happy Parisiennes tags along behind the parade.

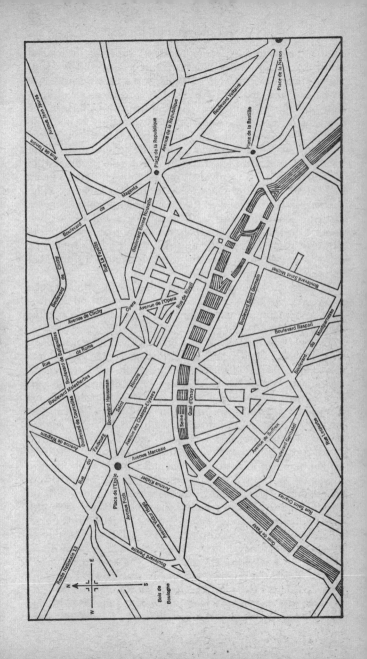

columns, moving on the southwestern corner of the capital along a front seventeen miles wide. The first and weakest, under Major François Morel-Deville, was a diversionary move down the axis the V Corps had originally assigned him, through Trappes, Saint-Cyr, past the haughty outlines of the Château of Versailles, onto the city through the porte de Sèvres. Its mission was "to make noise," to convince the Germans theirs was the main thrust. The second, under Lieutenant Colonel Paul de Langlade, five miles southeast of Morel-Deville's line of advance, moved through the rich green folds of the Valley of Chevreuse, to Toussus-le-Noble, Villacoublay and down to the city through the porte de Vanves. Leclerc's main effort, under Colonel Pierre Billotte, was an attempt to slam straight along the main southern entry to the city past the grimy industrial towns of Longjumeau, Antony and Fresnes, into the capital through its southern gateway of the porte d'Orléans.

In these first hours of the morning, with little German opposition, the 2nd Armored advance was a wild and delirious parade through a sea of ecstatic countrymen literally jamming their path.

Everywhere, their route was lined with cheering civilians, waving flags, singing, crying. Women and girls leaped onto the running boards of their trucks, vaulted over the treads of their tanks, to flood their liberators in a deluge of flowers, fruit, kisses, wine and tears. Jean René Champion, the Frenchman from Mexico driving the tank *Mort-Homme*, saw an elderly woman gesticulating wildly at him. He popped open his metal visor and a package came sliding through it. It was a casserole of stuffed tomatoes. Lieutenant Alain Rodel caught in midair a roasted chicken and a bottle of champagne tossed up to his tank by a baker. For some, the girls were simpler but no less touching, like the tricolor bouquet Corporal Claude Hadey plucked from the hands of a timid little girl.

In the packed streets of Orsay, Lieutenant Henri Karcher, who carried on the windshield of his half-track the picture of a son he had never seen, studied the mob of women and children he was passing. "You know," he said to his driver Léon Zybolski, "if my own kid was in that crowd, I wouldn't recognize him." He was. The next day Karcher would learn that his wife and his son Jean-Louis, born June 3, 1940, had been along that very street watching his column roll past,

Jean-Louis chanting to his mother, "Where is Papa? I want to see Papa."

To their astonishment, the troops of the 2nd Armored learned that the telephone lines to the city were up and functioning. As their columns paused in their roll forward, they swarmed into homes, bistros, and stores to demand telephone numbers they had not called in years. Patrick Deschamps, who had left Paris in 1940, was one of the first. "Mother," he gleefully cried, "get out the champagne. We're coming home!" A few men were so dumbfounded when they heard a familiar voice they could think of nothing to say. "Uh, uh," stuttered Private Étienne Kraft to his mother, "it's me." Some phones did not answer. Lieutenant Jacques Touny had to learn from his uncle that his father had been arrested by the Gestapo in February.

In Arpajon, Corporal Maurice Boverat, his column momentarily stopped, heard a woman in the building beside his jeep calling Paris. "Madame," he begged her, "call Élysées 60-67—it's my parents." The woman cut her call and placed his. But at that moment Boverat's column started forward. Over his shoulder he shouted, "Madame, tell my mother her son's coming home. I'm in a regiment with black berets!"

A few minutes later, in her apartment at 32 rue de Penthièvre, Mme. Yvette Boverat picked up the phone and learned her son was coming home "in a regiment with black berets." Numb with joy, she sobbed "Merci" and hung up.

Then Mme. Boverat started. "But which son?" she screamed. Mme. Boverat had two sons with de Gaulle. For three years she had had no indication of where either one was.

Suddenly, on this gray and cloudy morning, at Massy-Palaiseau, at the outskirts of Arpajon, and at Trappes, the three columns of the 2nd Armored ran up against the poised and waiting men of Generalmajor Hubertus von Aulock. At almost the same time, the first shells of the Germans' 200 carefully hidden 88s opened fire on each of Leclerc's advancing spearheads. For the 2nd Armored Division, the parade was over.

36

DIETRICH VON CHOLTITZ RECOGNIZED his caller's voice immediately. It was the ruddy-faced Luftwaffe major who three days earlier had offered to turn part of Paris into a "little Hamburg" for him. Choltitz was expecting his call. This time, Choltitz knew, the major was not calling on his own authority or that of his commander, Generaloberst Otto Dessloch. He was calling on the order of the Führer. In the upper right-hand corner of the cable order Choltitz had received at breakfast, right under his own name the general had seen the name of Luftflotte No. 3. It was the instrument Hitler had chosen to execute his command that the parts of Paris in which the insurrection persisted be "annihilated."

As Choltitz had expected they would be, the major's first words were the simple announcement that he was calling to coordinate plans for "the bombing of Paris." He informed Choltitz that since their last conversation his major occupation had been the evacuation of the Luftwaffe planes at Le Bourget. The idea he had originally suggested, a massive shuttle bombing of a part of the city, was therefore no longer possible. Instead, the major told von Choltitz, he now planned a single all-out terror raid on the city. Choltitz asked whether he planned to execute it by daylight or at night. Visibly irritated by the Paris commander's question, the major answered, "By night, of course!"

Choltitz remarked to the major that Paris was already swarming with German troops, and OB West had just informed him reinforcements were en route and due to start filtering into the city soon, perhaps that very night. A blind night raid without a clearly defined target, he acidly pointed out, "would kill as many Germans as Parisians." The major sighed. He told Choltitz he had no choice. His orders were "categoric." Luftflotte No. 3 had been instructed to bomb Paris, and they had no choice but to do it. Since they could not expose the few German bombers remaining in France to

Allied fighter attack, the raid would have to be made at night. In the present circumstances, he added, the loss of a bomber "was infinitely graver than the loss of a few men."

Choltitz fought to control his anger. Acidly, he told the major simply to advise him of the day and the hour he planned to stage his attack. Then he would evacuate his troops from the zones where they might be hit, in other words, the whole city of Paris. The Luftwaffe, he told his caller, could accept the responsibility for that at OKW.

Realizing the impasse at which they had arrived, the major told Choltitz he would consult his superiors further and pay a personal visit to him later in the afternoon. Then they would set the details for a raid as soon as possible, hopefully that night.

Von Choltitz hung up in disgust. Then he read again the last line of the cable before him, the order that had provoked the major's call. "The Luftwaffe," it said, "will annihilate any quarter of the city in which the insurrection persists." Von Choltitz shrugged his shoulders. To do that now, he reflected ironically, the major's Luftwaffe would have to "annihilate" most of Paris.

37

On a HILLTOP BEYOND Saint-Germain-en-Laye, over the western approaches of Paris, another German general studied the countryside with his field glasses. At the foot of the hill, in his black eight-cylinder Horch, Generalleutnant Günther Blumentritt's driver, First Sergeant Otto Pichler, waited with the general's ten pet parakeets. Like General Montgomery, Blumentritt adored the little birds. This officer who two weeks earlier had outlined a "limited scorched-earth policy" for Paris had decided, "just for sport" on this August morning, to give himself a little thrill. Before leaving the old headquarters of OB West in Saint-Germain to join his colleagues who had moved north a week earlier to their new headquarters near Reims, Blumentritt wanted to catch a glimpse of the first enemy tanks storming the French capital.

A few minutes before, Blumentritt had said goodbye to the French gardener at OB West, plucked a last rose, and climbed this hill. Now, in the distance, he saw the dust feathering up behind a line of advancing Shermans. He watched them until the echo of their cannon fire rolled up to his hilltop perch. An era in his life, he reflected, had ended.

Climbing into his car to leave this city he had so happily occupied for two years, Blumentritt heard his chauffeur announce a sad piece of news. "General," he said, "there's no more birdseed left. You'll have to ask Montgomery to send you some."

Twelve miles south of Blumentritt's hilltop, on a plateau over the airfield of Toussus-le-Noble, another German officer watched the forward progress of a column of Allied tanks. Twenty-two-year-old Lieutenant Heinrich Blankemeyer, of the 11th Flak Regiment, was not on his hilltop for sport. With the guns of the other men around him, he was supposed to stop those tanks, not look at them. The French advance seemed to the young Westphalian "like a parade." He could even see the rose-colored cloth panels stretched over the flanks of the tanks to identify them to Allied aircraft.

At the instant he gave his own tractor-towed 88 the order to open fire, the ridge of hills around him exploded. One by one, under his countrymen's shells, Blankemeyer saw the advancing tanks "like little toys" burst into flame.

In a ditch at one side of the airfield under Blankemeyer's glasses, Kenneth Crawford, war correspondent of *Newsweek* magazine, watched too. He cursed loudly. Five minutes before, "Papa" Hemingway had placidly assured Crawford that his FFI had scouted the way across the little airfield and found it clear. Farther on, his belly pressed into the same ditch, Major Henri de Mirambeau, the commander of an artillery batallion, stared in dismay at the line of Shermans of the 12th Cuirassiers spilling over the ridge onto the airfield "like a troop of cavalry on a charge." One by one, they exploded under the accurate fire of the Germans' still-hidden guns.

From his ditch, Mirambeau thought he had finally spotted the most menacing German emplacements. The fire seemed to come from behind a line of haystacks stretched along a wheat field beyond the airport. He ran to his jeep, still somehow intact, and ordered his motorized batteries to turn their fire on the wheat field. As the first shells tore over his head, Mirambeau watched in amazement as the whole line of haystacks began to move. Under each one, Colonel Seidel, the distinguished pianist from Dresden, had hidden an antitank gun.

When the far side of the field was finally cleared, Crawford found a smirking Hemingway coming up behind them. "You son of a bitch," Crawford said, "I thought you told me you'd scouted this place out and there weren't any Germans here!" Hemingway shrugged his shoulders. "I had to find somebody," he answered, "to be my guinea pig."

All along the three advancing columns of the 2nd Armored, tough and costly bottlenecks like Toussus-le-Noble slowed progress. On each of the division's lines of advance, the country ahead now flattened out into a network of villages and suburbs laced with intersecting crossroads, each offering the Germans an ideal emplacement for an antitank gun. In their rush to batter their way to Paris, the men of the 2nd Armored frequently tried to smash head on at those guns instead of nipping them out with infantry. It was a tactic that saved time. But it left behind each advancing column a sad and growing trail of blackened vehicles.

But time above all had to be saved this gray August day. In each column, relentless and unforgiving, the order was "Faster, faster." Rounding a curve just past the river Bièvre, Private Georges Simonin, leading a platoon of tanks in his Sherman *Cyclone*, saw five wounded Germans sprawled on the highway before his treads. One, frantically working the pavement with his elbows, tried to drag himself away. Simonin instinctively took his foot off the accelerator. As he did, he heard in his earphones the angry voice of his platoon commander crying, "*Cyclone*, nom de Dieu, get going!" Simonin shuddered, closed his eyes, and stamped on his accelerator.

38

LIKE THE CRASH OF distant surf, the echoes of the advancing 2nd Armored's shellfire drifted up to the capital from the southwest. As each hour passed, that welcome wave of sound grew closer, the muffled thuds it contained more distinct. This time it was true: the Allies were really coming.

Again the chimneys of the city's German headquarters poured out a stream of ash-flecked smoke as the last archives of four years of occupation disappeared forever. Running between the fireplaces at each end of the dining room of the Hotel Continental, Maria Fuhs, a secretary of the Wehrmacht's Paris Military Tribunal, burned one by one the hundreds of dossiers in the four filing cabinets shoved into the room. To speed their burning, she stirred her fires with a broom handle; and in a thin black veil of ashes, the last traces of 4,500 Frenchmen executed at Mont Valérien disappeared against a gray sky.

For the FFI, the distant thump of gunfire was the prod to a final drive forward. Despite their painful shortage of arms and ammunition, Rol's men pushed their insurrection into parts of the city in which it had not yet taken root.

The most violent fighting in the city was around the wide and open spaces of the place de la République. There the 1,200 troops of the Prince Eugène Barracks struck out at the ring of FFI closing in around them. The FFI fought back savagely. To take their foes from the rear, the Germans tried to pass through the blackened subway tunnels under the square. In those sweaty passageways, whistling to identify each other in the darkness, the two sides fought desperately, their combat lit by the flare of exploding grenades and quick, bright flashes of rifle fire.

But the FFI's most spectacular success of the day would pass almost unremarked. None of the Frenchmen waiting in ambush for the six-truck convoy rolling slowly toward the

Chamber of Deputies had any idea what they contained.

In the last truck, Warrant Officer Hans Fritz knew. He had only to peer through the rear window of his truck's cab to see the black and menacing stacks of torpedoes piled in the trailer behind him. They were the last torpedoes Captain Werner Ebernach needed to finish mining the Chamber of Deputies and the pont de la Concorde before it. In his nervous silence, Fritz could hear only one sound, and it symbolized his unhappy situation. It was the irregular ticking coming from the cardboard box of timing devices he held on his knees. All the way along the slow and painful ride back from Saint-Cloud, the ticking of those strange little devices had clocked off the passing seconds of the longest trip in Fritz's life.

The first burst of fire struck the driver beside him. The truck lurched to a stop and Fritz sprang out into the street screaming to the five other Mercedes trucks in the convoy. They did not stop. For a second, Fritz watched them disappear before him. Then, before his cursed truckload of torpedoes could explode, Fritz sprinted for cover. Hours later, when he finally worked his way back to the shelter of the Chamber of Deputies, Fritz learned that not a single one of those torpedo-laden trucks had reached its goal. One by one, they had been picked off by the FFI.

• • •

In the besieged Prefecture of Police, bearded law student Edgar Pisani had just learned that for the second time in five days, this central fortress of the Paris insurrection was almost out of ammunition. And three German tanks prowled the square before Notre-Dame like vultures, waiting, it seemed, for the instant the last of their reserves disappeared to attack.

Hearing the distant sound of gunfire, Pisani decided to call for help. He called the police commissariat at Longjumeau, 25 miles away. "Have the Allies arrived?" he asked the gendarme who answered.

To his astonishment, the gendarme replied, "They're here right now. They're going by the front door. Listen." Pisani told the gendarme to bring to the telephone the first officer he could find. It was Captain Alain de Boissieu. Pisani passed to him a desperate message for Leclerc. "For God's sake, hurry!" shouted Pisani. "We can't hold out much longer. Our ammunition is almost gone. We're going to be run over."

39

CORPORAL LUCIEN DAVANTURE drove his forehead against the lip of his periscope and desperately maneuvered his Sherman *Viking*, trapped in a crossfire of 88 shells on the edge of the gray-roofed village of Savigny-sur-Orge, 12 miles south of Paris. Suddenly, feet ahead of him, Davanture saw a spout of green, yellow and violet flames whoosh out of a house beside the road. Then his world went black. A German near miss had just sheared off his periscope. In a panic, he realized the *Viking* was now a blinded elephant, a target the Germans and their searching 88s could not miss.

At the same instant, Davanture heard in his earphones the calm, dry voice of his tank commander. "Lucien," he said, "do what I tell you. Back. Right. Back again. Faster." Like a machine, Davanture, choking in the oily smoke now filling the tank, executed the orders, wondering at what instant an 88 shell would rip him and the *Viking* apart. "Right. Left. Harder. Hard left. Faster. Now straight. Full left." The words rang on his ears with the crispness of rifle fire. Then, as he spun the *Viking* into a hard turn, he heard the tank commander shout out into his unbelieving ears, "Lucien, stop. We made it."

The tank was silent for an instant. Davanture slumped on his seat. Then, gasping for breath, his eyes sore and watering, he unbolted his turret and hoisted himself into the fresh air. Blinking at the sudden brightness, Davanture at first could see nothing. Then, rubbing the smoke from his eyes, he stared straight ahead, and as he did, he thought his heart would stop beating. There, graceful and proud as he had always imagined it would be, was a sight Corporal Lucien Davanture had never seen, the Eiffel Tower.

All along the three advancing columns of the 2nd Armored

at this same midday hour, these men, on whose arrival Police Prefect Charles Luizet so desperately counted, began to see that magic skeleton beckoning in the sky ahead.

To Colonel Louis Warabiot, it seemed as though his men had been "galvanized by an electric current" at the sight. In the turret of his tank, Captain Georges Buis stared solemnly at its distant outlines and thought that "the Crusaders seeing Jerusalem's walls or navigators catching their first glimpse of the Sugarloaf at Rio" must have experienced the same almost sensual delight he felt flowing through his body.

Like a magnet, the tower pulled the men of Leclerc's division toward its base, drawing their already bloodied columns forward with a new surge of energy.

But for some, the tower's spindly frame would be a promise forever unfulfilled. Private Patrick Deschamps, the boy who just hours before had jubilantly told his mother to "get out the champagne" because he was coming home, had seen it too, seconds before an 88 shell had torn apart his tank. Killed instantly, Deschamps lay crumpled in his steel coffin, his eyes closed forever on that image of the Paris he had come home to free.

● ● ●

But no soldier of the 2nd Armored would get closer to that holy stick of steel on this August afternoon than twenty-eight-year-old Jean Callet. The tower was now just under the wing-tips of Callet's Piper Cub as he scampered through the sky along the Seine toward the Prefecture of Police. Behind him, his observer Étienne Mantoux clutched a scrap of burlap tied to a chunk of lead. Stitched into that piece of burlap was the answer to Edgar Pisani's despairing call: four words of hope for the men in the beseiged building below.

In his ecstasy at the spectacle spread underneath his wings, Callet forgot even the danger of his slow and solitary progress over the capital. One by one, he numbered all its monuments from Sacré-Coeur to his left to the golden dome of Les Invalides directly under him. "Paris intact," he murmured, "Paris of my youth." He swung over Notre-Dame and the three tanks drawn up on its square. Callet saw the quick little flashes of their machine guns reaching up toward his plane. He could see the German soldiers running and, from rooftops, the waving white handkerchiefs of his countrymen. And for just a lovely second he caught the incongruous, beautiful sight of a couple embracing along the Seine.

Over the Prefecture, Callet pushed his Cub into a fake stall to convince the Germans he had been hit, and fluttered toward the ground like a fallen leaf. As he plunged toward its open courtyard, Callet saw a flag with the Cross of Lorraine spreading out under him, then, dropping like an arrow, Mantoux's weighted scrap of burlap. Callet pulled out of his stall and sprinted for safety over the city's rooftops.

Below, Abbé Robert Lepoutre, the priest who had become almost by accident the Prefecture's chaplain, was among the first to reach Callet's message. Someone tore it open and read it aloud. *"Tenez bon,"* it said. *"Nous arrivons."*

40

A SHOT OF COGNAC warming his stomach, his eyes fixed to the sight of the 88 dug into the main entry of Fresnes prison, Willi Wagenknecht listened and waited. The German prisoner who had so bitterly contemplated the sight of thousands of Frenchmen filing out of Fresnes to the concentration camps of Germany had been consigned now to the job of defending his own jailhouse. Somewhere down one of the five empty streets funneling toward the barrel of his 88, Wagenknecht could hear the slow clank of advancing tank treads.

From the window of her third-grade classroom at the Fresnes girls' school, well to Wagenknecht's right, just off National Highway 20, school-teacher Ginette Devray saw the tanks he heard. All day she had waited for this sight. "There they are!" she cried, tears running down her cheeks. "Oh, my God, there they are!"

One by one, three Shermans—the *Marne*, the *Uskub**** and the *Douaumont*, stole past her window. Pfc. Paul Landrieux,

---

* Named for one of Napoleon's battles in Russia.

the man who had left this town three years earlier to buy a pack of Gauloises, had come back. The treads of his tank *Marne* were tearing up the very pavement on which, as a boy, he had played soccer.

In this gray and fading afternoon, the three columns of the 2nd Armored had, like Landrieux's tank, reached the very doorsteps of Paris. The front of their advance, 17 miles wide in the morning, had shrunk now to less than 10 miles as they prepared to pry open the southwestern corner of the city. On its westernmost point, the column of Major Morel-Deville, assigned to "make noise" along the original line of attack, had run into heavy opposition beyond Trappes and halted. Next to him, the column of Lieutenant Colonel Paul de Langlade had been the most successful of Leclerc's three spearheads. After the costly fight at Toussus-le-Noble, Langlade's men had driven the Germans back across the Bièvre River, past Villacoublay airfield, through the grimy suburb of Clamart. Now they prepared to hook left down to the Seine itself where they would, before sunset, grab a foothold in the city, over the pont de Sèvres. But the main and easternmost column of Colonel Pierre Billotte had run into heavy opposition all along its approach to the city. Now, on the outskirts of Paris, Billotte fell onto a ferociously defended triangle that blocked his way into the capital like a cork sealing a bottle. It lay astride National Highway 20. Its right base, just east of the highway, was the prison fortress of Fresnes. Its other base, west of the highway, was anchored to the industrial town of Antony, and its apex was a mile ahead at the crossroads of Croix de Berny, where it barred the southern entry to the city just four miles distant.

Fresnes's gray stone walls, which only nine days before had housed Pierre Lefaucheux and his ill-fated companions, had been converted into an imposing roadblock by Wagenknecht and his 350 fellow German inmates, supported by a battalion of the 132nd Infantry Regiment. Flanking Wagenknecht's 88 in the prison's main entry were a pair of smaller antitank pieces and a protective brace of machine guns. The gate, set in the middle of Fresnes's long wall, gave Wagenknecht a perfect field of fire down three of the five streets leading to the prison.

Moving to the foot of one of them, the avenue de la République, Pfc. Paul Landrieux in the Sherman *Marne* pointed out

to his gunner the square bell tower of the church in which
he had been married. Beside it was the shuttered window
of a tobacco shop, the same tobacco shop toward which
Landrieux had headed three years earlier in search of his
phantom package of Gauloises. Then the two men fell silent.
The three tanks had turned and were starting warily up the
avenue de la République toward the mouth of Fresnes. There,
a thousand feet away, Willi Wagenknecht and his 88 waited.

Aboard the tank *Vieil Armand,* another Sherman moving
laterally along Fresnes's stone wall toward the prison gate,
Private Pierre Chauvet fixed his field glasses on the barricaded
entry and repeated to himself, "My God, what are they
waiting for to shoot?"

Crouched behind his 88, Willi Wagenknecht asked himself
the same question. Now he could see the tanks he had heard
before, three of them stealing toward him past the dingy
tenements of the avenue de la République. Holding the lead
tank in his gunsight, Wagenknecht decided to count to ten.
He had just begun when an officer behind him cried, "Shoot,
you silly bastard. Are you waiting for them to run over you?"

Captain Dupont and his adjutant Lieutenant Marcel
Christen, sliding on foot along the prison's wall to better
guide the action, heard the first roar of the 88. Christen saw
the lead tank moving up the avenue de la République lift
into the air under the shell's impact, then tumble to the
ground in a ball of flames. Dupont and Christen saw one man,
his legs shot off, hoist himself out of the tank and roll to the
ground, then another, his fatigues blazing, stumble from the
turret and run for cover.

Now, from all sides, Dupont's advancing tanks poured fire
into the mouth of the prison. Christen realized that "if we
don't get that *putain* of an 88 out of there, he's going to beat
up the whole company." Over his head Christen could hear
a stream of shells moving toward the gate as Pierre Chauvet
of the *Vieil Armand* cannonaded the entry. Suddenly there
was a terrific explosion. One of Chauvet's shots had hit an
ammunition truck just behind Wagenknecht's gun. Miraculously unhurt, Wagenknecht had only one thought. Abandoning the ruins of his 88, he sprinted for safety through the
smoke and debris choking the prison gate. Unseen, he dodged
past these tanks on which he had just been firing and ran
down the road paralleling Fresnes's walls to the village ceme-

tery. There he fell gasping into a ditch. As he panted for breath, one thought suddenly swept ex-prisoner Wagenknecht's mind. "Thank God," he told himself, "I'm free."

At the mouth of the prison, smoke and gunfire continued to pour out at the advancing Frenchmen. Barely 50 yards from the entry, pressed against the prison wall, Christen and Dupont continued their slide forward. Suddenly a German, his uniform torn and blackened, rose out of the smoke ahead and drove a quick burst of submachine-gun fire at them. Christen heard an "Oh!" beside him and turned to see Captain Dupont, his head neatly pierced, topple to the pavement. At the same instant, behind him, Christen saw one of his tanks, the *Notre Dame de Lorette*, sweep forward. Then at the gate to the prison it pivoted to the right and, all its guns firing, smashed head on over the ruins of Wagenknecht's gun and the German defenders still in the gate. For the driver of the *Notre Dame de Lorette*, Fresnes prison had no secrets. Pfc. Jacques Neal knew its courtyard as well as his Paris home. He had been a Gestapo prisoner there for thirteen months before escaping to join the Free French.

Following the *Notre Dame de Lorette*, the remaining tanks of Captain Dupont stormed the prison and silenced its defenders.

The price had been high. Charred and blackened, five tanks lined the streets around Fresnes. In one of them—in the middle of the avenue de la République, inside the burned-out carcass of the *Marne*—a pair of sightless eyes stared up through its open turret to the clouds drifting down to Paris. Paul Landrieux was dead, his chest ripped open by a shard of Willi Wagenknecht's first, well-aimed shell. In the pocket of his blackened fatigues was the unopened package of Camels he had brought home to Fresnes from his long voyage to eternity.

41

"MY GOD," THOUGHT THE stunned Frenchman, "this man is committing treason!" For the second time in less than eight hours, Lorrain Cruse, Jacques Chaban-Delmas's assistant, was standing by the bedside of Swedish Consul General Raoul Nordling, listening to Abwehr agent "Bobby" Bender's rich soft voice. A glass of whisky cupped in one hand, a pencil in the other, Bender was leaning over a frayed Michelin map of the Paris region, its folds spread across the foot of Nordling's bed. With a precise poke of his pencil, Bender was exposing, one by one, every German stronghold on the road to Paris.

"Here," Bender said, pointing to the outskirts of Clamart, "is a regiment reinforced by two companies of tanks. Your General Leclerc must bypass them." With swift movements of his pencil down the red and yellow lines of the map converging on the capital, Bender showed Cruse how it should be done. When his darting pencil had reached the limits of the city, Cruse saw Bender reflect for a moment, then sketch a line down to the Seine, across the river to the place du Châtelet and up the rue de Rivoli toward the place de la Concorde. That, he told Cruse, was the itinerary Leclerc's troops should follow if they wanted to get into the heart of Paris without opposition. It would, he said, take them "right to the Meurice without a fight."

The silver-haired German had just returned from the Meurice. There Bender had been able to measure the distance still separating Paris from disaster. It was 60 miles, the span separating the Hotel Meurice from the advance elements of the 26th SS Panzer Division waiting for darkness near the Napoleonic battleground of Montmirail. That night they would begin their next and probably last leap toward the capital. The Allies had to beat them into Paris, Bender warned Cruse. If the Shermans of Leclerc arrived on the doorsteps of the Hotel Meurice before those Panzers, Choltitz would be prepared to hand over the city after a symbolic resistance to satisfy his soldier's honor. But if the Panzers got there first, Bender warned, the little general would fight. Everything, he told the bronzed young resistant, depended on General Leclerc.

The once elegant playboy shook the hair of his graying temples and gulped down the last mouthful of his whisky. He fixed his piercing green eyes on the young officer before him. "If," he said, "I have made a number of revelations which have surprised you, it is because I sincerely believe they are in the best interests of my country."

Then Bender set down his whisky glass, reached down to his brown leather pistol belt and unbuckled it. "Now," he said, handing it to the Frenchman beside him, "I consider myself your prisoner."

Cruse did not take it. He did not have time. Tomorrow, he told Bender, he would take him prisoner; until then he should stay in Nordling's Consulate. Then Cruse bolted out to his bicycle.

42

ALL DAY, DISTANT AND lonely, the figure of Charles de Gaulle had prowled the flagstone terrace of the Château de Rambouillet. In the early hours of the morning from his simple attic apartment under the eaves of the château, de Gaulle had watched in moody retrospection as the imposing columns of the 2nd Armored moved on to Paris in a gray drizzle. He had reflected bitterly "what a difference seven divisions like it" would have made to France in 1940.

Now, hour by hour, de Gaulle followed the division's painful progress down the road to Paris. He had hoped to be in the capital by nightfall. But with one report of heavy opposition piling on another, it had become clear he would not be. The long journey home from exile would, for the chief of Free France, last one more night.

During the afternoon, the first of the Resistance papers

brought out from the city confirmed de Gaulle's suspicions of his political foes' motives. The chiefs of the insurrection, as he had foreseen, were now preparing to establish themselves as a kind of welcoming committee, to take him under their wing, to sponsor him to the city. De Gaulle was going to have none of it. He intended to have only one kind of investiture, and the leaders of the insurrection did not figure in it: It was the acclaim of the population.

To a suggestion, brought out from the city, that he be "received" on his arrival by the chiefs of the insurrection at the Hôtel de Ville, de Gaulle sent back a curt and cold reply. He would, he said, go directly to the Ministry of Defense and, in his own good time, receive the leaders of the insurrection there. As for those leaders and their committees, de Gaulle already had a future picked out for them: an honored place in "the glorious history of the liberation"—and oblivion.

As he had twice before in this day, de Gaulle beckoned his close associate Geoffroy de Courcel to walk with him in the gardens of the château. Puffing on an English cigarette, he retreated behind a wall of silence. Courcel knew enough not to interrupt his thoughts. For, like the other men around him, de Courcel knew de Gaulle did not follow the unexpectedly severe battle for the gates of Paris with a politician's eyes alone. He followed it also as a father. Proud and erect in one of the Marine tank destroyers that flowed out of Rambouillet that morning had been a young Marine lieutenant. It was Charles de Gaulle's only son, Philippe.

•   •   •

A dozen miles from the majestic towers of Rambouillet, in a collection of khaki tents near the village of Maintenon, another general displayed an impatience about Paris to rival de Gaulle's. Since midnight the evening before, Major General Leonard T. Gerow, Leclerc's American V Corps commander, had had no word from the advancing 2nd Armored. Worse, he had learned of Leclerc's personal decision to shift his division's line of attack 17 miles southeast, not from the 2nd Armored but from the U.S. division on its flank. In an angry telegram to First Army, Gerow reported, "2nd Armored . . . ordered an attack from the direction of Arpajon and Longjumeau to center of Paris. This is in violation of Field Order 21 of August 22 and disregards boundary between 2nd Armored and 4th Division."

Now, stalking through his command tent, Gerow vowed to his G3, Colonel John Hill, that if Leclerc were an American, he would sack him on the spot. Adding to Gerow's irritation were pressures from the Allied Command which, believing the defenses in front of Paris paper-thin, had expected Léclerc in the city by noon.

Bradley, worried by Nordling's report, was demanding hourly why Paris had not been taken. The soft-spoken American wanted to run no risk of its German commander's having a change of heart. Finally the exasperated Bradley issued a new order. "To hell with prestige," he announced. "Tell the Fourth [U.S. Infantry] to slam on in and take the Liberation."

To his embarrassment and anger, just after he had finished an unsuccessful search for Leclerc, Gerow received Bradley's command, translated into a toughly worded order telling him, "It is imperative your troops enter Paris without delay." The order instructed him to have the 2nd Armored speed its advance, and to send in the U.S. 4th Division "without regard" to the 2nd Armored's whereabouts. In other words, if the French were not capable of getting to Paris first, Gerow's GIs would.

Gerow relayed the order to the 4th Division, then wrote out a dry and severe message to Leclerc, ordering the 2nd Armored commander to "push your advance vigorously this afternoon and tonight." Then, still without any means of contacting Leclerc, he angrily ordered Hill to take the order to him personally. As Hill climbed into his jeep, Gerow told him, "I don't give a damn if you have to go to hell and back to do it. Find that Frenchman before you come back."

*   *   *

Jacques Philippe Leclerc was at that moment jabbing the brass tip of his malacca cane at the pavement of a country road, still ten miles from Paris. From his left, half a mile away, he could hear the shellfire of his armored columns trying to batter their way past the Croix de Berny. Neither Gerow nor de Gaulle had to tell Leclerc to hurry into Paris. He was ridden by the fear his troops would reach the capital after its German garrison had fired the explosives seeded through its streets. Angry and disappointed, Leclerc had had to accept the fact he would not reach the city for another twelve hours.

The red-haired captain jeeping toward Leclerc at the head of a little armored detachment was furious, too. Twice in the past half hour, Raymond Dronne had had the conviction that the road to Paris lay open before him. And twice he had been curtly ordered by his immediate superior to rejoin the main line of attack. Spotting Leclerc, Dronne vaulted out of his jeep and reported to his commander.

"What the hell are you doing here?" Leclerc asked. Dronne told him. "Dronne," Leclerc said, "don't you know enough not to obey stupid orders?"

Then, grabbing the elbow of this gentle-voiced captain who had served with him for four years, Leclerc said, "I want you to get into Paris. Take whatever you've got and go. Forget about fighting the Germans. Just get there any way you can. Tell them to hold on, we're coming tomorrow."

Dronne turned his little detachment around and in twenty minutes formed it up for his dash to Paris. To bring the standard of the French Army back to the capital of his country, Dronne had three Shermans, named for Napoleon's battles—the *Romilly*, the *Montmirail* and the *Champaubert*, and half a dozen half-tracks. The red-haired captain who had wanted to be handsome for the women of Paris was a grimy mess. He had not slept for forty-eight hours; his eyes were baggy and red, his beard clotted with sweat and grease. He was covered with oil, gunpowder and dirt, and his uniform stained dark with sweat. To a city whose memories of the French Army hung on the white-gloved officers of 1940 enjoying their last leaves of the *drôle de guerre*, Dronne was a fitting symbol of a new era.

With a last look at his column, this man destiny had chosen to be the first French officer to come home to the capital of France climbed into his jeep. Then, staring at the curious crowd gathered around him, he asked a last question.

"Hey," he shouted, "does anybody here know the road to Paris?"

43

A FEW MILES AWAY, in the crowded streets of Longjumeau, an American officer reached into a sack on the floor of his jeep. He pulled out two packs of cigarettes and handed them to a smiling civilian. The Frenchman passed him back a folded square of paper. Captain Bill Mills, G3 of the 2nd Battalion of the 4th Division's 12th Regiment, acknowledged it with a happy grin. It was a map of Paris, and it resolved Mills's most pressing problem this August evening.

So fast had the 4th moved up from Normandy, so unexpected had its Paris assignment been, that its headquarters had no detailed maps of the city or its approaches. A few minutes earlier its commander, Major General Raymond Barton, had learned that the 4th was now going into Paris. At that moment, he realized that he did not know the location of their objective, the Prefecture of Police.

Clutching the precious document in his hands, Mills started back to headquarters. In its upper left-hand corner, he read the name of the publisher, "A. Lecomte." Under it in neat letters was the title of this map with which, in a few hours, the advance elements of the 4th Division would race the men of the 2nd Armored into the capital of France. It was "A Practical Itinerary to the Monuments of the City for a Foreigner in Paris."

Exhausted by their long motor march in the rain in a tight blackout, with German planes probing the skies overhead, the men of the 4th were sprawled in three assembly areas on the city's southern flank. To some, like Technical Sergeant Milt Shenton of Taylors Island, Maryland, Paris "was a poor boy's dream come true." To others, like Rifleman Willie Hancock, of Lenox, Georgia, filled with the infantryman's dread of a built-up area, it was "just another big German-held city on the road to Berlin and home."

For some men, the city ahead already had a special meaning. Lieutenant Colonel Dee Stone patted the worn envelope inside his field jacket as he heard the news. The letter was Stone's talisman. He had carried it since the night he left his home in Forest Hills, New York, in November, 1943, to sail for England. It had landed with him on D Day, followed him through the bloody hedgerows of Normandy. It had brought him alive to the outskirts of Paris, and tomorrow Stone would keep faith with its author. He would deliver it in Paris.

First Lieutenant Jack Knowles, platoon leader of the 3rd Platoon of "I" Company, 22nd Infantry, and his platoon sergeant, "Speedy" Stone, were in a fury about the move to Paris. Their company commander told them it was going to be a "parade," and they would have to furnish their men with ties. Ties were something Stone and Knowles had not seen since leaving England. But Stone was the best scrounger in the division, and he promised Knowles he would have them by morning. Paris, to "Speedy" Stone, was worth a parade.

In a damp grove of poplar trees outside Trappes, Sergeant Larry Kelly was happy. This blond Irish giant from Altoona, Pennsylvania, had an almost mystic affection for France. In 1917, at the age of fifteen, he had lied about his age, enlisted, fought for eight months in France, been wounded twice. He had jumped into France with the 82nd Airborne on D Day, been wounded and transferred to the Field Artillery. Now, as a forward observer for the U.S. battalion backing up Major Morel-Deville's column, Kelly was delighted. He had promised himself he would be the first American into Paris. Now it looked as though he would be.

In the twilight that evening, Lieutenant Warren Hooker, a platoon leader in "A" Company, 22nd Infantry, climbed an aged medieval watchtower, just south of Orly Field. At the top, Hooker gasped in wonder at the sight spread out before him, the skyline of Paris, every sacred stone Hooker had read about in history books and Alexandre Dumas. Those outlines of Notre-Dame, the Eiffel Tower and Sacré-Coeur seemed to Hooker "like old friends." With an infantryman's grim wisdom, Hooker realized it would not be his lot to visit those sights he had dreamed about as a boy. His division's fate would be "to spill blood in the city and then move on." Sadly, Hooker thought of the lines of a poem by Robert Frost he had memorized in high school: "But I have promises to keep, and miles to go before I sleep/And miles to go before I sleep."

● ● ●

From a hilltop over Sèvres at one tip of Paris to the flanks of Orly Field, the exhausted and battered men of the 2nd Armored had paused for the night in their move on the city. Although they did not know it, they had knocked apart the last German strongpoints they would encounter until they reached the center of the capital. The road to Paris was now open.

In almost every one of Leclerc's units there were vacant places on this evening the men of the 2nd Armored had hoped to spend in triumph in Paris. Generalmajor Hubertus von Aulock had been true to his word. He had made this division pay a heavy price for the keys to Paris. Along the roads behind them, the division's three columns had left a sad trail of blackened vehicles and dead troops. One company of the Chad Regiment had lost fifteen of its sixteen half-tracks. The 3rd Company of the 501st Tank Regiment had lost a third of its tanks at Fresnes alone.

Their losses and their sheer fatigue dampened the spirits of the 2nd Armored's men. Their consolation now was the knowledge that Paris was just a stone's throw away, at the other side of the next row of rooftops. Their voyage home was almost over.

Now neither the Americans nor a motor failure could hold up Jean René Champion of the *Mort-Homme*. Paris seemed to him that night like "a sleeping mistress" waiting to be awakened. Beside his Sherman, *Norway*, Captain Georges Buis sang a song he had composed himself in the Libyan Desert while his gunner followed him on the harmonica. Its words began, "All our paths are only steps down the road to Paris." Stretched out behind the *Douaumont* near Fresnes, Sergeant Marcel Bizien gazed lazily at the sky and promised out loud that, the next day, he would make his Breton ancestors proud. He would. Tank driver Bizien would slam his Sherman into the flanks of a Panther on the place de la Concorde.

But none of the men of the 2nd Armored felt more emotion at the forthcoming liberation than a forty-year-old lieutenant of the Chad Regiment watching the elements that would lead the final push into the city moving into position. At the sight of the big blond kid standing proudly erect in a passing half-

track of the 97th Headquarters Company, Lieutenant René
Berth flushed with pride. It was his son Raymond. Two years
earlier, without a word to his mother, this bronzed twenty-
year-old had stuffed a few belongings into a knapsack and
walked from Paris to the Pyrenees to join his father in the
ranks of the Free French. Together, father and son had
fought their way to the gates of Paris in the 2nd Armored.
Waiting for them inside the city on this August evening,
Louise Berth did not know whether her husband and her son
were alive or dead—much less that they were a bare ten
miles from their home.

Watching his gangling son disappear down the road to
Paris, Lieutenant René Berth thought of the family reunion
they would have in a few hours. Then another thought struck
him. Tomorrow, August 25, was Louise Berth's feast day. "My
God," he thought, "it's going to be the happiest feast day of
her life."

At the gates of the Fresnes prison a pair of FFI herded
a sullen German prisoner past its 2nd Armored conquerors
into its debris-littered courtyard. For Willi Wagenknecht,
Fresnes's reluctant defender, this was the bitterest moment
of the war. He had been captured; his stay in Paris would end
this night where it had begun, in a Fresnes prison cell.

●   ●   ●

The last night of occupation fell on Paris just as the first
night had, to the distant din of cannon. At sunset that advancing wall of sound seemed to hang suspended along the
horizon like a cresting wave about to break over the city.
Paris's German defenders, almost isolated now by Rol's FFI,
braced in their strongpoints for the attack that could be only
hours away.

The commanders of each of those thirty major *Stützpunkte*
had pledged to defend them to "their last cartridge." It was
not an idle pledge. It had been exacted by Hitler himself
three weeks earlier. It was one of the rare occasions on which
the Führer had, in the west, ordered that pledge sworn on an
officer's oath. The last had been at Saint-Malo. There, carrying
it out to the letter, the island fortress had offered the Allies
as furious a resistance as any they would encounter south of
the German frontier.

In Paris, dug into some of the city's most handsome buildings, the Germans prepared to offer a resistance no less determined. At the surrounded SS barracks on the place de la République, a Sturmbannführer assembled his men to inform them two SS divisions were on their way to their aid. "We will," he told them, "hold on until they arrive to free us." In the École Militaire, Sergeant Bernhard Blache, whose men had been "cooking like sausages" before the Prefecture of Police a week earlier, heard Major Otto Müller inform them they would "fight to the end as the Führer has ordered." Then Blache was marched off for a pre-battle treat, a huge Westphalian ham. Müller's speech and the prospect of dying for the École Militaire had so sickened Blache that he could not touch it.

In the Palais du Luxembourg, Marcel Macary and his electrician François Dalby watched their German captors barricade the building for a final stand. Dalby knew that despite his efforts the Germans had largely completed their mining of the handsome structure. He was afraid they would, in a final Götterdämmerung, blow up themselves, the building and their prisoners. So were the palace's neighbors. In haste, they evacuated the blocks around it.

At the most important *Stützpunkt* in the city, in the sandbagged lobby of the Hotel Meurice, the man on whose shoulders the defense of Paris rested faced the officers of his command. Dietrich von Choltitz was burning in a rare public display of anger. A few minutes earlier one of his officers had asked permission to "get out of this rat's trap." Whatever his course of action was going to be, Choltitz was determined to do one thing. He was going to keep the hand of an iron disciplinarian on his troops.

He reminded the men before him that they were all under his orders. His orders were "to defend Paris and that is what I intend to do." He was going to force compliance with his orders, he warned, "with a pistol in my hand if I have to." He would, he told these shocked officers, "personally shoot down in my own office the next man who comes to me suggesting we abandon Paris without a fight."

In the silence that followed his last words, Klaus Engelmeier, a Westphalian doctor assigned to Gross Paris, thought to himself, "My God, he's going to force us all to die in this hotel."

44

UNDER THE FOLDS of an abandoned rock quarry just outside the village of Longjumeau, the commanding officer of the 2nd Armored Division stared at a map spread out on the hood of his command half-track. Rarely had Philippe Leclerc or the staff officers around him contemplated a map with the anguish with which they studied this one. It was a map of Paris, and it was covered with little red circles, each representing one of the German *Stützpunkte* Dietrich von Choltitz's officers had vowed to defend to "their last cartridge." In almost every instance those red circles fell around one of the architectural beauties of the city the 2nd Armored had come to free. If the Germans clung to these strongpoints as tenaciously as they had clung to their positions along this route this day, only heavy tank and artillery fire, Leclerc realized, would get them out. Tomorrow, he reflected bitterly, Paris would count the cost of its deliverance in the debris of the place de la Concorde, the Chamber of Deputies, the Luxembourg Palace and the rue de Rivoli.

To the silent staff officers gathered around him, Leclerc repeated a warning against using artillery or high-explosive shells in the city without his accord. They had, he told them, come here "to liberate Paris, not destroy it."

Then the little band of men moved off a few feet and sat down cross-legged on the ground around a katambouru skin Ahmed, Leclerc's Algerian orderly, had spread on a rock. To each man Ahmed passed a box of K rations. In silence, in the fast-falling dusk, with the simple ritual acquired in years in the deserts of Africa, these representatives of a new French Army ate their last meal in exile from the capital of their country. Rawboned and taciturn, these men who had burned the fat from their bodies and charred their souls in the furnaces of that Africa were distant cousins of those officers of "the phony war" of 1940, who dined by candlelight in

266

châteaux far from the battleground's disconcerting din. When they had finished, each wrapped himself in a jellaba and fell asleep on the ground.

* * *

A dozen miles away in the heart of Paris, in the mammoth basement refectory of the Hôtel de Ville, the chiefs of the Resistance, too, sat down to dinner. They sat on park benches, chairs, upended packing crates. Around them, their rifles and grenades tossed on the refectory's wooden mess tables, the building's exhausted FFI defenders fell in silence on the food before them.

They banged back and forth tin pitchers of raw red wine, while a dozen female collaborators, heads shaved smooth as billiard balls, served their only dish that evening, gray occupation noodles mixed with lentils.

It was, thought Jacques Debû-Bridel, the man whose timely intervention had prevented the Resistance's stormy meeting three nights before from disintegrating, a "dreary and depressing dinner." For forty-eight hours the men in the Hôtel de Ville had waited for disaster to fall on them. Now they too had heard the rumors that two SS divisions were approaching the city. To Debû-Bridel, as to many of the men in the room, it seemed at this solemn dinner as though fate was about to cheat them of the victory to which they had so precariously clung for five days.

* * *

Barely a mile away, at the other end of the deserted rue de Rivoli running past the Hôtel de Ville, Dietrich von Choltitz stood before his bedroom mirror and looked at the stiff collar cutting into his neck. He had, he realized, put on weight in Paris. This was the first time he was wearing a stiff collar since he had arrived in the city. On the bed behind him was the freshly pressed white jacket which, in a few moments, he would slip on over his field-gray trousers with their general officer's red stripe. Von Choltitz had worn that jacket only once before, at a reception behind the Anzio beachhead marking his promotion to major general. This evening he was wearing it to another reception, the last he would attend in many years. On the first floor of the Meurice, in one of the rooms of his office suite, his colleagues were offering him a farewell dinner.

There were few Germans left in the Meurice with any illusions about the fate awaiting them. All day, on the huge map of the Paris region in Choltitz's office, a set of red pins had marked the Allies' swift and unforeseen advance. Now those pins stood poised at the gates of the city itself. From OB West, the evening situation report for the whole front was no less depressing. It had told Choltitz something "Bobby" Bender did not know. The Americans had broken out over the Seine near Sens and were moving unchecked into German territory. To halt them, two divisions had been ordered to Nogent-sur-Seine and Troyes, the 26th and 27th SS Panzer Divisions. For Choltitz, there would be no reinforcements now.

Knotting his black tie before his oval mirror, Choltitz realized that in a few hours, at dawn probably, the Allies would move in for the kill. Even the Luftwaffe major, so menacing in their conversation that morning, had failed to show up at his headquarters. Bitterly, Choltitz thought of that major, of Hitler, of Jodl, of Model. Instead of reinforcements to defend this city, they had sent him only words and the pneumatic drills of the 813th Pionierkompanie. Incapable of defending Paris, OKW had chosen to offer itself instead the pleasure of destroying it.

Now they expected from him only one act: the order to detonate Werner Ebernach's carefully placed mines.

By tomorrow night, the conqueror of Sebastopol reasoned, he would be either dead in the ruins of this hotel or a prisoner. The May morning when he had leaped from his Junkers at Rotterdam airport he had dreamed of another end for himself, for Germany. Yet he realized he himself—by sending Nordling to the Allies—had helped bring on the end now facing him.

Picking up the eau de cologne Corporal Mayer had bought for him ten days earlier, Choltitz slapped a few drops on his face and resolved that on this mournful evening he would at least put up a cheerful front for his subordinates. He set the ornate flask back on its ledge. He had used it only rarely, and he noticed for the first time its name. It was "Soir de Paris."

Then, like a captain ready to go down with his ship in dress uniform, Choltitz left the room and strode calmly toward his farewell dinner.

•   •   •

In another room of the hotel, a pretty dark-haired girl slithered into a black silk dress sparkling with silver spangles. Decidedly, thought twenty-three-year-old Cita Krebben, looking at herself in the mirror, this last dress of her little Paris dressmaker was a great success.

The Munich secretary was one of the few German women left in Paris. Her natural elegance, and the regular patronage of her Parisian dressmaker, had made her a striking woman. A few minutes later, when she entered the candlelit room where Choltitz's staff waited, all eyes turned on her. Von Choltitz himself poured a glass of Cordon Rouge, then proposed a toast "to the health of all the magnificent German women whose solidarity during this war has softened its heavy blows."

Everyone in the little room raised his glass. It was, Count Dankvart von Arnim thought, "a moving moment." He studied the faces around him: von Unger, cold and distant as always; Jay, chipper and dashing even on this last evening; Clemens Podewills, a visiting war correspondent, despondent at having been caught in the city; Arnim's scholarly friend Captain Otto Kayser, a professor of literature from Cologne, the gloomiest of all. That afternoon Kayser had shown von Arnim a Resistance sticker torn from a wall near the Comédie Française. It was Rol's blunt slogan, "À chacun son boche."

As they chatted with forced gaiety, von Arnim noticed a messenger summon Choltitz out of the room to receive a telephone call.

At the other end of the line Choltitz recognized, faint and blurred, the familiar voice of General Walter Krueger, a prewar comrade, now commander of the 58th Panzer Corps. Krueger was calling from a field telephone outside Chantilly, 25 miles away. "I'm coming to Paris," Krueger joked. "We'll go to the Sphinx together." °

It was not, however, to make jokes that Krueger was calling. Model had ordered him to assemble all the 58th Corps' avail-

---

° The Sphinx was the most noted and popular of Paris's prewar brothels.

able tanks and send them urgently to Choltitz's aid. Krueger now had to confess to his old friend that on this August evening he had no available tanks. Of the 120,000 men and 800 tanks with which the 58th Corps had begun the Normandy campaign, barely a handful remained. They were streaming in defeat and disarray over the countryside south of Chantilly.

Krueger told Choltitz he had officers combing the area around the city at that very moment, trying to find the armor he had been ordered to send him. Sadly, Krueger admitted to his old friend that in the chaos of the collapsing front, he did not think he could find the tanks in time.

The two men fell silent. Then Krueger asked Choltitz what he was going to do. "I don't know," replied the Paris commander. "The situation is bad." Again there was a silence, and then the two men said to each other, *"Hals- und Beinbruch"* —"Break your neck and your legs." It was an old German Army term. It meant "Good luck."

• • •

Formal and proper, the maître d'hôtel of the Meurice passed the heavy silver tray bearing neat piles of asparagus. For this last dinner Annabella Waldner, the hostess who had arranged so many triumphant banquets for the Wehrmacht, had personally selected the best of the delicacies left in the Meurice pantries. After the asparagus in Hollandaise sauce, her guests would eat pâté de foie gras and the specialty of her Bulgarian chef, the profiteroles au chocolat that had been the favorite dish of Generalfeldmarschall Rommel.

Under the silver candlesticks Annabella Waldner had set out for the dinner, the little group began to eat. Seated between Cita Krebben and Hildegarde Grün, von Choltitz tried to play the diverting host for his staff. He told them of his days as a page in the court of the queen of Saxony. But cheer and conversation came hard. Slowly the group drifted into a somber and moody silence.

Count von Arnim daydreamed as he poked listlessly through his asparagus. Suddenly he was jolted back to reality by the image engraved on the bottom of his plate. It was the Arc de Triomphe. For this last dinner in Paris Dietrich von Choltitz was dining off a special porcelain service commanded by his predecessor from the centuries-old manufacturers of Sèvres.

Hand-painted on each plate of that service, capped with the seal of the Wehrmacht, was a monument of the city Adolf Hitler had ordered him to destroy.

45

IN THE DISAPPEARING DUSK, three words loomed ahead of Captain Raymond Dronne, along the same road that, 129 years earlier, Napoleon Bonaparte had followed home from exile on the island of Elba. They were PARIS—PORTE D'ITALIE.

With a rush, Dronne's tanks swept across the city limits into the gates of Paris. In a fleeting second, the red-bearded captain realized he had won a race four years in the running. He was the first French soldier to come home to Paris. Behind him, the men crammed into his little band of tanks and half-tracks cheered in wild delight.

Around the place d'Italie, hundreds of Parisians who had dashed for cover at the clatter of Dronne's approaching treads listened, and stared at these unfamiliar silhouettes slipping through the square. In a bewildering moment, they understood these soldiers were not wearing the squared helmets of the Wehrmacht. They were the first liberators of Paris.

"Les Américains!" someone screamed, and at those words a wild flood tide of humanity surged from every street corner and doorway of the square toward Dronne's vehicles. This red-bearded captain who had wanted to look handsome for his first Parisiennes was suddenly choked in a sea of them: old ones, young ones, pretty ones, ugly ones; redheads, blondes and brunettes; all scrambling to kiss him, hug him, shake his hand, or even stroke his dirty uniform. A heavyset girl wearing the red skirt and black bodice of Alsace jumped onto his jeep, smashing as she did the glass of his lowered windshield.

With the ecstatic girl singing and waving a tricolor, Dronne's men pushed through the square and swept in a new burst of speed down the avenue d'Italie. To avoid Germans, they slipped down the side streets, moving so fast that, by the time the Parisians along their route had glimpsed the white Cross of Lorraine on their Shermans, they had faded like a dream into the darkness. Only once did the Germans along their route have time to fire on them, at the Gare d'Austerlitz. Dronne's tanks rushed past without firing. They dashed over the unguarded pont d'Austerlitz, still intact despite all the orders Choltitz had received, and up the quais of the Seine. As his jeep curved along the quai des Célestins, the exhausted Dronne felt his first chill of emotion. There to his left, massive and majestic in this still-moonless night, was the ageless outline of Notre-Dame. He turned to the right, and in a shower of sparks and spinning treads, Dronne's three tanks and six half-tracks buckled a line of armor around the Hôtel de Ville, the symbol of the municipal authority of Paris. Dronne leaped out of his jeep at the enormous marble staircase of the Renaissance-style building, its façade chipped with bullet holes, its windows draped with the tricolor. On the open face of its clock tower, two golden hands marked the hour. It was 9:22. The French Army—1,532 days, 3 hours, and 52 minutes after the first troops of the Wehrmacht had passed through the porte de la Villette at 5:30 on June 14, 1940—had come home to the capital of France.

Seconds before, the frail figure of Georges Bidault had mounted a shaking wooden mess table in the crowded refectory below. Emotion pushing his voice into its upper ranges, Bidault cried, "The first tanks of the French Army have crossed the Seine and are in the heart of Paris!" The echo of his words still hung in the stunned room when, on the square outside, those men heard the scraping of tank treads moving toward the building. In a clatter of smashing crockery and clanging tin plates, they sprang to their feet to sing the "Marseillaise." As the anthem's last notes spent themselves in the refectory's rafters, the men inside, many of whom had spent four years in clandestine combat awaiting this moment, stampeded for the door. In a jubilant herd, they fell on the exhausted and speechless Dronne, smothering the stumbling captain in their wet embraces.

Pierre Crenesse of the French Radio, seized by the Resistance five days earlier from its collaborationist rulers, ran to the first exhausted soldier crawling from Dronne's lead tank, the *Champaubert*. A microphone in his hand, he shrieked in joy to his listeners, "You are going to hear the voice of the first French soldier, the first ordinary French soldier, to arrive in Paris."

Thrusting his microphone toward the stunned man, Crenesse posed the first question that came to his mind in this moment of triumph: "Where," he asked, "are you from?"

"Constantinople," replied Private Firmian Pirlian.

For almost an hour the radio had broadcast a frenzied series of reports, rumors, and proud French songs. Now, to spread the news of Dronne's arrival across the capital, the electricians of Paris power plants threw on all their switches to carry the radio's broadcast to every corner of Paris.

"Parisians, rejoice!" shouted Pierre Schaeffer at the radio's main studio. "We have come on the air to give you the news of our deliverance. The Leclerc Division has entered Paris. We are mad with happiness!" To express the depths of his own emotion, Schaeffer read the moving and apt stanza of Victor Hugo's *Punishments:*

Réveillez-vous! Assez de honte!
Redevenez la grande France!
Redevenez le grand Paris! °

Howling in happiness, people poured into the streets, banged open their shuttered windows, threw themselves into the arms of neighbors to whom they had not spoken for years. With all the power of Paris's electric plants behind it, the radio pushed one pulsating "Marseillaise" over the air. As it did, a remarkable thing happened. In hundreds of thousands of homes, Parisians spontaneously spun up their radios full volume and threw open their windows.

From balconies, doorways, windows; from sidewalks, streets and barricades, the whole darkened city, proud and alive again, sang with the radio. For a few moments Paris wrapped herself in the sound of that anthem rolling and reverberating through all her blacked-out streets.

For the bone-tired Raymond Dronne standing on the steps of the Hôtel de Ville, it was the most memorable moment of his life. That massive, mystic "Marseillaise" seemed to "lift up the whole city on a wave of sound." Tears forming in his

---

° Awake! Be done with shame!
Become again great France!
Become again great Paris!

bloodshot eyes, Dronne could think of only one thing. It was how wrong had been the propaganda of Vichy which had promised Dronne and his men through four years of exile that they were pariahs in their homeland.

Barely had the sounds of the "Marseillaise" faded when Schaeffer grabbed his microphone again. "Tell all the parish priests who can hear me, all the priests who can be alerted," he demanded, "to ring their church bells to announce the arrival of the Allies in Paris!"

For four years the bells of Paris had hung lifeless and silent. Not once during the occupation had their rich notes rung out to call Parisians to Mass, to proclaim the news that "A king is born," or "Christ is risen," or even to toll the passing of a departed parishioner. Now, on Schaeffer's call, they threw off that cloak and shook out the dust gathered in four years of silence and sorrow.

Already, from the south tower of Notre-Dame, the great 14-ton bell of the cathedral of Paris had launched the joyous peal. From the crest of Montmartre, the *Savoyarde*, the 19-ton bell of Sacré-Coeur, cast in prayerful thanks for the end of Paris's last German occupation, threw back its notes.

One by one, from one end of the city to the other, the churches of Paris joined them. Within minutes the whole skyline of Paris shook with the thunder of their majestic chorus. Parisians hanging from their windows wept in the darkness at the sound.

In Saint-Germain-des-Prés in their attic hideway, a pair of lovers turned to their record player at the sound. They set their little hand-wound machine to full volume and put on a record. Mixed with the proud pounding of the bells, their neighbors all around them could hear the blaring of a sound forbidden during four years of occupation: American jazz. It was a prewar recording of Louis Armstrong singing the "Basin Street Blues."

Rudolf Reis, the German MP who on Sunday had announced the short-lived truce of Consul General Nordling with a French policeman, understood the message in the bells. To his friend, Warrant Officer Otto Westermann, Reis announced simply, "We've had it." On the roof of the Postal, Telegraph and Telephone Ministry, Corporal Alfred Hollesch had watched the whole "unforgettable scene," hearing first the "Marseillaise" ringing up from the darkened streets around him, then the explosion of the church bells breaking like waves of surf all around him. Moved, Hollesch thought, "We are watching helplessly at the last hours of our own freedom."

There would be Parisians, too, who failed to hear the church bells. Furious that the bells of his parish church Saint-Philippe du Roule remained silent, thirteen-year-old Dominique de Serville time and time again called the curé of the church just off the Champs-Élysées. The line was always busy, and the bells remained silent. The angry little boy could not understand why.°

But nowhere in all the city did those bells ring with greater impact than they did in the little candlelit room on the first floor of the Hotel Meurice.

At their first echoes, light and distant, the desultory conversation of von Choltitz and his officers sputtered out. Like a wave running up a beach, the sound of the bells, building in depth and intensity, flowed toward their open windows.

Cita Krebben turned to Choltitz. "Herr General," she said, "the bells are ringing. Don't you hear them?"

Von Choltitz tipped back his chair and stared at her for an instant. In a voice that he had meant to be angry but was only resigned, he answered, "Yes, I hear them. I'm not deaf."

"Why are they ringing?" the pretty twenty-three-year-old asked.

"Why are they ringing?" repeated Choltitz. "They are ringing for us, my little girl. They are ringing because the Allies are coming into Paris. Why else do you suppose they would be ringing?"

Looking at the officers around him, Choltitz read shock and surprise on some of their faces, as though somehow, by some miracle, they had managed to convince themselves the Allies would not really arrive.

"What else did you expect?" he asked, his voice now rising in anger. "You've been sitting here in your own little dream-

---

° Sunday, at the Mass of the Liberation, young de Serville learned why. "My parishioners," announced Canon Jean Muller, beginning his sermon, "I want to thank all of you who thought Thursday night to call me to ask me to ring the bells of Saint-Philippe to announce the arrival of the Allies in Paris. I should also like to remind you of something you all forgot in your excitement that evening. There are no bells in the belfry of Saint-Philippe."

Then the good canon added, "Nothing seems more appropriate therefore than that at this Liberation Sunday, we should take up the collection to purchase a set of bells for the belfry of Saint-Philippe." They were indeed purchased and now ring daily from Saint-Philippe's bell tower.

world for years. What do you know about this war? You've seen nothing but your own pleasant life in Paris. You haven't seen what's happened to Germany in Russia and Normandy."

His tone turned scathing and bitter. "Gentlemen," he told them, "I can tell you something that's escaped you here in your nice life in Paris. Germany's lost this war, and we have lost it with her."

His brutal words ended what little gaiety had been left in their farewell dinner. Colonel Jay poured himself a last glass of champagne and swirled it thoughtfully under his eyes for a second. Then this habitué of Paris by night did the only thing left to do on this, his last evening in Paris. He went to bed.

Count Dankvart von Arnim, too, slid quietly to his room. In his diary he noted: "I have just heard the bells of my own funeral." Then the young count opened the *History of France* on the table beside his bed. Looking at the chapter he was due to start that night, he shuddered and closed the book. It was on the Saint Bartholomew's Day Massacre.

Alone in his darkened office, Choltitz took up his phone and placed a call, his second in twenty-four hours, to Army Group B. Von Unger had just confirmed what the commander of Gross Paris expected: A vanguard of the Allied armies was inside the city. The rest, he knew, would fall on him at dawn. In the crackling of his telephone line, he finally heard the voice of Army Group B's chief of staff.

"Good evening, Speidel," Choltitz said, his voice grave and heavy. Then he added, "Listen." With a brusque gesture, Choltitz thrust the receiver out into the night that vibrated with the solemn pounding of Paris's bells. In the neon-lit sterility of Speidel's underground command post 60 miles away, that sound seemed to pour through his little office. Speidel looked at his aide, Captain Ernst Maisch, listening with him, and then at the engravings of Notre-Dame over his head.

"Do you hear that sound, Speidel?" Choltitz asked.

"Yes," said Speidel, "I do. It sounds like bells."

"It *is* the sound of bells, my dear Speidel," answered Choltitz, "the bells of Paris ringing to tell the city the Allies are here."

There was a long pause. Then von Choltitz told Speidel that, as he had been ordered, he had prepared "the bridges, the railroad stations, the utilities, and their headquarters for destruction." Could he, he asked, "count on Army Group B" to extricate himself and his men from the city once that demolition work had been carried out? Again there was a long pause.

"No," answered Speidel, "I'm afraid not, Herr General."

Choltitz grunted wearily. Then he asked, "Do you have any last orders for me?" Speidel said he did not.

"Then, my dear Speidel," von Choltitz said, "there is nothing left but for me to say goodbye. Look after my wife and children in Baden-Baden, I beg you."

"I shall," answered Speidel, his voice tightening with emotion, "I promise you."

In the Hotel Meurice, the spent little commander of Gross Paris placed the receiver back in its cradle. He would not use it again.

46

IT WAS MIDNIGHT. ON the balcony of the first floor of the Meurice, two figures stood side by side in the darkness. For the fifteenth and final time in his brief command, Dietrich von Choltitz drew in the fresh night air of the city spread before him. At his side, blond and silent, was the girl whose laughter had lightened so many of occupied Paris's festive evenings in the past four years. Annabella Waldner, cut off from her own hotel, was going to spend her last night in Paris on a couch in Choltitz's office. At dawn, with the rest of the German women left in the city, Annabella was to be turned over to the Red Cross for repatriation to Germany.

Along the darkened skyline, another sound had replaced the jubilant pealing of Paris's church bells. It was the angry firing of Choltitz's 20,000-man garrison, reminding the city that the hour of its liberation was not yet at hand, and that Captain Dronne's three tanks were a symbol, not an army. A burst of their machine-gun fire had ripped into the happy celebration at the Hôtel de Ville, tearing off the marble wig

of a bust of Louis XIV, and almost shooting a glass of champagne out of the hands of Georges Bidault. The radio which
a few minutes before had urged the city into the streets now
begged Parisians to "go home, close your windows, stay off the
streets, it isn't over yet."

At the Prefecture of Police, Paris's first exhausted liberator,
the man whose arrival had stirred so much frenzy, prepared
to savor the one gift he wanted, a bath. As Raymond Dronne
stepped into its cold water, the shy young man who had just
drawn it for him introduced himself. His name was Félix
Gaillard, and the next time they met, he would be Prime
Minister of France.

Listening to the gunfire exploding along the horizon,
Choltitz said, "What shall I do? What shall I do?" It seemed
to Annabella Waldner that he spoke half to her, half to the
darkness before them.

Annabella looked at his hunched and worn little figure. "It's
too late to do anything now," she said, "except think of your
wife and children." Choltitz seemed to start at her words.
"They will need their father," she added.

For a long time Choltitz said nothing. Then, very softly, he
said to her, "Yes, my little girl, perhaps you are right." He
took her hand and, drawing it gently to his lips, kissed it.
Then Choltitz nodded good night and left to go up to his
room for an hour's sleep.

As he walked down the long corridor to the stairway,
Choltitz heard footsteps hurrying after him. He turned, and
found himself facing the young officer he had known on the
Mulde, Captain Werner Ebernach. Ebernach, too, had heard
the bells, and knew their meaning. He had no desire to be
taken prisoner here. He told Choltitz his work was finished,
and asked him if he had any further orders for him.

"No," Choltitz told him, "I have no orders for you, Ebernach."

Then Ebernach asked, since his unit was in Paris on de-
tached duty from First Army, could he have permission to
withdraw? He would, he told von Choltitz, leave behind a
section of men to detonate the charges he had placed.

Choltitz looked at the young officer. "Ja, Ebernach," he said,
gruff and angry, "take *all* your men and leave us." With no
further words, he turned his back on the captain and walked

off to his room. Three hours later, Ebernach and the men of his 813th Pionierkompanie left, riding out of Paris over the very bridges they had been sent to the city to destroy.

• • •

Five floors above Choltitz's bedroom, in a corner of the roof of the Hotel Meurice, a young couple clung to each other in gentle embrace. They were alone in a soft world of their own. From the rooftop of this hotel, with the skyline of Paris stretched just beyond their fingertips, they marked the end of an unforgettable evening in the unforgettable spectacle exploding before their eyes: a spiderweb of tracer bullets lacing the darkened sky with incandescent streaks of color.

Corporal Helmut Mayer, Choltitz's orderly, and Maria Schmidt, a pretty telephone operator of the Gross Paris switchboard, were perhaps the only Germans in the hotel who had not heard the bells of Paris toll the end of four years of occupation. They had been locked in the corporal's little room, banqueting on a final feast prepared for them by Mayer's friend, the Meurice chef.

Now, the edges of their sensibilities softened by the champagne he had provided, they stared in awe at the bursting chain of explosions dancing down the skyline of Paris to the distant horizon. It was, Mayer thought, the most memorable display of fireworks he had ever seen. Far off to the southeast, a whole hilltop seemed to soar into fire as an artillery battery on a hilltop above Meudon blew off the hundreds of 88 shells its cannons would never fire. In that shower of light and noise, the reality of the spectacle before him pierced Mayer's mind. Shuddering, he clasped the girl to his side and tiptoed quietly down to his room.

• • •

Choltitz was already asleep. So were Jay, Unger, Arnim, Kayser. The enormous hotel in which for four years the destinies of Paris and her people had been decided was silent. In the last fleeting hours of this brief August night, only the sound of sentries' boots and the occasional clacking of a teletype stirred its rest.

Annabella Waldner, too, was asleep when she heard the

ring of a telephone, harsh and demanding, cut through her light dreaming. In her stocking feet, she stumbled across Choltitz's darkened office and grappled in the blackness for his telephone. Faint and scratchy, a distant voice asked for the general.

"He's sleeping," she answered. "Shall I wake him?"

The phone fell silent. Then the caller spoke again. "No," he said, "don't wake him. It's too late now. Tell him . . ."

There was a pause as Annabella heard the distant voice hesitate.

"Tell him General Krueger called. Tell him that my tanks will not arrive."

PART THREE

THE DELIVERANCE

1

[AUGUST 25]

"Le jour de gloire est arrivé." Paris had waited four years for it. Now, on a breathless, blue summer morning, it arrived. Not a cloud disturbed the dawning of this day of glory. It was so beautiful, so perfect, nature and history seemed to have cooperated in its creation. In thousands of homes, Parisians prepared to greet it with the explosion of emotion that would stamp it forever in history and in the memories of those who lived it. Never again, perhaps, would a city know anything like the wave of sheer happiness about to break over Paris on this, its Liberation Day. It was August 25, 1944, the feast of Saint Louis, the patron saint of France. It was, thought a private American soldier named Irwin Shaw, "the day the war should have ended."

● ● ●

Somehow, everyone knew "they" were coming this morning. A people who had counted off the years now began counting off the minutes. Everywhere, Parisians took out the treasures long and secretly stored for this day: a dusty bottle of champagne buried in a closet corner; a dress painfully stitched up from scraps of black-market fabric; a tricolor, its forbidden folds hidden for four years; the Stars and Stripes, sewn together from a memory often as touching as it was faulty; flowers; fruits; a rabbit; almost any gift, in fact, that might convey a city's welcome and gratitude.

In her parents' apartment near the place de la République, twenty-one-year-old Jacqueline Malissinet slipped the pleated skirt of her dress over the blond hair piled high on her head. All winter, her fingers numb with cold, she had labored to make it for Liberation Day. As she put it on, a strange thought passed through Jacqueline's pretty head. She had just finished a course in English. Today for the first time in her life, she thought, she would speak to an American. She wondered what the first one would be like. He would be a dirty, unshaven captain from a steel town in Pennsylvania, and he would be laughing in a jeep on the pont de la Concorde. He would also be the man she would marry.

Across Paris, just around the corner from Saint-Philippe du Roule, the church whose belfry had been so silent the night before, a dark-haired legal secretary named Nelly Chabrier put on the rose dress her mother had given her for this day and, like any Spanish señorita waiting for a serenade, installed herself on her balcony to watch for the first tanks of General Leclerc. On one of them, too, would be the man she would marry.

Triumphant and exultant, the FFI on their barricades squeezed the Germans into their strongpoints and waited for the last push that would bring them the victory for which they had fought for five days.

On the outskirts of the city, in her pharmacy in the suburb of Saint-Cloud, Marcelle Thomas watched the fireman walk past clutching a new German Mauser in his hands. His name was Jean David. He had just been given the rifle, his first, a few minutes before at the Saint-Cloud town hall. It was to be his sad honor to fire it at the burial of a fellow FFI killed in the fighting the day before. Mlle. Thomas knew him as a simpleminded man with an affection for *vin ordinaire*. Looking at him stroll past, she told herself, "They shouldn't give guns to people like that."

For many in Paris, this would be a day of reunions with husbands, sons, fathers, lovers. In her apartment on the rue de Penthièvre, Yvette Boverat had not been able to sleep all night. At sunrise she, her husband and her daughter Hélène set out on their bicycles in search of "a regiment in black berets." Only when she found them could Mme. Boverat get the answer to the question that had haunted her sleepless night: Which of her two sons was coming home?

Not far away, in an apartment in Neuilly, a man looked at the American flag he had promised to deliver to his friends at the Ministry of Health near the Étoile. Norman Lewis had first carried that flag as a doughboy in France in 1917. Lewis, a banker, and his French wife had been caught in Paris at Pearl Harbor. They had lived the occupation first in an internment camp, then, after Lewis had been shot in the leg, in their apartment like any other Parisians. Now, the Stars and Stripes in a sack around his neck, his crutches under his shoulders, Lewis happily set out for the Étoile.

For Raymond Sarniguet, this was above all a day to keep a promise. Sarniguet, an officer of the Paris fire department, had promised he would put out a flag this day. It was a very special one. Sarniguet was determined he would be the first man to plant the tricolor on the top of the monument from which he had been the last to take it down, June 13, 1940— the Eiffel Tower.

• • •

In their isolated *Stützpunkte*, Paris's German defenders counted off the minutes too, the minutes separating them from the final Allied assault. Like many others, Warrant Officer Otto Kirschner, thirty-five, at the Kommandantur near the Opéra, heard a final exhortation to fight. "We must do our duty and fight to the end for the Führer," Colonel Hans Römer of Wiesbaden told him. That resolution, Kirschner would note, was not enough to prevent the colonel from disappearing when the fighting got hot in the afternoon.

Some received a last ration. For Willi Werner and his comrades in the Quai d'Orsay, it was a plate of bean soup. Sergeant Bernhard Blache at the École Militaire was luckier. He was given a tot of cognac.

Warrant Officer Hans Fritz, whose truckload of torpedoes had been ambushed the day before, was ordered to take a patrol from the Chamber of Deputies and find the missing truck. Fritz and his companions had walked only a few hundred yards from the building when they saw that the FFI had thrown up barricades on streets that, the day before, had belonged to the Wehrmacht. Caught in a cross fire, Fritz ordered his men to take cover and ran back to the Chamber for help. Its big gate was locked. Fritz pounded without success. By now, snipers were firing at him.

Fritz dashed across the street to cover in a doorway. As he stood there wondering what to do, an elderly woman came up and asked him to "please find some other place to do your shooting from." Fritz sighed, and decided he was not going to do any more shooting from any place. "For me," he told the old woman, "the war is over." With that, Fritz considered he had surrendered.

Of all the 20,000 Germans left around Paris, only one, perhaps, was moving of his own accord into the center of the city. Nobody had told Joachim von Knesebeck, the director of Siemens France, that Paris was about to fall. Knesebeck had just come back from a visit to Berlin. Dropped off near his apartment by a Luftwaffe truck, von Knesebeck walked home, only vaguely disturbed by the driver's warning that "there's lots of trouble in Paris."

At his apartment, his French concierge burst into tears. "You're mad," she said. "You'll be killed." She took him to the cellar where she had carefully padlocked a bicycle to a pole for him. She told him to get on it and flee. As Knesebeck pedaled away, she called after him, "Don't worry, you'll be back in two weeks!"

From a window in the Hotel Meurice, Captain Otto Kayser —the literature professor from Cologne who, the day before, had shown Dankvart von Arnim Rol's slogan, "À chacun son boche"—now looked at the early morning sun with the young count. "Paris," he told von Arnim, "is going to have a vengeance to take for these last four years. I wonder," he asked, "will we ever be able to come back here?" It was a question the scholarly professor need not have asked. He would never leave.

Below them, in the Tuileries garden, Dietrich von Choltitz and Colonel Hans Jay made a last inspection of their troops hidden in its three-century-old preserves. There were no children today around Lenôtre's pool. Instead, Choltitz saw his troops in their undershirts, their shaving equipment and towels spread along the pool's lip beside them, washing in its water. Looking at the garden, the blue sky, the sun climbing over the city, Choltitz thought with a trace of bitterness that "the Parisians are going to have a lovely day for their liberation." Then he walked to one of the Panther tanks at the entry of

the garden, its cannon pointing up the Champs-Élysées.
"Watch out," he told its crew. "Today they're coming for sure."

In the Gross Paris communications center, Warrant Officer
Otto Vogel was disconsolate. He had just tried to make a last
call to his family in Bad Wimpfen, but had been connected
only as far as Reims. Now the telephones of "Hypnose" were
buzzing every few moments with incoming calls. They were
all from the advancing Allies. Then, just before eight, Vogel's
teletypewriter coughed into action. It relayed a two-word
question from OKW to Choltitz. It was so simple that OKW
had not even bothered to put it in code.

It was "Demolitions started?"

2

FOR TECHNICAL SERGEANT MILT Shenton, the
GI to whom Paris had been "a poor boy's dream come true,"
the city was now an infantryman's nightmare. Shenton had
just learned he was going to be "point man" for his company,
and his company was going to have the job of leading the
whole 4th Division into Paris. That meant Sergeant Shenton
was going to be the first tempting target the division would
offer to the defenders of the city ahead. Shenton had had the
same job on another day, June 6, when he had led the 4th
Division across Utah Beach and survived unscathed. That,
figured Sergeant Shenton, was all the luck any man had the
right to in one lifetime. Strapping an extra canister of ammunition to his jeep near the little crossroads town of Nozay,
Shenton muttered to himself and wished he had never heard
the name of Paris.

At Fresnes, the Croix de Berny, the pont de Sèvres, and the
little villages of Orphin and Nozay, the men of the 2nd French
Armored Division and the 4th U.S. Infantry Division prepared,
like Shenton, for the last short thrust into the capital. They
would move in four columns. Three of them would move
through the southwestern edge of the city past Les Invalides,
the Palais du Luxembourg to the Chamber of Deputies, the

place de la Concorde, and the Prefecture of Police. The fourth was to flow through Saint-Cloud, the Bois de Boulogne and the fashionable Sixteenth Arrondissement to the Étoile.

The precious intelligence on the exact location of the German strongpoints in the city, given by Abwehr agent "Bobby" Bender to Lorrain Cruse, had not reached Leclerc. At dawn Cruse had leaped on his bicycle to ride out himself with the information. He found Colonel de Langlade near the pont de Sèvres, but Langlade, irritated by the mass of well-meaning but often ill-informed FFI that had swarmed over his headquarters all night, ignored Cruse. It was only after one of Cruse's college classmates on Langlade's staff had vouched for him that the colonel accepted his intelligence. By that time, Langlade's radio communication with Leclerc had broken down, and the three columns had already set out on their established attack plan. All along the southern rim of the city, in the early hours of the morning, the French and American columns had begun to slide forward. For them all, for the homecoming men of the 2nd Armored and the jubilantly curious GIs of the 4th Division, the order of the day was summed up in a terse command to Captain Billy Buenzle, of Roselle, New Jersey, leading the 38th Cavalry Reconnaissance Squadron into the city: "Put the show on the road, and get the hell into Paris!"

3

THE ROAD AHEAD OF Milt Shenton's jeep was empty and menacing. The drab gray shutters sagging from the stucco buildings that hung over the narrow sidewalks beside him were snapped shut. The only living thing ahead of Shenton was a stray cat sneaking along a building front. The only sound he could hear, it seemed to the sergeant, was the thumping of his own heart.

Ahead of him, Shenton saw a blue-and-white T-shaped road sign reading PARIS—PORTE D'ITALIE, the same sign Dronne had seen the night before. Overhead, Shenton heard a window creak open. He whirled around, snapping off the safety of his carbine. Then he heard another window open, and another. From somewhere he heard a woman's voice call "Les Américains!" Out of the corner of his eye, he saw a man in shirt-sleeves and two women in bathrobes, their slippers flapping, bolt for his jeep. The man threw his arms around the sergeant from Maryland and kissed him wetly on both cheeks.

Shenton never knew where they all came from, but within seconds each building seemed to vomit hordes of happy, shouting Parisians. Within minutes, the empty streets had become a clogged, cheering, impassable mass of humanity. Where instants before, he had felt uncomfortably alone, Sergeant Shenton now saw it was almost impossible to push his jeep through the screaming sea of faces barring the road ahead.

Everywhere, it was the same.

Along the route of the 2nd Armored, the crowds went mad. When they understood that the soldiers in these American helmets and uniforms were their own countrymen; when they saw the Cross of Lorraine on the Shermans, and names like *Verdun* and *Saint-Cyr* on their turrets, their joy at being liberated turned to pure frenzy. From each tank, armored car and half-track, girls and children hung like bunches of grapes. The drivers in the jeeps were at times crushed in the swarms of people leaping up to kiss them, touch them, talk to them. Crowds on the sidewalks threw flowers to them, and ripe tomatoes, carrots, radishes, anything they could offer. They ran after their columns on foot and on bicycles; they flooded toward them in screaming waves.

Lieutenant Touny, in his tank *El Alamein*, found so many people scrambling over his treads, diving into his turret, blocking his advance, that he had to fire his machine guns in the air to scare them away. To Captain Georges Buis, red-eyed and exhausted from two sleepless nights, his tank seemed to be "a magnet passing through a pile of steel filings." Jean René Champion, the Frenchman from Mexico, reached the place du Châtelet at 8:30 in his tank the *Mort-Homme*. He waited there for "the five most memorable hours" of his life. People sang, danced, cried, passed the soldiers wine and champagne, literally buried the vehicles of Champion's platoon until they were no longer visible. Nineteen-year-old Léandre Médori, a Corsican peasant who had never been to

Paris, stared at the crowds from his half-track and kept repeating, "My God, how big it is!"

Larry Lesueur, the CBS newsman, rode in with Langlade's
columns. As he watched these French tanks rolling irresistibly
into Paris, tears came to Lesueur's eyes. He thought of the
sight that had struck him in 1940, as he fled out of Paris down
this same road. It was a mother fleeing beside him, pushing a
baby carriage with a linden tree branch curled into its bonnet.
Someone had told her it would help camouflage it from the
Stukas ahead.

Along the route of the GIs of the 4th Division, the reception
was no less wild. To Captain Ben Welles of the OSS, sick,
exhausted, wet with a fever, it seemed that "a physical wave
of human emotion picked us up and carried us into the heart
of Paris. . . . It was like groping through a dream." Ankle-deep
in flowers, Welles leaned over to embrace a distinguished
gray-haired woman reaching up to kiss him. "Thank God
you're here," she said. "Now Paris will be Paris again." Three
weeks later, diplomat's son Welles met her officially. She was
the granddaughter of Ferdinand de Lesseps, the builder of
the Suez Canal. Master Sergeant Donald Flannagan of Pough-
keepsie, New York, thought the French "made each of us
feel like Lindbergh must have felt when he went up Broad-
way."

Major S. L. A. Marshall, of the U.S. Army's Military History
Section, counted 67 bottles of champagne in his jeep by the
time he reached the Seine near Les Invalides. For the men
who rode into Paris through that jubilant throng, there were
sights they would cherish forever. To Pfc. Stanley Kuroski of
Headquarters Company, it was "an old man with a handlebar
mustache and all his medals on, standing like a ramrod with
great big tears rolling down his cheeks." Major Barney
Oldfield of SHAEF's press section remembered an old woman
lying on a stretcher watching, through a mirror held over
her head, the liberators arrive. "Paris is free, Paris is free," she
kept repeating to the blue skies above.

Some of the sights were bizarre. Communications man Oren
T. Eason, attached to the 2nd Armored, saw a beautiful blonde
hanging from a lamppost repeating over and over again to no
one in particular, "Hey, I'm from Hoboken!"

But of all the experiences along their route, nothing stood
out more for these men than the sheer emotional impact of

the hundreds of thousands of exultant, overwhelmingly grateful Parisians swarming over them. Major Frank Burk, of Jackson, Mississippi, submerged in a sea of people, thought it was "without a doubt, the happiest scene the world has ever known." Burk reckoned there were "fifteen solid miles of cheering, deliriously happy people waiting to shake your hand, to kiss you, to shower you with food and wine."

A beautiful girl threw her arms around code clerk Brice Rhyne and sobbed, "We waited for you for four years."

The precise Virginian said, "But the United States has only been in the war three years."

"So what?" answered the girl. "We knew you'd come anyway!"

Everywhere along their route the happy, grateful French shoved everything they had at the passing GIs. Lieutenant Lee Lloyd from Alabama saw a woman beside his half-track yelling "Souvenir! Souvenir!" She suddenly spun around to the man beside her and yanked his pipe out of his mouth. With a gesture, she passed it up to Lloyd. Before the Alabaman could pass it back, his half-track rolled on. Lloyd saw the man's stricken face receding in the crowd. Finally, reluctant and resigned, the man broke into a smile.

A pretty girl holding a plate of cold, fresh grapes ran up to Lieutenant John Morgan Welch. A German, she said, had left them in her shop. As Welch began to eat them, a handsome woman watching him remarked, "Those are the first grapes I've seen in four years." Ashamed, Welch offered to share them with her.

"No," she said. "Today, young man, everything is for you."

Pfc. Mickey Esposito, an ex-prize fighter from New Jersey, and his company rolled straight through Paris in a six-by-six without stopping. As Esposito and his company passed, the crowds along their path reached up to slap their palms "to say thank you." Suddenly Esposito felt something being pressed into his hand. He pulled it up and, looking into it, saw a little white ivory elephant the size of a quarter. Esposito looked back at the faces in the crowd disappearing behind his truck. There Esposito saw an elderly woman—her white hair shrouded in a black shawl, her face thin and emaciated— watching him. This unknown Frenchwoman who had just offered her little charm to a passing GI cupped her hand and gave a timid wave as his truck disappeared forever. Esposito tucked the elephant into the pocket of his uniform, sure it would bring him good luck.*

• • •

In the wild delirium along the routes into the city, strange things happened to civilians, too. Paul Bertrand, a set designer, kept staring in disbelief at the 2nd Armored's jeeps. If the Americans, he thought, can design a machine like that, "the war is surely won." Like the Frenchmen running up to the GIs on the eastern part of town to try out their English, Robert Miller, an American lawyer interned in Paris since Pearl Harbor, ran up to the 2nd Armored soldiers passing his apartment on the place de la Muette and babbled a joyous welcome to them in French. They stared back at him in dumb confusion. They were all Spanish.

Eighteen-year-old Colette Massigny was sure this would be Liberation Day. She put on the blue silk dress she had saved for it and then set out to find the liberators. Parked on the rue de la Pompe, surrounded by shuttered windows, she saw a bizarre vehicle with three helmeted figures inside. She rode up to the first jeep she had ever seen and spoke to its occupants. They looked at her with as little understanding as Miller's Spaniards had looked at him. "Are you American?" she asked in English. "Hell, yes, honey," answered the driver. Colette threw herself on him. As she did, dozens of people watching the scene from behind their shutters swarmed into the streets. They buried the jeep in a human avalanche. Then a set of wooden shutters over Colette's head smashed open with a bang. From a window above, a young man leaned out with a silver trumpet in his hand. He played the "Marseillaise," strong and stirring. Never again, Colette thought, would she hear it sound so beautiful.

• • •

---

* Esposito carried the little elephant for weeks in the shirt pocket of his uniform, convinced it would get him safely through the war. At about 9 A.M. on November 19, crawling down the path of a tank tread in the Hurtgen Forest, Esposito was caught in a savage artillery bombardment. He felt for the elephant in his shirt pocket to reassure himself. It was gone. Eposito looked everywhere for it without success. "Now," he told himself, "I'm going to get it." One hour later, huddled under a tree, he did. A German shell tore through both his legs.

There were tragedies too, along this happy march. Lieutenant Yves Ciampi of the 2nd Armored, riding a half-track in a column moving past the porte d'Orléans, saw an aging German soldier on a bicycle, his uniform in tatters, his belongings pitifully stuffed into a knapsack, suddenly pedal in front of their fast-moving vehicles. The column ran over him. Looking back, Ciampi saw "a stain of red smashed into the pavement, all that was left of what, moments before, had been a man."

By and large, there was little opposition in the early advance. Dug into their strongpoints, hemmed in by the FFI, the Germans assumed the defensive, waiting poised and ready for the city's liberators to try to pry them out. Occasionally isolated pockets opened fire, scattering the excited Parisians like a covey of frightened pigeons and leaving the city's liberators alone in its streets.

By eight o'clock, the first troops reached the heart of the city. An exhausted Captain Georges Buis, catnapping in the turret of his tank, felt its engines stop. Mechanically, Buis raised his head and looked out. He experienced "the most memorable shock" of his life. Right in front of him, glowing warmly in the sunshine, was Notre-Dame. Captain Billy Buenzle of the 38th Cavalry Reconnaissance Squadron had come on Buis's tanks in a small side street on the other side of the Seine. Side by side, whooping with joy, the two columns, French and American, had raced each other for the honor of being the first into the square before Notre-Dame. It was a dead heat. Now Buenzle radioed his commander Colonel Cyrus A. Dolph that he was in Paris. "How the hell do you know?" asked old professional soldier Dolph. "Dammit, Colonel," answered Buenzle, "I'm looking right up at Notre-Dame!"

•   •   •

Everywhere along the lines advancing into the city were the women of Paris, lean, sun-tanned and, to these men who had fought their way to Paris from Normandy, almost unbelievably beautiful. Pfc. Marcel Rufin of the Chad Regiment of the 2nd Armored had boasted about them all the way to the capital. Now, leaning out of his half-track *Lunéville*, Rufin kissed dozens until, to his mates, his face "looked like a red

mushroom." Aboard his Sherman *Viking*, Corporal Lucien
Davanture felt he was "almost being assaulted by Parisiennes."
He established a priority for entry to his turret: prettiest first!
Pfc. Charley Haley of the 12th Regiment watched a blond-
haired buddy who wanted to see how many girls he could
kiss. "He must have kissed a thousand," Haley thought with
awe.

For the men of the 2nd Armored even more touching than
the wild uproar of the crowds was a sudden reunion with
family and friends. Aboard his half-track *Larche*, Georges
Buchet watched a woman on the rue des Bourdonnais bolt
through a burst of gunfire and fall on an advancing infantryman. "My son, my son," she sobbed. Near the place du
Châtelet, Corporal Georges Thiollat suddenly saw two familiar
faces before his tank. Fifty yards away, pedaling toward him
on a bicycle built for two, were his parents. Major André
Gribius thanked God he had a case of rations in his jeep when
he found his parents in Versailles. He could barely recognize
them. His mother had lost almost 50 pounds, his father 35.

Near the porte d'Orléans, a distraught woman pedaled up
and down a line of Shermans. Of each passing tank, she asked
the same question: Where could she find "a regiment in black
berets"? It was Mme. Boverat looking for one of her two sons.

No reunion would be more touching than that of Corporal
Lucien Davanture. Davanture knew his brother had gone to
Paris to escape deportation to Germany. All along his route
into Paris, the driver of the Sherman *Viking* had passed handwritten messages for him to the crowds around his tank. In
the heart of Paris, at the foot of the Pont-Neuf, the 75-mm
cannon of the *Viking* pointing at the Samaritaine Department
Store, Davanture noticed a figure making his way slowly
down the line of tanks behind him. He drew up to his tank
and Davanture stared blinking in disbelief. There, "unbelievably thin, in a policeman's uniform much too big for him, an
FFI armband on his forearm," was the brother he had not seen
for three years. These brothers who symbolized the two halves
of fighting France fell into each other's arms as though they
had been "pushed by an electric current." Their reunion was
brief. Minutes afterward the *Viking* was ordered to move forward. Davanture's brother tried to scramble into the tank with
him. He realized there was no room. The corporal hopped in
himself, slammed his turret shut and popped up his peri-

scope, grateful to be "alone in the darkness" with his tears. Behind his tank, a new figure joined the infantrymen advancing in its wake. It was Davanture's brother in his policeman's uniform.

Not all the reunions were so joyous. Spahi Robert Perbal, from the Lorraine village of Rombas, learned from a passing Lorraine woman in the Sixteenth Arrondissement that his father had been deported to Buchenwald two years earlier. A pale young man drew up next to the half-track of Lieutenant Henri Karcher, which had halted for an instant on its ride into town. "Excuse me," he said, "but do you by any chance know my brother Lucien Loiseau? We haven't heard from him since he left to join de Gaulle three years ago." Karcher looked in silence at the youth. "Yes," he answered, "I knew Lucien Loiseau. He was my best friend." Then, fixing his soft brown eyes on the young man, he added, "He was killed at Bir Hakeim." The youth whitened and vanished.

To dozens of these 2nd Armored men, the telephone they had so magically discovered the day before provided the first link with their families. Pfc. Jean Ferracci scrawled his sister's name and phone number on little scraps of paper and passed them into the crowd each time his half-track stopped. By noon, dozens of people had called to tell her her brother was coming home. Sergeant Pierre Laigle, tank commander of the *Montfaucon*, ran into a bistro near the Châtelet to call the fiancée he had neither seen nor heard from in four years. Tonguetied at the sound of her voice, Laigle at first could speak only two syllables, as beautiful as they were banal: *"Je t'aime."* Then he told her where he was, and she set off to find him.

For a few rare GIs, there were also this day reunions of a sort. Lieutenant Dan Hunter of the OSS was among the first Americans into the center of the city. His job was to requisition the Petit Palais for a collaborationist interrogation center. The frightened curator of the Champs-Élysées museum told him he could not have it. The building housed a precious art collection which, he said, could not be moved. "Move it," Hunter ordered; his unit was arriving at five o'clock. Impossible, pleaded the curator, the collection could never be moved so fast. It was a special gift, he told Hunter, offered France by one of his fellow Americans, a man named Edward Tuck. Hunter laughed. He told the curator to move it, and he would take the responsibility. Edward Tuck was his cousin.

On his way into Paris, Marine Corps Major Franklin Holcombe detoured past 72 rue de l'Université, the home of his engagingly eccentric aunt, Sylvia Sheridan, self-appointed protectress of Paris's White Russian colony. Holcombe took the most direct route. He stepped through the ground-floor window. The old lady, poised and dignified, was reading a book in her sitting room when Holcombe clomped in. She shrieked when she saw his green Marine uniform so close in color to the Wehrmacht's. Then she recognized Holcombe.

"Franklin!" she shrilled like a schoolmistress addressing a naughty child. "Is that what they've taught you in the Marines —to enter a lady's apartment through the window?"

• • •

Not everyone who entered Paris that day was greeted with kisses. Fifty yards from the Seine, in a shuttered home at Corbeil, 12 miles south of the city, an American officer peered through the mist rising from the river. It was Lieutenant Jack Knowles, the officer who had been ordered to get his men ties for the "parade" through Paris. Knowles's only parading had been down this riverbank where he had been ordered to prepare a crossing of the Seine. Seeing nothing, Knowles and his platoon sergeant, "Speedy" Stone, walked outside and cautiously edged down toward the riverbank. As they reached it, the Germans opened fire. Knowles dove behind a tree, its bark and branches already being ripped by machine-gun fire. Wounded in the shoulder and buttocks, he heard a voice behind him calling faintly, "Medic, medic." It was "Speedy" Stone dying at the edge of the Seine, the tie he had scrounged to parade in Paris still knotted around his neck.

• • •

Miles away, on the southwestern edge of Paris, near the Pilz torpedo depot at Saint-Cloud, the first columns of Major François Morel-Deville's troops moved in to the same thunderous acclaim the rest of the 2nd Armored was getting on the other side of the capital.

Roaring down the rue Dailly, past Morel-Deville's columns, a jeep shot toward the Saint-Cloud bridge. Max Giraud of the

2nd Armored watched it go and thought "the driver must be in a hurry to get into Paris."

He was. It was Sergeant Larry Kelly, the Pennsylvania Irishman, off to keep his promise to be the first GI into Paris. He swung through the square at the foot of the rue Dailly and, whooping with glee, pointed his jeep over the bridge. At its other end, Fireman Jean David, the man whose new gun the pharmacist Marcelle Thomas had noticed earlier, had just left the funeral he had been sent to attend. At the same instant that Kelly flung his jeep over the Seine toward Paris, David started across the bridge from the other side of the river.

When David saw the strange vehicle, the helmet, the uniforms, he knew those men could be only one thing: Germans. He shouldered his brand-new Mauser and, for the second time, fired it, point blank, every cartridge it held, right into the advancing jeep. Hit six times, Sergeant Kelly fell bleeding to the pavement, shot by mistake just 50 yards from the limits of the city into which he had wanted to be the first American soldier.[*]

* * *

All across Paris now as the advancing troops moved into the range of Choltitz's strongpoints, the sound of gunfire began to mix with the happy screams of the crowds. Those shots were a chilling reminder of the fact there remained in the Paris area, primed and waiting, almost 20,000 German troops, a number nearly equal to the arriving Allies.

Lieutenant Pierre de la Fouchardière of the 501st Tank Regiment looked astonished at the empty place de l'Observatoire before his tanks, a stark contrast to the wild crowds he

---

[*] Kelly was never to cross those last 50 yards. He was taken to the pharmacy of Marcelle Thomas, who gave him first aid. Kelly's behavior touched Mlle. Thomas enormously. Despite his intense suffering, Kelly told the people around him "not to blame" David and even passed out the contents of the pack of cigarettes in his uniform pocket. Kelly was moved to a nearby hospital where, three days later, a sorrowing David visited him, bringing him as a gift a bottle of wine. Paralyzed, Kelly was evacuated to the United States but kept in touch with Mlle. Thomas. He wrote her over twenty letters. The last said: "They still don't know when I'll be able to sit up, and the wounds still hurt, but it doesn't matter because we were helping a wonderful people and I shall keep you always in my memories."

Larry Kelly died from the wounds he had received in Paris in a Pennsylvania military hospital October 1, 1946.

had just left behind. Ahead of him, he heard firing. La Fouchardière got out of his tank and ran to the only Parisian he could see, an old man huddling in a doorway.

"Monsieur," he asked, "where are the Germans?"

4

THE GERMANS WERE JUST around the corner under the eight-faced cupola of the Palais du Luxembourg. There in its spacious garden between statues of Mary, Queen of Scots, and the Duchesse de Montpensier, La Grande Mademoiselle, 700 men waited ready to "fight to the last cartridge." To stimulate them, the SS Standartenführer whose tankers had used human shields to screen their turrets had issued each of his men a last combat ration of a pint of cognac and a pack of cigarettes.

Smoking one of them in a concrete pillbox opening onto the boulevard Saint-Michel, the "Boul' Mich," Sergeant Martin Herrholz, twenty-seven, of the 190th Sicherungsregiment, looked confidently at the weapon beside him. It was a "Panzerfaust," a German bazooka. With it, Herrholz had won the Iron Cross First Class near Rostov on the Don, knocking out four Russian T34 tanks with four shots. Today he would get his first chance to use it on an American tank.

Huddled in the trenches cut among the geraniums and begonias plump Generalfeldmarschall Hugo Sperrle had so carefully tended during four years of occupation, Lance Corporal Hans Georg Ludwig and his fellow parachutists of the 6th Fallschirm Panzer Jäger Division kept the garden's entries in enfilade with their machine-gun nests. Above them, on the roof of the palace, a spotter of the 484th Feldgendarme Company studied the streets around the palace with his field glasses. At the first sign of Allied troops moving against the building, he was to warn its SS commander, 30 feet underground in Sperrle's old air raid shelter. There the Standartenführer waited to direct the fight for the building. The core of his strength was his Panzer tanks of the 5th Sicherungsregiment, dug hull down into the garden approaches to the palace. In one of them, his turret pointed out onto the rue de Vaugirard, Tanker Willi Linke, who, five days earlier had led the first assault on the Prefecture of Police, moved his periscope back and forth. As he swept the scene before him, Linke could see the columns of the Théâtre de l'Odéon and beyond them the rooftops of the Sorbonne. The streets were empty, the shutters of the buildings above fastened shut. No liberators had passed by here yet. Linke thought of his native village by the Baltic and told himself this was certainly the "calm before the storm."

Barely 60 yards from his pillbox flanking that school, a group of civilians in a high-school study hall had waited all night to unleash the storm Willi Linke knew was coming. One of them, a bushy-haired young man not much older than a high-school student himself, prepared to start it. His name was Pierre Fabien. He was twenty-five, and in his short lifetime he had been wounded three times, twice in Spain, once in Czechoslovakia.[*] Twice he had escaped from the Gestapo, once only minutes before he was due to be executed. Two years earlier this youthful Communist colonel had, in the Barbès métro station, shot the first German soldier killed in Paris. Now, with the armor of the 2nd Armored in town, Fabien gave the order he had burned all week to give. He ordered his men to strike the Luxembourg, the first German *Stützpunkt* in the city of Paris to come under attack.

• • •

His dirty white shirt open to his chest, a tricolor on his arm and an aged Mauser in his hand, a young man slid along the wall of the rue de l'Odéon toward the Luxembourg Palace. He was one of Fabien's FFI. His name was Jacques Guierre and this exalting day was his twentieth birthday. His job was to spot the German troops in the area around the rue de Vaugirard for the attack on the palace. Guierre edged into the Café Arbeuf on the place de l'Odéon. From its windows he could see the helmeted silhouettes of the Luxembourg's defenders beyond the Théâtre de l'Odéon just opposite him.

"Have you at least eaten, *mon petit?*" the café owner, Ma-

[*] Where he fought against the German occupation of the Sudetenland with a group of French volunteers.

dame Arbeuf, asked. When Guierre shook his head, she
shoved a sandwich at him. "Eat that," she said. "It's better
to fight on a full stomach." The young FFI ate the sandwich
and swallowed the glass of Sancerre Madame Arbeuf gave
him to go with it. "Thank you," he said. "Vive la France."
Then, armed with his Mauser, he set out to cross the square
to the theater.

Three or four seconds later, Madame Arbeuf heard a roar
of gunfire. She saw the young boy she had just fed lying in the
square, a stain of red spreading across his white shirt. Jacques
Guierre, so proudly twenty this morning, was dead, the first
of Fabien's men killed attacking the Luxembourg.

Then, just ahead of her, Madame Arbeuf heard a series of
explosions. Two of the Standartenführer's armored cars, in a
brief foray out of the palace, were shelling a group of FFI
hidden in a little hotel at the corner of the rue de Vaugirard
and the rue Monsieur-le-Prince. Inside, choking in smoke, the
FFI hurled grenades on the vehicles below them. In the black
smoke and debris, two girls in the bright summer dresses
they had put on for this day dragged the wounded to shelter
in the hotel's corridors. On the ground floor a man in an under-
shirt hid in the doorway, a knife glinting in his hands. It was
the neighborhood butcher. He was waiting to slice open the
head of the first German infantryman who tried to enter the
building. Suddenly the besieged band of FFI saw the armored
cars back off and dart for cover inside the palace grounds.
Then down the boulevard Saint-Michel they heard the clank
of other tank treads. They were the Shermans of Lieutenant
Pierre de la Fouchardière. He had found his Germans. He
studied them now from his turret as he stole toward the
School of Mines.

Sergeant Martin Herrholz, the German sharpshooter,
studied de la Fouchardière, too, through the hairlines of his
bazooka sight. At almost the instant Herrholz decided to fire,
la Fouchardière spotted his pillbox. "Right!" he shouted to his
driver Lucien Kerbat. As la Fouchardière's tank skidded to
cover in the rue de l'Abbé-de-l'Epée, Herrholz's first shell tore
after it. It sliced over the Sherman's rear deck, bursting against
a doorway behind it. Cursing, Herrholz watched the tank
disappear from sight, and wondered how he could have
missed.

Getting out of his tank, la Fouchardière asked three of

Fabien's FFI to help him study the German positions in the School of Mines, cut like a wedge into a garden of the Palais du Luxembourg. The four entered a building whose façade gave on the school, and galloped up the stairs to the fourth floor. They rang the first doorbell they found. An elderly woman in black answered. "Lieutenant Pierre de la Fouchardière of the Leclerc Division," announced the young officer with a salute. Then, bending over slightly, he took the old lady's hand and kissed it. The four men walked past the stunned woman to her living-room window. From it they could look down onto the School of Mines 30 yards away across the boulevard Saint-Michel. There la Fouchardière saw the helmets of its German defenders bobbing up and down between the piles of sandbags heaped in the school's windows. Never in forty months of combat had he seen the enemy so close. Like the hero of a western, la Fouchardière took out his Colt, leaned against the window jamb and blazed away at the surprised Germans. The elderly lady's elegant book-lined salon filled with the acrid odor of gunpowder. She herself sat serenely in an armchair in one corner of the room, and watched with a combination of delight and horror as the four men turned her living room into a miniature battleground. When he had fired every round he had, la Fouchardière put his smoking pistol on the varnished surface of the woman's kidney-shaped Louis XVI antique desk and slumped in a happy daze onto her red velvet sofa.

By now, the tanks of the 501st Regiment to which la Fouchardière belonged were all around the Luxembourg. In his earphones, tanker Willi Linke heard the sharp, dry voice of his platoon commander, Lieutenant Klaus Kuhn, warn him, "Four enemy tanks moving up the rue Gay-Lussac." Linke asked himself, "Where in hell is the rue Gay-Lussac?" Moving his periscope slowly along his horizon, Linke finally discovered the silhouette of a self-propelled howitzer moving up a street to his right. At about the same instant Linke made his discovery, the howitzer commander, Lieutenant Philippe Duplay of the 12th Cuirassiers, discovered him. With a grimace, Duplay ordered his driver to back his howitzer, the *Mosquet*, down a side street before Linke could open fire.

Three hundred yards away, the jeep of Captain Alain de Boissieu, the commander of Leclerc's escort squadron, pulled up in the place de l'Observatoire. Determined to blow the

Germans out of the Palais du Luxembourg at any cost, Boissieu ordered his tanks to open fire on this building that housed the Senate of France. As he did, the young officer looked at the imposing building before him and thought it was as though he had "just given the order to fire on the government."

Above all, thought Boissieu, they had to get the tanks. This unexpected fight had forced Leclerc to move his command post into the Gare Montparnasse instead of the Hotel de Crillon as he had planned. If, thought Boissieu, the tanks in the Luxembourg decided to come out and smash for the Gare Montparnasse, nothing would stop them. "The tanks," he ordered, "for God's sake, get the tanks!"

In his self-propelled howitzer, Lieutenant Philippe Duplay heard the angry voice of Captain de Boissieu on his radio. "The Panzers, for Christ's sake, get me the Panzers," he ordered again. As he heard Boissieu's voice, Duplay saw a sweaty soldier climbing out of a half-track with a white star on its flanks. He was an American. Summoning all his command of the English language, Duplay asked the GI, "Excuse me, sir, do you have a bazooka?"

A few minutes later, like a pair of young men off for a drink at their neighborhood bar, the Frenchman and the American, lugging the GI's bazooka between them, set off for the boulevard Saint-Michel. Scornful of the sniper fire exploding around them, they strode off with a firm and resolute stride to settle accounts with Willi Linke's Panzer.

5

WHILE DUPLAY AND THE unknown GI advanced toward their target, the men of the 2nd Armored Division tightened the net around the other German strongpoints in the city: the Chamber of Deputies, the Quai d'Orsay, the massive complex of the École Militaire spreading over four city blocks, the Hotel Majestic and the area around the Arc de Triomphe, the place de la République, the Hotel de Crillon, the Kriegsmarine and the whole colonnaded sweep of the rue de Rivoli that enfolded Choltitz's headquarters.

Before launching a full-scale and costly attack on all those strongpoints, Colonel Pierre Billotte, who had finally received the intelligence passed the night before by "Bobby" Bender to Lorrain Cruse, decided to pass an ultimatum to Choltitz. Bender's words had convinced Cruse the 2nd Armored had only to announce its presence to Choltitz to effect his surrender. Billotte, promoting himself to Brigadier General, wrote a terse note for Choltitz, giving him half an hour to "end all resistance" or risk "total extermination" of his garrison.

Billotte sent the note in a half-track to Bender at the Swedish Consulate. Bender read it in distress. It was, he feared, too brutal in tone to be acceptable to Choltitz. But, on Nordling's insistence, the Abwehr agent, dressed in civilian clothes, set out for the Meurice with it. After arguing his way past the now trigger-happy Meurice sentries, he finally gave it to Count von Arnim, who passed it to von Unger. The cold and rigid chief of staff found it wholly unacceptable. He did not show it to Choltitz. Instead he informed the commander of Gross Paris that "the French want to give you an ultimatum." Faced with that blunt phrase, Choltitz answered, "I don't accept ultimatums." The note was passed back to Bender.

In his distress at Choltitz's refusal, Bender appended to his reply to Billotte a thought of his own. The general, he said, would order the Paris garrison to surrender if he himself had been taken prisoner first in a show of force adequate to satisfy his soldier's honor.

● ● ●

Nine hundred miles away, in the cool and unreal world of OKW, Adolf Hitler, on this August midday, faced up to the coming loss of the last prize left in an empire that was to have lived a thousand years. The evening before, General-feldmarschall Model, caught by the sudden onslaught of the 2nd Armored, had warned OKW that Paris was "critical." The little field marshal on whom Hitler had counted for miracles had failed to produce the miracle the Führer wanted above all else. He had lost his gamble for time by just twenty-four short hours. The 47th Infantry Division, which he had ordered to Paris to bolster Choltitz until the 26th and 27th Panzers could arrive, would, he had realized, not reach the suburbs of Paris until midday on August 26. Distressed, Model tried to rush into the city all the bits and pieces of his command he could find in the Paris area: a battalion of half-tracks, a regiment of infantry, all the armor left in one of his mauled Panzer divisions. They would, like the efforts of Hitler's enemies four summers earlier, be "too little, too late."

Now before the Führer, as the first OKW strategy conference opened, was the midday Army Group B operations report received at Rastenburg minutes earlier. The Allies, it reported, were in the heart of Paris, "attacking our strongpoints with artillery and infantry." The shocking news that the Allies were swarming into Paris—this attack that seemed to have materialized from nowhere—threw Hitler into a memorable fit of frenzy.

Angrily, he repeated to Jodl that for a week he had demanded Paris be defended to the last man. He had personally sent reinforcements to the city's commander. Now, almost without warning, he saw this symbol of his dizzying triumphs about to be snatched from his hands. Barely three years earlier he had ruled Europe from the tundras of Lapland to the flanks of the Pyramids, from the rocky coast of Brittany to the outskirts of Moscow. Now Paris, for which he had danced his little jig of delight, was now to be denied him. And, within days of Paris's fall, Hitler knew that the war he had launched must finally come home to the sacred soil of Germany.

Vengeful and bitter, he again shouted to Jodl that the Allies must find nothing in Paris "but a pile of ruins." He had issued orders for demolition in the city, he shrieked. He had ordered engineer units to Paris to carry it out.

Caught up in the hysteria of his mounting rage, Hitler began to scream. What had happened? Had these orders been carried out? Hitler wheeled on the chief of his general staff with a savage glare.

"Jodl!" he rasped. *"Brennt Paris?"*—"Is Paris Burning?"

A silence fell over the bunker. Even the usually imperturbable Jodl seemed taken aback. He sat upright and still in his chair.

"Jodl," Hitler repeated, smashing his fist on the table, his voice rising further still, "I want to know—is Paris burning? Is Paris burning right now, Jodl?"

Finally Jodl stirred. With a whisper, he sent one of his aides out of the bunker to telephone OB West for an immediate report on the state of destruction in the city. When the aide had left, Hitler ordered Jodl to call Model personally. He told Jodl to repeat again his orders that Paris be defended "to the last man." "Tell him," Hitler yelled, that Paris "must be reduced to a pile of ruins" before the Allies seize it.

Then after a pause Hitler made another decision. If the Allies were to deprive him of his rocket bases, he would find one last vicious use for them. Turning once again to Jodl he ordered him to prepare a massive launch of all available V1 and V2 bombs on the city of Paris, backed up by every available Luftwaffe plane in the West. If indeed Paris was to be taken from him, his foes would find nothing there but "a blackened field of ruins."

Moments later, slipping out of the conference, General Warlimont noticed Jodl's aide talking frantically on the special telephone connected to the distant underground command post at Margival. "The Führer," the young officer said desperately, "wants to know: is Paris burning?"

• • •

The Paris so quickly slipping from Hitler's grasp was already a scene of wild contrasts. On one street corner, crowds poured over the city's liberators in an orgy of delight. On the next, in a welter of smoke and gunfire, these same liberators slowly, and often painfully, had begun the job of prying Choltitz's men from their strongpoints. On a street corner near the Palais du Luxembourg, his body already covered with flowers, was the unknown GI who had set out with Philippe Duplay to settle accounts with Willi Linke's Panzer. A well-aimed rifle bullet had split open his head a few yards from their goal.

Not far away, a pair of half-tracks tore madly up the edge of the Champ-de-Mars toward the spreading base of the Eiffel Tower. Their treads clattering on the pavement, their crews yipping in glee, the two vehicles of the Spahi Regiment dashed for the tower like a pair of racing Roman chariots.

Seconds before, as, side by side, the two half-tracks had pivoted onto the allée Adrienne-Lecouvreur, their drivers, Corporal Pierre Lefèvre and Pfc. Étienne Kraft, had hurled a challenge at each other: a dinner at Maxim's for the first crew under the tower. Forgetting the war for an instant, the two huge half-tracks bolted hell-for-breakfast for the tower. As he swept under its supports at 30 miles an hour, Kraft thought to himself, "My God, what if it's mined!" Then, in a yelp of triumph, he realized it was not. He had won.

Far above the head of Pfc. Étienne Kraft, well up in the tower itself, another man, his lungs raw, his legs aching, ran another race. Under his arms he carried a heavy bundle knotted with a piece of laundry rope. It was the French flag. Ahead, through the patchwork of iron ribs above him, fireman Captain Sarniguet saw the plodding figures of the two men he was racing to the top of the Eiffel Tower. They too, Sarniguet knew, carried a tricolor they were determined to plant on the tower's summit. Almost dizzy with fatigue, Sarniguet chased them up the 1,750 steps to the summit, the same exhausting climb he had made at 7:30 on the morning of June 13, 1940, to bring the tricolor down for the last time.

His head pounding, his legs moving with the leaden slowness of a dream, Sarniguet pounded after the fleeting image of his two compatriots. Less than 200 steps from the top of the tower, he caught them. Their eyes popping from the strain, too tired to talk, the three men matched each other stride for stride in a final sprint to the summit. At the top, Sarniguet burst forward with a lunge. He had won his race. From his package he took out the flag he had made a week earlier and raised it to the flagpole of this, the very symbol of Paris.

It was made from three old military bed sheets stitched together. One was dyed pink, one a washed out blue, and the third was tattletale gray. But it was the French tricolor, and at noon of this August 25, 1944, it was back where it belonged at the top of the Eiffel Tower.

6

"Augen gerade aus! Attention!"

At these sharp words ringing out under the chandeliers of the dining room, the officers stiffened to attention. Strapped tightly into the same field-gray uniform he had worn nineteen days earlier to his meeting with Adolf Hitler, his Iron Cross hanging from his chest, his monocle fixed with imperious rigidity into its socket, Dietrich von Choltitz entered the room. With a solemn and ponderous air, he marched to his regular position at the head table just under the windows of the dining room. Despite the fatigue drawing at his features, Choltitz was neat and clean. He had just shaved and bathed before putting on this uniform Mayer had set out for him to wear as he performed his last act as a German general.

As Choltitz reached his table, Colonel Jay urged him not to take his accustomed seat with his back to the window. A stray bullet, Jay feared, might cut short his life. "No," said Choltitz softly, "today, of all days, I take my regular place." The little general sat down, and as he did, the pendulum of the dining-room clock swung out the short stroke of one.

For Captain Jacques Branet, thirty, and the 200 men of his command drawn up in the place du Châtelet less than a mile away, one o'clock was jump-off time. Branet, a tough gravel-voiced veteran of the 2nd Armored Division, had the order to capture the German general sitting down to a last spartan meal in the Meurice dining room. To attack his headquarters, Branet split his men into three groups. The first he ordered along the quai de la Mégisserie, into the garden of the Tuileries through the graceful passageways cut into the flanks of the Louvre. The second he ordered past the elegant shopwindows of the rue Saint-Honoré to the edge of the place Vendôme, where they were to attack the Meurice from behind. The third, under his own command, would go straight ahead down the 130-year-old arcades of the rue de

Rivoli past the Ministry of Finance. Branet was determined to walk into the headquarters of the commander of Gross Paris by the front door.

The attack began like a Sunday stroll. At the base of the rue de Rivoli, Henri Karcher, the lieutenant who the day before had searched for the face of his own son in the streets of Orsay, led his infantrymen and a section of Rol's FFI up the avenue to the cheers of a crowd so enthusiastic the police had to struggle to hold them back. Ahead, up the long and graceful street built to mark one of Napoleon's victories over the Austrians, was an astonishing sight. Up to the place du Palais-Royal and the edge of the Tuileries, every door and window was decked with the tricolor. Beyond the Tuileries, all the way to the place de la Concorde, another flag hung out over the street, the red-and-black banner of Nazi Germany.

As Karcher's men darted from column to column up along the street, women rushed out to kiss them and throw them a last bouquet of flowers. At the corner of the rue des Lavandières-Sainte-Opportune, noted for the abundance of its brothels, a husky redheaded girl bolted up into the arms of Pfc. Jacques d'Étienne, gunner of the tank *Laffaux*. Under the shock of her affectionate assault, d'Étienne tumbled over backward into the shell rack of his tank. The redhead fell right in with him. At that instant, d'Étienne heard a voice in his earphones shout "Get moving!" Looking up, d'Étienne saw his driver Jacques Nudd, a blonde beside him, shrug his shoulders and gun the Sherman forward. With its two new laughing crew members, the *Laffaux* set off to assault the Meurice.

Karcher's infantrymen had left the happy civilians behind. Now the street ahead was empty, still and menacing. Occasionally his men could hear a window spring open above them. They spun their weapons toward the sound. But they had not yet reached the Tuileries. They could still see their countrymen behind the windows, urging them forward from the safety of their living rooms.

Through the slits of his pillbox at the head of the Tuileries and the rue de Rivoli, Captain Otto Nietzki of the Wehrmachtstreife watched them too. To Nietzki the strange sight looked "like a Holy Week procession."

And in the dining room of the Hotel Meurice, someone

had seen them too. Corporal Mayer walked discreetly up to von Choltitz and, leaning over respectfully, whispered to his commander, "*Sie kommen, Herr General.*"

• • •

Outside, along the arcades of the rue de Rivoli, a German tank pivoted into the line of advance of Branet's tanks. As it did, his lead Sherman *Douaumont* swung its 75-mm gun toward it. The *Douaumont* blew it apart with one shot.

At the *Douaumont's* shot, the whole street exploded into fire. Inside the dining room of the Meurice, the windowpanes were blown out by the shock waves of the shells exploding in the streets below. Choltitz stoically finished his meal. Then, calm and emotionless, he rose to address a few words to his officers waiting for him to leave so they could bolt out of this now menaced chamber.

"Gentlemen," he said, "our last combat has begun. May God protect you all." He added, "I hope the survivors may fall into the hands of regular troops and not those of the population." When he finished, he walked slowly out of the room.

Climbing up the staircase to his first-floor office with von Arnim, Choltitz paused at the sandbags piled together at the landing. To the gray-haired gunner manning the machine gun behind them, its barrel trained on the hotel's entrance, Choltitz spoke a word of encouragement.

"In Münster," muttered the old soldier in reply, "my farm, my wife . . . they've been waiting five years for me."

As they stepped past, von Arnim looked sadly at the old man, and hoped for his sake he would one day see that Münster farm.

Outside, in his pillbox at the corner of the rue de Rivoli, Captain Otto Nietzki directed a sweeping fire onto Karcher's advancing troops. Watching his tracer bullets fingering their way down the graceful line of arcades, Nietzki counted Karcher's men tumbling one by one to the sidewalk.

From another sandbagged strongpoint at the place des Pyramides, Lieutenant Heinrich Thiergartner joined his machine gun's fire to Nietzki's, catching Karcher's men in a crossfire.

Nailed to the pavement by the machine gun, Karcher and

his troops were stymied. There were no cheers nor flowers now. "The *Mitouze,* for God's sake, the machine gun!" yelled Karcher. As his men fired on Heinrich Thiergartner's sandbag barricade, they suddenly noticed an old man with a goatee and an antique hunting rifle step out into their line of fire, shoulder his ancient gun and send a smoky blast toward Thiergartner's men. Then, his face radiant with happiness, he disappeared back down the street from which he had just appeared.

Seeing his infantry screen pinned down, Branet ordered his tanks forward to reduce the opposition holding up Karcher. Led by Sergeant Marcel Bizien, the little Breton in the *Douaumont* who had vowed to make his ancestors proud of this day, the five tanks moved past Karcher's men. Driving into the place des Pyramides, Jacques d'Étienne, the gunner of the *Laffaux,* saw three Germans sprinting past the statue of Jeanne d'Arc, a bare 30 yards ahead of him. D'Étienne fired. With a kind of horrified ecstasy he watched the Germans' severed limbs fly into the air like a wild bouquet garlanding for a second the gilded limbs of the Maid of Orleans.

•   •   •

Striding through his office, which was alive now with the sound of gunfire, Dietrich von Choltitz dictated a last letter. It was to Consul General Nordling. Since dawn, the pretty Cita Krebben and her female companions had been taken into custody by the Red Cross. There was no one left for the general to dictate this letter to except the faithful corporal. "My dear Mr. Nordling," it began, "I wish to send you my profound thanks." Choltitz interrupted himself and took a few steps to the window. He started. His enemy had arrived. Just below the balcony on which he had spent so many perplexed moments in the past two weeks, Choltitz saw a Sherman tank, its turret open, its cannon swinging in a graceful arc toward the entrance of the hotel. Choltitz looked with fascination at the black beret of its commander bobbing in the tank's open turret. He wondered if he was French or American. Then he thought to himself, whoever he was, he "wasn't taking this fight very seriously if he was leaving his turret open." Beside Choltitz, von Arnim peered at the gun swinging toward the door. "My God," he asked, "what's he going to do?"

Choltitz told him he imagined "he's going to use it. There'll be a little noise and we'll be in trouble." As they turned to go back into the hotel, a German on the roof lobbed a grenade into the open turret under them.

Lieutenant Albert Bénard, the commander of the *Mort-Homme*, felt it bang his head and slide down his back to bounce into his turret. Sliced from his forehead to his waist by its shards, his tank suit in flames, Bénard scrambled out of the smoking tank. His gunner went with him. Left alone in the choking machine, Jean René Champion tried to drive it forward, looking for cover.

Watching the flaming figures of Bénard and his gunner roll on the asphalt, the Germans held their fire for an instant. On the rooftop of the Kriegsmarine, Lieutenant Commander Harry Leithold told his men not to fire on the wounded Frenchmen. Then, emerging out of the smoke pluming up behind the *Mort-Homme* Leithold saw the rest of Branet's Shermans moving ponderously forward. In a few seconds, Leithold realized, they would spring on the flank of the Panther at the place de la Concorde entrance to the Tuileries. Leithold tried desperately to signal the Panther's commander. A flame burst from the mouth of the Panther's 88. The tank commander was too busy with another target at the head of the Champs-Élysées to see him.

At the top of the Champs-Élysées, at its juncture with the place de l'Étoile, the shell the Panther had just fired tore off the last gaslight on the broad avenue. The spray of broken glass spattered down on the turret of a tank destroyer passing at that instant in front of the Arc de Triomphe. It was the *Simoun*. In its cramped quarters, one odor dominated the smells of battle. It was the rancid stench of the crew's dead duck, still stuck into the *Simoun's* shell rack. Two more shells from the Panther sailed over the *Simoun*. The first chipped off the base of the statue of the Marseillaise. The second plunged under the largest triumphal arch in the world, right over the heads of Colonel Paul de Langlade and Major Henri de Mirambeau offering a hasty reverence to the tomb of France's Unknown Soldier before attacking the Hotel Majestic nearby.

At the Étoile, Second Mate Paul Quinion, commander of the *Simoun*, fixed the Panther in his field glasses. He ordered his gunner Robert Mady to load a high-explosive shell into

their cannon. He announced the range to Mady: 1,500 meters.
Mady clicked off the range on his gunsight. Then he hesitated.
Without informing Quinion, he clicked off three more stops,
setting his range at 1,800 meters. Parisian Mady had just
remembered reading long ago in the *Almanach Vermot*, the
standard French almanac, that the length of the Champs-
Elysées from the Arc de Triomphe to the Obelisk was 1,800
meters. Mady fired. The almanac was right. His first shot hit
the Panther. Watching a column of gray smoke seep up from
the injured tank, Mady suddenly said to himself, *"Bon Dieu,*
if I'd shot two meters to the right, I would have knocked down
the Obelisk!"

Behind his sandbagged window in the Hotel de Crillon,
Sergeant Erich Vandamm watched the smoke rising from the
spot where Mady's shell had torn off one of the Panther's
treads. As he did, he saw a column of Shermans slide out of
the mouth of the rue de Rivoli and turn toward the stricken
tank.

In the *Douaumont* leading the procession before Vandamm's eyes, Sergeant Marcel Bizien saw the Panther too.
"Boche tank to the left!" he yelled to his gunner. "Fire!" The
Douaumont's high-explosive shell burst against the armor
plate of the Panther without breaking it. Now Bizien watched
the German's turret slowly swing its deadly 88 toward him.
Inside the German tank, its crew was cranking it by hand.
Mady's shot had knocked out their electric system. "An armor-
piercing shell, for Christ's sake!" yelled Bizien. Below him
his gunner groped in the smoke filling the *Douaumont's* turret
for a shell. "Fire!" yelled Bizien.

The shell burst against the Panther. A coil of smoke spouted
up from it. In the darkness of his turret, Bizien's gunner had
rammed a smoke shell instead of an armor-piercing round
into the breech of his cannon. Now the Panther was barely
30 yards from Bizien's tank. In seconds, before the *Douaumont*
could fire again, the German 88 was going to find them and
tear the *Douaumont* to pieces. In a flash the little descendant
of a band of Breton sea raiders realized his only hope was to
smack into the German before that awful 88 could fire. "Ram
him!" yelled Bizien. Driver Georges Campillo slammed down
his accelerator and sent the *Douaumont* surging forward.
From his rooftop outpost on the Kriegsmarine, Lieutenant
Commander Leithold watched as the Sherman charged like

a locomotive through the smoke billowing around the Panther. He thought the sight looked like a "medieval joust."

In the turret of his tank, Bizien braced himself. Below him, Campillo pressed back against his metal seat to absorb the blow. Like lances, the cannons of the two tanks crossed. In a fountain of sparks and a thunderclap of sound, the seventy tons of metal smashed together in the center of the most beautiful square in the world. Then the echoes of their crash died and an eerie silence filled the square.

Stunned by the blow, half choked in the smoke, the crews of both tanks huddled dazed in their turrets. Coming slowly to his senses, Bizien stirred first. To driver Campillo he pointed to the slender outline of the Obelisk in the smoke "like the foremast of a boat in a fog" rising over them. The little Breton unbuckled his Colt and leaped out of the tank toward the Panther beside them. Inside the *Douaumont* Campillo heard the thump of an exploding grenade. Then he saw Bizien returning through the smoke, cursing. "The s.o.b.s all beat it," he said.

Still watching fascinated through his field glasses, Leithold saw the Sherman lurch backward under its own power. As it did, he heard a flurry of shots and saw the figure in its turret slump forward. It was Sergeant Bizien, shot through the neck by a bullet fired from a window. The triumphant joy of the little Breton who had wanted to make his ancestors proud had lasted only a few minutes, just the time to savor a promise kept and to die.

● ● ●

In the Meurice, grim and resigned, Choltitz had just reached a decision. It was the decision Bender has expected he would take when, on his own authority, he had told the French the commander of Gross Paris would surrender his strongpoints once he himself had been taken prisoner. A few moments earlier, Jay had said to his old friend, "Now, you must make up your mind. Are you going to sit here and play hide-and-seek with the Americans all day or are you going to surrender and get this damn business over with?"

Choltitz pondered. Sad and weary, he decided he could not condemn his men to death in a long and useless fight that would serve no cause. He called in Unger. If the FFI tried to take the hotel, he ordered, they would fight. If the regular troops entered first, the building commander was to surrender after a few shots had been fired. He ordered von Unger to take down the flag when the Allies entered the building. Then he left his office to wait for them in a small room in a sheltered interior court.

In Choltitz's bedroom Corporal Mayer, with the precise and meticulous gestures of seven years' training, packed a last valise for the commander of Gross Paris. Into it he put three shirts, a uniform jacket, socks, underwear, and a pair of the general's trousers, their bright claret-red stripes of office running down their outer seam. In another room Count von Arnim stuffed a few bars of chocolate, a heavy sweater his mother had knitted for him the winter before, and two books into a sack. One was the *History of France* by Jacques Bainville. The other was *War and Peace*.

In the streets outside, the French drew closer to the hotel. Darting across the rue de Rivoli in a cloud of smoke, three men slammed themselves to the ground at the gates of the Tuileries. Peering through the smoke around him, one of them, Lieutenant Henri Riquebush, saw with horror that he had chosen to hide himself right in front of the slit of a German pillbox. Groping through the smoke with his hand, he felt a burning piece of metal scrape his palm. It was the barrel of the pillbox's gun, abandoned seconds before by its defenders.

At the other end of the Tuileries Corporal Georges Thiollat of the Sherman *Francheville* saw his armor-piercing shell smack into the rear treads of its target, a Panther crouched before the Orangerie, its cannon leveled across the Seine. The alerted Panther's turret started to wind toward Thiollat's tank. The *Francheville's* second shot missed and Thiollat gulped in dismay. The next shot was going to be the Panther's. Then he saw the tank's cannon stop. Its slow sweep toward him had been arrested by the trunk of a tree beside the tank.

Across the garden, in the furious rain of grenades and bazooka shells pouring out of the buildings along the rue de Rivoli, three of the five tanks that had started to attack were already out of commission. Playwright Irwin Shaw, a private in the Army's photoservice, saw one of them limp out of combat, its rear deck blown open. Maddened by the death of their friends, the crew of the *Laffaux*, one of the two tanks left, went on a shooting spree, firing off all but a dozen of the 90 shells stuffed into their turret.

"*Laffaux*," ordered a furious Captain Branet, "stop that firing. You're shooting up the most beautiful square in the world." Almost at the moment his words died, another voice announced to the crew of the *Laffaux* that Pierre Laigle in the *Montfaucon* had been killed and his tank knocked out of action.

"*Merde!*" thought the *Laffaux*'s gunner, Jacques d'Étienne. "We're the last ones left."

7

BEHIND THE MEURICE, LIEUTENANT Marcel Christen looked at the line of vehicles blazing like torches all along the rue Castiglione and rue Saint-Honoré. "My God," he thought, "Stalingrad must have started like this!" Before him, the Hotel Continental was a shambles, its windows blown out, its façade battered and torn apart, the bodies of its German defenders spewed across the street. Grabbing his Colt, the young lieutenant who the day before had helped direct the attack on Fresnes prison leaped out of his tank. With his driver Henri Villette behind him, he slid from doorway to doorway toward the hotel entrance. From it a little German captain, his helmet in his hand, stumbled toward them. "Surrender!" cried Alsatian Christen in German. The dejected captain muttered "*Ja*" and raised his hands. Pushing him before them, the two soldiers entered the hotel. One by one a flood of Germans, hands over their heads, poured toward the pair. Each time he spotted a German wearing an Iron Cross, Villette ripped it off. He had been collecting them since Libya. He already carried seventeen in his tanker's belt, but never had Villette stumbled on a bonanza to match this one in the Continental.

Floor by floor, the two men cleaned out the hotel. On its fifth floor Christen heard a series of low groans coming from behind a door. Kicking it open, he found a group of American prisoners chained to a bedroom wall, weak with fatigue and hunger.

"*Eh bien, les potes* [O.K., pals], you're free!" said the astonished Frenchman.

Downstairs a troop of infantrymen had flooded into the hotel behind Christen. They rounded up the last Germans. It was 2:30. The first of Choltitz's *Stützpunkte* had fallen.

• • •

In front of the Meurice, the fight was as bitter as ever. Lieutenant Yves Brécard had been so busy ducking Otto Nietzki's bullets sweeping the Tuileries that he had just told a German officer who was stumbling out of the bushes to surrender, "Wait a minute, I'll take you prisoner later." At the corner of the rue Saint-Roch, gunner d'Étienne of the *Laffaux*, the last surviving Sherman of the tanks that had plunged so gaily up the rue de Rivoli ninety minutes earlier, saw an officer stumbling to the ground, his back torn open by a grenade. It was Captain Branet, who had wanted to walk into the Meurice by the front door. Seconds later, a grenade split apart a vent of the *Laffaux*, wounding d'Étienne and its driver. The tank turned and dashed back to an aid station at the Châtelet to join the *Montfaucon* and the *Villers-Cotteret*. The *Douaumont*, with the body of Marcel Bizien still inside, was abandoned in the place de la Concorde. On the Royale the *Mort-Homme* burned to ruins where Jean René Champion had taken cover.

For a few seconds a silence fell over the rue de Rivoli. Then the tank company of Captain Georges Buis moved across the place de la Concorde to take up the attack. Sweeping over the wide square, Buis saw to the left of the turret of his tank *Norway* the charred frame of the Grand Palais. To his gunner, Henri Jacques, Buis mumbled, "What a dump!" The gunner agreed. "Suppose we finish it off?" said Buis. Chuckling, Jacques began to feel through his shell racks for an incendiary shell.

Seconds later he announced sadly to his captain that he had none left. An explosive shell, he said, wouldn't do any good.

"Pity," answered Buis. Disappointed, they rolled on toward the Meurice.

* * *

Ahead of him Henri Karcher read the words printed on the oval plaque: HOTEL MEURICE—THÉ—RESTAURANT. Seconds before, the lieutenant had had the closest brush with death he had ever known. At the instant he turned his head to pass an order to the soldier behind him, a tracer bullet had singed his left eyebrow. Had his head not been turned, he realized, the bullet would have cut into his eye and furrowed through his brain. Now, moving toward the door ahead, Karcher remembered he had been here before. It was just before the war, when a newspaperman friend had invited him to "have a drink with the Queen of Romania."

His submachine gun in his hand, Karcher and the three men behind him sprang into the door of the hotel. Ahead of him Karcher saw a huge portrait of Hitler crowning a showcase of jewels, evening bags, and compacts. It shattered to bits. Karcher's first gesture in the headquarters of the German commander of Gross Paris had been to fire on the Führer. From behind his sandbags on the first landing, the old soldier from Münster opened fire on Karcher. The Frenchman ducked behind the reception desk and plucked a black ball from his belt. It was a phosphorous grenade. Biting out its pin, he hurled it into the lobby. Behind Karcher, Pfc. Walter Hermann, an Alsatian, turned his flamethrower onto the elevator cage. At that instant, Hermann saw a Wehrmacht helmet come bouncing down the stairway before him. It belonged to the old farmer from Münster, killed by Karcher's grenade.

Through the mass of acrid smoke filling the lobby appeared the figure of a German officer, his hands in the air. Karcher leaped for him, jabbing the snout of his submachine gun into his belt. While Hermann translated, Karcher ordered, "Everybody, one by one, hands up and arms thrown away!" The German yelled a command. The firing stopped, and one by one, covered with blood and sweat, the defenders of the ground floor of the hotel streamed out of the smoke toward Karcher and his three men. Down the stairs, stepping past the body of the old soldier from Münster, Karcher saw a German officer in the red-striped trousers of the general staff approaching him. Karcher sprang at him. "Where," he asked, "is your general?"

• • •

The general was seated behind a long table placed at an angle in a little room just one flight above Karcher. His head in his hands, Dietrich von Choltitz seemed lost in his thoughts. Before him on the table, resting inside the lining of his officer's cap, was a brown leather holster containing the 6.35 pistol with which he would shortly surrender his command. Choltitz had had to borrow it; he did not own a pistol of his own. Beside him, Unger, Jay, Bressensdorf and Arnim waited with him. They, too, had laid their pistols on the table before them like medieval fighters tossing their swords into the shields of their conquerors. It was a cruel and painful moment which each of them felt in his own way. In the heavy silence weighing on them, these last representatives of a command that had for four years locked in its ruthless power one of the world's most beautiful capitals reckoned up their personal balance sheets.

Calm and resigned, Choltitz waited now for the final denouement without emotion. He had nothing, he thought, for which to reproach himself. His soldiers were at this moment executing the orders of his Führer to "fight to their last cartridges." His soldier's honor was intact, and once he himself was a prisoner, he could in honor order his men to surrender. At the same time, he could now await the judgment of history without fear or shame. He had not allowed a vengeful Hitler to force him to play the executioner of this city to which fate had sent him nineteen days earlier. In these last moments of liberty, Choltitz felt with perfect sincerity that he had properly served his name and his nation in Paris.

Standing to his left, the dapper and urbane Colonel Jay had a different thought. He was making an imaginary trip. In the debacle awaiting Germany, when the Allies had split among themselves the ruins of his country, there would, he thought, be little room left for people like him. Where, Jay asked himself, would he go?

For young Ernst von Bressensdorf, this end seemed to bring "the marvelous promise of a new beginning."

Beside him, his young friend Count von Arnim thought that at last this war, which had "taken the best years of life," was over. But strangely, at this approaching end, no one seemed more serene than the cold, distant and austere von

Unger. Arnim noticed the colonel, at Choltitz's right, his features suddenly softened, the rigidity seeping out of his martial figure, gently thumbing through the pictures of his children tucked into the billfold he had just taken from his pocket.

When the door opened, Choltitz raised his head. Corporal Mayer stood in the doorway. For the second time in just over two hours, the corporal clicked his heels lightly together and announced, *"Sie kommen, Herr General."*

• • •

This time "they" were at the other end of the corridor. At the head of the Meurice staircase, Karcher had just found a group of silent officers, their hands in the air. As Karcher had appeared, one of them burst into hysterical laughter. It was a bald little lieutenant, and in perfect French he shouted, "It's the happiest day of my life! I'm Austrian. I hate these Nazis. All during the war I managed to keep away from the front. Three days ago they sent me here. Am I glad to see you!" With those words the bald officer threw himself at Karcher's feet and began to kiss his boots.

Walking down the smoky corridor toward his waiting prize, Karcher felt his temples throbbing. Ahead of him, hands in the air, the officers who had staggered down the stairs showed the way. "You can't put on a bad show now," Karcher told himself. At that thought a stream of memories flashed through his mind. He saw the faces of the friends he had left behind on the road to this hotel corridor: Loiseau, whose brother he had seen earlier; the man whose Colt he clutched in his fist; the men whom, in a sense, he was about to represent in the glorious instant just ahead in which he would accept the surrender of the German general occupying the capital of his country. Karcher opened the door to the room indicated by the officer before him. Choltitz stood up. Karcher came to attention and saluted.

"Lieutenant Henri Karcher of the Army of General de Gaulle," he announced.

"General von Choltitz, commander of Gross Paris," answered the German.

Karcher asked Choltitz if he was ready to surrender.

"*Ja*," Choltitz replied.

"Then," Karcher said, "you are my prisoner."

"*Ja*," answered Choltitz.

At that moment a second French officer entered the room. At the sight of Major Jean de la Horie, Colonel Jay's eyebrows raised slightly. Before the war these two men had waged a different kind of combat in the riding rings of Europe where each had ridden on his army's equestrian team. Now as their eyes met, the two men nodded almost imperceptibly. La Horie turned to Choltitz. Through an interpreter he told him, "General, you wanted a fight. You've had one and it has cost us a heavy price. I demand you order all resistance to cease in the rest of your strongpoints in the city."

Ceremoniously, La Horie turned to Karcher and said, "My dear fellow, will you take care of the others?" He ordered Choltitz to come with him. The Prussian shook hands with Jay and Unger, murmured to each a "*Hals- und Beinbruch*," and, his hat now fixed on his head, marched off.

After they had left, Karcher demanded a tour of inspection of the Gross Paris headquarters. Von Unger stepped forward to accompany him. In Choltitz's old office, Karcher noticed a bundle of cloth neatly piled on the general's desk.

"What," he asked Unger, "is that?"

"It is the flag of the Gross Paris Command," answered Unger. It had been taken in, he explained, when Karcher entered the building.

"Then," said Karcher, "you shall give it to me."

The two men were alone in the smoky room. Outside the intermittent clatter of gunfire rose up to its windows from the Tuileries and the place de la Concorde. From the sidewalks below came a more disconcerting mumble. It was the mob, already drawing close to the doors of the Meurice. Face to face, the two officers stiffened to attention, saluted, and then, with a solemn gesture, the elderly Unger handed his young French captor the enormous red-and-black banner that for four years, two months and ten days had hung in triumph from the flagpole of 228 rue de Rivoli.

That brief ceremony over, Karcher picked up the Paris telephone on Choltitz's desk and dialed a number.

"Auteuil 04.21?" he asked when his number answered. "*Eh bien, Papa*," Karcher announced to his stepfather, a retired general who had not shared his affection for de Gaulle, "I present you my respects. This is Lieutenant Henri Karcher. Despite the unfavorable predictions you made on my military

career, I am happy to announce to you that I have just captured a German general, his staff, and his flag."

In the streets below, Major de la Horie, his revolver in his
hand, fought to protect his prisoner. Dignified and inscrutable,
Dietrich von Choltitz accepted the fury of the vengeful crowd.
Women, their faces contorted in hatred, clawed at his uniform,
trying to rip off his shoulder boards, and spat on him as he
marched past. Men shouted "Son of a bitch!" At the satisfying
sight of this German general, his hands held high in surrender,
a people brutalized, chained, and repressed by four years of
Nazi occupation took a crowd's instinctive revenge.

"They're going to lynch me," Choltitz thought. At his back
he could feel the panting of his faithful orderly Corporal
Mayer. In one hand Mayer clutched the valise he had carefully prepared for this unhappy journey to a prisoner's cage.
With each step, a weary Choltitz felt his arms drooping.
"Higher, higher, General," Mayer whispered. "If you don't
keep them up, they'll kill you!"

All along the rue de Rivoli ahead of them, a triumphant
phrase preceded their march: *Le général boche, le général
boche!* At the place des Pyramides, a woman of about forty,
her face twisted in hate, burst before him. "Bastard!" she
shrieked. Then she drew her head back, and snapping it forward like a snake, sent a wad of spit sloshing onto his cheekbone just below his monocle.

At that moment a woman in a Red Cross uniform stepped
beside him, and, indignant and angry, placed her body between him and the crowd. Touched by this rare gesture of
compassion, Choltitz—passing at that moment behind the
gilded statue of Jeanne d'Arc—murmured to his benefactress,
"Madame, you are as Jeanne d'Arc."

La Horie finally spotted the sides of a half-track, to which
he guided his prisoner. In the crush the Frenchman forgot
about Corporal Mayer. Terrified, the orderly saw the half-track
start to leave without him, abandoning him alone in the
middle of a vengeful mass of Parisians.

At that moment an FFI smashed the general's valise from
Mayer's hands with the butt of his rifle. The Frenchman
began to batter it apart and rip out the spare uniform trousers
and tunic Mayer had carefully packed for this journey. Mayer
left it behind and, beating at the hands already clutching at
his uniform, pushed forward with a frantic lunge until he

seized the tail gate of the rolling half-track. Relieved, he saw above him the figure of Choltitz.

Choltitz, for once, did not notice him. Transfixed, he was watching a sight he would never forget. Behind him, as he rolled off to captivity, was a grotesquely ugly Parisienne dancing a wild carmagnole on the pavements of the rue de Rivoli. Over her head she jubilantly flourished her personal trophy of the liberation of this, her city. It was a pair of trousers, and down their seams ran the proud claret stripes of a general officer of the Wehrmacht.

8

AT THE VERY HEART of Paris, in the paneled banquet hall of the Prefecture of Police opposite Notre-Dame, another general, his crumpled uniform flaked with dust, had just sat down to a late lunch. For once, a smile rested on his dour Picardian features. Jacques Philippe Leclerc had kept the promise he had sworn to himself in the Libyan Desert. He was a liberator of Paris. By one of history's happy chances, his moment of final triumph was about to arrive exactly four years to the day, almost to the minute, from the instant he had set out on his journey back to his nation's capital. It had begun under a sweltering African sun in midafternoon of August 25, 1940, on the banks of the Wouri River in Cameroun when he had set out to reconquer in the name of Charles de Gaulle a first corner of France's empire. Leclerc had started this journey in a pirogue with seventeen men: three officers, two missionaries, seven farmers and five civil servants. He had finished it with 16,000 men and the most modern unit in the French Army.

For the commander of the 2nd Armored, this triumphant lunch progressed only as far as a plate of hors-d'oeuvre. One of his aides tiptoed up and whispered in his ear. Leclerc rose and went into the room next door. It was the billiard room. There Leclerc prepared to accept over a billiard table the formal act of surrender of the capital of his country from its last German commander.

Outside he heard the howls and whistling of the crowd massed in the courtyard of the building Choltitz had decided to reduce to rubble five days earlier. Then the door opened. Red-faced and puffing, the German came in. The little general walked up to Leclerc and the two men identified themselves: Choltitz, freshly scrubbed and shaven, stiff and sweating in his dress uniform; Leclerc, his khaki collar open, a crumb at the corner of his mouth. Looking at this first French general he had ever seen, Choltitz thought "how incredibly informal" he was. Leclerc, for this historic occasion, wore a dirty khaki shirt and a pair of GI boots. He wore no decorations, and his only insignia were the stars of his rank pinned to his shoulder panels.

The two men discussed briefly the terms of the typewritten surrender document. As they did, there was a stir in the room. The Communist "Colonel Rol," angry that he had not even been asked to watch the surrender of the city for which he had fought for six days, was demanding admission to the room. Leclerc acquiesced. Then Maurice Kriegel-Valrimont, the garrulous Communist member of the COMAC assigned to act as a party watchdog on the Prefecture, insisted Rol's name appear on the surrender document with Leclerc's. Exasperated, Leclerc agreed.

Leclerc demanded that Choltitz order all his strongpoints to cease fire and, to put his order into effect, send a German, a Frenchman and an American to each strongpoint. Then, with Choltitz beside him, Leclerc set out for his Gare Montparnasse headquarters. As they climbed aboard his command car, Leclerc's driver stared disdainfully at this panting red-faced general who only hours before had still held much of Paris's destiny in his chubby hands. "*Tiens,*" he said, "the *gros cochon* is still agile."

• • •

As rumors of Choltitz's surrender spread across Paris, the city, already wild with delight, seemed to soar off into an ecstatic trance all its own. Never before, perhaps, had a city so completely opened its heart as Paris did this day. To war correspondent Ernie Pyle, the city's massive display of joy was "the loveliest, brightest story of our time." "Describing Paris in words today," wrote his colleague Ed Ball, "is like trying to paint a desert sunset in black and white."

Paris lived and loved, cheered and cried, danced and, on occasion, died, all through this magnificent day with a vigor that did honor to even its gay and Gallic heart. Caught up in the delirium, Captain George Knapp, a Protestant chaplain from Dyer, Indiana, thought it was "the greatest experience" he had ever lived. (His fellow chaplain Captain Lewis Koon of Woodstock, Virginia, driving in a jeep with his function painted on it in white letters, heard the crowds murmur, "Ah, Charlie Chaplin.") Everywhere, people broke out bottles of champagne long set aside for the Liberation. Huddled underneath a truck on the avenue de la Grande-Armée while a fire fight flared around him, Colonel David Bruce suddenly saw a well-dressed Parisian crawling through the gutter to join him. Bruce, the European head of OSS who had accompanied Ernest Hemingway to Rambouillet, stared in surprise at his elegant visitor. "Excuse me," the Frenchman said, "but I wonder if you'd like to come to my home for a glass of champagne?"

For most of the exhausted and dirty soldiers of the 2nd French Armored Division and the 4th U.S. Infantry Division, few of the gifts Paris might offer could rival a bath. Pfc. Charley Haley of "B" Company, 4th Engineers Combat Battalion, got his in an apartment at 2 avenue Léon-Bollée. Stripped to his skivvy shorts, Haley stood in a tub while a Frenchwoman, her two daughters and her son scraped the dirt of Normandy off him. When his company drew up at the avenue d'Orléans, Captain Jim Smith, of the 12th Regiment Antitank Company, was invited by a lovely blonde to take a bath. She had neither a tub nor a shower, but she stood the lanky captain in a wooden bucket in the center of her kitchen, and, while he drank champagne and asked himself if he was dreaming, she scrubbed him down from head to foot.

Everywhere among the wild and happy crowds, nothing touched the city's liberators more than the spontaneous generosity of a city anxious to share the little it had left after four years of occupation. Over and over again, the crowds shouted, "Merci, merci," to the passing troops. "Ah, Paris," Sergeant Douglas Kimball of Franklin, New Hampshire, could still recall twenty years later, "her *Mercis* will ring forever in my ears."

Scampering in a box on the back seat of Master Sergeant Don Flannagan's jeep as he entered Paris was his company's pet rabbit, Jeannie, a skinny animal liberated in a Normandy farmyard. Stopped for a few moments in the midst of a crowd, Flannagan noticed a Frenchman edging toward him, a big fat rabbit flopping in his arms. The Frenchman had noticed the bony Jeannie, and in a touching gesture thought he would offer Flannagan a rabbit that promised better eating than the skinny animal in his jeep. With some difficulty, Flannagan convinced his astonished benefactor that Jeannie was not for eating.

But more than any of these gifts from an anonymous crowd, it was the immense gratitude of an entire people that humbled the incoming troops. By the time he had reached the place de l'Étoile, Pfc. George McIntyre of "B" Company, a New Jersey man, had been hugged so often he "thought his ribs had been cracked." McIntyre, "short, nearly bald, with only half a set of teeth," hopped down for a rest from his tractor-towed bulldozer. As he did, he saw the figure of "a beautiful girl of eighteen" push her way into the circle of people around him. For fully ten seconds she stared at the unshaven, dirty little GI. As she did, the people around them hushed. Then, suddenly, her face alive with happiness, she cried, "The people of France can raise their heads again. Thank God for our liberators. *Vive l'Amérique. Vive la France!*" She threw herself on the open-mouthed GI and kissed him. Then, covering his hands with kisses, she sank to her knees before him. Profoundly touched and just as profoundly embarrassed, McIntyre drew this beautiful girl up and kissed her again, this time to the cheers of the crowd around them. To the little GI from New Jersey, tears smarting in his eyes, it seemed as though "all the hardships of the war had been canceled by the touching gesture of one girl."

• • •

In her neat two-room apartment at 102 rue de Richelieu, Mme. Jacques Jugeat listened to the happy howls of the crowds in the street below. The seventy-one-year-old widow smiled with just a touch of sadness at the noise. She was

alone in Paris, cut off from her family, and she was spending
Liberation Day as she had spent most of the occupation, alone
with her thoughts. So lost was she in those thoughts that she
failed to hear the first knock on her door. At the second she
started and was sure it was a mistake. At the third, timid and
afraid, she went to answer it.

There, standing before her, was a smiling giant in a strange
uniform. He reached into his pocket, and on this Liberation
afternoon, the first American Mme. Jugeat had ever seen
handed her a letter. It was from her only son 3,600 miles
away in a country she had never known. The soldier before
her was Lieutenant Colonel Dee Stone. Mme. Jugeat's son
was Stone's next-door neighbor in Forest Hills, New York.
The night Stone had left the United States, Jugeat had given
him this letter to deliver in Paris. "It'll bring you luck," he
had said. It was the letter Stone had carried as a talisman
across Utah Beach, through Normandy's hedgerows to this
dim Paris apartment.

*   *   *

In the gay carnival now reigning in the streets of Paris,
everything seemed to be happening at the same time. Excited
FFIs, a bottle in one hand and a rifle in the other, chased
over the city's rooftops looking for German snipers. On the
Champs-Élysées an excited fireman's band alternated cho-
ruses of the "Marseillaise" and "God Bless America." Around
the German strongpoints still resisting, the troops of the 2nd
Armored fought and died while just blocks away their comrades, their fighting over, celebrated.

Lieutenant Colonel Ken Downes and Lieutenant John
Mowinckle decided to have a welcome-home drink in the only
place that, to ex-newsman Downes, seemed fitting for such
an occasion—the Hotel de Crillon. Downes shoved aside the
hotel employees barring the iron grille to its lobby and stalked
inside. He stopped with an abrupt jerk at the sight before
him. Stretching from one end of the lobby to the other was
a sullen mass of Germans, haversacks slung over their shoulders, sidearms strapped to their waists. They stared at the two
Americans. Then one of them stepped forward. "Are you
American?" he asked.

Downes replied that they were.

"Then," said the German, "we surrender to you, and not"—he gestured disdainfully to the crowd beyond the hotel gates—"to *that* out there."

"How many are you?" asked Downes.

"One hundred and seventy-six," answered the German.

Downes thought for a second. Then he turned to Mowinckle. "Lieutenant," he said, "take care of the prisoners." With that, Downes left to find a more congenial bar. Alone with his 176 prisoners, Mowinckle decided to disarm them like a gentleman. He told them to check their arms in the cloakroom.

As they did, Mowinckle found he had an ally, an enormous French lieutenant in the uniform of the Spahi regiment. Like Mowinckle, he had entered the hotel with a distinctly exaggerated notion of the state of its liberation. He had thought it was Leclerc's headquarters. The Frenchman decided to tour the hotel. Pulling his Colt from its holster, he cleared a passage to the stairs by bopping the Germans in his way with the butt end of his pistol. The American followed him. Upstairs was a huge banquet hall still littered with the remains of the Germans' last feast. The two young officers entered by different doors, and at almost the same instant spotted a prize left behind by the Germans, a case of champagne. With as much speed as a sense of dignity would allow them, they raced each other for it. They reached it together. Face to face, they stood at semi-attention over their prize.

"Lieutenant Jean Biehlmann, French Intelligence Service," said the Frenchman.

"Lieutenant John Mowinckle, American Intelligence Service," answered Mowinckle.

"I propose," said the Frenchman with a sweep of his hand, "six for you and six for me." Mowinckle bowed a polite assent and the two young officers scooped up the champagne. Then, side by side, their arms crammed with champagne bottles, they marched solemnly down the grand staircase of the hotel, past their popeyed prisoners, and, laughing like two schoolboys who had just played a prank, they strode out of the hotel.

A few blocks away, two truckloads of FFI drove up at the main entrance of an equally famous Paris hostelry. Dirty and dusty, in berets, undershirts, and grease-stained blue-denim work clothes, they strode like the workers' battalions that had marched out to defend Madrid into the very citadel of old-world luxury, the Hotel Ritz. At their head marched the imposing general of this one-man army, Ernest Hemingway, and his two volunteer aides, the distinguished Colonel David Bruce and "Moutarde," a prewar engineer on the French-owned Ethiopian railroads who had served as chief of staff of Hemingway's FFI army for the past four days.

In the Ritz's deserted lobby they found only one person, a frightened assistant manager. He recognized his distinguished American visitors, frequent prewar guests at the hotel.

"Why," he gasped, "what are you doing here?"

They informed him they had come with some friends for a short stay. Recovering from his surprise, the assistant manager asked Hemingway if as a welcoming gesture there was anything the Ritz could offer him. The writer looked at his happy, scruffy horde of FFI already milling through the lobby.

"How about seventy-three dry martinis?" he answered.

* * *

All morning, Yvette Boverat, her husband and her daughter Hélène had pushed their bikes through the laughing throngs, looking for the regiment in black berets. From the porte d'Orléans where they had watched the first troops moving into Paris, past the Luxembourg, down the boulevard Saint-Michel to the Hôtel de Ville, they had pressed their search. Now, at least, they knew the name of the regiment they were looking for. It was the 501st Regiment des Chars de Combat, the unit whose tanks had led the assault on the Meurice.

Finally, on the place du Châtelet, the Boverats found their first soldiers in black berets. But none of them knew a Raymond or a Maurice Boverat. They told them to look on the Ile Saint-Louis. There were other units from their regiment over there, they said.

For an hour the three Boverats rushed up and down the crooked streets of the little island hooked like a barge onto the Ile de la Cité behind Notre-Dame. They asked everyone they could find if they had seen "any soldiers in black berets." No one had. Finally, in front of a café, two FFI guarding a jeep told the discouraged family there was a black-bereted soldier sleeping in the courtyard of the café behind them.

Hélène reached the courtyard first. In the corner, wound

up into a ball, was a soldier, sound asleep in the sunshine. He was too big to be one of her brothers, she thought. Her mother and father joined her. The three Boverats bent down and peered with beseeching eyes at the dirty, unshaven man snoring at their feet. Then Mme. Boverat reached over and with the same gentle caress with which she had stirred him from his sleep as a child, she shook the shoulder of the sleeping soldier. It was her son Maurice.

Maurice stretched into wakefulness. The first person he saw, as he opened his eyes, was his sister. "How beautiful she is," he thought. The girl, tears in her eyes, leaned closer to stare at this enormous man she had last known as a gangling adolescent. She saw the regular metallic glint of what seemed to her a familiar object stuck into his belt. It was a clip of cartridges for his Colt .45.

"Oh," she asked in a voice soft with shy admiration, "do you still play the harmonica?"

* * *

Captain Victor Vrabel's jaw muscles "were sore from laughing and kissing so much." The thirty-year-old captain, the 12th Regiment's ammunition officer, was bogged down in a happy mass of Parisians swarming over his jeep on the pont de la Concorde. As Vrabel tried to understand the grammar-school English of a polite fifteen-year-old boy, a pretty blonde emerged from the crowd. "Can I help you?" she said.

The laughing captain said she could. He asked her for a date. Only, she said, if her mother standing beside her came along. They exchanged addresses, and, seeing the list of names already filling his address book, Jacqueline Malissinet thought to herself she would never see this laughing captain again. She was wrong. He would come back, and in two years the man with whom she had just exchanged her first phrases of secretarial-school English would become her husband.

* * *

A mile and a half away, on the fourth floor of a rough stone apartment house on the avenue Mozart, another young French girl, a dressing gown wrapped over her shoulders, watched the passing parade of Paris's liberators and wept all the tears in

her frail body. To Antoinette Charbonnier, the half-tracks of
Major Jacques Massu tearing at the pavement below her
window meant "the end of the world," the end of her life with
Captain Hans Werner, the handsome victor of 1940 with
whom she had lived the gayest days of her life, the occupation. With a brusque gesture, she bolted shut her window
blinds.

Sprawled on his bed in the scabrous hotel on the rue Henri-
Rochefort where she had hidden him as a Polish resistant fleeing the Gestapo, Hans Werner listened, too, to the triumphant
arrival of Paris's liberators. He smoked a cigarette and watched
a cluster of flies dance around the bare and lifeless light bulb
hanging over him. Then he, too, heard the sound that meant
"the end of the world," the clatter of Allied tank treads passing
below his window.

•   •   •

Cita Krebben, the pretty Munich secretary, also heard the
tank treads outside the Faubourg Saint-Honoré apartment in
which she'd been detained with the other German women left
in Paris. For her short walk into captivity, the twenty-three-
year-old Cita had proudly put on her most elegant outfit, a
pale-beige shantung suit topped by a chestnut cape. Taken
in charge by the Swedes of Consul Nordling's staff, Cita and
her countrywomen had been led first to the Hotel Bristol.
There, a swift search had emptied their carefully packed suitcases of a storehouse of chocolate, silk, silverware, hotel
linens and even a few pocket revolvers.

Then they had been marched off to this assembly point
through a crowd only slightly less hostile than that which
had swarmed around Choltitz. Of all the gestures of wrath
along her route none had cut Cita more cruelly than one just
a few blocks from this apartment. There, her face distorted by
hatred, a woman spat on the beige suit in which Cita was
being led off to prison camp. She was Cita's dressmaker.

At the sound of the tanks, Cita edged to the window. Over
the blue-uniformed shoulder of a gendarme, she saw five dirty
Shermans pull to a stop at the foot of the rue Jean-Mermoz.
Watching the happy crowds mob around these, her conquerors, Cita thought resignedly that "the war was really
over." As she stared out, the name on one of the tanks caught

her eye. It seemed almost German, and Cita wondered what such a name was doing on a French tank. It was the *Hartmanns Villerkopf.*

A whole neighborhood was swarming over Lieutenant Marcel Christen and the five tanks of his platoon still marked with the gut and gunpowder of their fight for the Hotel Continental. It was a scene being duplicated on hundreds of Paris streetcorners this liberation afternoon. There was Antoine, the shoemaker, Leclerc, the butcher, Fillon, a jeweler from the rue Rabelais, Paul Andréota, a young writer, and his American wife, Gloria. There was Robert, the policeman, and the elderly Mme. Chassaigne-Goyon whose late husband had left his name on the square just ahead of Christen's tanks.

There was Thérèse, the deaf concierge from 19 rue Jean-Mermoz, and her fortune-telling rival from across the street at number 20, who faithfully, each New Year's Day for the past four years, had predicted the Liberation for "next spring." There was Canon Jean Muller, whose bells at Saint-Philippe du Roule had not rung the night before, and 13-year-old Dominique de Serville, still angry because they hadn't. And, in front of the bakery of Daloyau, there was Nelly Chabrier, the dark-haired legal secretary, in the rose dress her mother had given her for Liberation Day.

Nelly Chabrier, like Cita Krebben, was attracted to the *Hartmanns Villerkopf.* In mute admiration, she stared at the tall, dark and dirty young officer commanding the tank. Unable to pass through the crowd of her neighbors surrounding him, Nelly scrawled a note for the young officer.

"You are," she wrote, "the kind of a Frenchman we need to know and see. If you pass through Paris again one day, you will be welcome at 20 rue Jean-Mermoz, Élysées 09-82." With a desperate gesture, she passed the note over the heads of the crowd to the young lieutenant. Fifteen months later, Canon Jean Muller, now observing her act, would marry Nelly Chabrier and Lieutenant Marcel Christen in the church of Saint-Philippe du Roule, just a few yards down the street from the spot where, on this Liberation Day, a tank named *Hartmanns Villerkopf* had paused briefly on its journey to the Rhine.

9

ELSEWHERE THE FIGHT WENT ON. From their strongpoints, the Germans, still unaware of Choltitz's surrender, continued to throw up a bitter opposition to the 2nd Armored. As each hour passed, they took a growing toll of these young soldiers who had ridden into Paris in triumph a few hours before, and of the FFI fighting beside them.

From an attic window in the Ministry of Health, a spectator watched the fighting around the place de l'Étoile and the Hotel Majestic. Norman Lewis, the American civilian who had set out on crutches to deliver the Stars and Stripes to this building, had come up to the top floor to get a better look at the fighting. Just after he arrived, firing broke out all across the square. In the first outburst, the doughboy of 1917 paid a high price for his desire to watch again the sight of battle. Half a dozen bullets tore through the thin wall before him, killing him instantly.

• • •

Pfc. Léandre Médori, the Corsican peasant who had thought Paris was so big, thought the plane tree behind which he was hiding in front of the Quai d'Orsay was the smallest tree he had ever seen. With a deadly accurate fire, the Quai's German defenders kept Médori and his company nailed to what little cover they could find. Next to Médori, his back pressed against his, was Pfc. Jean Ferracci, the boy who had passed a dozen notes for his sister to the crowd on his way into town. Each time they moved, the pair could hear the German rifle fire tearing off the bark of the tree sheltering them.

Inside the Quai d'Orsay, Willi Werner heard a Luftwaffe major announce he had refused to surrender. He was sure, he said, he had "spoken for them all." He had not spoken for Willi. Groaning at the major's "stupidity," Werner slid off to get drunk in the cellar and "wait for the end of the war in peace."

In front of the building, another 2nd Armored soldier set out on a little war of his own. With his Colt in his hand, his red Spahi garrison cap jauntily perched on his head, Corporal Serge Geoffroy set out to find himself some Germans.

He found his first timidly waving a white handkerchief on the pont de la Concorde. Geoffroy agreed to follow him to take the surrender of thirty of his mates hidden behind a garden wall on the rue de Bourgogne. Before the stupefied eyes of a concierge huddled in a nearby doorway, the Frenchman and the German stopped halfway down the garden wall. The Frenchman bent over, cupped his hands together, and boosted the German to the top. Then the German reached down and pulled Geoffroy up after him. Leaping down into the little garden, the German led Geoffroy to a set of glass doors opening onto a salon. Inside was a bar and thirty Germans. Twenty-nine of them raised their hands. The thirtieth walked up to Geoffroy, a glass in one hand, a bottle of dry vermouth in the other, and offered him a drink.

*   *   *

On the first floor of the École Militaire, Sergeant Bernhard Blache watched the attack on his strongpoint. He was sprawled on a mattress in front of a window. Beside him, groaning softly, his arm torn off by one of their shells, was a comrade of this, his last day of the war, a baker from Munich. Looming up before him on the greensward of the Champ-de-Mars, he saw a flood of Shermans. Blache started to count them. When he got to seventeen, he gave up. The blacklash of one of their shells exploding nearby tore off his helmet, and suddenly, for this twenty-four-year-old Berliner who had entered Paris with the first troops of the Wehrmacht in June, 1940, "the war had become hell."

Behind the École Militaire, in the Postal, Telegraph and Telephone Ministry from which he had heard the bells of Paris the night before, Corporal Alfred Hollesch decided with the men around him it was time to give up. Hollesch found an original way to do it. He smashed a fire-alarm box in the cellar of the building and authoritatively announced to the fireman whose voice came squawking over it that the PTT was ready to surrender.

In front of the building, Captain Georges Gaudet, commander of the 4th Squadron of the 12th Cuirassiers, nicknamed "The White Elephants," decided it was time to end the fighting. Backing up his Sherman *Verdun*, Gaudet set it in line with the door. Then at full speed he slammed it straight at the silent mouth of the 88. From his window, Bernhard Blache watched Gaudet's charge and the shower of debris as the *Verdun* bolted over the barricade. Blache had had enough. He broke his Mauser in half and ran into the basement.

A few minutes later, Blache and a dozen fellow Germans, hands over their heads, were driven to a small room. There an enormous soldier with a machine gun, crying "*Hitler kaput!*" drove them one by one through a window to the sidewalk just below. Blache heard firing outside. He whitened with fear as he waited his turn.

Pushed toward the window, Blache saw below him the bodies of half a dozen of his comrades crumpled on the pavement. The FFI had been gunning down the prisoners one by one. Before his guard could act, Blache spun to his left and ran out of the room. In the corridor outside he fell gratefully into the hands of a group of 2nd Armored men.

10

As, LITTLE BY LITTLE, the sound of gunfire slackened in these streets spilling over with sunshine and joy, the occupiers of Paris began a last, sorry parade through the city they had ruled for four years. At the sight of their first sweaty and haggard files, the people of Paris exploded with all the hatred pent up during their long, bitter months of occupation. They beat and pummeled, cursed and spat on them, and, on occasion, killed them.

Some, like a Panzer lieutenant at the place de la République, killed themselves rather than face the vengeful crowd. Some found easier ways to escape. Private Georg Kilber put on civilian clothes and slipped into the crowd to acclaim the liberators along with the rest of Paris. Captain von Zigesar-Beines, who had already spent two days in captivity at the Grand Palais, put on pajamas and persuaded a friend to commit him to the American hospital in Neuilly "to wait for the Americans in peace."

But for most, there was no escaping the harsh and humiliating experience to which their commanding general had been exposed earlier on the rue de Rivoli. MP Sergeant Rudolf Reis, who five days before had been announcing a truce to the city, instinctively thought of the carts of the French Revolution as a 2nd Armored Division truck hauled him through a jeering, menacing mob to the Prefecture of Police.

For Sergeant Werner Nix, Choltitz's reluctant parader, fate reserved a special irony. It was another parade through the place de l'Opéra less defiant than the first. Hands over his head, Nix was clubbed and pummeled all the way from the rue de Rivoli to the white marble staircase of the Opéra.

On the place du Châtelet, Lance Corporal Paul Seidel saw a sight that seemed to him even more painful than his own ordeal. His captors stopped him to make sure he would not miss it. It was a line of twenty-odd girls, their heads shaved, naked to the waist, the swastika painted onto their breasts. Around each one's neck was a sign reading: I WHORED WITH LES BOCHES.

Even the wounded were not always spared. In the ambulance carrying him to the Saint-Antoine hospital, Jacques d'Étienne, the gunner of the *Laffaux*, woke up to find a wounded German lying unconscious beside him. With his one free hand, d'Étienne reached over and strangled him. Then he ripped the German's Iron Cross from his tunic and stuffed it into his pocket. A few moments later, that trophy almost cost him his own life. In the hospital's emergency room, a nurse hung it to his blanket. An overworked surgeon, determined to operate on his own countrymen first, passed along the line of stretchers, ticking off "boche, boche, boche" before each German patient. Seeing d'Étienne's Iron Cross, he said "boche" and passed on. The Frenchman, sliding into unconsciousness, struggled to one elbow at his words. "Me—boche?" he screamed. "Are you nuts?"

But of the thousands of Germans taken prisoner this sunny day, the sorriest lot of all were the officers of the Gross Paris general staff. For those men who symbolized the heart of the Nazi tyranny that had oppressed them for four years, the people of Paris reserved a particular violence. All along their path the crowd jeered, spat at them, struggled to leap past the screen of FFI guards to rip at their uniforms, club them, kick their shins.

In the middle of the long column, an overcoat tossed over his shoulders, Count Dankvart von Arnim shuddered as he looked at the crowd and thought of the few lines he had read the night before of the Massacre of Saint Bartholomew. Arnim was sure he was going to die. Vividly, lucidly, he told himself, "I'm going to have to pay for all our crimes here." To clear his mind, the young aristocrat forced himself to think of something agreeable. In the midst of this screaming mob that had just ripped his little sack from his hands, Arnim thought of the sprawling acres of his family estate in Brandenburg where, as a boy, he had hunted wild boar and deer.

His dream was split apart by the sight of a screaming man in a blue beret breaking into their ranks. For a second, the Frenchman stood before Arnim, screaming and waving his pistol. Then he pointed it at the German head nearest him and fired. It was the head of Captain Otto Kayser, the literature professor from Cologne who the day before had shown him Rol's poster bearing the phrase "à chacun son boche." White and sickened, Arnim looked down at the beseeching eyes of his dying friend. He paused and an FFI, with a jab of his rifle, told him to move on. Gingerly, Arnim stepped over Kayser's body. "My turn is next," he thought.

11

SILENT AND UNSMILING, CHARLES de Gaulle sped toward his rendezvous with history in an open black Hotchkiss. As the last miles separating him from the capital of France flashed past his car, de Gaulle felt himself "overwhelmed by emotion and a sense of serenity." He was coming home over almost the same roads he had followed out of

Paris in the chaos and collapse of June 10, 1940. He was entering Paris while fighting still raged in the city—without the knowledge or consent of his Allies, in a French car with a French driver—to assist at the climax of a liberation which had been, as he had desired, largely a French operation.

It was just before 4:30 when his little procession of three cars—headed by an armored car of the 2nd Armored—drew toward the porte d'Orléans "black" with "an exultant tide" of people. His exile was over. He had left France as an obscure brigadier general in a beaten army; he was home a hero.

At the other end of the avenue d'Orléans leading out of the square by which he entered the city, under the state-rimmed façade of the Hôtel de Ville, the leaders of Paris's insurrection waited to put their official stamp on his triumphant entry into the city. They would wait a good moment yet. De Gaulle's procession swung left away from the Hôtel de Ville toward another destination, the headquarters of the 2nd Armored Division at the Gare Montparnasse.

As he walked into the station to the cheers of the horde outside, de Gaulle met a familiar figure. It was his son Philippe, off with a German major to force the surrender of the Chamber of Deputies.

Leclerc was waiting for the general on Track 21. He handed the general a copy of Choltitz's surrender. As he read its first lines, de Gaulle started, disagreeably surprised. Rol's name, he coldly pointed out to Leclerc, had no business on that document. Rol, as his subordinate, had no reason to sign. Above all, de Gaulle saw in the gesture a move by his Communist rivals to appropriate for themselves the credit for Paris's deliverance. It was not a title he envisaged for them.[*]

The inclusion of Rol's signature on the surrender document stoked a cold anger already rising in de Gaulle. Its source was a proclamation published earlier in the day by the Conseil National de la Résistance, hailing the liberation of Paris. Not once did that document mention de Gaulle or his government. Moreover, in it the CNR assumed the right to speak in "the name of the French nation." That was hardly among the rights

[*] In one respect, however, Leclerc had faithfully executed de Gaulle's order. Leclerc had accepted the surrender not in the name of the Allied Command on which he depended, but in the name of the Provisional Government of the French Republic. It was the only major surrender of the post-D-Day Command in which the Allied principle was ignored.

de Gaulle was ready to accord this committee he had in his own mind consigned to oblivion. To de Gaulle, the proclamation read like a blunt challenge to his authority. He was ready to answer it bluntly.

Outside, he shook hands with the officers of Leclerc's staff. When he came to Rol, red-eyed, weary, a strange figure in his Spanish Civil War uniform, de Gaulle paused and cast an appraising eye at the young Breton. Almost as an afterthought, it seemed to Rol, he took his hand and shook it. Then, as his aide would later note, de Gaulle stepped out of the station through a doorway marked BAGAGES—ARRIVÉE, to return to the same building from which he had left Paris on the chaotic evening of June 10, 1940, the Ministry of War.

Protected by a lone armored car, his brief convoy set out through the streets of the Left Bank, almost past the house in which he had played as a boy. Passing the rue Eblé just above Les Invalides, the convoy came under fire. While his escort returned it, de Gaulle left his car to watch. Calmly puffing a cigarette, he stood beside the car, six feet four inches of defiant challenge to the marksmanship of the Wehrmacht. Two shots clanked into its trunk. He ignored it. To Geoffroy de Courcel, who had ridden out of Paris with him in 1940, de Gaulle remarked in his mocking tone, "Eh bien, de Courcel, at least we're coming back to better conditions than those in which we left."

At the Ministry his advance party barely had time to gather up a few offensive busts of Marshal Pétain before his car drew up at its gate. With a slow and formal pace, he strode up the stairs and glanced for a nostalgic instant at the office he had occupied four years before. Then he entered the Minister's office. Not a table, not a rug, not a drapery had been moved. The same usher who had bidden him farewell that June evening four years earlier now welcomed him back. Even the names neatly written on the call buttons of the Minister's antique telephone were those he had seen in 1940. "Gigantic events had shaken the universe. Our army had been annihilated. France had almost perished" in the days since, he thought. But, as de Gaulle noted with irony, in the Ministry that had sent an unprepared and untrained army off to the debacle of 1940, "nothing had changed."

12

ARMED WITH A WRITTEN order from Choltitz,
the officers of his staff set off to force the surrender of the
strongpoints still resisting in the city. The elegant Colonel Jay
was assigned a fortress in the quarter of Paris with which he
was least familiar—the place de la République. Striving to
maintain his dignity in the thickening stream of spittle sailing
into his jeep, Jay could find one consolation in his ordeal. The
mob's aim left much to be desired. His escort, a Parisian captain, seemed to be getting about as much of the saliva as he
was. Jay was guiding them. As the Frenchman had coldly explained to him, he had been away a long time.

In front of the Chamber of Deputies an American photographer, Pfc. Phil Drell of Chicago, joined Lieutenant Philippe
de Gaulle as the Frenchman negotiated the building's surrender with an emissary sent out by its 500-man garrison.
In the milling crowd, de Gaulle's interpreter got lost and the
sweat-stained American volunteered to replace him. Drell
addressed the splendidly uniformed German in the only
foreign language he could speak that the German could understand. It was Yiddish.

One by one, the strongpoints fell, and the heavy stutter of
gunfire faded from the streets of Paris for the first time in almost a week. In the cool darkness of the Swedish Consulate
at the rue d'Anjou, an exhausted man slumped in an easy
chair. Slowly, aching with fatigue, "Bobby" Bender got up,
went to his coat tossed on the Consulate's coat rack and pulled
out his revolver. Then, for the second time in less than twenty-
four hours, he offered his surrender to Lorrain Cruse. This time
Chaban's young adjutant accepted it.

By the end of the day one strongpoint still resisted, the one
that had opened fire first, the now charred and shell-pocked
Palais du Luxembourg. Stiffened by SS troops, its defenders
had refused to yield an inch of ground all day. To force its
garrison to end its resistance, Choltitz sent his chief of staff

Colonel Friedrich von Unger to the palace. With them went
Colonel Jean Crépin, the 2nd Armored Division's artillery
commander. To hide Unger from the mob, Crépin stuffed
the austere colonel onto the floor of his half-track.

Inside, Crépin stared aghast at the confusion and disorder
in the parquet corridors of Marie de Médicis's palace. Helmets,
cartridges, overturned ammunition boxes littered the floors.
Its draperies and murals were shredded and torn. The dead
and dying rolled together on its Persian carpets. The palace's
SS commander, the Standartenführer, his monocle in his eye,
his Iron Cross proudly pinned to his chest, listened to Unger
and Crépin's terse command. Beside him a band of young
SS officers, furious and adamant, threatened to kill him,
Unger and Crépin if he ordered a surrender.

Angry and impatient, Crépin saw their efforts falling apart.
He told the commander and the SS around him they had one
hour to surrender. If they refused to do so, he said, they
"would not be treated as prisoners of war." For a few seconds
the Germans argued. Then the Standartenführer, "red as a
beet," roared to the SS that "in the name of the Führer" he
was ordering the surrender. Paling, they ripped off their decorations and, shouting "Heil Hitler," stamped out.

During the last hour left them, the SS fired off their ammunition. As they did, the rest of the garrison assembled in the
palace's debris-spattered courtyard. Their prisoners drifted up
with them. Looking with delight at the mass before him, Paul
Pardou, the little hijacker, saw the red-necked form of his
mess-sergeant captor, Franz. Franz caught his eye and
beckoned to him, reaching into his pocket. Summing up his
last reserves of the French language, the man who had so
often mumbled to him "Today you make kitchen clean, tomorrow you shot" handed an envelope to Pardou. "It's for my
wife," he hissed.

Like a miner coming out of a cave after days underground,
François Dalby, the electrician, came up from his control
room to watch the sight. Dalby was going to stay behind. For
the next forty-eight hours he would remain in the Senate,
supervising the demining of this building saved largely
through his own clever sabotage.

At precisely 7:35, exactly one hour after Crépin's ultimatum, the gates of the great court swung open. His monocle
defiantly clamped in his eye, his Iron Cross on his chest, a

huge white flag between his hands, the palace's SS commander stepped out to surrender the last German strongpoint. Formally and definitively, Paris was free.

Now the last lines of German prisoners began to shuffle off before the exultant crowd. Among the 700 men and ten tanks taken in the Luxembourg, Eugen Hommens, whose pistol had been stolen at a Marneside swimming pool two weeks earlier, looked with sullen indifference at the victors. As he did, he started. Hanging from a tank of the 2nd Armored, her arms garlanded around a French soldier, was Annick, the mistress for whom he had refused to desert.

No German was stung more deeply by the fickleness of the female than the cook marching down the avenue Victor-Hugo beside Lieutenant Johannes Schmiegel. Over and over again, with a kind of dumb animal assurance, the cook told Schmiegel that if his girl friend Jeannette could see him, "she'd do something to get me out of this." In front of the church of Saint-Honoré-d'Eylau on the avenue Raymond-Poincaré, she did see him. She ran up to the frightened cook and spat on him.

●　●　●

Now, in the first soft strokes of twilight, the only angry sound left was the occasional snap of sniper fire. The occupiers' guns had been stilled, but not without their price. Almost 20,000 Germans had been taken prisoner in the past forty-eight hours; 3,200 had been killed and wounded. On this day alone, the 2nd Armored Division had lost 42 killed and 77 wounded. Of civilians, 127 had been killed and 714 wounded. Each of those figures produced its island of sorrow in the waves of happiness sweeping the city.

Behind the Quai d'Orsay, an excited girl rushed up to the men of Captain Charles d'Orgeix's company. It was the little sister of Pfc. Jean Ferracci. One of the flood of notes he had passed to the crowd during his triumphant march into the city had found her in her butchershop in the suburb of Ménilmontant. She had arrived too late. Her brother had been killed behind a plane tree bordering Les Invalides, its trunk torn apart by machine-gun bullets. At the place du Châtelet, an anxious girl summoned by a joyous phone call a few hours earlier moved down the line of black and broken tanks, the survivors of the attack on the Meurice. To each she asked the same question: "Do you know my fiancé Pierre Laigle?" None of those exhausted men in black berets had the courage to tell her Pierre had been killed just two hours earlier.

And on the doorstep of her apartment in the suburb of Choisy, Louise Berth looked in awe at the man in uniform approaching her door. It was her husband. He threw himself into her arms, his body shaking with sobs. The joyful reunion on which the proud René Berth had counted so much would not take place. His son Raymond had been killed by a sniper's bullet near the Dupleix métro station below the Eiffel Tower, on this, the day they were to come home together to surprise Louise Berth for her feast day.

13

FROM THE FOOT OF the pont d'Arcole, spilling down the quais of the Seine, pushing over the rue de Rivoli up to the steps of the city's most popular department store, a dense, black mass of Parisians packed the place de l'Hôtel-de-Ville. Here, in this historic square, where the Third Republic was proclaimed in 1870 and the *Commune* a year later, thousands had waited for hours for an event no less historic: the city's first official glimpse of General de Gaulle, the first chance to hear directly this man who for four years had given voice to the stifled soul of France.

De Gaulle almost did not come.

In his office at the War Ministry, de Gaulle had just met for the first time the man who had been his political representative in Paris, Alexandre Parodi. To the slim and soft-spoken Parodi, the meeting was a jarring experience. De Gaulle indicated in his forthright manner the displeasure he felt over the CNR's proclamation of the evening before, a proclamation which Parodi had unhappily made the mistake of signing.

But above all, Parodi was stunned by de Gaulle's view of the Paris situation. It seemed to Parodi that de Gaulle expected nothing less than "a direct, Communist-led challenge to his authority" in Paris. The CNR and the organs like it were, in de Gaulle's eyes, little more than the unwilling tools of the party.

De Gaulle informed Parodi coldly that he had no intention of being "received" by the CNR or the CPL. There was no reason why, in his eyes, he should pay a visit to a building that was a symbol of municipal authority. He was, he reminded Parodi, the head of the French government. He would receive the CNR and the CPL when he was ready to. And he would receive them in a government building.

Distressed by the bitterness and shock de Gaulle's failure to appear would cause, Parodi urged the general to reconsider. De Gaulle was adamant. He would not go. Finally Parodi, sensing that perhaps someone who knew de Gaulle well might succeed where he had failed, sent for reinforcements. He called for Charles Luizet, the Prefect of Police.

After a long discussion, Luizet finally persuaded de Gaulle to change his mind by stressing the bad impression de Gaulle's refusal to go would have on the masses waiting to see him. But first, de Gaulle announced two things. He would visit the Prefecture of Police, a symbol of the Gaullist Resistance and the authority of state, before he went to the Hôtel de Ville. And before he would leave, he issued the orders for his own reception, the only reception he considered valid, a symbolic communion between himself and the masses. The next day, he announced he would make his "official entry." He would parade down the Champs-Élysées from the Tomb of the Unknown Soldier to the Cathedral of Notre-Dame, symbols of the traditions and continuity of the France he meant to represent. It would be his answer to the pretensions of the CNR, a blunt demonstration to his foes, he hoped, of where the masses' support lay. And it would be a party to which the CNR was not invited. Then he dourly announced to those around him, "All right, if we must go, let's go!"

● ● ●

Inside the Hôtel de Ville, a rising sense of irritation and frustration seeped through the leaders of the insurrection. De Gaulle's failure to show up had at first surprised them, then irked them. Now they were angry. Stalking through the office of the President of the Municipal Council, Georges Bidault, pale and upset, mumbled, "No one has ever kept me waiting like this before." De Gaulle's decision to visit the Prefecture, "the house of the cops," before the Hôtel de Ville, "the house of the people," had provoked, as perhaps de Gaulle had expected it would, a high state of indignation among the adherents of the CNR. Fernand Moulier, a newsman who had slipped into the city a week ahead of the Allies, heard one of its members mumble, "Those s.o.b.s have been arresting us for four years and now de Gaulle goes and pays tribute to them."

If de Gaulle would not come to the Hôtel de Ville, Bidault told the men around him, the CNR "would hold a liberation ceremony without him." Gesturing to the crowds outside, Bidault boasted, "This is where the people of Paris are, not at the *maison des flics.*"

In fact, de Gaulle's appraisal of the ambitions of most of the members of the political Resistance milling around the Hôtel de Ville was largely accurate. For most of its members, the insurrection had been political in character. It was indeed their aspiration to formally "present" de Gaulle to the people of Paris, a gesture which would subtly assign the CNR a kind of role as his sponsor. They were prepared to invite him to "assist" at their meetings. They expected an important "national palace" would be put at their disposition. Most important, they had drafted a solemn "proclamation of the Republic" which they wanted de Gaulle to read to the crowd, a gesture in keeping with the hallowed tradition of this square. Bidault had it in his pocket. It was a clever political gesture which would, officially, mark an end to Vichy. It would also in a much more subtle way mark an end and a beginning for de Gaulle's own government. It would allow the CNR to pretend to the role of sponsors of the new republic with de Gaulle as their executive officer. It was an ambitious and naïve set of dreams, and the first awakening would not be long in coming.

It came, in fact, at the foot of the white marble staircase of the Hôtel de Ville where, tall and imposing, Charles de Gaulle now moved through the cheers of the crowd toward the waiting members of the CNR.

In his simple khaki uniform, wearing only the Cross of Lorraine and the red-and-blue badge of fighting France, de Gaulle strode past the shirt-sleeved honor guard before him to the waiting Georges Bidault. Brusquely, he rushed through Bidault's introductions.

In the office of the President of the Municipal Council, the two exchanged brief addresses. Bidault was moving and emotional. De Gaulle, no less moving, burst forth into his own stately eloquence.

"Why should we hide our emotions?" he asked. "We're living minutes which transcend each of our individual lives, our poor lives."

Then he told the men around him, "The enemy is shaken, but he is not beaten . . . more than ever our national unity is a necessity. . . . War, unity, *grandeur*—that is my program."

As he finished, Bidault drew his proclamation from his pocket. "General," he said, "would you step to the balcony and solemnly proclaim the Republic before the people here assembled?"

De Gaulle looked down at the little man before him. "No," he said. "The Republic has never ceased to exist."

Then he stepped to the window. Below him, from the Seine to the rue de Rivoli and all the streets flowing into it, the place de l'Hôtel-de-Ville was a black, throbbing mass of people. As he appeared, the crowd came alive. Wave after wave of cheering broke over him. Then, in rhythmic chants, the crowd began to yell "De *Gaulle*, de *Gaulle*, de *Gaulle*." Behind him his aide, Captain Claude Guy, noting that the balcony railing was no higher than de Gaulle's thighs, hooked his hand into the general's Sam Browne belt. If a sniper shot de Gaulle, Guy reasoned, he might topple to the pavement below. Over his shoulder, in a voice for all the room to hear, de Gaulle said, "Would you be kind enough to let me the hell alone?" Guy lightened the pressure on de Gaulle's belt but did not let go. The general turned and addressed the crowd.

Finally, his speech to the crowd over, de Gaulle turned to leave. He looked at Guy and winked. "Thanks," he said.

With a few hasty handshakes, de Gaulle left. Not once had he mentioned the CNR or the Resistance. There had been no victory toast. The champagne waiting for him still sat cooling in the next room. He had avoided formally meeting the CNR. Bidault's proclamation, unread, rested in the little resistant's pocket.

As de Gaulle left, the stunned and bitter members of the CNR heard the roar of the crowd outside rattle the few windows still intact in the Hôtel de Ville. Beside him, Pierre Meunier, one of the CNR's two Communist secretaries, heard a friend mumble angrily, "It's simple. We've been had."

● ● ●

His little triumph at the Hôtel de Ville was not the only victory de Gaulle was to have this day. In a half-furnished office at Les Invalides, with the sound of gunfire still echoing outside, two men initialed a lengthy 37-page document. In the jubilation of the Liberation, their action went almost unnoticed by the world. Yet the same happy circumstance that had placed the liberation of Paris on Saint Louis's feast day had selected this day for another event, the signing of the Franco-American Civil Affairs Agreement. It had been urged by Eisenhower before D Day, agreed to in principle in Washington by de Gaulle and F.D.R. in July, haggled over weeks thereafter, its final signing pushed back half a dozen times.

Finally, on this Liberation Day, Brigadier General Julius Holmes had flown out of SHAEF in Eisenhower's L-5 and landed in a wheat field near Paris to bring the document to General Pierre Koenig for signing. Even at this last minute, this long-delayed first official United States recognition of de Gaulle's authority in France had its barbs. Eisenhower was instructed by Washington to announce he was "authorized to make these agreements on the understanding that it is the intention of the French authorities to afford the French people an opportunity to select a government of their choice." It was not a statement chosen to improve relations with de Gaulle. And unlike the British, who signed the agreement on the Foreign Ministers' level, the United States insisted on its being signed between military men. F.D.R. wished to make sure that the document was not confused with formal recognition of the French government.

Looking at the situation in the city as he signed, professional diplomat Holmes reflected on the gap between this document and reality. No one in Washington, he knew, had planned to see de Gaulle's government installed and functioning in Paris for some time. Yet here, he realized, was de Gaulle, already digging in, and "nothing short of force was going to budge him out." The State Department, he mused, was already going to have to start agonizing over changes in this document on which the ink literally was not yet dry.

De Gaulle, Holmes thought, "never had had any intention of being anyplace else tonight but where he is right now—in Paris." Smiling ironically to himself, the American diplomat mused, in a thought not unlike that of the resistant on the steps of the Hôtel de Ville, that "once again, we've been politely had by de Gaulle."

•   •   •

In the Kriegsmarine on the place de la Concorde, one German had escaped capture. Lieutenant Commander Harry Leithold knew the corridors of Gabriel's palace intimately. After watching the fighting in the place de la Concorde, Leithold had ducked into this small room on the corner of the third floor of the building to hide until nightfall. Outside, Leithold heard the crowd in the square roaring. Peering out, he saw a black open car coming into the square from the rue de Rivoli. Leithold reached down and drew up his MP submachine gun. Cautiously he leaned it on the window ledge and peered down the gunsight. "What foolish chances these Frenchmen take," Leithold thought. There, barely 200 yards away, in the back seat of the open car, Leithold saw the kepi of a French general. He fixed the man in his sight and prepared to fire. Shooting a French general, Leithold thought, would be a distinguished way to end his war. As he watched and waited, the crowds waving at the passing car broke and rushed out to it. Another thought struck Leithold. If he fired, that crowd was going to hunt him down and beat him to death. Leithold paused. Then he reluctantly lowered his submachine gun away from the window ledge. Whoever that general was, Leithold decided, his life was not worth his own. The black car slipped under his window ledge and disappeared across the place de la Concorde.

Two years later, in a prisoner-of-war camp, the naval officer learned from a newspaper photograph the identity of the general he had held in his gunsight for those fleeting seconds on an August evening. It was Charles de Gaulle.

14

Dusk dropped softly over a free Paris. Like a body spent by love, the city drifted into a kind of ecstatic numbness, the natural hangover of the day's emotional outburst. It was a moment of tenderness after a storm of joy.

Sergeant Armand Sorriero of Philadelphia, bodyguard of the 12th Regiment's commander, tiptoed into Notre-Dame, his carbine flung over his shoulder. Inside, the Philadelphian knelt in the semidarkness and prayed for a moment until he suddenly thought that he "did not belong in the house of God with a weapon to kill." As he hurried away, half ashamed, a pair of nuns beckoned Sorriero to a three-legged milking stool. Chirping like happy sparrows, they washed the grime from his face with a porcelain potful of warm water. Sorriero was moved; he thought it must "be the Lord's way of thanking me for going to church."

Just off the Champs-Élysées, a priest walked up to Pfc. George McIntyre. He told McIntyre that one of his parishioners, an old woman dying of cancer, wanted to see an American soldier as proof that the Allies had arrived and that at least she could die in a free Paris.

The priest led McIntyre through a maze of side streets to an ordinary apartment house. There on the third floor, in a spare two-room apartment, was the woman. Her room, McIntyre recalled later, was "just big enough to contain a double bed, two high-backed wooden chairs, a small table with a statue of Saint Anne, a vase of wilted flowers and a candlestick." The woman, gaunt, "with a white lace bed jacket and a cap on her head," asked McIntyre, through the English-speaking priest, "How soon will you reach Berlin?"

"Soon," answered McIntyre.

Despite the difficulty with which each sentence passed her lips, the old woman insisted on talking. She asked McIntyre about the invasion, the damage in Normandy, whether "the

346

people were hospitable to you," and finally, with the fervor of the Marne, "How many boches did you kill?"

Behind him, two of her neighbors slipped in with a bottle of cognac. They drank a toast. "Vive l'Amérique," whispered the old woman.

"Vive la France," McIntyre answered. Then the balding GI left behind the only things he had in his pockets: two Hershey bars and a cake of Ivory soap. From the table beside her, the woman gave him a crucifix "to protect you through the rest of the war." He bent over and kissed both her thin cheeks. He promised he would come back the next day. When he did, she would be dead.

Count Jean de Vogüé had a gesture to accomplish this evening too. With the mustache that had carried him through his long months in hiding shaved off and a bouquet wrapped in his hand, this distinguished aristocrat and Resistance leader walked up to the massive town house at 54 quai d'Orsay.

A maid answered the door. She stared at him and then, clapping her hands over her face, screamed, "Monsieur Jean has come home!" De Vogüé stepped into his mother's mansion, and on to the sitting room where his awed and unbelieving mother staggered from her chair. Gently, de Vogüé handed his bouquet to this woman from whom, as a resistant, he had hidden on a street corner in the rain.

"When did you get back from London?" she asked.

"I haven't been in London, Mother," de Vogüé said. "I was a leader of the Resistance."

She drew back, stunned. "Jean," she asked, "how could you have done that—associate with all those ruffians and Communists?" She sank back into her armchair in dismay.

• • •

A twenty-nine-year-old former Georgia farmboy named Leon Cole stared in wonder at the sight. There, spread at his feet below the balcony of this fifth-floor Montmartre apartment, were all the sights he had read and dreamed of for years, their contours barely visible now in the sinking dusk: the Eiffel Tower, the twin towers of Notre-Dame, the lazy loops of the Seine. His host brought him a glass of cognac, and, side by side—the elderly French couple who had invited him for a drink and the gangling GI with a

carbine hitched over his shoulder—watched the darkness
settle over Paris.

Suddenly, as they watched, the whole magnificent sight
spread before them burst into a blaze of light: the lights
of Paris shining defiantly forth for the first time since
September 3, 1939. In one brief gesture of celebration, its
electricians had just flooded the city with power.

Cole gulped at the beauty of that sight. The woman beside him gasped. Slowly, half in a trance, she lifted her
glass out across her iron balcony toward the city below.

"À la Ville Lumière," she said in a whisper. Cole looked
down at her, and, peering through the darkness, he realized
she was crying. Then the farmboy from Georgia realized
something else. He was crying too.

15

OF ALL THE JOBS he had held in his life, the
one ahead, thought Major Robert J. Levy, was going to be
the most difficult. The New York stockbroker had just been
assigned to Charles de Gaulle as his American liaison officer.
After three days of searching, he had finally caught up with
de Gaulle in Paris on this Liberation night. He waited now in
his outer office to be presented to the general. From the faces
of the men streaming out of the great man's office, it was
apparent to Levy that the general was in a high state of ill
humor. He could understand why. The Ministry of War headquarters, occupied just three hours earlier, was bedlam. The
lights did not work. The telephones worked only now and
then, and when they did, only for local calls. No one seemed
to know where anything was.

Finally Captain Guy called Levy into de Gaulle's office.
The general rose behind his plain, flat desk and peered at the
five-foot eight-inch Levy.

"Eh bien, Levy," he said, "I hope you speak French. I
speak English but I don't intend to."

The formalities that followed were brief. When they were

finished, de Gaulle thrust out his hand in an angry gesture at the noise, the faltering lights and the confusion around him.

"How," he thundered at Levy, "can I govern France in chaos like this?"

Without waiting for a reply, he listed for Levy the three items he considered essential for the effective government of France that night: cigarettes, C rations and Coleman lanterns.

Levy saluted and, convinced of the urgency of his mission, began to ransack the streets of Paris for these precious items de Gaulle deemed indispensable that night to the orderly administration of France.

The cigarettes—Players—he got from a British colleague, the C rations from a truck of the 4th Division near the Hotel de Crillon. The lanterns were more difficult. He found them in a quartermaster convoy pulled off the road outside the city. The GI on guard duty at first refused to surrender any of his cargo. Finally Levy convinced the GI to turn his back while he performed a "moonlight requisition" for the lanterns that would illuminate Charles de Gaulle's first night in Paris.

At about the time Levy rushed away from the Ministry of War, another figure glided down the staircase of a building only a few blocks away on the rue de Grenelle. Larry Lesueur of CBS had just made, as he had promised himself he would, the first broadcast out of Paris. He had done it by using the French radio's transmitters to get his broadcast out of the capital. He was the only radio correspondent in the city to think of it.

In a tiny bar in Pigalle, next to the Bal Tabarin, Lesueur's colleague Charles Collingwood had finally found refuge among the prostitutes and petty gangsters of Montmartre. They seemed to be the only people in Paris that evening who did not know his name. All day long Collingwood had winced each time he had uttered it and reaped in return a storm of abuse for his unfortunately premature announcement of Paris's liberation.

• • •

On this first festive night of freedom, Paris sat down to a gay, if not always copious, victory banquet. All across the city, the men of the 2nd French Armored Division and the 4th U.S. Infantry Division reached into their sacks to share with the city's population whatever they could find. Sometimes it was a product that was, for Paris, only a memory. In the place de la Bastille, a little girl asked a GI "for another red ball" like the one he had just given her. It was an orange. She had never seen one before. The Parisians shared with their liberators the little they had been able to save themselves or pillage from German stocks. In some areas, like the rue de la Huchette where a huge black-market cache had been discovered, there was butter, tinned meat and sugar. In other areas, it was just another plate of rutabagas, garnished with a bottle of long-hidden wine. But whatever it was, it was served with verve and spirit. Hundreds of GIs learned this night that, passed through a French kitchen, even a can of C rations could become appetizing.

In the Ministry of War, a cook hastily pressed into duty prepared General de Gaulle's first meal in the capital. The cook, too, had just arrived in Paris—from Vichy. He had been one of the cooks of Marshal Pétain.

In the dining room of the Hotel Meurice, just feet from the spot where Dietrich von Choltitz had sat down to his last meal a few hours earlier, his captor, Lieutenant Henri Karcher, installed himself in front of a sumptuous feast. It was his reward from the manager for "not having caused too much damage" while liberating his hotel.

Around the corner in the Ritz, another diner screamed in outrage. The waiter had just handed Ernest Hemingway the bill for his Liberation dinner.

"Millions to defend France," he declared, "thousands to honor your nation—but not one sou in tribute to Vichy." At the bottom of the check, the waiter had automatically included in the price of the meal the Vichy sales tax.

At the Prefecture of Police, Charles Luizet gently guided his dinner guest to a tiny balcony. There Luizet and Brigadier General Julius Holmes, the man who had signed the Franco-American Civil Affairs Agreement, sipped a brandy together.

There was, Luizet told Holmes, who was a friend of some months' standing, "a terrible danger in Paris now." It was not the Germans or the Vichyites, he declared; "it is the Communists." He added, "I can tell you one thing. Right now, we can't control them." If the Communists made a bold move, the de Gaulle government, he warned, might not be able to stop them. He asked Holmes to get arms for the police and gendarmes. Forty-eight hours later, a convoy drove discreetly up to the Prefecture. Inside were 8,000 carbines, submachine guns, ammunition and a few bazookas for good measure.

• • •

Few of the men of the 2nd Armored or the 4th Division had such serious thoughts on their minds that night. Most were too busy enjoying what Pfc. John Holden of Maysville, North Carolina, remembered as "the greatest night the world has ever known." Holden spent it in "a glorious world of wine, women and song." Technician David McCreadil of the 12th's Antitank Company went "to a café where everything was free, the French were wild with joy, the women danced on the piano tops, we all got high and kept singing the 'Marseillaise' even though we didn't know the words."

From every tank, armored car and jeep of the two divisions, it seemed, came the happy laughs of soldiers and Parisiennes. In hundreds of café's, behind blacked-out doors, they drank, danced, sang, laughed and loved.

Robert Mady, the gunner who had remembered the length of the Champs-Élysées, stopped for the night with his crewmates of the *Simoun* halfway down the avenue. They liberated the Lido. On its deserted dance floor, Mady and his mates received a gift that made them forget their rotten duck: the best champagne in the most famous nightclub in the world.

On the rue de la Huchette, near the 12th Regiment headquarters, an outdoor Bastille Day type of ball was in full swing with the firemen's band for music. An excited middle-aged woman was led up to Sergeant of the Guard Thomas W. Lambero. She wanted to know if all the men had girls to sleep with. Lambero assured her the situation was well in hand.

In the Bois de Vincennes, worried about discipline, the commander of one of the regiment's infantry battalions ordered his men to pitch their pup tents in squad lines and ordered a reveille formation for dawn. When it was staged, he took the measure of his failure. Out of virtually every tent staggered a tired GI—and a sleepy-eyed girl.

Language was no barrier that happy night. Still scanning his army phrase book for something to say to the pretty girl beside him, Pfc. Charlie Haley of "B" Company, 4th Engineers, thought what a stupid institution the army was. "Imagine," he told himself, "saying to this girl, 'Have you any eggs?' "

Technical Sergeant Ken Davis, a tough Pennsylvanian, had memorized one practical phrase: "Vous êtes très jolie." As Davis prepared to put it to use, an excited group of FFI rushed up to his truck looking for a few GIs to help flush out a sniper. Davis went.

On the way back, a truck hit the car in which he was riding, throwing the sergeant unconscious onto the pavement. As he came to, Davis saw a group of faces forming and re-forming over his head. One was female and very pretty. To his chagrin, his carefully rehearsed phrase deserted him. Instead, he kept repeating over and over again to the pretty Parisienne above him another phrase. It was one he and his buddies had used in Normandy to justify the occasional pilfering of a chicken or a duck: "It's a cheap price to pay for liberty."

In the gaiety, the laughter, the happiness of this evening, no one noticed the pickup truck, its canvas flaps snapped shut, rolling quickly down the avenue d'Italie. Inside, a passenger peered through a flap at the carnival outside. He saw a GI lean down and haul a girl up to the turret of his tank. The crowds around them cheered. Sadly, Dietrich von Choltitz closed the flap and thought "a whole era in his life" was ending. Beside him, Colonel Hans Jay remarked to console him, "The war will be over in eight weeks." "No," answered von Choltitz, "in Germany there'll be a madman to shoot at them from behind every tree. You'll see." Then, smoking his first American cigarette, Dietrich von Choltitz leaned back and, lost in a melancholy silence, rode out of the city he had helped to save toward two years and eight months in Allied prison camps.

Outside the city, far from the ring of its celebrations, a lonely GI noted a few lines in a diary. It was Corporal Joe Ganna, the medic who, two days earlier, had complained of the rain in his face, his coffee and his fatigues.

"This should have been written in Paris," he scrawled, "but they decided going through was good enough for us. There were women and children kissing us, men handing us tomatoes and wine. It was a grand day until we met the Germans. Then it was the same old story, firing, more killed and wounded, digging, and to bed in a foxhole." One of Ganna's buddies was among the killed. It was Pfc. "Davey"

Davison. He had been shot in an open field near a pair of old factories. Before Ganna could get back to claim his body, the FFI had buried him in a churchyard cemetery. The little GI would sleep forever on the edge of the city in which he had hoped to find "one night's sleep in a real bed."

*   *   *

For most of the men of the 2nd Armored and the 4th Division lucky enough to survive this fabulous day, the memory of its emotion, its tenderness, its beauty, would remain in the face of a woman. For Technical Sergeant Tom Connolly, it was a beautiful blond girl in a white dress. He first saw her timidly edging her bicycle toward the circle of children clustered around him in the cobbled courtyard of the old château where his battalion had set up its command post. Her name was Simone Pinton and she was twenty-one. Her blond hair hung down to her shoulders, and to the twenty-seven-year-old soldier from Detroit she was the most beautiful girl he had seen since he left the States.

Never would he forget her first words. "May I wash your uniform?" she asked in her hesitant English. "It is very dirty." At those words, Connolly felt "awkward, tongue-tied, very dirty, and very grateful." Just after dark, Simone brought him back his clean uniform, and, arm in arm, the two set out through the neighborhood around them. It seemed to Connolly he "toasted to a million Frenchmen" that night. Everywhere people ran up to them laughing, and crying *"Vive l'amour," "Vive l'Amérique,"* and *"Vive la France."* They offered them wine and flowers and affection. Finally, happy and exhausted, the couple slid away from admiring crowds. Alone, the lanky sergeant from Detroit and the beautiful French girl in her white dress ran up a little wooded hillside. Laughing, they flopped on the grass at the top. Overhead, Connolly could see a forest of stars, and, in the distance, in the heart of Paris, the dark silhouette of the Eiffel Tower poised against the lighter night sky. Simone gently took his head and put it in her lap. She leaned over and kissed him, and her blond hair spilled over his face. Then, in a gesture as old as men and women and arms, she began to softly caress his hair. "Forget *la guerre,*" she murmured quietly. "For tonight, *mon petit* Tom, forget *la guerre.*"

16

[AUGUST 26]

DAZED AND STILL WONDERING, Paris awoke to its first full day of liberty. Stiff, sometimes heavy-headed, still alive with the enthusiasms of the day before, liberator and liberated alike blinked in the warm sunshine flooding Paris this Saturday, August 26.

Lieutenant Bob Woodrum sprawled in the bedroom behind Louis Berty's kitchen. The day before the Nanterre pork butcher had been released from Mt. Valérien prison by his fleeing captors. Woodrum felt a rough stroke on his shoulder. Through the haze of his champagne-inspired sleep he had one instinctive thought: Germans. He sprang up. Before him was a clean-shaven young U.S. Army lieutenant.

"O.K., buddy," he said, "you're back in the army now." The day before, during a brief foray into Paris, Woodrum had made the error of registering at a temporary Army Air Force headquarters at the Hotel Windsor Reynolds.

For many GIs, the most memorable moment of this post-liberation day took place early in the morning at Notre-Dame Cathedral. There, on the side altar of Saint Joseph, in borrowed French vestments, Father Leonard Fries said Mass "for the men of the 12th Regiment we left behind on the road to Paris." Kneeling in the somber sunlight filtering down into the great cathedral, over 300 GIs, their M1s or carbines in one hand, their helmets cupped under the other, were present at the Mass.

Even more moving perhaps was another religious service held in the main synagogue of Paris this same sunny Saturday. There Captain Morris Frank, the Jewish chaplain of the 12th Regiment, a group of Jewish GIs and the sad survivors of four years of oppression and deportation joined together in a memorial Sabbath service. To Rabbi Frank, "the sight of those pale, gaunt faces, the remnants of our decimated people" was an image he would hold forever in his memory. After the service, Frank and the GIs were "hugged, carried aloft, mobbed by crying women . . . who poured out their hearts with stories of children killed before their eyes, husbands and daughters torn from their arms."

As they left, the grateful Jews of Paris gave to these Jewish GIs a souvenir, a gift of gratitude for what was to them not just a liberation but a delivery from a sentence of death. It was almost invariably the same, the yellow cloth Star of David that symbolized the four years of horror from which they had just been delivered.

●   ●   ●

At V Corps headquarters in the suburb of Chilly-Mazarin, a German colonel handed Colonel Arthur Campbell an envelope. "It's the key to General von Choltitz's room in the Meurice Hotel," Hans Jay explained. "He won't need it for a long time."

In Baden-Baden, a shawl thrown over her shoulders, Uberta von Choltitz hurried to the apartment of a close friend, a retired officer who, minutes before, had called her to come "urgently." As she stepped into his apartment, he embraced her. Then he told her what he had heard the night before on the forbidden BBC: Paris had fallen and its commander had been taken prisoner.

Outside the château which had been his battalion's headquarters for one brief night, Sergeant Thomas Connolly strapped his last belongings onto his jeep. Beside him, Simone Pinton watched silently. When he was ready to leave, she pressed a small gold locket into his hands. "I may never see you again," she said simply. "I hope that you will remember last night."

She asked him to come see her if ever he came to Paris. He promised he would. They kissed, and Connolly drove off. In his rear view mirror he saw her standing by her bicycle in her white dress, just before the château gate, until, a distant white speck, she disappeared from sight. For miles down the road, he could still smell her perfume. Then, ahead of him, he heard again the sounds of the war she had helped him to forget for a night. He never came back.

• • •

Above all, this August 26 would belong to Charles de Gaulle. All night the radio had announced his march down the Champs-Élysées. Thousands of banners reading "VIVE DE GAULLE" had been printed on presses kept running until dawn. It was to be de Gaulle's rendezvous with history, the culmination of his four-year crusade, the unofficial plebiscite in which he would read the authority to silence his political rivals.

For his march to Notre-Dame, de Gaulle considered it essential to have the 2nd Armored Division along his route. He needed them for security. But, more important, he wanted them there, massed and imposing, to impress the population with the authority supporting his government. Bypassing the Allied chain of command, de Gaulle gave his own orders to Leclerc to assemble his troops for the parade. As his only concession, he agreed to allow one combat team to move northeast to Le Bourget, where a body of German troops threatened a counterattack.

The whole plan was incredibly dangerous. In a city not yet cleared of German snipers, with only a regiment of United States troops and a combat team of the 2nd Armored between the capital and the German rear guard, de Gaulle proposed to assemble well over a million people and the cream of his country's leadership. Not since the invasion armada had stood off the coasts of Normandy would the Luftwaffe have before it so tempting a target, nor one so carefully announced beforehand.

Yet, despite those risks, de Gaulle was determined to go ahead. His political future—and that of France, he was sure —depended on his taking them. He had to impose his authority, his leadership, immediately, while the capital stood at the crest of the emotional wave its liberation had produced.

The first result of his decision was a conflict with his American Allies. At 10 o'clock, unaware of de Gaulle's orders to the 2nd Armored Division, an officer of the V Corps appeared at 2nd Armored headquarters with the division's orders for the day. The V Corps commander, General Leonard T. Gerow, was concerned with the exposed approaches to the city; he wanted the division to take up a screening position on the capital's northeast flank. The V Corps was informed that the 2nd Armored Division was not available for the day.

Angrily, V Corps radioed First Army: "General de Gaulle has ordered Leclerc to hold a big parade today from the Arc de Triomphe to Notre-Dame. French division staff furious at being diverted from operations. They say Leclerc has been given orders and nothing can be done about it. It will get 2nd Armored so tangled up they will be useless for an emergency operation for at least 12 hours or more."

When Gerow returned from a troop inspection, he boiled over. He sent to Leclerc a tough handwritten order reading: "You are operating under my command and will not accept orders from any other source. I understand you have been directed by General de Gaulle to parade your troops this afternoon at 1400. You will disregard those orders and continue on present mission assigned you of clearing up resistance in Paris and its environs. Your command will not participate in any parade this afternoon or at any other time except on orders signed by me personally."

The unhappy Leclerc, caught in the cross fire, felt he had no choice but to obey de Gaulle. To minimize his breach with V Corps, he tried to make himself unavailable so Gerow's orders would not catch up with him. Finally, a lieutenant colonel from Gerow's staff found him in a restaurant near Les Invalides. Handing him Gerow's order, the colonel added that if the division took part in the parade, Gerow would consider it a "formal breach of military discipline." Exasperated, Leclerc took the officer to de Gaulle.

"I loaned you Leclerc," de Gaulle grandly declared. "I can perfectly well borrow him back for a few moments."

• • •

As the last preparations for the parade were being finished, a telephone rang in the underground command post of Army Group B at Margival. It was the "Blitz" line of Generalfeldmarschall Model. It did not answer. For the first time since he had returned from his initial inspection of the front, the little field marshal was absent from his headquarters. That morning Model had left to inspect his forces around Compiègne.

His caller was upset. He had instructions from the Führer to pass an order to the field marshal Hitler knew to be among his most devoted disciples. Reluctantly, Generaloberst Alfred

Jodl asked for Model's second-in-command, Army Group B's chief of staff Generalleutnant Hans Speidel. To Speidel he gave the order for the execution of the attack Hitler had ordered prepared the day before, the V-bombing of Paris. From the 100-odd V bases in the Pas-de-Calais and northern France, the Führer, Jodl told Speidel, wanted rockets "rained" on Paris. For that night, he informed Speidel, the Luftwaffe in Reims had been ordered to launch an attack on Paris "with all the forces at its disposition."

Speidel hung up. As the first of the two million people who would soon swarm through the center of Paris began to assemble, the general who had received this message destined for the most faithful of Hitler's field marshals wondered what to do with it. Speidel decided to forget about it. Barely a week later, Speidel was arrested by the Gestapo.°

* * *

In Paris, de Gaulle himself furnished the final definition of the parade he was about to stage through the city. He gave it to Major Robert J. Levy, his new American liaison officer who had the delicate job of presenting General Gerow's objections to de Gaulle.

Militarily, de Gaulle told Levy, Gerow was right. The risks, he admitted, were "great." But, he told the little major, "we must have this parade." The goal was worth it.

"This parade," de Gaulle said, "is going to give France political unity."

° Neither Speidel nor OKW was aware of the demonstration planned for Paris that afternoon. After his arrest Speidel was questioned for his involvement in the July 20 plot against Hitler. He spent the rest of the war in a German prison.

17

TALL AND POISED, TOWERING above the crowd around him, Charles de Gaulle stood at the Arc de Triomphe before the tomb of France's Unknown Soldier. He laid a wreath of red gladiolas on the simple stone slab above the tomb. Then, with a symbolic gesture, de Gaulle relit the grave's eternal flame, the first Frenchman to perform that hallowed act in freedom since June, 1940,

After a moment of silence, de Gaulle turned and inspected the tanks and armored cars of the 2nd Armored lined up around the Étoile. From balconies, rooftops, windows and curbs, thousands cheered him. Then he returned to the base of the Arch. Before him was the Champs-Élysées. All the way to the Obelisk its borders were black with cheering crowds. Overhead, a warm sun shone out of another cloudless sky, brightening a rainbow of summer dresses, flags and banners.

Rarely in history had it been given to a man to live a moment of triumph as dizzying and exalting as that that now awaited Charles de Gaulle.

A surprise enemy air attack could, he knew, end this glorious moment in bloodshed and tragedy, a tragedy for which his foes would be quick to blame him. But at this moment, looking at that mass before him, de Gaulle "believed in the fortune of France"—and in Charles de Gaulle.

A police car announced to the crowd that de Gaulle was "confiding his well-being to the people of Paris." Four tanks of the 2nd Armored set off down the avenue. On each of its flanks, two chains of FFI, police, firemen, their hands linked, moved along the curb to hold back the crowds. Behind de Gaulle the leaders of a new France assembled in a haphazard line: Generals Juin, Koenig, Leclerc, the chiefs of the Resistance, the CNR, the CPL, the COMAC, Parodi, Chaban-Delmas.

De Gaulle turned to them. "Messieurs," he said, "one step behind me."

Then, on foot, alone, the thunderous acclaim of his nation rolling over him, Charles de Gaulle strode off down the grand and broad expanse of that handsome avenue.

Behind him, without shape or rank, the rest of the parade flowed down the avenue in an uneven mass. De Gaulle had designed it that way. He did not want the formality of a military review. He wanted no artificial barriers between him and the masses, and there were none.

All along the avenue, the crowds lined the rooftops, windows and balconies, packed the sidewalks, screamed their support as de Gaulle walked by. Little girls ducked out to hand him bouquets which he hastily passed back to the men behind him.

In that crowd, it seemed to de Gaulle, "was one thought, one spirit, one cry." Looking at these happily crying children, these men crying *"Merci,"* the "elderly extending me the honor of their tears," de Gaulle felt "more than ever" that he was "the instrument of France's destiny."

But, as de Gaulle knew, no joy is untrammeled. The first shot rang out as de Gaulle turned out of the Champs-Élysées into the place de la Concorde. At the sound, thousands of people fell to the pavement or scurried for cover behind the vehicles of the 2nd Armored in the square. Sergeant Armand Sorriero, the GI who had visited Notre-Dame the day before, hid behind his jeep. Peering out, this D-Day veteran "felt ashamed." Before him, moving indifferently through the gunfire, was de Gaulle, "very straight, standing tall for his country," Sorriero thought.

Across the square, Lieutenant Yves Ciampi of the 2nd Armored had the same instinctive reaction as Sorriero. He too had ducked for cover, and as he did, he felt the prodding of a cane in his back. "Monsieur l'officier," exclaimed a distinguished-looking old man, "at your age you should get up and stop this stupid shooting."

• • •

At the base of the north tower of Notre-Dame, an angry man pounded on the door before him. Lieutenant Burt Kalisch had been promised by a cathedral priest that he would be allowed to place a photographer in the tower to photograph the *Te Deum* service. Behind the door Kalisch could hear voices. He pounded again. Suddenly the door sprang open and the unshaven face of a middle-aged civilian in a white shirt appeared. In an angry shout, he told Kalisch something in French, then slammed the door. At almost the same instant, Kalisch heard the roar of the crowd announcing de Gaulle's arrival. Then he heard shots. Kalisch instinctively looked up. From between the slits of the tower above him, he saw very clearly the tips of three gun muzzles firing straight into the crowd. As he watched, the three muzzles drew back into the tower. "My God," gasped Kalisch, "they're going to assassinate de Gaulle!"

In front of the cathedral, de Gaulle's open car had just arrived. De Gaulle calmly stepped over to receive a tricolor bouquet from two little girls dressed in Alsatian costume. Then, imperious and outwardly indifferent, de Gaulle marched toward Notre-Dame's great main Portal of the Last Judgment. As he did, firing swept across the square. FFI and soldiers of the 2nd Armored raked its rooftops and sent chips of granite flying off the gargoyles lining the balustrades of the cathedral. Leclerc's officers desperately tried to restore order. The quick-tempered general himself swatted one of his wildly firing soldiers with his cane.

Imperturbably, de Gaulle strode on. In the half-darkened cathedral, the assembly invited for the *Te Deum* had heard the cheers of the crowd outside and the sharp sound of rifle fire. Now, as de Gaulle moved through the Portal of the Last Judgment, firing began in the cathedral itself. In the hushed, cool interior of the great church, the sound of the gunfire echoed into a roar. The congregation spilled to the floor, trying, it seemed to Captain Guy, "to pull their *prie-dieus* over them like covers." Down the 190 feet of the aisle separating him from his seat, de Gaulle moved at his steady, unchanging pace, the unvarying single step still setting him apart from the now shrunken official party behind him. André Le Troquer, one of de Gaulle's ministers, murmured, "I can see more rear ends than faces." One woman popped her head from behind her seat just long enough to cry *"Vive de Gaulle,"* then ducked back to cover. At the head of the nave, Jeannine Steel, secretary of one of de Gaulle's senior officers, thought, *"Les salauds,* they've killed him." Then, seeing his head bobbing in the rear of the church, she thought, "What a target." Finally, as he continued to move forward "erect and rigid, a shaft of light falling through the shadows struck his shoulders." At that moment, the pretty blonde, never an ardent Gaullist, felt "tears of pride over the man" fill her eyes.

At the head of the transept, de Gaulle moved calmly to his place of honor at the left of the main aisle. Behind him, General Koenig surveyed the congregation, and in a compelling roar the victor of Bir Hakeim shouted, "Have you no pride? Stand up!" His hymnbook in his hands, the sound of firing still sweeping the cathedral, de Gaulle stood before the officiating priest and bellowed back each phrase of the *Magnificat!*

Realizing it was folly to go on, he ended the service after the *Magnificat* was over. With the same steady pace with which he had entered the cathedral, de Gaulle left.

No gesture he could have made, no phrase he might have spoken, could have earned for de Gaulle the admiration of his countrymen that that display of physical courage had just won him. "After that," said an American newsman who watched him, "de Gaulle had France in the palm of his hand."

There remained the question of who had done the shooting. It would never be fully answered.° But among an already growing number of Gaullists was the suspicion that it had not been done by just Vichy's Milice and German snipers.

At the end of the pont au Double, two young colonels watched Leclerc's troops firing at the rooftops around the cathedral. "I see," said Communist "Colonel Rol" to Colonel

---

° It was at first assumed the firing was done by the Vichy Milice and German stay-behinds to sow panic and insecurity among the population. Supporting this theory was the fact the firing broke out simultaneously in several parts of Paris. Yet none of the snipers was taken alive in the act of shooting. Three characters loitering behind Notre-Dame were arrested; one was beaten to death and no involvement in the shooting was ever pinned on the other two. The few snipers caught were either shot or beaten to death before they could be interrogated. De Gaulle at one point remarked to Achille Péretti, his chief of security, "Those imbeciles are shooting in the air." He, as many, had noted the absence of the whistle of passing bullets. The Paris hospitals, however, admitted over 300 wounded August 26, most of them suffering from gunshot wounds (the rest from breaks and bruises occurring in the crush of the crowd). Much of the sound and fury was caused by the sometimes panic-inspired answering shots of the FFI and the 2nd Armored.

Many came to believe that firing inside Notre-Dame was an exchange of shots between zealous guards. The experience of Kalisch tends to disprove it. Others are convinced the firing was done on Communist instigation to inspire an air of uncertainty which would serve as a party pretext to justify continuing the police role of the Communist segments of the FFI.

Jacques de Guillebon of the 2nd Armored Division, "that your men don't know much about street fighting."

"No," replied Guillebon, calmly looking at the leader of the Paris insurrection, "but they're going to learn."

18

THOSE AROUND HIM may have been perplexed about the origin of the shooting; de Gaulle had no doubt about who was behind it. He was convinced it was the work of the Communists. Riding back to the Ministry of War, he remarked to his aides, "*Eh bien,* messieurs, there are forces in this country that are ready to destroy me to prepare their own road to power." At worst, de Gaulle suspected these shots had been meant to kill him; at the best, it was to sow the seeds of a chaos that would serve his rivals' political ends.

By the time he arrived at the Ministry of War, de Gaulle had reached a decision. The crowd's acclaim had given proof of the support he enjoyed; the firing had demonstrated the dangers he ran. He decided to reach out immediately, at the height of his popularity, and break his foes. His first decision was to disarm the FTP and split it up into small units in the Regular Army under army discipline.

A few hours later General Koenig told Colonel Richard Vissering of SHAEF, "The worst danger in Paris at the moment is the FFI." De Gaulle, he said, wanted "to relieve the situation by getting the most disturbing elements into uniform and under military discipline." To do it, Koenig asked Vissering "urgently" for 15,000 uniforms. After Koenig's briefing, Vissering added his own weight to Koenig's request by reporting to SHAEF, "The situation from a public safety standpoint is alarming. Citizens of all kinds go about in fear of being arrested by one gang or another. It appears most of these groups are political, the most powerful among them being Communist. The [Paris] region is rapidly becoming a terrorist one and the general opinion on all sides is that a state of civil war may break out any moment."

De Gaulle wrote to Eisenhower telling him it was absolutely necessary to leave the 2nd Armored Division in the city until order had been fully restored. The next day he asked Eisenhower to parade an American division through the city to demonstrate to its population the depth of Allied support behind him.°

Two days later de Gaulle announced the dissolution of the higher echelons of the FFI command in Paris. He announced "such elements of the FFI as may be useful" would be incorporated into the army. All members of the FFI were ordered to register with Koenig. Their arms and equipment were ordered stockpiled under the supervision of Koenig's command.

The CNR, instead of its "National Palace," was assigned a nondescript villa belonging to an English lord for the few meetings that would precede the organization's swift march to oblivion. De Gaulle, of course, never "assisted" at its meetings. He received its members once, briefly. They expressed their intention to transform their organization into a permanent body, functioning alongside his authority, to hand over to the COMAC as their military arm the control of the Communist Milice. De Gaulle politely but bluntly informed them their functions had ceased. The police would take over law and order, he said. There was no longer any need for the Communists' "Milice Populaire." They were dissolved, as was the COMAC whose members he never received.

"The iron," de Gaulle later wrote with eloquent understatement, "was hot. I struck it."

° De Gaulle passed his request to Eisenhower when the Supreme Commander came to call on him at the Ministry of War, Sunday, August 27. The day before, still unaware of de Gaulle's plans, Eisenhower's headquarters had combed the front looking for de Gaulle so that Eisenhower could address to him his congratulations on the liberation of Paris. More concerned with keeping order behind his fast-moving front than he was with the political niceties of Franco-American relations, Eisenhower did not share his State Department confreres' consternation on learning that de Gaulle had installed himself in Paris. Recalling his visit to the French leader, Eisenhower said: "What I wanted was to see the situation in Paris under control, and as far as I was concerned de Gaulle was the best man to do that. I wanted my visit to show the people he had my support, that as far as I was concerned de Gaulle was the boss of France. That's the effect I wanted and that's the effect I got."

Eisenhower assigned the 28th Infantry Division the task of meeting de Gaulle's request for an American show of force in the capital. On August 29, two days later, the division staged one of history's most unique parades. In full battle dress, the division marched down the Champs-Élysées, then kept right on going out the other side of the city. It was engaged in combat before the end of the day.

19

LOW AND STRONG, THE sound of airplanes filled the night. They came from the northeast, rolling awesomely down the river until they seemed to shake the terra-cotta walls of the sleeping village of May-en-Multien. From the Romanesque belfry of the church of Notre-Dame de l'Assomption, the aging German sergeant watched in wonder as they thundered past, dozens of them, flying wing to wing, breaking through the sky barely a thousand feet over his head. It had been a long time since he had seen a sight like that. These planes were German, and they were plunging straight down the Marne to Paris, 48 miles away.

From the park of the old château just northeast of Paris where General Hubertus von Aulock had installed his new headquarters, Captain Theo Wulff saw them too. At the first sound of those engines, Wulff started to run for cover. The skies of France, this veteran of Normandy knew, belonged to the Allies. He listened to the roar of the planes sweeping overhead. The rumbling of their engines seemed different to Wulff than those of the Marauders and B-24s that had haunted Normandy. He thought for a moment they might be Heinkels of the Luftwaffe. But Wulff knew the Luftwaffe would not put in the sky an assembly of planes like those passing over his head. The captain was wrong.

The German Luftflotte No. 3 had indeed returned to the skies of France for one brief and final farewell. There were no "forgetful" generals at the Reims headquarters of Generaloberst Otto Dessloch. Finally, thirteen days after he had issued his first orders for its defense, twenty-four hours after its fall, Adolf Hitler was about to inflict on Paris a small measure of the destruction he had vowed would be its destiny. Speidel had stilled the V-bombs, but the Luftwaffe was faithful to the Führer's command.

Wulff listened to the planes, almost 150 of them, sweeping gracefully over the Bois de Vincennes toward the northeastern corner of Paris. In a few minutes he heard the distant echoes of their first bombs exploding and saw, creeping slowly into the sky, the glow of the fires set by their incendiaries. Almost reverently, Wulff thought to himself that "never again will we see so many of our planes in the sky at one time."

In Paris, the piercing screech of air-raid sirens cut through a city celebrating its liberation as though it meant the war had ended. All across the city, lights were on, people were dancing in the streets, cabarets and bars shook with laughter. The first bombs fell before the sound of the sirens had died.

Corporal Bill Mattern of the 20th Field Artillery had just started to dance with a lovely redhead at a block dance near the Château of Vincennes when he heard the planes. His girl, and all the girls around her, vanished, "leaving about fifty cursing GIs in the middle of the town square." Captain Bill Mills, the officer who had bought the map of Paris in Longjumeau, was in the battalion CP he had chosen in a *café dansant* near the lac Daumesnil. A few hours earlier Mills had realized the CP had served a wider range of interests than just social dancing before his battalion's arrival. There had been a bordello upstairs. Huddled under a table, listening to the roar of bombs exploding around him, Mills remembers praying, "Dear Lord, if You get me out of this, I'll be more careful about where I put the battalion CP in the future."

For thirty minutes at low altitude, General Dessloch's planes drifted unmolested through the Paris skies. To oppose them, there was not a single Allied antiaircraft gun functioning in the city. Within twenty minutes, half a dozen huge fires lit up the night sky. The biggest was accompanied by the pop of bursting bottles. In this, the heaviest air raid Paris suffered during the war, the Luftwaffe had set fire to the wine market. They also killed 213 people, injured 914, and damaged or destroyed 597 buildings, most of them tenements between the Gare de Lyon and the Bois de Vincennes.

In his prison at the fire station of the boulevard du Port-Royal, Count von Arnim heard above the distant burst of bombs another sound, closer, more chilling to the young German aristocrat. It was the vengeful howl of a mob streaming toward the fire station. Already von Arnim could hear its leaders beating on the door three flights below, screaming, "Les boches, les boches, give us les boches." Von Arnim knew the handful of indifferent firemen guarding them would stand aside at the mob's first determined rush. With war correspondent Clemens Podewills at his side, Arnim looked over the railing of the staircase to the cement fire station floor four flights below. The two young noblemen vowed to each other that if the mob started up those stairs, they would leap to their deaths rather than fall into the mob's hands.

Silently they stared down at the cold cement as the shrieks outside rose to an insistent howl of hate. Then, above the explosions and the mob's yells, Arnim heard another sound, the metallic splashing of tank treads. He ran to the window and saw half a dozen tanks drawing up in front of the fire station, the white star of the United States Army stamped on their turrets. For the young Brandenburg nobleman there would be no Saint Bartholomew's Massacre this August night.

* * *

Their bare feet slapping on its wooden parquet floors, two men in skivvy shorts ran down the dark and dusty corridors of Les Invalides toward an open window. Breathless and silent, they stared out over the esplanade des Invalides. There, arm in arm in their undershorts, Pierre Koenig and Jacques Philippe Leclerc watched in dumb fury as the distant explosions of the Luftwaffe's bombs flashed along the horizon. Then the general who had raced his tanks to Paris to save the capital from destruction began to mutter over and over again one angry phrase: *"Les salauds, les salauds, les salauds."*

* * *

From the window of a darkened anteroom in the Ministry of War, Captain Claude Guy watched, too. Down the skyline he could see the wink of exploding bombs and, soft and red, the glow of half a dozen fires splotching the darkened horizon. To his left, from behind a row of shuttered apartments, drifting through the noise of the attack, came the sound of laughter, free and happy. It was a group of Parisians, ignoring the air raid in a noisy celebration of their liberation.

In the darkness Guy felt a figure glide up beside him. It was de Gaulle. Moody and silent, he stared out at the spectacle before the window. He turned his head and caught the sound of laughter in the night.

"Ah, Guy," he sighed, "they think that because Paris is liberated, the war is over. *Eh bien,* there you see—the war goes on. The hardest days are ahead. Our work has just begun."

Then de Gaulle moved off through the blackened room back to his office. There, by lantern light, he went on with work that had just begun.

Paris was free—fifteen days earlier than his Allies had planned. Ahead of their timetables, before his friends had hoped or his enemies had feared, Charles de Gaulle had returned to keep his rendezvous with history. Now, while Paris slept, he prepared to impose his authority on the capital of France. It was already past midnight. Another day was beginning.

On August 28, 1944, at 12:45 A.M., three days after
the surrender of General von Choltitz, Field Marshal
Model, Commander in Chief of the Armies of the West,
transmitted the following message to Adolf Hitler's
headquarters.

28.8.44—12.45
P.C. BLITZ
        DESTINATION: OKW, General Staff Command Personnel

                    Command Affair
                    To be transmitted only by an officer
                    Top Secret

                    To the GS: First Bureau, Judge Adv.

                        Third Bureau (original)

                        First carbon to Army Grp B

I have asked the president of the Reich Tribunal to open a
criminal procedure for breach of discipline against General
der Infanterie von CHOLTITZ and his accomplices.

General von Choltitz failed to live up to what was expected
of him as the general assigned to defend Paris.

I cannot say if his failure was due to a wound caused by
shellfire, or a weakening of his will to resist and his capacity
to act by an intervention of the enemy by special arms. Such
a possibility cannot be excluded.

                        MODEL
                        Commander in Chief/West
                        3rd Bureau No. 770/44

SOURCES

BOOKS AND PERIODICALS

FRENCH

ABEL, JEAN-PIERRE: *L'âge de Caïn. Nouvelles Editions latines,* 1949–1950.

AMOUROUX, HENRI: *La vie des Français sous l'occupation.* Arthème Fayard, 1961.

ARNOUX, ALEXANDRE: *Hélène et les guerres.* B. Crasset, 1947.

ARON, ROBERT: *La libération de la France.* Arthème Fayard.

D'ASTIER, EMMANUEL: *Sept jours.* Editions de Minuit.

AUBRAC, CECILE: *La Résistance, naissance et organisation.* Robert Lang, 1945.

AUDIAT, PIERRE: *Paris pendant la Guerre.* Hachette, 1946.

AURY, BERNARD: *La Délivrance de Paris.* Arthaud, 1945.

BARDOUX, JACQUES: *La Délivrance de Paris.* Arthème Fayard, 1958.

BARRAT, PIERRE: *Pavés Sanglants.* Arthème Fayard.

BARREYRE, JEAN: *Images de la Libération.* Les Oeuvres Libres No. 227, 1944.

BERGIER, JACQUES: *Agents secrets contre armes secrètes.* Arthaud, 1955.

BERTAUD, JEAN: *Saint-Mandé dans la Libération.* Le Comité l'Ombre et la Lumière, 1945.

BLANCHOT, ISIDORE: *Libération de Paris.* A. Lahure, 1945.

BLOND, GEORGES: *D'Arromanches à Berlin.* Arthème Fayard, 1954.

BONNAMY, GEORGES: *Souvenirs d'un pseudo-vaincu.* Debresse, 1945.

BOUCHER, FRANÇOIS: *La Grande Délivrance de Paris.* Jacques Haumont, 1945.

BOURDAN, PIERRE: *Carnet de Retour avec la Division Leclerc.* Paris-Trémois, 1945.

BRAIBANT, CHARLES: *La Guerre à Paris.* Corréa.

BROCQ, PIERRE: *L'Hôtel Dieu pendant les Journées du 19 au 27 Août 1944.* Mason & Cie, 1945.

BRUCKBERGER, RÉVÉREND PÈRE RAYMOND-LÉOPOLD: *Si Grande Peine* . . . Gallimard.

CAMPAUX, SIMON: *La Libération de Paris—Récit de combattants et de témoins.* Payot, 1945.

CANLORBE, PIERRE: *Le Service de Santé de la Résistance.* Amédée Legrand & J. Bertrand, 1945.

DE CHEZAL, BERTRAND: *A travers les Batailles pour Paris.* Plon, 1945.

CORDIER, REMY: *Mémorial des Journées d'Août.* Cordier, 1944.

COUROUBLE, ALICE: *Amie des Juifs.* Bloud et Gay, 1946.

CRENESSE, PIERRE: *La Libération des Ondes.* Berger-Levrault, 1944.

DAIX, PIERRE: *"Explosions" à Rive Gauche.* France-d'Abord (Jeunesse Héroïque), 1947.

DANSETTE, ADRIEN: *Histoire de la Libération de Paris.* Arthème Fayard, 1946.

DENIS, HENRI: *Le Comité Parisien de la Libération.* PUF.

DUBOIS, EDMOND: *Vu pendant la Libération de Paris.* Payot-Lausanne, 1944.

———: *Paris sans lumière.* Payot-Lausanne, 1946.

DUCLOS, JACQUES: *Les Communistes dans la Bataille pour la Libération de la France.* Report presented to the Central Committee of the French Communist Party.

———: *Préface de "l'Insurrection Parisienne."* Printed and circulated by the French Communist Party.

DUHAMEL, GEORGES: *Images de notre Délivrance.* Editions du Pavois, 1944.

DUMAY, RAYMOND: *Les Chaleurs d'Août.* Julliard, 1945.

DUNAN, RENÉ: *Ceux de Paris.* Editions du Milieu du Monde, 1945.

DUPIN DE LACOSTE, SIMON: *Les Journées d'Août.* L'Expansion Scientifique Française, 1945.

DUPUY, FERDINAND: *La Libération de Paris vue d'un Commissariat de Police.* Librairies Imprimeries Réunies, 1945.

DUPAYS, PAUL: *Libération de Paris.* Hachette, Londres, Editions de la Critique, 1954.

EPAGNEUL, DR. LOUIS: *Dans les Geôles Allemandes.* F. Soulisse-Martin, Niort, 1945.

FABRE-LUCE, ALFRED: *L'Enfermé.* Editions de Midi, 1945.

FERON, YVONNE: *Délivrance de Paris.* Hachette, 1945.

FLEURY, EMMANUEL: *La Participation des Postiers Parisiens à l'Insurrection Nationale.* Speech delivered September 2, 1944, at the Mutualité Hall.

FLORIAN-PARMENTIER, ERNEST: *Le Règne de la Bête ou la Tragique et Sublime Epopée de 1939–1946.* Ed. Pierre Clairac, 1949–1950.

GALTIER-BOISSIERE, JEAN: *Mon Journal de la Grande Pagaïe.* La Jeune Parque, 1949–1950.

————: *Mon Journal pendant l'Occupation*. La Jeune Parque.

————: *Mon Journal depuis la Libération*. La Jeune Parque.

HENIN, ABBÉ P.: *M. R. Nordling, consul de Suède, et son rôle pendant la Libération de Paris*. Editions du Foyer Français, 1946.

————: *La Résistance dans le VIIe arrondissement*. Editions du Foyer Français, 1949.

HERRIOT, EDOUARD: *Episodes 1940–1944*. Flammarion, 1949–1950.

HERVAL, RENÉ: *La Bataille de Normandie*. Editions de Notre Temps, 1947.

HOSTACHE, RENÉ: *Un gouvernement Clandestin: Le Conseil National de la Résistance*. Thesis for doctorate, Paris, 1957.

HUGONNOT, JEAN: *Les Journées d'Août 44 à Paris*. Cahiers Internationaux de la Résistance.

JACQUE, ANNE: *Journal d'une Française*. Editions du Seuil, 1946.

JAMET, CLAUDE: *Fifi Roi*. Editions de l'Elan, 1947.

JOLY, MARCEL: *Petits Episodes de la Grande Semaine*. Imprimerie M. Brenner & Cie, 1944.

JOUBERT, JOSEPH-GUSTAVE-MARIE: *La Libération de la France*. Payot, 1951.

JUIN, ALPHONSE: *Mémoires*. Arthème Fayard, 1959–1960.

LAVAL, PIERRE: *The Diary of Pierre Laval*. Charles Scribner's Sons, New York, 1948.

LECLERC, MME. THÉRÈSE: *Preface: "Le Général Leclerc vu par ses compagnons."* Alsatia, 1948.

LEFEVRE, GEORGES: *"Et Paris se Libère."* Hachette, 1945.

LE HARDOUIN, MARIA: *Celui qui n'était pas un héros*. Ed. du Nyete.

LEPERC, AIMÉ: *Manuscrit de l'Allocution prononcée le Vendredi 25 Août 1944 à l'Hôtel de Ville*.

MALRAISON, COLONEL GEORGES (LUDO): *Résistance et Contre-attaques en Uniforme*. Privately circulated.

MASSIET, RAYMOND: *La Préparation de l'Insurrection et la Bataille de Paris*. Payot, 1945.

————: *La Carnaval des Libérés*. Ed. J. Vautrain, 1952.

MAUDRU, PIERRE: *Les Six Glorieuses de Paris*. Société Parisienne d'Edition, 1944.

MAURIAC, FRANÇOIS: Texte de présentation d'un album de photos "La Libération." Flammarion, 1944.

MERLE, GUY: *À l'Assaut avec la IIe D.B.* Imprimerie Malesherbe, Caen, 1949–1950.

MICHEL, HENRI: *Histoire de la Résistance*. Presses Universitaires de France (collection "Que sais-je?"), 1949–1950.

MONOD, DR. ROBERT: *Les Heures Décisives de la Libération de Paris*. Ed. Gilbert, 1947.

NORD, PIERRE: *Leclerc et ses hommes*. Editions G.P., 1952.

OUZOULIAS, COLONEL ANDRÉ: *La vie héroïque du Colonel Fabien*. Editions Sociales. 1945.

PONCHARDIER, DOMINIQUE: *Les pavés de l'enfer*. Gallimard, 1949–1950.

REPITON-PRENEUF, LT. COL.: *La IIeme D.B.* Arts et Métiers Graphiques.

REYBAZ, G. JEAN: *Le Maquis Saint-Séverin, ou comment fut libéré le quartier Saint-Michel*. Maison du Livre Français, 1945.

ROY, CLAUDE: *Les yeux ouverts de Paris insurgé*. Sequana, 1944.

————: *Les Parisiens reprennent Paris*. Édité par les Francs-Tireurs, Partisans Français du Lot, 1944.

SAINT-BENNET, GEORGES: *Sang de Paris*. Fasquelle, 1945.

DE SAINTE-PIERRE, CECILE: *Des Ténèbres à l'Aube*. Arthaud, 1945.

SEREAU, RAYMOND: *L'armée de l'Armistice*. Nouvelles Editions Latines, 1961.

SOREL, JEAN-ALBERT: *La Résurrection 1944–1945*. Julliard, 1945.

TAITTINGER, PIERRE: *. . . Et Paris ne fut pas détruit*. Editions de l'Élan, 1948.

TAUZIN, JEAN-HENRI: *Quatre ans dans les bagnes hitlériens*. Imprimerie Crété à Corbeil, 1945.

TERRENOIRE, ELISABETH: *Combattantes sans uniformes, les femmes dans la Résistance*. Bloud et Gay, 1946.

THARAUD, JEAN ET JÉRÔME: *Discours sur la Libération*. Le Divan, 1945.

THOMAS, EDITH: *La Libération de Paris*. Méllottée, 1945.

THOSAC, J.: *Missionnaire et Gestapo*. Les Trois Nefs.

TILLON, CHARLES: *Les F.T.P.* Julliard, 1962.

TOUCHE, MME. FIRMIN: *Mon Fils Jean-Claude*. Bloud et Gay, 1945.

VIANNEY, PHILIPPE (INDOMITUS): *Nous sommes les Rebelles*. Collection Défense de l'Homme.

VILAIN, CAMILLE: *Quand le canon tonnait aux Gobelins*. Meyer-Ruelle, 1945.

WELLERS, GEORGES: *De Drancy à Auschwitz*, Editions du Centre, 1946.

WICHENE, SIMON, ET DARVILLE, JACQUES: *Drancy-la-Juive*. A. Breger Frères, 1946–1948.

GERMAN

ABETZ, OTTO: *Histoire d'une politique franco-allemande*. Stock, 1953.

_____: *Pétain et les Allemands*. Ed. Gaucher, Paris.

VON CHOLTITZ, DIETRICH: *Soldat unter Soldaten*. Konstanz, Zürich, Wien, Europa-Verlag.

_____: *Brennt Paris?* UNA Weltbücherei, Mannheim.

EPTING, KARL: *Generation der Mitte*. Bonn, Bonner Universitäts-buchdruck Schour.

EPTING-KUHLMAN, ALICE: *Zwischen Paris und Fluorn*. Burg Stettenfels bei Halbronne N. Hunenburg-Verl.

FRASCHKA, GUNTER: *Gnade Für Paris*. Rastatt/Baden e. Pabel Verl.

JACOBSEN, HANS ADOLF: *Der zweite Weltkrieg in Chronik und Dokumenten*.

JUNGER, ERNST: *Strahlungen*. Tubingen, Heliopolis-Verlag.

_____: *Jahre der okkupation*. Stuttgart, E. Klett.

MICHEL, KARL: *Der Kriegsrichter von Paris*. Wiesbaden, UNA Euripaische Verlagsgesellschaft.

SPEIDEL, HANS: *Invasion 1944*. Henry Regnery, Chicago, 1950.

WESTPHAL, SIEGFRIED: *The German Army in the West*. Cassel & Co., Ltd., London.

Die Stimme des Menschen: A collection of personal letters and documents of combatants and members of the Resistance of thirty countries. Some of this material pertains to the entrance of the Allied Forces into Paris.

AMERICAN AND BRITISH

BLUMENSON, MARTIN H.: *U.S. Army in World War II—Break-out and Pursuit*. Office of the Chief of Military History, Department of the Army.

_____: *Duel for France*. Houghton Mifflin Company, Boston, 1963.

BRADLEY, GEN. OMAR N.: *A Soldier's Story*. Henry Holt, New York, 1951.

BUTCHER, CAPT. HARRY: *My Three Years with Eisenhower*. Simon and Schuster, New York, 1946.

CHURCHILL, PETER: *The Spirit in the Cage*. Hodder & Stoughton, London.

DOUGLAS, S.: *Liberation of Europe Operation Overboard—May to August 1944*. London Gazette suppl. 38111, 1947.

EISENHOWER, DWIGHT D.: *Crusade in Europe*. Heinemann, London, 1949.

ELLIS, MAJ. L. F.: *Victory in the West,* Vol. I.: *The Battle of Normandy.* Edited by Sir James Butler. Her Majesty's Stationery Office, London, 1962.

FRIZELL, BERNARD. *Ten Days in August.* Simon and Schuster, New York, 1956.

GILBERT, FELIX: *Hitler Directs His War.* Secret records of his daily military conferences from the manuscripts in the University of Pennsylvania Library. Oxford University Press, New York, 1960.

HART, LIDDELL: *The German Generals Talk.* The *New English Review.*

HATCH, ALDEN: *The de Gaulle Nobody Knows.* Hawthorn Books, Inc., New York, 1960.

HOEMBERG, ELIZABETH: *Thy People, My People.* J. M. Dent & Sons, Ltd., London.

HUDDLESTON, SISLEY: *France, the Tragic Years.* Devin-Adair, New York, 1956.

LIEBLING, A. J.: *The Road Back to Paris.* Harcourt, Brace & Co., New York, 1944.

MacMILLAN, RICHARD: *Le Miracle devant Paris.* Plon.

MONTGOMERY, FIELD MARSHAL SIR BERNARD: *The Memoirs of Field Marshal Montgomery.* Collins, London, 1958.

PATTON, GEN. GEORGE S.: *War As I Knew It.* Houghton Mifflin Co., Boston, 1947.

PERLES, A.: *Round Trip.* Dennis Dobson Ltd., 1946.

POGUE, FORREST C.: *The Supreme Command.* Office of the Chief of Military History, Department of the Army, Washington, D.C., 1946.

PYLE, ERNEST TAYLOR: *Brave Men.* Henry Holt, New York, 1944.

SHIRER, WILLIAM L.: *The Rise and Fall of the Third Reich.* Simon and Schuster, New York, 1960.

SHULMAN, MAJOR MILTON: *Defeat in the West.* Secker & Warburg, London, 1947.

WERTH, ALEXANDER: *France 1940–1955.* Hale, London, 1956.

WHITCOMB, PHILIP: *France During the German Occupation.* The Hoover Institute, Stanford University, 1959.

WILMOT, CHESTER: *The Struggle for Europe.* Collins, London, 1952.

DOCUMENTS

(In departmental Records Branch, A.G.O. Washington 25, D.C.)

G2 Files of First US Army (FUSA)

On an intelligence officer of the Economic Branch of the U.S. Service dispatched to Choltitz:
FUSA Memo, Info elicited from the German Commandant of Paris, 31 Aug.; FUSA G2 Jnl and File.

On Choltitz and destructions in Paris:
FUSA Rpt. 2055, 26 Aug.; 4th Div. G2 Periodic Rpt. 2000, 26 Aug.; FUSA AAR (After Action Report), Aug.

On Choltitz and Paris:
Interrogation of Colonel Paul Krause, Mil. Comdr. East of Paris, FUSA PWI Rpt. 12, 29 Aug. (cited as Krause Interrogation); FUSA (Tactical Echelon) G3 File.

On defense inside the capital:
XII Corps G2 Per. Rpt. 19 Aug. XII Corps AAR, Aug.

An agreement Bradley/Patton on sending the French Second Armored Division into Paris:
12th AGp Memento for Red, 19 Aug. M. L. 205

XV Corps Chiefs of Staff Journal and Files

On Leclerc wanting to start toward Paris:
Telecon, Gaffey and Menoher, 1715, 14 Aug. and Ltr, Leclerc to Patton (16 Aug.), XV Corps CofS Jnl and File; Notes (16 or 17 Aug.), XV Corps CofS Jnl and File

V Corps Documents (From "The V Corps in the ETO"). *(Memo dictated by Bradley for Hodges. The memo is also included in V Corps Field Order 21, 23 Aug., and a photostatic copy appears in V Corps Operations in the ETO p. 200. This document contains all the information then known by the Allied command on the situation in Paris.)*

On Gerow's orders that no troops were to cross the Versailles-Palaiseau line before noon, 23 Aug:

V Corps Letter of Instrs, Gerow to Leclerc, 22 Aug., and V
    Corps Field Order 21, 23 Aug.
On Gerow/Leclerc and Leclerc's selected point of attack:
    Msg, Gerow to Barton, 0840, 24 Aug. V Corps Operations in
    the ETO p. 203.
Instructions to allied troops in case of strong resistance from the
    Germans:
    V Corps Ltr of Instrs, Gerow to Leclerc, 22 Aug., and Dir,
    Gerow to 102nd Cav Reconnaissance Gp (Mechanized), 23
    Aug.
On Eisenhower's request to Bradley to meet him on 22 Aug.:
    V Corps G3 Memo, 21 Aug.
On de Gaulle's request to Eisenhower to hold the French Armored
    Division in the capital:
    V Corps Operations in the ETO p. 210.
On Leclerc's wish to progress toward Paris:
    V Corps Dir, 21 Aug., and Ltrs of Instrs, 21 and 22 Aug.
On Gerow's order that the French division pursue the Germans
    North of Paris on Aug. 26, 1944:
    V Corps G2 Msg, 1303, 26 Aug.; V Corps AAR, Aug.; Msg,
    26 Aug., probably from V Corps Liaison officer with the
    French division.

CAPTURED GERMAN MICROFILMS

(Furnished by U.S. National Archives)

Wehrmachtfuehrungsstab, file containing a handwritten report on
    the situation of the war in the West, from April 1 to September
    17, 1944. We find also part of this report written in pencil,
    on the war in the West, from July 31 to September 16, 1944,
    in the collection OKH, Item H 48/5. See also the Kriegstage-
    buch of the Oberkommandos der Wehrmacht (Wehrmacht-
    fuehrungsstab) 1940–1945. Volume IV, January 1, 1944, to
    May 22, 1945. Foreword and commentaries by Percy Ernest
    Schramm. Frankfurt am Main, 1961.
File of uncertain origin containing Sonderbefehle and Wehrmacht-
    berichte, February 3, 1943 to May 9, 1945.
Generalstab des Heeres, Operationsabteilung/II, files entitled
    "Tagesmeldung OB. West," daily reports on the situation by
    the operational officers of this command, July 25, 1944, to
    September 30, 1944.
"Tagesmeldungen Heeresgruppe B," file of Genst.d.H. Opabt/II,

containing the daily reports of Army Group B, from June 6 to September 30, 1944.

Generalstab des Heeres, Organisationsabteilung, daily reports of operations from July to September, 1944.

Chef Heeresnachrichtenwesen, file containing reports on enemy situation in the West (Feindlage Westen), from May to September, 1944.

Files of unknown origin containing reports on the situation in the West, from January to December, 1944, sent by OKH, Genst.-d.H., Fremde Heere West.

OB. West radio orders, uncoded text, registered by H GrD/Information service, August 10-16, 1944.

War log and weather reports, July 1 to August 31, 1944, Items H GrD 75144/24, 24a, 25, 25a.

War log, appendices: orders and reports, December 27, 1943–December 31, 1944.

Ibid.: information on enemy and reports on the morale of the German troops, July 1-31, 1944.

Information section, daily reports from July 1 to September 30, 1944.

Information section, appendices to the daily reports, July 1 to September 30, 1944.

Appendices to the daily war log of OB. West: orders and reports of the operational section, July 1 to September 30, 1944.

H Gr.B, war log, information annex section, reports on the enemy situation and probable plans, from July 1 to December 31, 1944.

Reports on the situation of the operational branch and weekly reports, including the coded correspondence of Rommel, Kluge, Model and Rundstedt with Jodl, Keitel and Hitler, from May 20 to October 11, 1944.

File of the operational branch containing Hitler's orders and H Gr.B's answers, from June 17 to September 25, 1944.

Daily reports, operations officer, from June 6 to August 31, 1944.

Operations orders and pertaining papers, from June 9 to September 13, 1944.

Daily reports of OB. West operations, from June 8 to September 30, 1944.

Index